Road to Civil War, 1625–1642

Road to Civil War, 1625–1642

The Unexpected Revolution

Timothy Venning

Pen & Sword
MILITARY

First published in Great Britain in 2023 by
Pen & Sword Military
An imprint of Pen & Sword Books Limited
Yorkshire – Philadelphia

Copyright © Timothy Venning 2023

ISBN 978 1 39905 588 8

The right of Timothy Venning to be identified as
Author of this Work has been asserted by him in accordance
with the Copyright, Designs and Patents Act 1988.

A CIP catalogue record for this book is
available from the British Library

All rights reserved. No part of this book may be reproduced or
transmitted in any form or by any means, electronic or mechanical
including photocopying, recording or by any information storage and
retrieval system, without permission from the Publisher in writing.

Typeset by Mac Style
Printed in the UK by CPI Group (UK) Ltd, Croydon, CR0 4YY.

Pen & Sword Books Limited incorporates the imprints of After
the Battle, Atlas, Archaeology, Aviation, Discovery, Family History,
Fiction, History, Maritime, Military, Military Classics, Politics,
Select, Transport, True Crime, Air World, Frontline Publishing, Leo
Cooper, Remember When, Seaforth Publishing, The Praetorian Press,
Wharncliffe Local History, Wharncliffe Transport, Wharncliffe True
Crime and White Owl.

For a complete list of Pen & Sword titles please contact

PEN & SWORD BOOKS LIMITED
47 Church Street, Barnsley, South Yorkshire, S70 2AS, England
E-mail: enquiries@pen-and-sword.co.uk
Website: www.pen-and-sword.co.uk
or
PEN AND SWORD BOOKS
1950 Lawrence Rd, Havertown, PA 19083, USA
E-mail: Uspen-and-sword@casematepublishers.com
Website: www.penandswordbooks.com

Contents

Introduction	vi
Part I: The Calm Before the Storm – Or Ominous Subcurrents? 1625–1640	1
Chapter 1 Introduction to the English Situation pre-1640. Ominous Subcurrents or Not? Religion, Law, Finance and the Outbreak of Conflict – the Deciding Factors?	3
Chapter 2 The Scots Crisis: The Tipping-point which Ruined an Otherwise Strong Position in 1637–9?	74
Chapter 3 1640: Missed Opportunities for Compromise?	118
Part II: The Drift to War, 1640–2	147
Chapter 4 November 1640–May 1641. Reform, Retribution and Confrontation	149
Chapter 5 May 1641 to January 1642. Missed Chances or Inevitable Showdown?	211
Notes	263
Bibliography	282
Index	289

Introduction

The outbreak of the first internecine military conflict in the newly combined 'dual monarchy' of England (plus Wales and Ireland) and Scotland was far from the most expected outcome to the political struggle between the King and a majority of Parliament which commenced in November 1640. Nor was the fact that when the struggle for control of the British polities resorted to armed conflict this would not be settled (even temporarily) in one campaign – as had been the norm for all civil wars since 1216. The outcome of a three-and-a-half-year civil war across three kingdoms (longer in Ireland) and a second subsequent outbreak in 1648, plus the Anglo-Scottish war of 1650–1 ending in Charles II's invasion of England, has tended to cast an air of 'inevitability' over what happened in this complicated conflict (or rather three conflicts). In Scotland there was a primarily religious Protestant revolt against London-based 'centralism'; in Ireland a Catholic revolt, against Parliament rather than King.

Similarly, the monarchy of Charles I has been seen as inevitably 'doomed' and the King as a poor political leader whose rashness and unwillingness to compromise – or to stay faithful to his promises to opponents – caused the seemingly stable edifice of his state in the 1630s to collapse into political confrontation then to civil war. The nineteenth and twentieth-century 'Whig Historians' indeed developed a determinist theory that it was Charles' aggressive imposition of autocratic centralization and denial of the 'democratic' rights of his subjects (or at least the political elite) in Parliament that inevitably caused this. Implicitly or explicitly, Charles was the enemy of 'progress' towards the evolution of democracy, as fulfilled in the nineteenth-century constitution, and was thus rightly to be defeated by the 'progressive' Parliamentarian opposition. His government was thus 'reactionary' and 'un-British' in a deliberate and systematic policy of centralization – and in Scotland the evidence of his pro-Anglican, 'Anglicizing' reforms of the Presbyterian Church certainly appeared to spark off a 'revolution' by affronted Presbyterians. To students of twentieth-century revolutions like Christopher Hill, Charles 'caused' revolution in England too.

His policies could also be compared to those of the centralizing early mid-seventeenth-century continental European monarchies who took on 'vested interests' among regional elites and the nobility, e.g. in France and Spain. These monarchies often faced a backlash and revolt, e.g. in the 'Frondes' in France and the 1640 Catalan and Portuguese revolts in Spain, and a 'wave' of political breakdown into civil wars or attempted revolutions broke out across Europe in the 1640s – a 'mid-seventeenth-century crisis' visible as far afield as the Ottoman Sultanate and Russia, culminating in 1648. In recent years, this has been linked not only to the stresses of systemic modernizaton of government but to 'climate change' in the 'Little Ice Age' causing famine and public discontent, providing the 'cannon fodder' for armed opposition. Thus Charles I's policies could be presented as trying to create a 'modern', bureaucratic, centralised state in England and to impose 'central control' on traditionally autonomous systems in Scotland and Ireland. This was imposed against fierce resistance that the King tried to ignore – and he failed where Cardinals Richelieu and Mazarin succeeded in France. It involved inadequate resources and mechanisms and botched planning, plus inadequate consultation and unnecessary stoking of opposition – particularly over latent fears of 'Popery'. This has superficial attractions – indeed, Charles' character can be compared to those of two other well-meaning but politically inadequate 'autocrats' who fumbled their way into and failed to react subtly to multi-faceted crises and ended up executed in revolutions, Louis XVI of France and Nicholas II of Russia.

Modern 'revisionists', however, would argue that this picture is far too simplistic – for one thing, Charles had no 'grand plan' for an autocratic monarchy in 1629–40 and did not set out to subvert traditional rule through Parliament. Summoning the latter was often suspended for as long as a decade when there was no need of their services to provide finance, e.g. by Elizabeth I and James VI and I. There was no Royal 'plan' for confrontation with Parliament by Charles from 1625, but rather a continuing series of sporadic clashes between a tenacious monarch and a usually co-operative political elite that encroached on Royal prerogatives and/or sought to use its 'power of the purse' for political coercion. These instances had been apparent as far back as the 1560s – as had resistance to Royal financial demands without any *'quid pro quo'* and agitation by 'lobby groups' of militant 'Puritan' MPs for further reform of the Anglican Church and coercion of Catholics, plus a vigorous but cheap 'Protestant' foreign policy. Similarly, resistance by 'Presbyterian' sympathisers to coercive centralizing powers in the Anglican Church – seen as still half-Catholic – were as apparent under Elizabeth as under Charles – and both monarchs harshly punished 'impertinent' criticism of their policies by subjects, e.g. John Stubbes in 1581 and Prynne, Burton and Bastwick in 1637. Charles however, unlike Elizabeth, was suspected of undue sympathy to Catholicism, and the tone of criticism of Church centralization after c. 1620 shifted to specific allegations of 'Popish' theology as well as practices (e.g. by Laud) which could not be made against Elizabeth's equally vigorous centralizing disciplinarians (e.g. Archishop Whitgift).

Charles' search for money when he was without Parliament and accompanying aggressive reassertion of his traditional feudal 'rights' were in contrast to his predecessors', but were within the existing legal framework (albeit 'bending the rules' somewhat). Elizabeth and James invented as many non-Parliamentary sources of taxation. He always saw himself as acting within his legal rights rather than innovating, and indeed restoring traditional 'order' and harmony, as reflected in the propaganda of his Court masques, though there was increasingly an air of unreality about the latter. To him, his critics were ungrateful and disobedient, which stern 'fatherly' control would counter-act. Indeed if we see the problems of government and religious 'control' in the 1630s in the light of the reigns of Elizabeth as well as James, it can be seen that neither the government's and Church's policies nor the nature of the 'opposition' were new, with the notion of disaffected aristocrats endeavouring to coerce the monarch by political then armed opposition traceable back to the medieval period (as shown by John Adamson). Coercing the King by great nobles' ancestors by rebellion or Parliamentary action had been a major factor in politics under John, Henry III, Edward II, Richard II, and Henry VI, and these were the parameters of the 'mindset' of opposition magnates like Warwick and Essex and Bedford in 1639–42 rather than a democratic assertion of Parliamentary rights. Forcing themselves into office and their policies onto a reluctant government was their intention, not overturning the political order – though a plan did emerge to permanently 'control' the unreliable King, as modelled on the oligarchy of Venice. This study will show how the Parliamentary crises of 1625–9 and Royal policies of the 1630s appear in a different light if viewed through the prism of Elizabeth's and James' reigns, with struggles for political influence and religious 'control' and for Royal financial consolidation as 'normal' not due to new confrontational policies by Charles. To some extent he was 'reaping the whirlwind' of his father's compromises and failures to find long-term solutions. He certainly adopted a confrontational manner that his two predecessors, both brought up in a hard political 'school', tended to avoid. His actions in Scotland were at least naïve and misjudged his political strength, mistaking image for reality. But he was unlucky in his timing as well as incompetent, particularly concerning heightened fears of international Catholicism arising from European events, and on several occasions in 1640–2 a (temporary?) solution to his problems was possible but was missed due to bad luck or his misjudgements. His demands arguably put too much stress on the ramshackle edifices of 'control' in England and Scotland at once and his timing was poor, but his failure was far from inevitable. So was the 'slide' to civil war, and his failure to achieve a quick victory in 1642.

Part One

The Calm Before the Storm –
Or Ominous Subcurrents? 1625–1640

Chapter One

Introduction to the English Situation pre-1640. Ominous Subcurrents or Not? Religion, Law, Finance and the Outbreak of Conflict – the Deciding Factors?

(But would the level of opposition have been manageable without the Scottish revolt?)

(a) **An inauspicious opening to the reign or misinterpreted? The 1625 Parliament and the previous indications of Charles' political profile**

Charles I's character has to be considered as a major factor in the way that the 'Three Kingdoms' of England/Wales, Scotland, and Ireland headed for crisis – and failed to get out of it – between his accession and 1642. This was after all an era of personal monarchy where the monarch not only 'set the tone' but determined much of policy either themselves or indirectly by setting parameters within which their subordinates operated and against which their critics reacted. In addition, when it came to working out what to do and negotiating within the 'art of the possible' flexibility was at a premium – and Charles' stubbornness, high self-regard for his 'divinely-appointed' office, and desire for unquestioning conformity to his will were assets in some circumstances but a recipe for disaster in others. These covered secular/political as well as religious issues, as did his unhesitating harshness towards opponents. This has duly impacted on his reputation, as compared with that of his more 'consensual' father James VI and I; he could be seen by historians as actively seeking conflict – setting his kingdoms on the road for confrontation?

From his accession he could be seen as confronting his Parliaments, setting the pattern for his reign. The tension and repeated breakdown in relations between King and Parliament (temporary or not) in 1625,

1626 and 1628–9 duly feeds into the basic question of whether or not there was a rising 'arc' of what may be termed political opposition to the King – and this King in particular – in the 1620s. If there was, then this political crisis in the mid-late 1620s can be seen as the foreshadowing of 'Personal Rule' without Parliaments in 1629–40 and Charles' apparently 'autocratic' and innovatory resort to doing without the main forum of the nation, in contrast to his predecessors. The King's reluctant calling of Parliament again in April 1640, his dismissal of it as political stalemate resumed, and the even more reluctant calling of the 'Long Parliament' that November would thus appear to be a steady progress (inevitable or not) towards confrontation and Civil War. This picture of a rising 'arc' of confrontation between King and Parliament from 1625 was favoured by the great constitutional historians of the 17th-century crisis in the late 19th and early 20th centuries, the so-called 'Whig Historians' (e.g. Bishop Stubbs and Samuel Rawson Gardiner) who sought to present the growth of Parliamentary opposition to the King – and thence of Parliamentary power to constrain the executive – as 'progressive' and by definition 'good'. Thus Charles I was to be presented as the 'regressive' and autocratic 'villain' of the narrative, in the manner of his treatment by the Parliamentarians in the 1640s, and the crucial political confrontations of the mid-late 1620s showed the assertiveness in rival directions of a 'tyrant' (or at least arrogantly assertive) King and a bloc of MPs (and often side-lined peers) in contrast to earlier co-operation under Elizabeth I and James VI and I.

In reaction to this simplistic 'Whig History' viewpoint, more recent historians in the later 20th century such as Conrad Russell, Kevin Sharpe and Mark Kishlansky sought to show that there was not an 'inevitable' clash between two implacably hostile 'power-blocs' (Royal prerogative vs Parliamentary liberty), or even a steady evolution of confrontation from the 1620s to the Civil War. There had always been tensions between the rival rights and claims of the sovereign and 'opposition' in Parliament, but only over specific issues in short-term crises and usually ones that both sides sought to resolve – and Elizabeth and James had dissolved unco-operative Parliaments and arrested MPs for infringing their prerogative too. The creaky nature and inadequate finances of the Early Modern English (and indeed British) state were more to blame for crisis and confrontation than increasingly implacable rival views of Royal vs

Parliamentary power, especially when issues of religion or financing a war occurred. These 'revisionists' have had the better of most of the arguments in recent decades, though their rivals have managed to identify issues where there were both rival views of major constitutional issues and a new assertiveness over these in the years after 1625. The questions of subjects' legal rights and of Royal legal prerogative powers 'trampling' on these were increasingly aired in this period, as seen in the debates over the legality of non-Parliamentary taxation and detention without trial (e.g. of the 'Five Knights' arrested for not paying the forced loan of 1626–7) in 1628. 'Magna Carta' was now cited against the King's arbitrary and unquestionable legal decisions, and these problems gained a new urgency after Charles' accession.

It will be shown that the circumstances of crisis in 1625–9 were not all Charles' own fault, or an allegedly ominous sign of his lack of political skill or willingness to compromise – though he avoided chances to back down or be consensual which his far more subtle (or less principled) father would have used. In any case it was not unreasonable to anticipate a degree of naivety from the 'sheltered' new King who was only twenty-four and unlike his late elder brother Henry (d. 1612) had not had a long apprenticeship in 'man management' in charge of his own household. His father James VI and I, by contrast, had succeeded to his first (Scots) throne aged nine months, as a malleable Protestant puppet installed in a coup by a faction of rebellious nobles to replace his unpopular Catholic mother Mary Stuart – and had been at the mercy of his regents until he was thirteen and even after that had been occasionally kidnapped by rebel lords. James had been under threat of being ignored, countermanded, or even deposed (or at times killed) throughout his reign in Scotland to 1603, and after he had come to an unfamiliar new throne in England had once nearly been blown up with his entire elite in Parliament in 1605. All this bred insecurity and a nose for survival plus cunning in dealing with the great men of his realm, if at times ruthlessness too – he had been in a 'hard school'. But Charles was not intended to be the heir until his much more astute, physically fit, and confident brother Henry died suddenly when he was twelve, he had been kept under strict control at court by his protective father into his twenties – and been referred to dotingly as 'Baby Charles' and allowed little chance to develop as a political actor. Indeed, it can be argued that by 'infantalising' him and preventing him from developing an independent and confident presence at court as a young man James had made it likelier that he would commit mistakes when he achieved full power, as he had had no suitable 'apprenticeship'. (Was this due more to James accommodating his younger son's shyness and lack of confidence, or to his fear of the Prince rivalling him politically and outshining him as Henry had done?) When Charles did emerge into politics around 1622–3 it was as a 'pupil' of the dominant figure at Court, the overwhelmingly handsome and confident but much-resented 'favourite' George Villiers, Duke of Buckingham, on whom his sentimental father relied for advice and emotional support to an embarrassing degree – and who Charles had initially resented as such before falling under his 'spell' as well.

It had been Buckingham who inveigled the naïve and romantic Charles into his well-meant but foolhardy and probably inevitably unsuccessful 'secret' journey to Madrid in 1623 (initially in inadequate disguise) to woo the Prince's intended bride, King Philip IV's sister the Spanish 'Infanta'. James had been seeking this marital resolution to the long Anglo-Spanish confrontation as a means to bind together the leading Protestant and Catholic powers in a now once more war-hit Europe and cement his own hoped-for role as the great international peacemaker, but progress had been slow and Buckingham hoped to speed it up with a personal mission to the Spanish court. In reality, both King James and Buckingham underestimated the practical difficulties in arranging the match, which the Spanish were interested in more as a means of tying England to an alliance against their hereditary foe France than in helping James' plans for European reconciliation. Nor was King Philip IV's Spanish government prepared to help James out by pressurising its ally the Holy Roman Emperor Ferdinand II (as fanatical a Catholic as his cousin Philip) into restoring the recently-confiscated German electorate of the Palatinate to James' daughter Elizabeth and son-in-law Elector Frederick, which was James' main hope. (see in detail later for this crisis.) The Spanish had totally different priorities to the English and would not sacrifice them just to marry off their Infanta to Prince Charles. However, this mistake – which made Charles' naïve mission to Spain futile – was not solely the fault of Charles and his enthusiastic mentor Buckingham; both the English ambassador in Spain, John Digby, and the recently-departed former Spanish ambassador to England, Count Gondomar (who had got on well with King James due to their mutual love of hunting) had encouraged the idea, which Digby had first thought up. Nor did James quash the plan as risky and unlikely to end Spanish delays when Charles and Buckingham begged him for permission to go. Once in Spain, where his arrival astonished the English embassy, Charles predictably could not get near the well-chaperoned Infanta, who the Spanish 'dangled' in front of him as a bait to his making concessions with excuses about her strict Catholic upbringing inhibiting any meeting, and at one point he was driven to climb a wall and trespass in her garden to see her like a romantic lover from a contemporary chivalric poem. His leading role in the mission and determination not to go home quickly when he was frustrated from progress by the Spanish negotiators were recognised by contemporaries at the time, though later Clarendon blamed it all on Buckingham; apparently he felt inspired by his timid father's having journeyed by sea to Oslo to collect his Danish bride in 1589 to do the same with the Infanta, ignoring the differences between the two courts' culture. All this argues for his complete lack of worldliness when he first emerged in politics, at an older age (22–23) than his brother Henry had been (16–18) as a political 'newcomer' in 1610–12 – when Henry had been corresponding with leading thinkers and cultural figures, restructuring his court, designing buildings, and planning to join in a 'Protestant vs Catholic' European war.

Possibilities such as the hard-nosed Spanish using the talks to demand public and legal guarantees for tolerating Catholics in England or 'stringing along' an eager Charles with excuses and tempting him into written concession after concession were not considered. Nor did any of the principals – James, Buckingham, and Digby as well as himself – consider the visceral Protestant English hatred of 'Popery' in general and Spain – the national foe and would-be invader of England in the now revered 1588 Armada 'showdown' – in particular, which would undoubtably transfer itself to a hatred of any Spanish Catholic Queen of England. Any Spanish demand for legal toleration of English Catholics would create a political 'firestorm' and not get through Parliament. Crucially, when the marriage-plan and general Anglo-Spanish reconciliation were becoming problematic in English political circles as early as 1617–18 – and James arrested and executed Elizabethan hero Sir Walter Raleigh at Gondomar's request for attacking a Spanish colony in South America on his exploration voyage there – the King had purged Charles' household of Scots Presbyterian opponents of the match rather than listen to or take note of their fears. Charles was thus served by fewer Scotsmen and fewer anti-Catholic Englishmen than his elder brother Henry had been in his formative teens, so did this isolation from a major strand of British opinion lead to his constantly underestimating this factor? And did this feed into his miscalculations of the strength of opposition to 'toleration of Popery' (as anti-Catholics saw it) from 1623 right through to the 1637–42 crises? If so, Charles sowed the whirlwind of James' miscalculations, though James' own naivety was due to 'inclusive' idealism (as it would now be seen) rather than incompetence.

The over-confident expectations by the impulsive Prince on his 1623 visit to Spain that he would be allowed to meet and charm the strictly-chaperoned princess in a court governed by stifling protocol – or be allowed as a Protestant to marry her, a Catholic, without either converting himself or agreeing to their children being brought up Catholics – set the course for Charles' lack of political shrewdness once he was King. So did the way that he failed to realise the overwhelmingly hostile reaction in the fiercely Protestant England to the possibility of his marrying a Catholic princess, from a country that was best known in popular memory for trying to invade England and convert it by force in 1588. He was also planning to marry a Catholic less than twenty years after the 'evil Papist mass-murder plan' sensation of the Gunpowder Plot, so this would necessitate careful planning and plenty of reassurances to his father's paranoid subjects – and it needed to be dealt with by expert diplomats used to wily and uncompromising Spanish ministers. Charles dashing off to Spain on his own initiative without proper 'back-up' also 'short-circuited' his father's more careful attempts to arrange the marriage and its concomitant Anglo-Spanish rapprochement through hard-headed negotiations. The sudden and unannounced departure of the Prince to Spain indeed roused panicked fears across England of another Catholic plot, this time to kidnap or brainwash the heir into acting as a Catholic agent. It was accompanied by farce over poor planning as his and Buckingham's fake beards and false names ('Mr John Smith and Mr Thomas Smith') were seen through by local authorities as they rode across Kent and led to their temporary detention in Canterbury en route to Dover. Once in Spain, Charles had the advantage of surprise in announcing his arrival to the startled Spanish court and thus pushing the slow negotiations into a 'higher key' of action – he even asked James for permission to agree a deal without having to refer everything back to him. But he let the Duke (charming and courtly but not experienced in dealing with wily Spanish civil servants) take the lead in talks, sidelining the experienced Digby who had had years of dealing with current chief minister the Count-Duke of Olivares and his minions, and indeed after the talks failed he 'cold-shouldered' Digby as if unfairly blaming him rather than blaming Buckingham for naïve impetuosity. He gave way on politically dangerous matters such as his bride bringing up her children as Catholics to the age of twelve and assuring that his father would pass pro-Catholic laws through Parliament (wholly impractical), and when even Buckingham realised that they were being played along and withdrew from the negotiations Charles pressed on for weeks alone. Eventually even he had to give up. Charles' return to England unmarried was greeted with mass –relief and celebratory bonfires that showed how unwise the marriage-plan had been from the point of domestic security.

Similarly, once he was denied his intended bride by predictable 'stone-walling' on terms and had the sense to return home, Charles turned on Spain and used his patronage over Parliamentary seats as Duke of Cornwall in the 1624 Parliament to back an alliance with Spain's long-term foe France and war with Spain instead. This put him back on the same political ground as the majority of the nation's elite which had a visceral distrust of Spain as the principal source of 'Counter-Reformationary' Catholic aggression. Fears of the latter had been revived recently, particularly in the manoeuvrings of the hated Spanish ambassador Count Gondomar in London and Spain's alleged role in encouraging the Spanish Habsburgs' relative Emperor Ferdinand II to overrun Protestant-seized Bohemia and evict its new rulers (James I's daughter Elizabeth and son-in-law Elector Frederick of the Palatinate) in 1620 – thus commencing the long-term 'Catholic vs Protestant' struggle of the Thirty Years' War in Germany. The Emperor and Spain then overran Frederick's own Palatinate lands, and looked ready to seize Frederick's crucial Electoral vote in future Imperial elections for a pro-Habsburg Catholic. This gain for centralising Imperial/Habsburg power under the fanatical 'Counter-Reformationary' Ferdinand, who was busy trying to exterminate Protestantism in conquered Bohemia, was to the detriment of 'moderate' German Catholic states as well as Protestants, and so revived the French plans of King Louis XIII's late father Henri IV in 1610 to intervene – and brought an alignment between France and England. Now Buckingham switched from organising a 'rapprochement' with Spain to fighting them instead, and Charles assisted. When James died in March 1625 a French alliance was being arranged instead of the originally planned Spanish one.

But Charles also inherited the creaky and unreformed Stuart administrative machine and military infrastructure, that would prove inadequate to fund or run the war successfully. The inadequacy of the English army and its commissariat had been shown in the Spanish Armada crisis of 1588, but despite this neither Elizabeth I nor James had taken up drastic reform. The only English soldiers who had crucial experience of 'modern' European warfare (as opposed to fighting poorly-armed Irish rebel guerrillas) and knew what supplies and training were needed were those who had joined in the long-running Dutch campaigns against their former overlord Spain, though these included a number of well-connected scions of the nobility and gentry families. Stocks of weapons and ammunition and supposedly regular training had been technically available for the 'Trained Bands' militia in each English county since the Spanish crisis in the 1580s, but muddle and a lack of direction were notorious and the Spanish had a large and well-trained army of infantry 'tercio' regiments who had been fighting in Europe under skilled generals since the 1560s. The resources at the disposal of the English King and the technical capability of the English state to wage the popular Spanish war were wholly inadequate to the major task ahead, while the elite in Parliament had little idea of the scale of financial commitment that would need to be made for success – or preparedness to assist the government generously. Charles had already proved his naivity in Spain in 1623 and was now to prove his stubborn inflexibility on matters where his father had been more prepared to negotiate, but his lack of adequate training was at least partly James' responsibility. Charles had been able to lean heavily for advice as the adult heir on the reassuring (though widely hated) figure of Buckingham, and indeed he now continued to keep the latter on as his principal adviser and arguably only emerged as 'his own man' after the latter was murdered in August 1628. In political terms, Buckingham's concentration of power and influence in his own hands since the late 1610s – and his propensity for quarrelling with other figures at Court – made him a divisive figure who would inevitably face rival courtiers (in his case in the early 1620s led by the Earl of Pembroke). In fact he was more competent as an administrator, more interested in financial retrenchment and other reforming measures, and less personally venal or lazy than his predecessors as royal favourites, James' handsome and feckless Scots male confidante Robert Carr and the latter's wife's English Howard dynasty. But his lack of 'established' connections to major noble dynasties – he was a younger son of a minor Leicestershire gentry family – added to his problems, as did his having Catholic close relatives (his wife Katherine Manners, until she converted to Anglcanism, and his mother) and international Catholic cultural tastes. All this made it controversial for Charles to keep him on as chief minister on his accession, at a time when many observers had been hoping that Buckingham's 'rule' would end with James' death. But discontent at any failures by the new government in the forthcoming war would now focus on the Duke, and the gap between what was available to the State and what was needed for success in administrative and financial terms was a looming problem. This could have been narrowed dramatically – if not resolved entirely – and Charles' situation would have been better if James had taken such reforming initiatives as were attempted by his ministers Sir Robert Cecil pre-1612 and Lionel Cranfield in the early 1620s, both in administration and finance. (Buckingham was to be blamed for Cranfield's being frustrated and impeached by Parliament as he turned on him, but originally the latter had been his protégé and backed by him.) The failure of the vigorous if brusquely confrontational Cranfield certainly lay with James for not defending him in 1624, and it will be argued that in many ways Charles reaped the whirlwind of his father's hesitant and erratic policies and failures to confront long-term problems. James indeed warned him after he used MPs to attack Cranfield (to help Buckingham's cause) that they would turn on him next.

The clashes between what the King and what Parliament saw as an adequate financial settlement began with the refusal of the Commons to meet Charles's full financial demands for the supposedly popular Spanish war and to agree to the usual life grant of tonnage and poundage in early summer 1625. Only a poor £160,000 (two subsidies plus the usual 'fifteenths') and a year's grant were given, which could seem to be a sign of distrust or dislike of the new King as this meant that the latter would be forced to consult Parliament again soon for more money. Complaints were made about the new King continuing to 'illegally' collect a non-Parliamentary commercial levy, the much-contested 'impositions' introduced by James in 1606. However, the superficial impression this gives of 'King vs Commons confrontation' was misleading, as by the time of the crucial vote many MPs had gone home early in a panic over the plague in London; only around a quarter were in attendance at the time. Those who voted for it did not reflect majority opinion in the House, though arguably Charles slipped up in not having a united body of Privy Councillors and their clients in the Commons (throughout its sitting) to try to direct voting. Instead, some of the Council were resentful of Buckingham and failed to support his financial requirements – deliberately, to embarrass him? The disappointment of Buckingham's Court enemies and critics in the country (the former often egging on the latter in the Commons) that the Duke had not been dismissed on King James' death in March 1625 was an added problem. Some people evidently believed the libellous allegations made after James' death that the greedy Buckingham and his family had poisoned the late King to remove him and save themselves from dismissal and ruin – the story was unrealistic but its existence shows what was rumoured at the time. To that extent Charles had already committed his first political mistake, by not removing the Duke from at least some of his posts to reassure other factions. The latter reflected his naivity as well as his generosity although he was only twenty-four and inexperienced – and was a parallel to the case of the disappointing 'no change' manifesto of new young Czar Nicholas II in Russia (another overthrown and executed autocrat) in 1894.

But the responsibility for giving full control of patronage and overwhelming influence in policy-making to the acquisitive Duke lay with the ageing, doting James in the period 1618–25, and insecure and immature Charles merely compounded his mistake out of relief to have a friendly 'expert' to hand. Charles inherited a political system with one 'favourite' dominating the scene. Possibly Charles was also keen to imitate the political situation in the era's 'great power' Spain, which he had visited in 1623, with one dominant minister (Count-Duke Olivares) on whom the even younger King Philip IV, born in 1605, relied. Did Charles forget that the harmony between Duke and Commons in 1624 was unlikely to be repeated now the bills for war had to be met?

The late King James's assessment of the money needed for the Spanish war, as of his request of 14 March 1624 to the Commons, had been for five 'subsidies' – each of which was approximately £70,000 in value – and ten 'fifteenths' – each of which was around £20,000. This amounted in effect to around £550,000, without adding the extra annual money that James thought necessary to wipe out his current debts (which were partly due to his extravagance and partly due to an ongoing deficit of expenditure outweighing income). The current deficit between annual income and annual expenditure in 1624 was around £100,000, with the monarch having £900,000 of unpaid debts – a sum which had been building up for years and which war would make worse. Hence cost-cutting Lord Treasurer Cranfield's opposition to a Spanish war in 1623–4, and Buckingham's success in stirring up MPs against him as unpatriotic and pro-Catholic. Parliament had failed to meet the late King's financial request in 1624, and costs were escalating as now France and Denmark were involved in the wartime plans too. By Sir John Coke's reckoning for the 1625 situation, six subsidies (£210,000?) and 'six fifteenths' (£120,000?) would be needed to pay for the English fleet and bringing Denmark into the planned anti-Habsburg war in Germany. The navy needed around £113,000 more and Denmark £40,000, plus £30,000 a month for bringing in the Danish army to attack the Habsburgs and £20,000 a month for Count Mansfeld's army. The actual grant made amounted to £127,000. Other Privy Councillors then failed to back Coke up, making his request seem less urgent and be ignored.

There was an overall lack of direction and unity in the government 'case', with some Councillors as well as disgruntled sidelined senior MPs (e.g. Charles' later minister Sir Thomas Wentworth, at this point an 'opposition' figure, and Sir Robert Phelips) resenting Buckingham's monopoly of power and seeking to embarrass him. Buckingham was at odds with the Lord Keeper, Bishop John Williams, for a start, suspecting him (probably correctly) of underhand intrigues to remove him, and at Court the Lord Chamberlain, the Earl of Pembroke (owner of Wilton House, near Salisbury), was a potential foe and had control of various Parliamentary seats in Wiltshire. Pembroke had previously used the rising Buckingham, then plain George Villiers, to undermine the influence of the pro-Spanish, Catholic Howards at Court and probably resented his protégé getting beyond his control. To make matters worse, in 1624 Buckingham had manoeuvred both Williams and Pembroke out of the crucial Privy Council foreign policy committee – and James and later Charles had not stopped him. Where Buckingham did put out 'feelers' to the critical MPs or their patrons for co-operation in return for later rewards in 1625, these failed – though Wentworth was to be lured into office after 1628 and become ultra-loyal so arguably the fault for this failure lay with the inadequately conciliatory Duke. The most notorious failure of the latter to keep a potential critic loyal was to be Sir John Eliot, a spokesman of the Duke's in the 1624 Parliament (and his Vice-Admiral for Devon), who turned on him in 1626.

To the problems of a divided Council and one of its members having undue prominence in decision-making – a legacy of James' reign – was added the inefficiencies of the haphazardly-managed Navy, which Buckingham had inherited not caused but which his enemies could use to attack him and so annoy the King. His main Commons critic in 1625 was a disappointed rival admiral, Sir Robert Mansell. Buckingham being Lord Admiral (James' decision not Charles') thus made the Duke vulnerable to accusations of corruption and incompetence in a vital area in wartime. The critics forgot – or deliberately ignored – that the Duke was young, no naval expert, had only recently taken over a creaky and inefficient system riven with local autonomy by the dockyards managements, embezzlement, and inefficiency, and was no more 'out of touch' with the minutiae of administration than his predecessor, the octogenarian Elizabethan commander Lord Howard of Effingham. But it was still a risk to appoint a man with no naval background as Lord Admiral as James did in choosing Buckingham in 1624.

There were also overseas factors beyond the King's control – the cost of the Spanish war estimated in 1624–5 was bound to be too low, bringing in Continental allies (e.g. Denmark) would be expensive, the land-expedition to Germany led by mercenary general Count Mansfeld was proving a chaotic failure, and England's ally Louis XIII of France was demanding help from English ships to put down a Huguenot rising in La Rochelle (by the MPs' Protestant co-religonists, so enraging them). The French alliance – Catholic as with Spain – was not popular, not least as Louis required the suspension of English penal laws banning Catholic services and arresting all priests. (This was partly due to his insecure new chief minister, Cardinal Richelieu, needing to reassure ultra-Catholic *'devots'* in France.) This clashed with Charles' promises to Parliament as Prince of Wales in 1624 that he would not accept any softening of the penal laws to appease France. Some MPs such as Sir Robert Phelips then made untimely demands for a comprehensive survey of the government's precarious finances, which were due to two decades of neglect by the profligate James and to the 1624 impeachment of 'cost-cutter' Treasurer Lord Cranfield. MPs eager to use their right to hold up supply until demands were met backed him. The result was deadlock as Parliament reassembled in Oxford after leaving London due to the plague, and a delay in voting money to the King despite his urgent needs. To him, as seen by his and his mouthpiece (Chancellor of the Exchequer) Sir Francis Weston's arguments, it was a matter of loyalty and respect to him to grant his civil requests. To legalistic and suspicious Phelips, backed up by Wentworth, it would set a bad precedent to vote a second sum of money in one Parliament – at least without major concessions first. Charles promised to hold a second Parliament the following winter if MPs would come up with the money now and thus save the 1625 campaign; this was refused so he abruptly dissolved Parliament (10 August). Buckingham's critics blamed the Duke, but in fact he pleaded with Charles not to do this.

Bishop Williams had advised a delay to no avail; he had also advised Charles to carefully secure the election of a compliant 'bloc' of Privy Councillors and their MP clients first.[1] When Charles decided to close Parliament in August Williams also advised, to no avail, that it would only lead to an even more fractious Parliament – bees from the same hive, as he put it – when money-worries soon required the next one to be called. The inexperienced Charles was in a hurry to raise money, and so hastened to a confrontation which was unfortunately timed to coincide with the arrival of his Catholic bride Henrietta Maria of France. Williams was a political foe of his closest adviser and personal confidante, Buckingham, so he probably already mistrusted him even if Williams' rival Bishop Laud was not accentuating this yet. But Charles was only impetuous and too hasty to regard normal political manoeuvring and suspicion as personal insolence to him, not antagonistic to Parliaments 'per se'.

The politically difficult start to his reign was combined with the immediate Commons onslaught on his religious policies one of the major causes of trouble in 1625–42 – over his suspending the anti-Catholic penal laws on 1 May 1625 and pardoning some Jesuits. But this again is misleading. His marriage in June to a Catholic princess, Henrietta Maria of France (his ally against Spain), exacerbated the King's seeming 'pro-Catholicism' for insular, fiercely Protestant MPs who were at fever pitch about the 'Papist threat' at a time of visible Catholic aggression on the Continent following the expulsion of his sister and brother-in-law, Elizabeth and Frederick of the Palatinate, from their dominions by Habsburg troops in 1620–1. Charles seems to have naively assumed that the popular euphoria over the collapse of his mission to Spain to marry the Infanta in 1623[2] only referred to dislike of a Spanish – not of any Catholic – marriage. Significantly, he had not even considered the possible public backlash in his enthusiasm for the Spanish match in 1623, a sign of his isolation at Court from public hatred of Catholics. The French marriage provided basic political reasons for his unpopular toleration of his Catholic subjects, which the French had insisted on putting in a clause of the marriage-treaty in November 1624 (though this was not generally known). Was Buckingham, as the inexperienced chief negotiator, hoodwinked by France into giving too much away or caught in a trap whereby he needed French help so urgently that he could not walk away from the talks, as French chief minister Cardinal Richelieu knew? The timing of Louis' requirement for English ships to help him against Huguenot rebels was unfortunate, and possibly the Anglo-French problems were added to by the King's choice of Buckingham to head his first embassy to France in spring 1625 as the Duke was supposed to have been caught flirting with Queen Anne in compromising circumstances. (This incident was used later by novelist Alexandre Dumas for 'The Three Musketeers'.) More prosaically, the Duke was unimpressed by Richelieu's alleged goodwill and decided that the French were unreliable. France was thence seen as an untrustworthy ally, as it was to prove in 1626 by agreeing peace with Spain. The crisis of summer 1625 thus had special features and cannot be simply ascribed to an early sign of Charles' unbending arrogance; though he mixed the personal and the political to a significant extent, refusing to dismiss Buckingham in 1625 or 1626 to save his relations with the Commons. Arguably relying less on one, contentious minister would have eased Charles' path – though some of the most persistent MPs in criticising him, such as Sir Nathaniel Rich (cousin and probable spokesman of the aggressively Calvinist, anti-Catholic Earl of Warwick), were far too militant on religion ever to have reached accommodation with him on this issue.

The Parliamentary crises come to a head: March 1629 and after

The special reasons for the initial problems with the 1625 and 1626 Parliaments have thus tended to be ignored, as Charles' 'intractable' character has been seen by many as a fundamental reason why the Royal disputes with parts of the 'political nation' from his accession failed to end in accommodation, unlike the clashes which his predecessors Elizabeth and James had with their Parliaments. This was so again when it came to another crisis in 1640–2 and this one ended in war. The onlookers' attitude to Charles was inevitably influenced by the known outcome to Charles' confrontations – civil war and regicide. The classic 'Whig History' determinist liberal approach to the mid-17th century crisis duly presented him as the villain of the narrative, implying that Elizabeth and James had been able to handle their political clashes skilfully but Charles – arrogant and tactless? – lacked their abilities. This will be explored later.

'Prima facie' and dramatic evidence of Charles' uncompromising behaviour is not lacking, however. A 'high-profile' instance of this was his treatment of Sir John Eliot, following the final confrontation with Parliament on 2 March 1629 when his group of eleven leading 'opposition' MPs held up the dissolution by slamming the door in the Royal messenger 'Black Rod's face (still commemorated today). Three of them – Eliot, Denzel Holles, and Benjamin Valentine – physically prevented the Speaker from standing to close the session until their group had passed the critical votes they wanted to register.[3] One of the offenders, Denzel Holles, was to be among the 'Five Members' who the King tried to impeach in January 1642. Eliot was also the member of this group who wrote and that day unsuccessfully presented to the Speaker a 'Protestation' about the recent rise of 'Popery' and arbitrary government – its exact contents are unclear as he later destroyed it (thus denying evidence to his prosecutors) but it was clearly inflammatory. Worse, he was at this point of the Parliament verbally attacking the Lord Treasurer (Richard Weston, Earl of Portland) as a promoter of crypto-Catholic 'Arminianism' and ruinous economic meddling by abuse of the law (in collecting tonnage and poundage). He had also accused Attorney-General Sir Robert Heath over his failure to prosecute the 'Arminian' enthusiast Dean Cosin for denying the Royal Supremacy over the Church (which amounted to taking a Catholic theological stance), implying that Heath was a 'crypto-Catholic' sympathiser. He was thus 'targeting' current senior ministers by name and could expect them and their master to retaliate for this 'impertinence' beyond his immediate 'crime' of riotous behaviour in Parliament. The use of force and open disrespect to the King in the Commons by manhandling the Speaker and slamming the door in the King's messenger's face went beyond normal 'accepted' procedure, not to mention being what was still technically in a Royal palace – the Commons sat in the 14th century-St Stephen's Chapel within Westminster Palace – so it was legally within the 'verge of Court'. A harsh punishment for insulting the King's officers was to be expected, as with 'brawling' at Court – which latter offence had sparked off several 'high-profile' cases involving physical confrontations in the past (such as the Duke of Norfolk threatening Elizabeth's favourite Leicester on the royal tennis-court in the 1560s). Any sovereign had a duty to clamp down on brawling in his palaces, whether by assaulting the Speaker or by an inter-noble quarrel. The excuse that Eliot and his two colleagues made to the Court of King's Bench was that it was in the House of Commons, i.e. covered by Parliamentary privilege – and hence that the latter outweighed any judicial rights of the King's courts, which was politically and legally provocative.

The context of the events of 2 March 1629 indicates that though the blame for the violence was the MPs', Charles had provoked an unnecessary confrontation with them, as in June 1625. The unexpected resolution to his refusal to accede to MPs' demands to sack or impeach the hated Duke of Buckingham by the latter's (hugely welcomed) assassination in Portsmouth while he was visiting the fleet in August 1628 had opened a window of opportunity for a settlement to current disputes. Charles had indeed told his Privy Council on 27 November that he would anticipate Commons attacks on his attitude to Catholics and 'Arminian' Anglicans by arresting some 'high-profile' Papists (which he did, albeit only priests) and allowing a Council commission to investigate the latter (which he did not do).[4] He would not budge on his right to continue to levy tonnage and poundage without Parliamentary consent and to arrest non-payers, including MP John Rolle (whose arrest undoubtably antagonised MPs as trespassing on their supposed immunity during Parliamentary sittings). When the customs-men who had arrested Rolle were summoned before the Commons Charles made it clear that he backed them and that arrests of non-payers would continue[5] – legally justifiable but politically inflammatory.

This duly led to predictable Commons objections when Secretary of State Coke introduced a bill for the tax's legitimization in February 1629, and a counter-attack against Catholics and 'Arminians' led by arch-Presbyterian Francis Rous, a Cornish MP and half-brother to future Parliamentary leader John Pym. Charles offered no concessions; the most he would do was assure MPs in his personal address to the new session as it opened on 24 January that he had collected tonnage and poundage due to the military emergency rather than just out of prerogative right.[6] Events duly moved to confrontation; possibly Charles' abandonment of conciliation was linked to the rising power of his new Lord Treasurer Sir Francis Weston, a crypto-Catholic and so at risk if the King was pressurised to hunt down such men at Court to satisfy MPs. The linked double question of Catholics and 'Arminians', the two being seen as part of the same 'Papist' conspiracy by suspicious MPs, was to form the centrepiece of Eliot's verbal tirade against Royal policy in the final showdown in the Commons on 2 March.

The offenders of 2 March 1629 were all arrested, eventually arraigned before the Court of King's Bench, and sentenced to hefty fines (which Eliot refused to pay) and imprisonment during the King's pleasure – which was normally terminable by apology and a grovelling request for pardon. They were also denied access to visitors, books, and writing-materials for a time, which was more usual for serious political offences than for their charge of riotous behaviour in the Commons. (Eliot, however, had written provocatively against the King's rights and ministers, so reasons for his treatment were arguably not that different from those for the equally troublesome Sir Thomas More's in 1535.) There was an ominous sign of the King's personal involvement in drawing up the list of charges, in that he examined and amended the drafts for the legal indictments and added his indignant personal comments. He also used abusive language about the accused in his speech to the Lords as he dissolved Parliament on 10 March, calling them 'vipers' and fulminating about the insult to him personally in their disorderly behaviour[7] – mixing fully precedented anger at violence within the verge of Court (which had also annoyed Henry VIII and Elizabeth) with the political nature of the offence. The fact that Eliot, unlike the others, refused to apologise or to accept an offer of his release on license if he would agree to be 'bound over to keep the peace' and was thus kept in the Tower indefinitely showed that he was determined to make a stand. But the monarch was content to let him rot there and to keep him there for years if necessary – though this was standard practice for 'seditious' and stubborn enemies of an extant government (albeit usually for more serious offences) such as Sir Walter Raleigh in 1604–16. Apparently the cautious counsel of Royal ministers Lord Keeper Coventry and Lord Privy Seal Manchester concerning Eliot's treatment lost out to Weston concerning the 'hard line' taken; and for good measure some merchants who were suing for the return of goods seized over non-payment of tonnage and poundage were arrested too.[8]

Eliot's arrest for his anti-Royal agitation in the Commons in 1628–9 was not unusual – Elizabeth behaved similarly towards 'insolent' MPs like Peter Wentworth, and James I as well as Charles arrested Parliamentary critics as a Parliament ended in the 1620s. Wentworth, like 'Puritan' pamphleteers Prynne and Burton who were punished by Charles, was once arrested for impinging on the sovereign's dignity by his 'libels' – in his case, his 1590–1 pamphlet on the need for Elizabeth to be pressurised to name a successor. Like Eliot in 1629–32, he faced staying in prison until he apologised; but Elizabeth, unlike Charles, eventually released the culprit. Charles, moreover, had 'form' for stretching his authority into questionable areas – during Parliament in May 1626 he had briefly arrested Eliot and his fellow-critic of Buckingham, Sir Dudley Digges, and the Earl of Arundel and had been induced to release them after strong protests. Arrest and prosecution for verbal or written abuse of the government and the Church extended to other former 'elite insiders' too (Eliot could be categorised as a marginal 'insider' as he had been a client and employee of Buckingham as Lord Admiral). In 1637 the regime turned on and prosecuted the King's late elder brother Prince Henry's vociferously 'Puritan' ex-chaplain Henry Burton, who had also served Charles until he was sacked in the early 1620s for abusing the then junior but influential bishop William Laud. Being lower down the social scale than respected (if impoverished) minor Cornish gentleman Eliot, Burton ended up publicly flogged and having his ears cropped in the pillory for his 'seditious' religious writings.

Arrest during a sitting of Parliament was legally dubious, as infringing MPs' immunity – though this had already happened in the 1628–9 Parliament to Rolle. At the time, the only possible charge was for words or actions in Parliament, which should have been covered by Parliamentary privilege; at least in March 1629 Eliot and his group had assaulted and intimidated the Speaker. But Charles did take matters further than his predecessors. His ominous mixing of the personal reaction to an insult with the 'administratively' legal in his actions was not normal for a sovereign, and it was typical of his rashness that when Eliot's faction had indicted Buckingham on various charges (some clearly malicious) in 1626 Charles complained to the Speaker that some of it touched on his own honour. By contrast, when MPs drew up equally malicious charges against Lord Treasurer Cranfield in 1624 James had stayed out of the matter, whatever his personal annoyance at it.

A spell in the Tower or another London prison for *'lese majeste'* was an occupational hazard for opposing the monarch's wishes, and Charles had sent peers such as Arundel there before for co-ordinating Commons attacks on Buckingham. His punishment of the Earl of Bristol (the former ambassador to Spain, John Digby) in the mid-1620s was particularly partisan, and seemed to be stepping down into the political arena to come to the embattled Buckingham's aid in the House of Lords. Bristol had been a personal foe of the Duke since the latter and Charles had stayed at his embassy in Madrid in 1623; Charles seemed to be endorsing the Duke's grudges. He tried to keep Bristol away from the Lords in 1626 so the Earl would have no public forum to attack Buckingham, and arranged for the Lord Keeper to send Bristol a note with his (legally required) Lords summons asking him not to turn up; Bristol took no notice.[9] In retaliation, as soon as Parliament had been dissolved the Earl was thrown in the Tower.

Elizabeth was well-known for threatening disobedient or impertinent courtiers with the Tower, and sent those who defied her there from time to time – such as her cousin and potential heir Lady Katherine Grey and her 'illegal' husband Lord Hertford for marrying without her permission. Her harsh treatment of Katherine (who remained under supervision at isolated country houses until she died of tuberculosis in 1568) and her sister Mary (arrested for marrying without the Queen's permission to a man of inferior rank) went beyond the politically necessary to indicate personal grudges against her would-be heirs. Her arbitrary imprisonment encompassed personal as well as political misdeeds – e.g. Sir Walter Raleigh for impregnating her lady-in-waiting Elizabeth Throckmorton – and she was as renowned for standing on her rights to obedience as was Charles.

King James, by contrast, was usually more tolerant, and ignored rather than punished critics of his policies and his ministers – his few targets were 'political' risk-takers who might be plotting subversion with foreign powers as (dodgy) 'evidence' claimed, e.g. Raleigh. Charles' use of arrests as a first not a last resort when facing trouble in Parliament in 1626–9 was a shock to the elite after James' leniency and as such was more harshly regarded than if such measures had been normal in 1605–24, though it was not so much 'tyranny' as a desire for seemly respect for the sovereign, as seen in tightening up Court regulations. But he stood on his 'rights' in other matters too. After the 1626 Parliament's failure to provide enough funds for the government and its French war plans Charles resorted to an unusual 'voluntary' loan of money from his wealthier subjects – not illegal as such and previously practised by cash-strapped English kings for their campaigns in the medieval period, e.g. Edward I and Edward III. As with the 1630s revival of the royal 'Forest Laws' and other dormant kingly legal powers (again more as a money-making mechanism than as a legal principle), the means chosen had adequate legal precedent but had not been exercised often in recent centuries. It was also inflicted on larger than usual numbers of the nobility and gentry who had the ability to express their disquiet in Parliament, with local royal officials required to draw up lists of all those who had the necessary wealth before the Council sent out demands to them. The nobility had been exempt from paying such loans for centuries, and their inclusion in 1626–7 was a sign of the extent of the King's financial crisis rather than a 'sinister' encroachment on their liberty. (Only one peer, the Earl of Lincoln, held out against paying long enough to be arrested.) The navy and the soldiers used in the 1625 Cadiz and Continental campaigns and Charles' Danish allies needed to be paid, with rioting unpaid sailors already demonstrating in London. The King had already used up his wife's dowry and sold or pawned most of the Crown Jewels, with some of Queen Elizabeth's most iconic jewellery recently having been auctioned. As far as the King was concerned he was acting in the national interest, ultimately for a matter of national defence (as he was to do in raising non-Parliamentary funds for the Navy via 'Ship-Money' later), and in any case it was up to him to define the national interest. Disobedience must be punished and refusing to pay up was undermining the nation's safety, and his vigorous and unhesitating use of the courts quashed the resulting 'tax strike' over the 'Forced Loan' with five leading opponents who held out being gaoled as an example. The latter included figures connected personally or by family to the future 'opposition' of 1640–2, e.g. Dorset 'Puritan' MP Sir Walter Earle (a recent critic of Buckingham and a client of anti-Catholic Calvinist peer Lord Saye and Sele) and the uncle of future 'Ship Money' protester Sir John Hampden. The resort of those accused in the resulting legal cases against the 'Five Knights' to arguments that Magna Carta invalidated taxes imposed without consent were a sign of intellectual boldness and a newly coherent legal 'defence', and have accordingly gained iconic status – which was played up in the 1628 Petition of Right and in 1640–2 by Parliament. The King was accused of violating the legal rights of Englishmen, i.e. the constitution, and Magna Carta was cited as protecting *'habeas corpus'*. But this obscures the facts that the forced loan was mostly paid up (some £250,000 by early 1628), only a few 'dissidents' held out, and their legal arguments were soundly 'trashed' in court by the King's tame lawyers led by Attorney-General Heath. Moreover, this time the King had the sense to release the accused after a short spell in gaol in spring 1628 as a sign of his graciousness, as Elizabeth and James had usually done to their critics.

Charles' obstinate treatment of Eliot (and to a lesser extent Holles) in 1629–32 was not just a sign of his 'tyrannical' and/or politically risky habits of stirring up resentment by his manner of proceeding. Compared with the situation facing him over the 'Five Knights' in 1627–8 or with James in 1621 and 1624, he was not facing an immediate or immanent expensive war that would necessitate another appeal to the 'political nation' and would make mercy expedient. But his drastic action was a sign of extra harshness, probably exacerbated by bitterness over the assassination of Buckingham who Eliot had vilified in 'libellous' terms for tyranny. Eliot, unlike earlier dissidents, was kept in the Tower until he died – normally a fate reserved for especially dangerous or obstinate figures, such as Philip, Earl of Arundel (a Catholic) under Elizabeth and Raleigh (an alleged plotter) under James, and then only after legal process. A short spell in gaol was more normal for criticising the monarch in Parliament or in writing. Other arrested members of Eliot's group of MPs who had participated in the rowdy scenes in the Commons on 2 March 1629 did in fact apologise and were released; but Charles would not even let Eliot out on bail as his health deteriorated.[10]

(b) A long tradition of angry Royal reactions to criticism plus harsh punishment – was Charles unfairly singled out for this, or was his reaction demonstrably worse?

The same situation of Charles' 'extreme' and supposedly draconian reactions to his critics not being new occurs with royal punishments. The ear-croppings and public floggings of 'libellers' such as the abusive 'moralist' Protestant pamphleteer William Prynne in the mid-late 1630s may have been notorious at the time, but they were perfectly legal – and occurred earlier to less fanfare. The most extreme punishment for past 'lese majeste' had been that of the pamphleteer John Stubbes for violently abusive writing against Elizabeth's proposed Catholic marriage to the French Duc d'Anjou in 1581 (in *'The Gaping Gulf wherein England is like to be swallowed if Her Majesty forbid not the banns'*.) Whether the ever-cautious Elizabeth was serious about Anjou, her main concern was strategic – to tie Anjou, then heir to the French throne, and his devious elder brother King Henri III to help her defeat Spain in the Low Countries. As a result, she sought to lure France into taking on the cost and risk by fighting King Philip's forces in the region on her behalf – and Anjou was the likeliest commander for a French expedition there so marrying him would tie him to assisting her and be the lynchpin of a lasting Anglo-French alliance. But Anjou was a Catholic, whose late brother King Charles IX and mother Catherine de Medici had arranged the notorious 'St Bartholomew's Day Massacre' of French Protestants in Paris in 1572. Stubbes probably had secret encouragement from senior political figures who his punishment was intended to 'warn off'. He had his hand cut off by the public executioner, as was legally permissible for extreme libel.[11]

This was no harsher than Charles having 'libellous' 'Puritan' pamphleteers Burton, Bastwick and Prynne put in the pillory and having their ears cropped in the late 1630s (Prynne twice). The aggressively anti-Catholic pamphleteer William Prynne infringed on the Royal dignity by abusing Queen Henrietta Maria for acting in public, implying that she was no better than a a whore. But Stubbes' punishment was done by due legal process and was accepted as such, without any short-term or long-term political damage to the sovereign; indeed, Stubbes loudly declared his loyalty to the Queen just after the sentence had been carried out. Charles, by contrast, suffered politically from his punishments for opponents, which were dredged up in Parliament years later; had the 'national mood' among the politically active part of the people changed since 1581? Or had political determination by 'opposition' leaders to exploit memories of the monarch's behaviour hardened? (The Prynne episode was made much of in 1640 by Charles' foes – but it had unluckily for him coincided with 'evidence' for concerned 'Puritans' of other 'pro-Catholic tyranny', e.g. in Scotland.) The impression given by the attitude of Stubbes towards Elizabeth appears to be that of ultimate loyalty to the Queen and a desire to persuade, not insult her. Zealous Presbyterian pamphleteer William Prynne and his fellow-writers were far more abusive in the 1630s, had an obsessive desire to sniff out evidence of 'Arminianism' and its sinister allies at Court in the manner of McCarthyites hunting 'Communists' in the 1950s, and showed no sign of ultimate goodwill. Prynne practically accused Queen Henrietta Maria of being a prostitute for acting on the public stage (in fact appearing in decorous and ideologically tinted Court masques) in his *'Histiomastix'*. Elizabeth had benefited from being the personal embodiment of the Protestant cause, by restoring the 'Reformed Faith' in 1559 after the horrors of Queen Mary's reign; Charles had no such benefit. He also had the problem of Prynne's (and equally harshly treated Burton's and Bastwick's) noble patrons, e.g. Warwick, being alienated from him at the time and out to cause trouble; Stubbes' backers were not hostile to the then monarch.

Charles probably felt that Eliot's intemperate attacks on (his ex-patron) Buckingham for corruption and causing national humiliation in the badly-handled French war of 1627–8 had incited the Duke's murder; Eliot had compared the Duke to famous tyrannical ministers who had died by violence, such as Emperor Tiberius' favourite Sejanus.[12] Worse, Eliot was not exactly a long-term, principled critic of Buckingham; he had been a client of his at the Admiralty in the mid-1620s until he lost out in the question of advising him in 1625, and he only turned on the Duke in the 1626 Parliament (over the issue of the incompetence of the recent attack on Cadiz and general Naval waste of money). The fact that the public and balladeers had celebrated Buckingham's killer Felton as a hero would have exacerbated Royal fury. But making a link between the killing and the Duke's Commons traducers was legally unprovable, though the 'loner' assassin had probably been influenced indirectly by the abusive attacks on the Duke as the cause of the failure of his 1627–8 naval campaign to save the rebel Protestant port of La Rochelle in France from the Catholic government's siege. If the King's intention was to force Eliot to beg for his release as his health declined, his bluff was called by a man as stubborn as him and he was undismayed at any adverse reaction when Eliot fell ill and died in custody. Elizabeth had always known when to give way graciously, or at least show the open appearance of forgiving her insolent subjects without giving in – as over the issue of her marriage, where she issued vague promises to consider and act on all the importunate Parliamentary pleas for her to announce her choice of husband (1563, 1566).[13]

James had also reacted furiously to criticism in Parliament for infringing on his prerogative, as when he tore out the page of the Commons 'Journal' containing the 'Protestation' (an attack on his foreign policy which was seen as too even-handed between Protestants and Catholics) in 1621.[14] The issue, again, was Royal anger at MPs meddling in matters which he thought were his concern alone. James was regarded by more rabidly Protestant sections of the 'political class' as being 'soft' on the international Catholic menace like Charles, with the Court-feted Spanish ambassador Count Gondemar being regarded as a sinister Catholic mastermind who was duping the King with the aid of a cabal of Howard-led courtiers. As with Charles courting the French in 1625, what seemed reasonable international *'realpolitik'* at the Council table seemed a 'plot' to suspicious observers. The King was seen as the victim of a scheming and corrupt clique, linked to Catholicism. The powerful courtier Howard dynasty in the 1610s (led by Lord Treasurer Suffolk and the Earl of Northampton), like Buckingham in the 1620s, were denounced by MPs as hugely corrupt crypto-Catholics; the 'opposition' belief in 1625–8 that their King was under the malign influence of a corrupt pro-Catholic minister was not new. However, Charles was in a worse – public – position than James was in the 1610s, as when Buckingham was the target in 1625–8 Parliament was more often sitting; criticism had a public 'forum'.

James had eventually sacrificed his unpopular 'favourites' when pressure became overwhelming, even sending his protégé Robert Carr and the latter's wife Frances Howard to the Tower over their part in the murder of Frances' ex-ally and potential blackmailer Sir Thomas Overbury. James had stretched legal procedure in seeking to keep Carr and his lover from prosecution for as long as possible. Indeed, James had probably had been involved behind the scenes in arranging Frances' divorce from her previous husband, the Earl of Essex, on the dubious grounds of impotence, so she could marry her lover.[15] (One of the many ironies of Early Stuart politics was that Essex later commanded the Parliamentary army against the King's son.) The crucial difference between James and Charles was that the anti-Buckingham attacks of 1625–8 occurred during wartime, when the King needed money for his campaigns, and in 1625 became tangled with the initial financial settlement of the new reign; in the mid-1610s James did not have to meet Parliament and thus face a public 'forum' debating his loathed crypto-Catholic favourites as it was peacetime. Parliament had ended in stalemate over finance in 1614 and did not meet again until the Bohemia crisis forced this in 1621; the Howards were thus spared violent denunciation by MPs. The drama of the exposure and trial of Carr and Frances Howard in 1615–16 proceeded without a popular 'forum' for it in Parliament.

A partisan King aiding his personal favourites and violent attacks on the latter were thus not new to the Buckingham ascendancy in the mid-1620s. Buckingham indeed used Parliament to 'trash' his rival Cranfield in 1624 – with James warning him that he could be the next victim of such a weapon. James also warned Charles of the counter-productive nature of his enthusiastic use of Parliamentary pressure in arranging a Spanish war in 1624, according to Clarendon.[16] Arguably a new factor was the 'lead' taken in such matters by the senior (ex-Attorney-General) legal expert Sir Edward Coke, a former government figure 'gone rogue', who provided the legal expertise and eloquent leadership that encouraged MPs to interfere more in State matters. A 'culture' of Commons judicial enquiry into alleged misdeeds by lay and religious elites alike emerged, with Coke providing learned 'proof' that this was Parliament's historic role – and in 1640–1 famous Late Medieval cases of the latter taking on royal officials, e.g. Chief Justice Tresilian in 1387, were to be cited by opposition leaders such as Oliver St. John. This new boldness in turn clashed after March 1625 with a King who was more inflexible than the equally irritated but less consistent or harsh James.

James' failure to intervene openly in the 'Thirty Years' War' to save the Protestant cause in central Europe after his daughter and son-in-law's eviction from Bohemia in 1620 was criticised by MPs in 1621 and 1624

– at a time of paranoia about the 'Catholic threat' every bit as heightened as that which faced Charles in 1641–2. Elizabeth and James had however both faced Commons attempts to blackmail them over policy by refusals to vote subsidies, and Parliamentary assaults on the current 'unreformed' condition of the 'semi-Catholic' State Church. Both Elizabeth and James had kept Parliament prorogued or unsummoned for as long as possible after disagreements, as in 1566 and 1614 – but there is no plethora of historians regarding the lack of Parliamentary sessions in the 1570s and early 1580s as evidence of 'Royal tyranny' as there is for the situation when Charles did this in 1629–40.

Parliament had ended in deadlock over supply and was dismissed prematurely and not recalled for years before, in 1614 (the 'Addled Parliament'), as in 1625, 1626, and 1629, and the exigencies of crisis and immanent war forced James to recall it in 1621 and 1624 as Charles also had to do. Luckily for James, the 1624 Parliament was in a belligerently anti-Spanish mood and was prepared to vote a reasonable sum of money for war with Spain – though the talk then was of concentrating on a naval war, not on Continental entanglements (as in 1625 with Mansfeld) which were more costly and unpopular.[17] The decision to launch a Continental campaign rebounded on the government as it became bogged down – which James would have had to face had he lived. Continental entanglements had not been very successful under Elizabeth either, as seen by the frustrating English attempt to assist the Huguenots in the French civil war in 1563. This had ended in a stalled campaign to occupy Le Havre, which the English eventually had to evacuate; and the losses to English troops there from plague and desertion were as bad as those that the Mansfeld campaign faced in 1625. In 1625, however, despite Charles' usefully anti-Habsburg Low Countries campaign his French alliance meant that he was an ally of a Catholic King currently fighting Protestant rebels, which MPs also complained about.

James, like Charles, was in a rocky financial position for much of his reign, a situation inherited from Elizabeth, and indeed made worse by conspicuous Court expenditure although he had the excuse of having a marital partner and (in 1603–12) three children's Households to pay for. His most competent early minister, Sir Robert Cecil who he had inherited from Elizabeth and who he put in charge of the Treasury in 1608, had endeavoured to negotiate a long-term arrangement for increasing Crown revenues with Parliament in 1610 (the 'Great Contract') and had been blocked by both Royal and Commons opposition. Cecil's reduction of the Royal debts as Lord Treasurer in 1608–12 (£597,000 to 500,000) had been reversed by his prodigal successor Howard – and the long-term effects of this failure were to be felt by Charles. So was Charles in a poor position due to the 'bad luck' of capable Cecil dying early (aged 48) and James relying on a policy of loyalty-inducing high spending on his court elite?

Charles' situation and attitudes were thus not unique, and yet his stormy relations with the majority of the 'political nation' in 1625–40 have been traditionally written up as presaging the 'inevitable' clash between King and Parliament after 1640. Similarly, the King was seen as the 'guilty party', bearing in mind the fact that he was to take up arms against Parliament and end up executed on charges of tyranny. It can be suspected that this was an example of unconscious 'wisdom after the event' – regarding the chain of events that led to civil war as inevitable and seeking to present a seamless narrative in which every incident is seen with the wisdom of hindsight. The 'progressive' approach of the predominant school of 'Whig Historians' in the later 17th century and 20th century indeed saw the cause of Parliament in its own contemporary terms – as that of 'good', democratic political development – and thus regarded the King's non-Parliamentary rule in 1629–40 as inevitably 'wrong' and dictatorial. The King stood in the way of political 'progress' and had shut down Parliament in 1629; his cause was thus, as Sellars and Yeatman were to satirise mid-20th-century historians' attitudes in *1066 And All That*, 'wrong but romantic'. To the 'progressive' Victorian writers and their heirs, the cause of Eliot or, in 1640–3, Pym and Hampden was that of democracy against a tyrant and the ultimate authority in 17th-century England, as later, should have been Parliament. The intellectual concept of the King seeing himself as God's appointed representative at the head of the hierarchy of the world's 'natural order' seemed proof of his arrogance and outdated attitudes – in 19th-century and 20th-century terms – rather than the actual 'world-view' of almost all those living in 1640, his opponents included. The foundation of the 'ideal' British constitution was the 1688 'Glorious Revolution' against 'Divine Right', and an autocratic sovereign who ignored Parliament was automatically a villain. In this secure age of democratic confidence, it was forgotten that the King as the 'keystone of the arch of government' was a guarantor of stability, quite apart from 17th-century people's 'mindset' being heavily influenced by notions of a hierarchy of authority established by God. The 'revisionist' historians of the later 20th century, led by Conrad Russell and John Adamson, duly reversed the simplistic and determinist 'Whig' interpretation of events.

(c) Were Charles' attitudes especially liable to cause political disaster? Why was he so naïve or inflexible, and why the high level of offence taken at this?

Charles was not known for his ability to compromise or for his political skills at winning over his critics; and part of this can be plausibly ascribed to his lack of serious 'education' in the world of high politics. Again, he was in a different position from his two predecessors – and had had a less harsh 'training'. Elizabeth had grown up in the turbulent world of Tudor Court factions, bastardised and her mother executed at the age of two-and-a-half and herself threatened as the centre of two serious plots against her predecessors (the plans of Sir Thomas Seymour in 1548 and the Wyatt rebellion in 1554); she had been interrogated by angry Councillors on both occasions and had nearly been executed before she became Queen. James, king at nine months, had grown up as a pawn in the bloody world of Scottish noble feuds over control of his regency government and had been kidnapped and used as a political puppet. He had sacrificed the chance to defend or avenge his mother, who he had not seen since he was an infant, to the political cause of good relations with Elizabeth and the probable succession to the English throne. Charles, by contrast, had had no youthful experience of the difference between formal deference to the King and real political power, of conspiracy or rebellion, or even of serious reverses; he had grown up within the cocoon of English Court life (and been kept in the background until his early twenties). His older brother Henry – regarded by contemporaries as far more intelligent and dynamic, and physically fit to take part in arduous sports unlike Charles – had left Scotland at nine so he had some knowledge of a world beyond the Court; Charles had left as a 'backward' child of two. Henry had run his own establishment as Prince of Wales from the age of sixteen, and had had pronounced views different from his father on important matters; Charles had had no such independence until his surprise decision to seek out his potential bride in Spain at twenty-two. He heavily depended on Buckingham in his mid-twenties, even as King; James had shown a similar emotional dependence on a good-looking, glamorous and more experienced male mentor of pro-Catholic views (Esme Stuart) in his late teens, infuriating Protestant nobles who then forced the exile of the latter, but had matured to balance factions more expertly.

The impression provided by Charles in his crucial formative years as a political 'actor' is of a decidedly naïve character, heavily dependent on the physically and politically impressive Buckingham. Like his brother he was morally opposed to the laxity and debauchery of James' rather louche and easy-going Court, but Henry had not been at all dependent on older figures to guide him. Charles had no idea of the potential political 'pitfalls' of marrying a hugely unpopular Catholic Spanish bride in 1623, for example, or even of the way the Spanish government would use his presence in Madrid to endeavour to win unwise political concessions from him. He soon showed more confidence as King, as with the politically wise order to his new French wife Henrietta Maria to send most of her Catholic entourage home; and his unbending defence of Buckingham in 1626–8 showed that he preferred loyalty to the 'easy course' of dismissing an unpopular minister. He was less flexible than James, who did sacrifice ministers to the Commons and sections of the Lords (Lord Chancellor Bacon in 1621 and Lord Treasurer Cranfield in 1624); ironically Cranfield had owed his fall to Buckingham turning on him over his opposition to the Spanish war and arranging for a move for impeachment.

Charles had an unfortunate flair for mixing the personal with the political – but he backed this up by his use of harsh and 'privileged' public pronouncements, which reflected his (honestly stated) beliefs as well as the 'dignity' which he felt owing to his status as King. In his 'official' published explanation for the problems of the 1625 and 1626 Parliaments, 'A Declaration of the True Causes which moved His Majestie to assemble and dissolve the last two meetings of Parliament', he (or more probably Secretary of State Conway, writing subject to his approval) made space to abuse the 'violent and ill-advised passions' of a few MPs who had maliciously attacked Buckingham. He also falsely claimed that it had been MPs, not him or Buckingham, who had wanted the Spanish war and that they were legally obliged to pay for it, and condescendingly (if sincerely) insisted that he did not have to render account to anyone but God. He had graciously agreed to explain his actions to Parliament out of goodwill to allay their fears, not because of legal requirement.[18] In a similar vein, on 29 May 1626 he reminded MPs that 'Parliaments are altogether in my power for their calling, sitting and dissolution; therefore as I find the fruits of them good or evil they are to continue or not to be'.[19] His own view of recent international constitutional history, set out by Secretary of State Carleton to Parliament on 12 May 1626, indeed had it that it was MPs who had needed reining in for transgressing on Royal prerogatives, not vice versa: '(monarchs) seeing the turbulent spirits of their parliaments at length they, by little and little, began to stand upon their prerogatives, and at last overthrew the parliaments throughout Christendom except only here with us'.[20]

Charles and his defence of Buckingham: a misunderstood case?
But has Charles' stubbornness and obsession with his rights been too easily condemned out of hindsight? Or seen through the prism of the Civil War? The case of his fierce defence of Buckingham is a crucial early example; and it can be argued that he showed commendable loyalty to his closest allies unlike the devious (if more realistic) James. The Duke's competence and energy as an administrator have been reviewed more favourably in recent years, as in Roger Lockyer's biography;[21] did his foes unreasonably blacken his name and ability? Nor was naval administration a paragon of efficiency in the much-praised Elizabethan 'heroic' era; the government had faced similar problems of incompetence, slackness, and embezzlement then and Elizabeth had placed a non-expert senior courtier (Lord Howard of Effingham, whose father had also held the post) in charge of the navy at the time of the Spanish wars. Howard's advantage had been having a highly efficient subordinate who could run the shipyards adequately, Sir John Hawkins; Buckingham lacked an equivalent and did not take the gamble of putting the zealous, prickly but capable Sir John Eliot (another Plymouth 'local') in charge. To anticipate the quip of US President Lyndon Johnson about a promoted potential foe, Eliot was one of those vituperative characters who it was better to have 'inside the tent' aiming out rather than 'outside the tent' aiming in. But Buckingham preferred to exclude potential rivals or critics, as seen by his treatment of unreliable fellow-Councillors who he marginalised in 1621–6. He served his sovereign loyally to his best ability despite –

justified – misgivings about the people he was negotiating with on his disastrous Spanish mission in 1623. In an age when personal charm and courtly manners mattered a great deal in high-level politics, he proved a quick learner and held his own on the international 'stage'. Much of the criticism of him can be explained by his monopoly of power under two successive monarchs and the grants lavished on his large family, which as usual aroused jealousy and intrigue in those denied influence by his role.

As with many Commons campaigns against Royal ministers and policies in this era, the hand of frustrated 'opposition' peers seeking to dislodge their rivals from power can be seen behind the attacks. The Earls of Pembroke and Arundel were the prime suspects. (The recent work of John Adamson even presents the crisis of 1640–2 in this context; see below.) This is not to deny that resentment of Buckingham was genuinely widespread, not least over his attitude to Catholicism and his many Catholic relatives; the public rejoicings at his murder showed that. It was not helpful for his reputation that he was famous for his conspicuous consumption, and in Westminster he not only bought up prominently-placed Wallingford House (at the entrance to Whitehall) but took over the Lord Chancellor's usual residence, York House (near modern Charing Cross Station). The fear of his greed for power and unscrupulousness extended to lurid claims that he had James poisoned in March 1625 as the latter was tiring of him – the 17th century equivalent of modern tabloid journalism. Parliament duly examined the stories in 1626, calling on the eminent physician Wiliam Harvey and other Royal doctors for evidence.[22] Arguably the attempts to remove him from power were merely the latest in a long line of attacks on ministers assisted by their would-be supplanters in the Lords, most recently those on Bacon and Cranfield under King James. Accusing ministers of abusing their position for financial gain was common practice, and in an era of perquisites and regular financial 'sweeteners' it was accepted practice – connived at by Elizabeth as well as by the Stuarts. If Lord Treasurer Howard built his new mansion at Audley End out of the fruits of office, so did Elizabeth's Secretary of State/Treasurer William Cecil (Burghley House) and Lord Chancellor Christopher Hatton (Holdenby House). But Elizabeth was not seen as a patron of corrupt ministers, despite her failure to act on her promises to Parliament (e.g. in 1601) to reform abuses – did hindsight knowledge of what led to civil war in his case make Charles more vulnerable?

Charles was well aware of the personal and political reasons for attacks on his minister by rivals, as shown by his 'targeting' of the Duke's principal Lords critics Arundel and Bristol. But unlike Elizabeth or James he stepped in to the political 'arena' to defend them, openly – loyal but risky? His decision to put Bristol on trial before the Lords in May 1626 was counter-productive, as the Earl made counter-charges against Buckingham (e.g. taking Charles to Madrid in 1623 to turn him Catholic) instead of giving way and begging pardon as Charles probably expected. This fanned the lurid public fears of Buckingham as pro-Catholic. Similarly, when Charles arrested Arundel to deny his vote to the anti-Buckingham Lords faction the House refused to sit until the Earl was released.[23] Charles' actions went beyond normal Royal actions in showing displeasure to a politically provocative peer, and mixed the personal and political again. Elizabeth was luckier or shrewder in her choice of targets for personal revenge – Leicester, thrown out of Court on several occasions after quarrels, was hated by many nobles and the banned/arrested Duke of Norfolk and eighth Earl of Northumberland were Catholics.

The turbulent Parliaments of 1625–9 served as a public arena for struggles for power and influence among major peers and ministers rather than as portrayed in 'Whig History' – namely as a unified, 'democratic' resistance to the King and the corrupt, monopolistic Buckingham. But so had the Elizabethan Parliaments of 1563 and 1566 which debated the succession. In Charles' case, it was not a case of 'united' and 'principled' attacks on Buckingham which he unfairly objected to – some of Buckingham's critics had links to current ministers who had fallen out with the Duke and may have wished him ruined, e.g. Sir Dudley Digges with the Archbishop of Canterbury, George Abbot. It should not be forgotten that in winter 1625–6 there was 'orthodox' Calvinist pressure on the King and Duke to endorse the decrees of the Dutch Synod of Dort (1618), denouncing the dissident anti-Calvinist theologian Jacob van Arnim, 'Arminius' (of which more later). The resultant 'York House Conference' had seen Buckingham take the lead in refusing this as unnecessary, thus leaving him – a former patron of Calvinist preachers such as John Preston – open to charges of being 'pro-Arminian'. Did this 'desertion' by him[24] spark off the hatred of anti-'Arminian' MPs in the Commons in 1626–8? The anti-Buckingham abuse can thus be seen as a 'political' move by enemies of his recent religious 'stand', not a principled attack on a dangerous and incompetent minister backed up by a 'tyrant' king. The Earl of Warwick and Lord Saye and Sele, later 'opposition' leaders in 1637–42, were involved in this abuse.

Nor was the case of Sir John Eliot's opposition to the Duke one of straightforward, long-term principled suspicion of a 'corrupt' minister by a public figure with no 'axe to grind' in doing this. Eliot had started as one of the Duke's clients in 1624–5, acting as Vice-Admiral of Devon to assist naval activities at Plymouth. But he had fallen out with the Duke and gravitated to the opposition; the bungled naval attack on Cadiz in October 1625 seems to have been a major reason for his resultant hunt for evidence of incompetence and bribery at the Duke's Admiralty. This would imply that if the Duke had appointed the less lackadaisical Sir Robert Mansell as commander for the Cadiz expedition, instead of the courtier Sir Edward Cecil,[25] Eliot would not have had this 'ammunition'. And would he have been so vehement had the Duke not had him dismissed as Vice-Admiral for Devon in late 1625, thus stimulating his hatred? If Eliot was right in his emotive speech to Parliament in February 1626 about one man being behind the Cadiz disaster, that was Cecil not Buckingham though the latter had advised Charles to choose him. In fact, disaster and triumph were often a matter of luck and timing in a 17th-century naval expedition not of sinister Court-sponsored embezzlement; the expedition only narrowly missed capturing part of the Spanish 'Plate Fleet' bringing treasure from Mexico, which would have silenced critics. The Duke's failed attack on Cadiz in 1625 was not a unique example of bad management of a naval campaign; under Elizabeth the 'Isles Voyage' of 1597 and other occasions had seen the English ships missing their target and achieving little.

It was the Duke's bad luck that the La Rochelle campaign of 1627–8 to rescue rebel Huguenots from the French government's attack exposed a multiplicity of problems that only a far more experienced and diligent administrator, with far more money granted by Parliament, might have lessened. Crucially, this was England's first major naval war since the 1590s, so there had been no time to overhaul the usual inefficiency of the naval and military administration and assess what was needed and how to provide it quickly in advance. The most that can be said about Buckingham's responsibility for the failure at La Rochelle is that he missed several chances to take the initiative when in personal command on the adjacent island of Rhe during the expedition to relieve the

Huguenots besieged in La Rochelle by Louis XIII's army in 1627. Most notably, when he landed on Rhe and launched his attack on the town of St Martin on 12 July 1627 (which was meant to secure the entire island in one blow and thus overawe the Rochellois into admitting his army to their town) he failed to follow up his impressive victory outside St Martin. The defeated French general, the Marquis de Toiras, was able to pull back into the citadel adjacent to St Martin, rally his demoralised men, and hold out until Cardinal Richelieu could send help.[26] Equally, Buckingham was over-confident that his imaginative 'grand strategy' to bring in restive anti-Richelieu French nobles to attack the French army outside La Rochelle in the rear would work. Other factors were beyond the Duke's control – the town authorities at La Rochelle did not agree to admit his troops when his fleet arrived and he sent his deputy Sir William Beecher to inform them. The populace were in favour of the English, but the mayor and council refused to do as they wished. Thus he had to continue to camp in the open on Rhe, exposed to the weather and thus demoralising his troops. Similarly, when Buckingham failed to take the citadel of St. Martin in mid-July and blockaded it the garrison were nearly starved out, but the great 'chain'/stockade which he placed between boats across the bay outside the fortress to block off sea-access to them was broken up by the tide so food and later reinforcements could arrive. The English government was supposed to send 2,000 or so military reinforcements by sea from Plymouth to him, which would have demoralised the defence even if they did not give in quickly. Instead, none arrived. The supply-ships were still loading up in the Thames and their officials did not have enough money to provide quick loading; the Lord Treasurer, Sir James Ley (Earl of Marlborough), had not found or released the money to pay for men or supplies. Nor had the local county authorities mustered volunteers or sent them to Plymouth on time – hardly unusual, as even when facing invasion in 1588 musters had had a habit of running late. Not enough men volunteered, and the troops did not arrive – which was not the Duke's fault. The French King's army outside La Rochelle then landed reinforcements at St Martin at night despite the English naval blockade. Buckingham then had to evacuate Rhe under fire, losing many men in a humiliating withdrawal 'under fire' along a causeway to the embarkation-site. Buckingham may have been an indifferent general with no military experience, but the La Rochelle campaign was dogged by bad luck. In any case, the Duke's assassination in August 1628 abruptly ended the political deadlock over that issue.

(d) **Religion: not a new 'flashpoint' for a disciplinarian monarch after 1625. But was Charles an innovator and so made his situation worse? Or were his foes (the anti-'Arminians') innovators – with a new weapon?**

The next clash with the Commons, over religion in 1628–9, had been foreshadowed by similar anti-State Church agitation by factions of MPs under Elizabeth. Elizabeth as well as Charles was unwavering in her defence of the Church as established in 1559 and against any further 'reform', ignoring the militants' demands in the Commons. So did James, despite (or because of?) his Presbyterian Calvinist upbringing – though the main 'arena' for his obduracy was the clerical Hampton Court Conference of 1604, where he shouted down radicals who had dared to refer to a State Church containing presbyters. Like Elizabeth and Charles, James preferred a hierarchical Church where the junior clergy obeyed orders and a 'chain of command' – reflecting the order of the Universe – led up to the King at the summit. James' view of kings' rights over the Church was as exalted as Charles', albeit due to personal experience of the Calvinist alternative in Presbyterian Scotland – ministers such as Andrew Melville haranguing the King like any other parishioner and meetings of the clergy ignoring Royal orders if they seemed 'ungodly'. Charles' unbending attitude to his rights was at its most imflammatory to a substantial body of important provincial opinion (and to a group of leading nobles) in religion. These may have been a minority in statistical terms, and Elizabeth and her ally Archbishop Whitgift had driven many outspoken Presbyterians out of the Anglican Church – but they were vocal and had the ability to focus on gaining seats in Parliament (often within a Calvinist peer's gift, e.g. Warwick's hold on Essex borough seats). Charles' devotion to an episcopal form of Anglicanism was to prove a major problem in acquiring his consent to 'Root and Branch' reform of the Church by the victorious Parliamentarians after 1646, and helped to prevent an agreement that would have saved his throne – and his life. He duly became the 'Royal Martyr', as played up in propaganda after 1649 and enshrined at the Restoration with the day of his execution a political equivalent of a saint's day. But this is not evidence of his unique and counter-productive 'High Anglican' antipathy to 'Puritan' elements in the Commons and the clergy, or indeed that all his opponents favoured abolishing the bishops. This ideological antipathy to bishops 'per se' surfaced with 'Root and Branch' petitions to Parliament in 1640–1 – but would it have done so if more bishops at that date had been as firmly Calvinist as Williams?

The problems lay in whether the sort of Church Charles envisaged was that of his father's and Elizabeth's reigns, continuing without major change – and whether the policies and practices he backed under Laud's ascendancy amounted to doctrinal innovation. In that sense, perception was as important as fact – which is where the added post-1618 problem of 'Arminianism' comes in, to his detriment and to the benefit of his critics. The Church, as established in 1559, had been doctrinally 'Calvinist' like the 'Reformed Church' established by Lord Protector Somerset in 1547–9, while continuing the administrative and disciplinary frameworks of the pre-Reformation Catholic Church. It was thus a hybrid – and its opponents had complained of that under Elizabeth and James too. It was organised in bishoprics, with local 'grass-roots' religious networks frowned on and suppressed (as seditious if not heretical) by Elizabeth and her favoured clerics – indeed, the disciplinarian zeal of Archbishop John Whitgift in the 1580s was a foretaste of that of Laud. A firm hierarchy was maintained, and – as in society and in the contemporary concept of the universe – order and harmony were vital. It was thus seen by radicals, loosely referred to as 'Puritans', as incompletely reformed and its Catholic-style bishops, vestments, and disciplinarian mechanisms as 'Papist'. There was already an implication that any actions by the hierarchy that did not meet the approval of the radicals would be tarred with this brush; disciplinarian action by the imperfectly reformed Church establishment would be placed in the category of Catholics persecuting the 'godly', as seen in the immensely popular *Book of Acts and Monuments* by John Foxe on which generations of Englishmen were brought up.[27] This popular glorification of the persecutions of 1554–8 fostered a culture of victimization for any opponents of the Church's hierarchy, with their prosecutors cast in the mould of sinister agents of international Popery. By extension, any sovereign who backed such attacks on the 'godly' was comparable to 'Bloody' Mary – and a King who was already married to a Catholic wife like Charles was at particular risk. James' wife, Charles' mother Anne of Denmark, turned Catholic; but this was before the 'wave' of aggressive international Catholic advance seen in Germany and Bohemia after 1620 and James himself was always firmly Calvinist in his theology.

Any disciplinarian sovereign would thus face suspicion unless his orthodoxy was impeccable – as James I's was due to his Scots upbringing by John Knox's party. Luckily for James' reputation, he had been taken away from his Catholic mother and her priests as an infant. James allowed suspected or semi-open Catholics prominence at Court and maintained good relations with Spain. He saw himself as a trusted mediator and peacemaker in Europe, which made him equally approachable to Catholics and Protestants – hence the idea of his obtaining a Catholic wife for his heir to bind Spain to him. .But he could not be accused of being a crypto-Catholic, and his estranged wife Anne of Denmark's Catholic sympathies and possible conversion did not damage him. Charles could not escape such suspicions, although he had sent almost all his Catholic wife's potentially missionary entourage home despite her protests. (Ironically, when Henrietta Maria was resisting this it was the supposedly 'pro-Papist' Buckingham who reminded her of the fate that Henry VIII had meted out to obstreperous wives.)[28]

James was doctrinally Calvinist but attracted to the political advantages for stability and monarchy of the orderly and ceremonial English Church, whose administrative structure he did his best to impose in Scotland. He shared this approach with Charles – but the latter was operating in a different situation. The lack of Protestant doctrinal innovations in the period c.1559–1618 had been followed by a state of flux, with new possibilities arising from the theology of the Dutch writer Jacobus van Armin ('Arminius'). The latter had been condemned by orthodox Dutch Calvinist theologians at the Synod of Dort as a crypto-Catholic, and the same allegations were thrown at his supporters in England from the early 1620s. The first theological 'cause celebre' to scandalise the vigilant Calvinists in the Commons was that of Richard Montague – who James, backer of the Calvinists against 'Arminius' at Dort, firmly believed to be fully orthodox. Charles appointed the already controversial Montague as a Royal chaplain in July 1625, probably mainly to protect him from his Commons inquisitors.[29] But there was not a deterministic 'Royal policy' from 1625 to promote 'Arminians' and drive out their enemies;

simultaneously with this Buckingham was trying to persuade the leading anti-'Arminian' John Preston to become Lord Keeper. According to one modern analysis, Charles was not committed to promoting the 'Arminians' until 1628.[30] Certainly, as Prince of Wales Charles had collections of anti-Arminian polemics dedicated to him by two men in a position to know his basic beliefs – the new Archbishop Abbot's brother Robert Abbot (1621) and Dr John Prideaux, Professor of Divinity at Oxford (1625).

Charles sought to restore order and decorum and impose discipline at his Court, with a mass of new rules and regulations and enthusiasm for hierarchy. This belief in the natural order of things in Nature, as in politics, being a hierarchic order headed by the monarch was also played up in his elaborate Court entertainments. The 1630s saw a series of grand (and expensive) masques at Court feting the King as a semi-divine figure in a usually pastoral Classical setting, most notably by the poet Thomas Carew (e.g. 'Coelum Britannicum' on Shrove Tuesday 1634).[31] There was clearly an overall didactic purpose to the portrayal of a munificent and all-wise King who brought the benefits of peace (post-1630) and banished dissenting troublemakers, acting like an Olympian god (often Neptune, showing his naval concerns)[32] and overseeing the harmonious revels below him. Sedition, lewdness (and homosexuality), and alcoholism were all targeted, and the love of King and Queen celebrated. Charles' personal commitment to this was crucial; his concern for the correct 'spin' on Court iconography extended to taking down the embarrassingly anti-Spanish De Vroom tapestries at the Guard Chamber, Whitehall, which celebrated the victories of 1588 and banishing them to rural Oatlands Palace.

The question of the monarch believing that such idealised entertainments represented (or at least should represent) reality has been raised in Charles' case,[33] but not in that of the equally enthusiastic James. Did he confuse image with reality? It is a fair point, and comments can be made about the obtuse 'make-believe' image of Their Majesties easily vanquishing the seditious goddess Discord in William D'Avenant's masque 'Salmacida Spolia' in the midst of political chaos at Twelfth Night 1640.[34] D'Avenant's flattering picture of a King governing by love as much as by power can easily be ridiculed – but was all this ever meant to do more than reflect back the Courtly elite's idealised vision of themselves to the (limited) audience? The notion of the King as 'divine' was not new or a sign of megalomania – the learned James had explained to Parliament in 1610 that Kings were rightly regarded as divine because they exercised God's power on earth. In political terms, the picture of a 'divine' ruler does tie in with Charles' demands for unquestioning loyalty and obedience from his subjects as seen by his harsh treatment of those who defied him, such as the Earl of Bristol in 1625–6 or Eliot in 1629–32. This extended to merchants who would not pay tonnage and poundage or complained that he treated his subjects worse than the Sultan did the Turks in 1628–9, so it was all-encompassing not just aimed at the elite for political resistance.

Charles had been brought up in the rarified world of isolated country residences until his late teens, with limited access to Court, and had not had his father's (or Elizabeth's) experience of savage political 'in-fighting' in his youth. His desire for seemliness, order, and 'control' can be welcomed after the coarse buffoonery and rampant drunkenness that marred James' court.[35] Psychologically, comments have been made on Charles seeking to compensate for his small stature or his being an overlooked second son, a 'late developer' who his brother Henry had reputedly said was fitted to be Archbishop of Canterbury.[36] His extension of 'seemliness' and 'order' to the religious sphere was more problematic than restoring such behaviour to Court, but was pursued no less earnestly. As seen by a group of concerned senior 'High Anglican' clerics (including the future Archbishop Laud) in the first serious debate about his religious intentions in 1623, his interests were for order and stability within the existing framework of the doctrinally semi-Calvinist Church, not innovation. Matthew Wren, the future disciplinarian ally of Laud, recalled that the Prince's chaplain Neile assured the other debaters that the Prince was keener on 'upholding the doctrine and discipline and right estate of the Church' than his father was.[37] A 'confession' dated January 1626 which he probably wrote reveals him as what he called a 'Catholic' Christian, in the sense of being a supporter of the idea of a universal Church and reverencing the saints but not accepting that they had any holy powers of intercession, and as respecting the Pope but not allowing that he had any secular power.[38] His main influences as a small boy were not at all 'High Church' – his guardians Sir Robert and Lady Carey were conventional Anglicans and his tutor Thomas Murray was pro-'Puritan'. He seems to have developed his ideas in his mid-twenties, but was as exposed then to the anti-'Arminian' John Preston as he was to Laud – though his chaplain Neile was to turn out a disciplinarian as a bishop and so may have encouraged him in that direction.

Charles would have seen no 'innovation' in his actions to enforce Church ceremony and punish controversialists in the 1630s, merely asserting the proper running of the Church as he did the State. It was never portrayed as stepping beyond the theological or ceremonial boundaries laid down in the 1559 Prayer-Book, or the 'media res' between the Catholicism of Rome and the austere Calvinism of Geneva upheld by Bishop Richard Hooker in his *Laws of Ecclesiastical Polity*. The enforcement of official rules on wearing correct apparel – proper vestments, not a plain 'Geneva gown' – despite objections about this being allegedly 'Catholic' was not new to Charles' campaign. The desire to be more 'pro-active' about discipline than his father – or the lax and ineffective rule since 1611 of Archbishop Abbot – coincided with the fact that his most eager and effective clerical allies in carrying out this work were interested in the new intellectual currents at work in theology since 'Arminius' challenge. The crucial factor was that he quickly found a more than willing but temperamentally controversial instrument in William Laud, a minor figure in the Anglican Church with no powerful patrons as of 1625 (and disliked by James, who only gave him the minor see of St David's) but dedicated and zealous – and one who did not care about making enemies. The crucial sponsor in Laud's rise was Buckingham, to whom he was chaplain from 1622–8 and whose mother he endeavoured to 'save' from turning Catholic at King James' request. It was also through Buckingham's sister Lady Denbigh that Laud met the most famous 'Arminian' controversialist of the time, Richard Montague, according to the disapproving John Preston. Thanks to Laud's rise his personal enemy Bishop John Williams – a far more shrewd politician – lost the King's ear, though Williams' dealings with Buckingham's enemies (e.g. Pembroke in 1626) also doomed him anyway. Thus Charles came to rely on a divisive figure in the Church around 1627/8, as he had already done in secular matters.

The Laudian 'control' mechanisms: 'innovation' as opposed to a revival of Elizabeth's disciplinarian attitude? But did 'Arminianism' (real or rumoured) make Laud's problems much worse by tainting his allies with semi-Catholicism?

Another problem for Laudian disciplinarianism was its linkage to greater ceremonial and rigidity in both theology and the 'appearance' of both churches and clergy. This was all part of the same project – but the latter was seen by its foes as semi-Catholic. Here events in the Protestant Church in Holland rebounded on that in England. Was the Dutch reformer Jacob van Arnim ('Arminius'), an inspiration for English Anglican disciplinarians as they attacked 'extreme' Protestant clerics who defied the Church hierarchy, really theologically Protestant, as understood by the boundaries set for the English Church in 1559? The Dutch religious authorities at the synod of Dort in 1618 ruled that he was non-Calvinist i.e. not an orthodox Protestant thinker, which set down a 'marker' and provided a weapon for enemies of his perceived sympathisers. (In fact there had already been Armin-style theological attacks on predestination within the Church in the latter years of Elizabeth's reign, when the strict Calvinist inflexibility of thought at the intellectual 'power-house' of Cambridge colleges had lapsed, without punishment.) The authorities had taken a more relaxed view of such speculation then than in the 1560s, when the Anglican Church was newly-established and more hesitant. Elizabeth had had to appoint the 'pro-Genevan' Edmund Grindal as Archbishop of York in 1570 and later of Canterbury due to his theological and administrative 'stature' – though his lack of discipline towards the 'Puritans' among the clergy had caused her to suspend him from his functions. But under the stricter Archbishop Whitgift from 1583 – a former Calvinist theology professor at Cambridge, but a disciplinarian on matters such as vestments – the Royal battle to secure a disciplinarian higher clergy seemed to have been won. James and Charles duly profited from this and Whitgift and his zealous successor Bancroft could not be accused of being crypto-Catholics; but open 'Puritan' doubts about the orthodoxy of senior clergy resumed around 1620. The Arminius controversy was the obvious signpost to this renewed tension within the Church, as giving critics of disciplinarian 'moderates' a useful target to aim at. The nature of the Synod of Dort's reaction to the perceived threat from van Arnim in 1618 was to lay down strict and precise theological 'lines in the sand' defining acceptable doctrine, backing 'Predestination' and other 1550s Calvinist doctrines – which horrified the attending English clerics. The result had a long-term impact in England – it was to land the English Church with an unwanted definition of what doctrine was acceptable. Without this outcome, would Laud have had such problems in the 1630s? He would not have been called 'crypto-Catholic' on theological grounds, which added to the level of reaction in 1640–2.

It was no more than slander by the victims of Laud's zeal to allege that there was crypto-Catholicism on the part of King or clerics. Charles had carefully sent most of his wife's Catholic entourage home. Charles continued to enact the anti-Catholic penal laws in the 1630s and paid no attention to efforts to convert him by the Papal envoy Panzani, and all the optimistic emissary could recall was that the King had deplored the effects of schism in the Christian Church and approved of the furnishings of the Queen's new Catholic chapel.[39] He was careful to drop legal cases against lay Catholics and even to release arrested Jesuits, allegedly telling Panzani that he wanted no martyrs in his reign[40] – but, as with James, he had no reason to punish loyal if errant subjects. The alleged 'arch-villain' to the victorious anti-'Arminians' of 1640–2 was Laud, but it is doubtful if Laud was ever theologically Arminian, despite the hopeful claims of his biographer Peter Heylyn.[41] He was recalled as having attacked Arminius in a sermon at Christmas 1632[42] which is more significant than his denying being an 'Arminian' at his trial in 1645 when any 'smear' was useful – and Prynne, his victim, was leading the attacks. Laud's vigorous condemnation of Catholicism in his 'Conference with Fisher'[43] showed that he was no Catholic apologist. But it is significant that he 'abhorred too rigid definition' of the correct theological position to take to be an Anglican,[44] and believed that the Church of England could accommodate theological differences if these were not publicly aired.[45] This was to him in line with Hooker's late 16th-century doctrine of 'idiaphora', i.e. not forcing the exclusion of those who dissented on matters that were not vital for salvation.[46] He was profoundly annoyed by public debates on theological differences within the Church, seeing them as unnecessarily disruptive.[47] But this laid him open to attack over his concern for hierarchy and discipline, while adding to his 'common ground' with the King.

Charles' desire for 'order' at Court, as paralleled in religion, implied undertaking a vigorous 'clean-up' of inefficiency and unseemliness in the Church – and finding a disciplinarian Archbishop of Canterbury to do it when the next vacancy occurred. Such 'symbolic' matters such as placing rails in front of altars was as much to do with practical tidiness and dignity – including keeping stray dogs away from the Communion table – as it was about a move to 'Romish' ceremony. Equally important was Charles' interest in the 'beauty of holiness' – which meant his personal sympathy for the more ceremonial aspects of Church ritual and a desire to increase them. This coincided with his interest in the beauty and orderliness of Continental Catholic art, of which he was now a major patron in succession to his mentor Buckingham. His desire for traditional Church ritual was as much aesthetic as religious, and the spectacle of 'message' implicit in inspiring Church ceremonial coincided with the propaganda in favour of Divinely-backed order in a hierarchic world seen in Court masques. All this could be interpreted as 'Papist' by obsessives like Prynne, who gleefully interpreted the 1630s Royal theatrical spectacles as Popish orgies and denounced the participation of Court ladies as showing that they were Papists and strumpets. The challenge posed by Prynne's *Histriomastix* in 1632 was particularly crucial as it criticised the Queen for taking part in theatricals and made comparisons to Nero – who had been overthrown as a despot, which implied that Prynne was being seditious and disrespectful to Charles too so his harsh punishment was legally justifiable.

The Laudian ecclesiastical 'innovators' of the 1620s/1630s did not regard themselves as such; nor was a disciplinarian crackdown by a zealous Archbishop on unorthodox and scurrilously abusive 'grass-roots' critics new, as seen by similar controversy in the 1580s. The extreme 'left wing' of the Anglican Church (in modern terms), led by local enthusiasts among the clergy who owed their appointments and freedom of expression to sympathetic lay patrons and feared control by disciplinarian bishops, indeed rejected the very notion of bishops. The latter were seen as an ungodly Catholic survival that must be purged, and the example of the bishop-free Scottish Church was cited with approval as a model to follow, which was to be important after 1637 when Charles was confronting an autonomist revolt in Scotland led by anti-episcopal zealots. The desire to rid a 'true' Protestant Church of bishops had been played out across the border in Scotland under Mary Stuart and James VI, and despite the leadership of energetic publicists like Knox and the Melvilles the anti-episcopalians had eventually lost. But the theological attacks on predestination by Arminius in the 1610s gave a handle to those who argued that such 'innovators' had turned against Protestantism. This could be added to disquiet in the 1630s at the new emphasis on the beauty and holiness of Church ceremonial, symbolised by moving the communion-table to the east end of the church – all practices followed in Catholic churches. Charles, given his enthusiasm for Southern European

– Catholic – aesthetics with their use of the senses to promote religious devotion, was bound to take the side of the ceremonialists.

There is still debate among historians as to whether the beliefs and practices of the group of theological enthusiasts and disciplinarians around Laud amounted to a deliberate attack on the more 'inclusive', less rigidly-defined Anglican Church of the earlier period. Campaigns on discipline and a 'semi-Catholic' promotion of vestments as required clerical wear were carried out in the Elizabethan Church as well as by Laud – by men who were doctrinally strict Calvinists, including Whitgift. His principal lieutenant in hunting down 'seditious' theological writers, Richard Bancroft, then succeeded him as Archbishop (1604–10). So was Laud's work just a return to this meticulous 'purge' by Bancroft (who had not been attacked as pro-Catholic for this)? But now a theological element had entered the question of whether the disciplinarians – this time, connected to the use of ceremony too – were fully Protestant and/ or innovators. As defined by Nicholas Tyacke, main proponents of the aggressively disciplinarian approach in the 1620s, the 'Laudian' faction – initially centred around Bishops Richard Neile and Lancelot Andrewes, not their junior Laud[48] – were 'Anti-Calvinists'. Tyacke also points out that the Dutch controversy over 'Arminius' (see below) made more rigid differences in theology between Calvinists and their foes apparent, and this spilled over into the English Church – making accommodation between them more difficult. But was the 'Anti-Calvinist' movement comprehensible within the Church established in 1559, and was Laud less wise about the Church as a 'big tent' (in modern terminology) than Elizabeth or James had been?

Whether or not Charles' religious reforms of the 1630s were perceived by him as 'innovation' rather than refinements within the framework of the Anglican Church settlement, this was how it was seen by his critics. The Church settlement of 1559 had been a political as much as a religious one, designed by Elizabeth and the more 'moderate' wing of the Protestant religious community as encompassing as many Protestants as possible within the Church. It retained elements of traditional English religious doctrine and ritual which were seen as 'Catholic' by the more radical Calvinists, together with the old disciplinary structures of the Church with 'top-down' doctrinal and canon law controls by the bishops. But there was a difference between the Elizabethan situation and that after 1625. Great Elizabethan noble patrons of 'Puritan' religious radicals, such as the Earls of Leicester and Huntingdon, had had close personal ties to and were continuously employed by their Queen. The 1630s earls of Essex (the son of Leicester's stepson, the earl of Essex who had in 1601 rebelled against Elizabeth and been executed) and Bedford and their 'Puritan' reformist noble allies had little to do with and rarely attended Court in the 1630s. Those peers who caused mischief in Parliament to put pressure on the monarch were not usually punished by Elizabeth; Charles, by contrast, made his personal animosity to objectors obvious in 1625-9. By extension, the 'normal' concept for great nobles of pressuring the monarchy into concessions was seen differently by Charles to how his predecessors had behaved.

The useful myths of 'Bloody Mary' and 1588: stoking up paranoia and a political danger which Charles ignored?
What happened when the State failed to reconcile two antagonistic religious parties was only too apparent from the early 1560s in the rounds of civil war and mass-bloodshed in France. Whatever personal sympathy Elizabeth retained for the order and ceremony of Catholicism, the experiences of persecution that England had suffered under Mary – enshrined in national literary mythology for future generations by Foxe's *Book of Acts and Monuments* – made the Church of Rome an object of irreconcilable popular hatred and fear. This was duly worsened by the development of the association of Catholicism with bloody repression in France and the Netherlands in the 1570s and 1580s, the threat of regicide and civil war linked to the cause of Mary Queen of Scots, and the climactic experience of the threat of invasion by the Spanish Armada in 1588. The myth of heroic national resistance to a tyrannical foreign empire in 1588 was as powerful in the national memory for early 17th-century England as the threat of Nazi invasion and the heroic national resistance to it was to be after 1940. Catholicism was entwined with both foreign aggression and the apocalyptic notions of the Pope in Rome as the 'Antichrist' foretold in the Book of Revelation. For the more radical English Calvinists, indeed, any retention of Catholic elements in the Church was a sign of the sinister influence of 'Popery' which had to be extirpated – and the Episcopal role in religious authority was of questionable origin given that the 'pure' original Church of the 1st-century AD was supposed to have been governed not

by bishops but by local boards of autonomous presbyters elected by their godly congregations. The retention of the traditional pre-1534 Church disciplinary mechanism of courts was congenial to a State and episcopate fearing uncontrolled radicals but was seen by the latter as unfinished business for reformers to pursue. A 'return' to an autonomous Church governed by presbyters in Britain was successful in Knox's Scotland after 1560, backed by the local nobility – and after it was threatened by Charles his English foes, who he saw as seditious, rallied to the Scots so this factor made the post-1637 interlocking Anglo-Scots crises worse.

James VI and I had been brought up as a firm Calvinist in the first years of the Scottish Reformation's post-1560 triumph, and had experienced the threat posed by powerful and argumentative Presbyterian clerics to Royal authority in Scotland. He had done all he could to bring that Church under Royal control once he came of age, and was equally alive to the uses of a disciplined and hierarchic Church in England. The Elizabethan disciplinary mechanisms continued under his rule and the traditional vestments and other 'semi-Catholic' practices continued unchanged, though he appointed more firmly Calvinist intellectuals as bishops (e.g. Archbishop Abbot in 1611). The lapse in aggressive ecclesiastical disciplinary enforcement against all 'unsound' clerics was largely due to the unexpected early death of the vigorous Archbishop Bancroft in 1610. The King had no concern to promote men of one particular ideology, nominating candidates from a variety of theological backgrounds and of varying competence. Enthusiasts whose views were potentially controversial – particularly Lancelot Andrewes – did not achieve the success that their reputation might have led them to expect.[49] Significantly, the Calvinist James was alarmed when 'Arminius' friend Grotius visited England in 1613 and grilled him on whether 'Arminius' was theologically 'sound';[50] and he never made the eminently learned but not clearly Calvinist Lancelot Andrewes an archbishop.

By extension, the events of 1610–11 had a major impact on the Church (and politics) in England in the 1630s, as Bancroft's unexpectedly early death left James with an archbishopric to fill and he appointed an obscure candidate (George Abbot) who was to 'let things slide' in terms of ecclesiastical discipline, enforcing rules on official vestments and ceremonies, keeping churches physically tidy and well-decorated, and sacking theological dissidents. Abbot lived until 1633 but was increasingly ineffective and was apparently depressed after accidentally shooting a keeper while out hunting in 1621 – but he did not resign and he was not replaced. By 1633 the impatient Charles was in a hurry to restore discipline and proper order in the Church, and chose a vigorous but tactless disciplinarian in Laud – but if Abbot had died or James had replaced him pre-1625 he would not have had the arch-see available to fill at that juncture as probably a younger man would have been appointed and would have lasted through the 1630s. Laud's biographer Peter Heylyn reckoned that a longer-lived Bancroft and a less controversial (but disciplinarian) replacement already in place before 1630 could have saved the Church. Even in 1625–8 Laud was only a junior Court cleric, though congenial to the King for his views and his vigour, and the 'front-runner' to be archbishop if the vacancy had occurred then was the equally disciplinarian and 'anti-Puritan' Richard Neile, in real life archbishop of York from 1631. Neile was theologically Calvinist, unlike Laud, so less open to attack – though he was equally committed to greater 'seemliness' and ceremonial in church (which would make him congenial to Charles) and he had a circle of younger clerical proteges who were sympathetic to Arminius and critical of dogmatic Calvinism (e.g. on predestination). The Church under Neile, or possibly the older and less vigorous but theologically expert preacher Lancelot Andrewes, would have been in a different position from what it was under Laud, and with a less easily attacked archbishop – so Charles suffered politically from the bad luck of having no vacancy at Canterbury to fill until 1633. With a different archbishop, Laud would probably have had to make do with his real-life early 1630s see of London, prosecuting and sacking 'Puritan' clergy there and so open to MPs' condemnation in 1640 but less crucial a figure.

Catholic-inspired foreign plots before and after the accession of James fed national paranoia, with the English Catholics seen as a sinister and alien 'fifth column' incited to rebellion by their foreign priests in the manner of English Moslem agents of Al-Qaeda after '9/11'. The Gunpowder Plot in 1605 seemed to confirm that James I's initial desire for a moderate approach to Catholicism had only led to attempted mass-murder, and regular calls were to be made in Parliament to hunt down priests as the agents of ungodly Romish aggression. The government – more specifically James' Secretary of State, Sir Robert Cecil – may have exaggerated the seriousness of the 'Gunpowder Plot' to end the chances of any compromise with Catholicism by King or ministers and to whip up public hatred.[51] Some MPs talked of solving the Catholic problem once and for all by seizing the Papists' children and forcibly educating them as Protestants, but the situation worsened further after 1619–20 as the new Catholic-Protestant conflict in Germany led to calls for English intervention to assist the latter against the threat of annihilation. The timing of the wars in Germany coincided with the rigid definition of 'acceptable' Protestant views set out at Dort – which was no coincidence as Maurice of Nassau, 'Arminius' enemy, was an ally of the anti-Habsburg coalition that challenged the Empire in Bohemia in 1619–20.

The perceived revival of Catholic aggression on the Continent was made more important to the English by the fact that the Protestant revolt against Catholic Habsburg rule in Bohemia, the catalyst for the Thirty Years War led to the rebels' choice of King James' son-in-law, the Elector Palatine, as their new King (and thus his daughter Elizabeth as Queen) in 1619. Their swift ejection by Habsburg troops made the 'Winter Queen' and her husband, already very popular in England as leaders of the international Protestant cause, seem innocent victims of Catholic aggression and led to Parliamentary calls for intervention to force the Habsburgs to return Elector Frederick's seized principality – and Spain, James' hoped-for ally, assisted the seizure of the Palatinate and thus had a stake in keeping it from him in any peace-settlement. In this context, James' good relations with the old Elizabethan enemy, Spain, were much criticised. The panic over Charles' and Buckingham's futile mission to Spain to secure a Spanish bride for the Prince in 1623 added to hysteria, and the resultant war with Spain in 1624–30 was duly popular – though the messy European situation ended up in Charles fighting Spain's foe France too in 1627–8, over their repression of the Protestant Huguenots.

All this complicated the chances of a limited reaction to Royal religious initiatives in the 1630s, as well as providing early evidence of Charles' capacity for misunderstanding and alienating his subjects. Elizabeth and James had both been brought up in a harder political school and were shrewd realists, aware of the potential and dangers of rebellion. In religion as in politics, Charles sought to impose an ordered ideal on a far harsher reality. Comparisons may be drawn with two other sovereigns isolated at hierarchic Courts who proved incapable of facing up to the challenges that their regimes faced – Louis XVI of France and Nicholas II of Russia.

Charles was based closer to political events than the other two, usually residing in his capital, and at Whitehall he had a public right of way to Whitehall Stairs running directly through his palace. But all three showed politically counter-productive hostility to their subjects' resurgent popular assemblies and ignorance of the depth of public feelings (or prejudices) – and none made concessions easily.

The element of resistance to 'centralism' in resistance to Laud – and in other criticism of the regime. Misconceptions, and false accusations of it being 'illegal'
Any hint of doctrinal innovation among English theologians which questioned Calvinist views was to be seized upon, and the accused to be kept out of Church office or evicted from any offices which they held at all costs. The vicious struggle over jobs and accusations of Catholic sympathies were not new, as seen in Oxford and Cambridge theological controversies in Elizabeth's reign. But the 'Arminian' controversy in Holland and the anti-Arminius rulings at the 1618 Synod of Dort gave the Calvinist zealots who continually denounced episcopacy new impetus. The new Archbishop Laud (appointed 1633) was already known for his vigorous disciplinary action against all clerics in his previous dioceses who defied the current canons. His actions to curb dissenting theologians as the new Chancellor of Oxford from 1630 notably affected the main 'power-houses' of activist Calvinist theology, colleges – and his strict rule as Bishop of London affected the capital with its émigré European Calvinists. But how much of the opposition was a case of 'sour grapes' by his defeated opponents? In the case of university appointments, for example, the pre-1630 strategic 'high ground' usually belonged to militant Calvinists who were not slow to try to remove their enemies. In 1595 the new Lady Margaret Professor of Divinity at Cambridge, Huguenot refugee Peter Baro – a pioneer of the 'Anti-Calvinists' – had been subject to a vicious campaign and eventual forced resignation for attacking Predestination. But when Laud tried the same level of theological discipline it was seized upon – a case of double standards? Laud did not obsessively exclude all 'Puritans' from Oxford appointments in a 'purge'; an analysis of his work there by Kevin Sharpe has shown that his main concerns were discipline and order, not 'fixing' appointments.[52] The ultra-Calvinist Professor of Divinity, John Prideaux, was not 'purged', and the King let him preach at Court.

Laud's imposition of uniformity was in fact based on enforcing identical modes of worship, not of doctrine – he was to declare that he followed Tudor theologian Richard Hooker in not seeking to exclude people by defining doctrine too narrowly. Laud's timing was risky, as seen above – but he was only reacting to the abeyance of archiepiscopal discipline under the long and increasingly feeble rule of Archbishop Abbot since 1611. Arguably Laud reaped the results of his predecessor's inefficiency by reacting to this – he was 'only doing his job' as Whitgift had done before him, but in a more dangerous era. Also, given the sympathies of many of the local gentry for and promotion of radical preachers, the zealous Calvinist watchdogs who abused Laud and his allies, any disciplinarian Archbishop would need to wrest control of patronage from them. As in Elizabeth's time, this would also entail tackling pro-Calvinist nobles who were used to controlling local religious patronage and appointing 'godly' clerical protégés to parishes and lectureships. The Laudian attack on local patronage of dissident clergy, the system of 'feofees', was a belated and resented reassertion of central control over disruptive autonomy. Significantly, Laud opposed lay appointments of local theology lecturers: 'by reason of their pay (they) are the people's creatures'.[53] He wanted them controlled by the Church whose experts could check on their orthodoxy, not by 'suspect' lay patrons. By extension, Laud desired to advance the local and national careers and influence of reliable Churchmen – and Clarendon reckoned in retrospect that this reversal of the secularising gains of the Reformation was a major cause of the Civil War.[54] But this does not mean the establishment of a 'Laudian' monopoly of office within the Church – plenty of 1630s appointments of anti-'Arminians' can be detected, such as Ralph Brownrigg as head of St. Catherine's College Cambridge and (at a junior level) the well-known 'Puritans' John Dury and Richard Sibbes. For that matter, under Laud as Archbishop some of his colleagues (e.g. Bridgeman of Chester, Wright of Coventry and Corbet of Norwich) were lukewarm in enforcing central orders or evicting troublesome clergy. There was no 'blanket Laudianisation' of the Church across the country; this was not a full-scale 'purge' as Laud's enemies asserted.

Stricter central control over local authorities in non-theological matters also arose, in the question of the King reissuing James' 'Book of Sports' in October 1633.[55] The late King's arguments that Sunday sports fostered physical fitness, martial skills, and neighbourliness had cut no ice with the sabbatarians who wanted no 'sinful' games on the Sabbath, and Charles held Council meetings and attended Court plays on the Sabbath but banned public performances and the selling of food and drink then. The stricter 'Puritan' sabbatarians, JPs as well as clergy, resisted or ignored the new orders to allow games and other non-religious activities on Sundays, and had to be checked up on or coerced. The issue indeed first arose over a sabbatarian Royal justice (Richardson) failing to obey orders to halt legal cases against Sabbath-breakers in Somerset. Richardson was called before the Council to be rebuked and personally blamed Laud for this,[56] and the radical preacher Henry Burton wrote up a self-righteous collection of all the alleged disasters that the resulting rise in lewdness caused.[57] The orders did give 'great distaste to many... others' as well as 'those who are usually termed puritans' according to later Parliamentarian moderate Bulstrode Whitelocke,[58] with perception of Episcopal interfering and encouragement for riotous behaviour evident. In fact most bishops did not hunt down all clerics who avoided their legal duty to read the 'Book' out in church, provided that some parish official did so or it was shown to the parishioners. Bishops Davenant and Wren were the main zealots for mass-prosecution rather than tolerating evasion.

So why the fervent public criticism of the King's actions? Again, the circumstances were different this time round. The lay legal machinery of the State was to be more notorious than usual in the 1630s for other reasons – its aggressive activity in raising money by ruthless and often petty enforcement of the law including utilising the King's dormant feudal rights as in Forest Law. In the case of the latter, it appears that the decisive move to resume all the King's ancient 'rights' within what had been 'Royal Forest' in medieval times was taken at the time of appointing a new Attorney-General in autumn 1634, with the rival candidates competing to show their useful zeal for the King's enrichment by looking up his ancient Forest financial rights in the late Sir Edward Coke's confiscated library of manuscripts. A 'test case' was then tried out in the ancient, virtually defunct 'Waltham Forest' in Essex, and success led to extensions of this to other medieval Forests. There was sheer surprise at reviving long-dormant rights in areas assumed not to have been Forest for centuries; £67,000 was raised by fines on those who had 'illegally' encroached on Rockingham Forest in Northamptonshire. An active search was made for legal precedents, however ancient, to enforce and maximum fines imposed for (accidental) encroachments – with the combination of centralisation, ruthlessness, and pettiness enraging victims all round. This would all add up to increase anti-government attitudes in the long term, so arguably combining secular and religious 'Thorough'(or official meddling) was counter-productive. In fact, the King's motives over the Forests would appear to have been honest and useful enough in practical terms, not just looking for extra cash – to conserve 'stands' of woodland to provide timber for building his new fleet in the 1630s. A possibly less controversial alternative source of funds would have been to sell off the rights to own and exploit what was still legally Royal Forest land to entrepreneurs, as suggested earlier to James I by Sir Julius Caesar, but this would not have preserved trees.[59] The imposition of a similar perfectly legal but financially exploitative and disastrously resented policy by the Church through its courts was to be expected from a government keen on its rights and determined to resort to any expedient to collect revenue in the absence of Parliament. That would increase the number of local gentry irritated – and thus mean a backlash whenever Parliament met. But in reality it seems that the volleys of hatred aimed at the reinvigorated ecclesiastical 'Court of High Commission' in 1641 for its 'abuses' in the 1630s have been exaggerated, and that it was not as active or as vindictive as suggested by the myths.[60] As with the Forests, the unwonted 'centralised' interference in local affairs was built up into an impressive list of 'oppression' by complaints to Parliament in 1640–1. Laud, an enthusiast for 'Thorough' and loathed as what would now be called a 'micro-manager', was correctly targeted by angry MPs – but was probably not its mastermind.

Legal matters. A creeping road to tyranny or just efficiency? And was the 'Star Chamber' unjustly vilified?
As analysed by Conrad Russell in his study of the 1620s Parliaments, there was no new and irreversible deterioration in 'Monarch vs. Parliament' relations in the 1620s, culminating in a decision to rule without Parliament. There was at most a shift in the legal grounds of contention. A systematic 'programme' of Royal response to financial challenges was however new in the 1630s – and a specific word, 'Thorough', and specific ministers were linked to it. There had been no such ideological obloquy attached to the fund-raising efforts of equally zealous and imaginative Lord Treasurer

Cranfield for his measures in 1621–4 as a systematic attack on the citizens' rights, as he had concentrated on efficiency and cutbacks at Court and duly been undermined by angry courtiers.

The King's reaction also had a 'constitutional' legal element, unlike Elizabeth's and James's – but was this partly a reaction to 1620s MPs, led by Coke, 'weaponising' the law to attack his policies' legality? The King's tame lawyers, led by the Attorneys-General, were wheeled into action to back up Royal actions against the King's critics – and these actions, as argued below, included deliberate attempts to seize control of potentially embarrassing legal 'evidence' that challenged the King's decisions (e.g. the lists of historical precedents in Sir Robert Cotton's papers). But the State seizing 'illegal' or libellous literature was not new, as seen by bans on importing 'heretic' Protestant literature from the Continent under Henry VIII and Mary and on Catholic literature (and Papal Bulls) under Elizabeth. All books had to be licensed by ecclesiastical commissioners or the Privy Council under regulations of 1559, 1566, and 1586, the number of licensed printing-presses was restricted, and from 1613 a new law allowed the commissioners to search for banned material. The machinery of enforcement was thus already in place, and was sporadically used – usually against Catholics.

Charles was suspicious of the anonymous popular news-sheets ('corantos') that sprang up during the post-1618 international crisis and Thirty Years' War – their promotion of anti-Catholic Continental warfare could be seen as criticism of his government. He intervened in 1629 to warn the Stationers' Company to be more pro-active in banning them.[61] In a modern sense, the King sought to control the 'news' and present a 'narrative' that did not get out of control and criticise his policies. As is well-known, a Star Chamber decree of 1637 extended and regularised the current restrictions to limit and list the approved printers, ban most imported material, license ballads for the first time, and require all new books to be examined by relevant experts for subversion.[62] This was duly played up by Prynne and his allies as sinister 'Arminian' censorship aimed at the godly, with warnings that pro-Laudian theological books could always get published unlike Calvinist ones.[63] But it was the Stationers' Company not Laud who decided which printers to license, rules could be evaded, and Prynne and others had no difficulty in continuing publishing as did illegal printers.[64] Even the supposedly 'lax' Archbishop Abbot had only licensed twenty printers in 1630 (Laud allowed twenty-four).[65] That is not to deny a deterrent effect of the harsh punishments such as public floggings and brandings, a climate of fear, or a mythology of oppression which was to explode in public in 1641 – and logically helped to rally indignant would-be printers to take part in the eruption of publishing thereafter.

The seizure of papers under Charles was more drastic (and efficient) – it extended to those of private individuals, as with those of the late expert antiquarian Sir Robert Cotton. The documents in question however usually had a political context. It is also arguable that the dangerous new element to 'State vs. individual' controversies was not of the King's invention, but a response to the controversial, 'anti-arbitrary governance' interpretation of the Common Law put forward in the 1610s and 1620s by the leading legal expert Sir Edward Coke (a former Attorney-General).[66] This first articulated the idea of inalienable and 'fundamental' rights under law, which did not originate in the Sovereign's gracious grants and so could not legally be cancelled. It was thus a basic challenge to the Royal right to interpet the law and linked in to the notion of venerably antique, pre-1066 Parliaments since restricted by the 'Norman Yoke'. Arguably, given the circumstances of veteran legal expert Coke's turning his formidable powers against the State his decision had as much to do with disappointment in his career as with immutable principle. His feuds with Bacon and Buckingham thus had drastic long-term consequences for the Crown. Elizabeth and James had not faced this sort of 'expert opinion' interpreting the Common Law so as to challenge arbitrary State decisions and put the 'community of the realm' as a constitutional force independent of the personal whims of the monarch. Coke 'weaponised' legal resistance to the State, and added to royal anger at this 'impertinence'.

Whoever originated the dangerous new area of legal conflict, there are two essential points to bear in mind. Firstly, the legal arguments made and precedents cited by Coke were used by the King's critics in Parliament in the 1620s as a weapon of justification for resistance and 'free debate' and so invited retaliation. 'Rogue' legal experts like Coke (in his later years) and John Selden, a man as committed to English naval power as the King but critical of his domestic constitutional claims, were now available to challenge the King in the Commons. The collection of ancient legal documents by Sir Robert Cotton (situated in his house next-door to the Commons) provided useful precedents.[67] The muddled and 'ad hoc' nature of the evolving English constitution made matters worse. As Parliament was technically a court as well as a debating forum – a position used to great effect in 1640–1 to terrorise opposition – the issue of the Commons' (and subjects') rights was able to be used to great effect by MPs, many of them lawyers trained in the Inns of Court. Legal matters were second nature to them, and they were familiar with the language and concepts used by writers like Coke and Selden. Physically, it helped that there was a large archive of legal material available to them in the library of Sir Robert Cotton a few yards from the Commons – which the King duly endeavoured to seize and shut off from unauthorised access when Cotton died in 1631.[68] In 1632 State agents carted off Coke's papers concerning Magna Carta from his house near Stoke Poges to preempt a politically embarrassing new book by him.[69] As Coke was dying a few months later Secretary Windebank had his house ransacked; in 1640 Parliament investigated and found that the Attorney-General had taken possession of them.[70] The seizure of papers by Royal agents was thus a reaction to an innovation by the King's critics, not unprovoked intimidation, but still part of a political 'crackdown'. Second, this toxic new element gave a tone of legal justification and venerable constitutional precedent to the demands of MPs. The latter had been criticizing Royal actions before, but now their behaviour could be backed up with 'expert' legal justification and the monarch's retaliation seen as illegal interference.

What of the alleged government censorship and legal oppression by means of the notorious court of 'Star Chamber' at Westminster Palace – that is, the judicial committee of the Privy Council sitting in a special room with a pattern of stars on the ceiling? This was the centrepiece of the propaganda attack on Charles' so-called legal tyranny in Parliament in 1640–1, and was played up by 'opposition' MPs as harsh, unrelenting, and biased in favour of the government. In fact, as analysed by Kevin Sharpe, this was grossly exaggerated and gave a misleading impression of the purpose of this 'fast-track' court, set up originally to deliver swifter justice than the costly and cumbersome mainstream judicial process.

Contrary to the assumption that all or most prosecutions were brought by the State to terrorise opposition, most cases were brought by private individuals seeking redress, usually in cases involving property (theft, burglary, embezzlement, forgery of papers, or conspiracy to defraud). In

1603–25 only nearly 600 out of 8,228 cases involved 'official' information delivered to the committee by the State's leading judicial prosecutor, the Attorney-General (under 1 per cent); around 3 per cent involved an 'official' prosecution launched by State officials. During the 1630s the figure for 'official' prosecutions rose sharply, but was at most 18 per cent and was usually between 6 per cent and 12 per cent. In the 100 cases heard before the Earl of Bridgewater (whose private notes survive) in 1630–5, the Attorney-General was prosecutor in 22; of the 239 cases listed by one analyst for February 1632 to October 1640, the height of the 'Royal tyranny', 85 were prosecuted by the Attorney-General but 16 of these were on behalf of an absent State official (e.g. Wentworth in Ireland). Quite a few of these 'official' cases were in fact brought on behalf of a private individual, often one unable to afford litigation – thus the court's original role as aiding humble petitioners to afford justice continued from the Tudor era. Some cases continued to involve complaints of abuse of power or private vendettas by provincial justices.

The number of 'political' cases was small, though notorious – e.g. the prosecutions of Long, Chambers and others after the 1629 Parliament, Eliot in 1629, and later of anti-'Arminian' agitators Alexander Leighton (author of 'Sion's Plea Against the Prelacie', 1628), of Prynne for libellously abusing the Queen in Histriomastix in 1633, and of Prynne, Burton and Bastwick in 1637. There is no evidence of abuse of process by biased and vituperative judges in these cases, in contrast to the antics of the regicide trial judges in 1660 and of Judge Jeffreys in the 1680s, or of the judges with more staunchly Protestant commitment (e.g. Coke) having any sympathy for the accused who were allegedly defending Protestant values against 'Popish innovation'. Indeed, the trials were scrupulously legal and the accused repeatedly committed what would now be called 'contempt of court', clearly keen to make themselves martyrs. Nor were the whippings and brandings meted out to the accused in the 1633 and 1637 'political' trials of the anti-Arminians unusual for cases where defendants had abused the judges or refused to plead – and they were commonplace for 'whores' or vagrants of low social class. Only 19 of the 236 known sentences passed between 1630 and 1641 involved corporal punishment, and the fact that Prynne and Leighton were technically 'gentlemen' so usually exempt from this sort of punishment was noted. Prynne was remitted part of his sentence for his first libel in 1633 at the request of his victim, the Queen. The eye-catchingly heavy fines issued to other defendants were usually to be paid in instalments or were partially remitted later, though their size clearly implied 'making an example' to alarm others.

Probably the exaggerated reputation of the Star Chamber for savage vindictiveness comes from a mixture of the eye-catching punishment of Prynne's group in 1637, a 'one-off' demonstration of government firmness given at a time of rising religious tension (and evidence of resistance to 'Arminian' reforms) shown by the Scots rebellion, and clever 'spin' by the anti-government MPs in 1640–2 to play up the outrages.[71]

Charles and 'order': exaggerated or misinterpreted? A necessary reaction from James' laxity?

The imposition of rules of conduct in the interests of seemliness and dignity was apparent from the start at Charles' Court, in contrast to the rowdiness, disorder, and promiscuity of James' Court. Orders were issued to tighten up access to the King and ban disorderly persons within a fortnight of Charles' accession.[72] It should be noted that physically the King did not live in an isolated palace in the middle of a park, safe behind manned gates, but in a jumble of Tudor buildngs between the public King Street and the River Thames at Whitehall, and public access to the courts and outer rooms of his palace was easy; proper rules and security were reasonable. If anything, the reforms were widely welcomed; the behaviour of certain of James' intimates had been demeaning to Royal dignity and 'seemliness', with the King indulging the excesses. The drunken behaviour at Court on occasions such as the State visit of the King's brother-in-law Christian IV of Denmark in 1606 were written-up by critics, as was criticism of James' slovenly habits and coarse language – though it is arguable how wide an audience this reached. The disorder of James' Court – and the need for action in 1625 – was not merely a matter of morals and prestige. Nor was the criticism new; Charles' elder brother Henry set up similar rules for his new residence and Court at St. James' Palace at the age of sixteen in 1610, banning foul language and drunkenness.

In practical terms, James' indulgence of the more extravagant and irresponsible of his courtiers had serious financial implications for the position of the monarchy – he protected the Howard clan, led by Lord Treasurer Suffolk, as they leeched off his revenue and undermined his shaky financial position through the 1610s. The corruption and waste at the Royal Wardrobe was particularly irresponsible, and even after the end of Howard influence the new 'favourite', Buckingham, made the most of the many Royal offices, perquisites, and gifts which he collected for his family and sold his goodwill to petitioners in c. 1619–25. In this arena of waste and mismanagement, the attempted cutbacks and rationalisations by the new Lord Treasurer Cranfield – a man not averse to collecting perquisites himself – in 1621–4 only served to stir up resentment among courtiers who combined to undermine him. Buckingham duly led the conspiracy of affronted courtiers and their MP clients which saw him impeached in 1624, halting retrenchment. The defeat of Cranfield's painstaking efforts to make the Court solvent was a defeat ultimately due to the ageing James indulging Buckingham's personal hatred of Cranfield. In that respect, James' financial imprudence was largely to blame for Charles' problems.

Similarly, Charles' attitude was a 'reaction' to the effects on the reputation of King and Court by such matters as the scandal of the Overbury murder in 1615–16, which his critics tended to forget. As with the Royal indulgence of Howard and Villiers extravagance, King James' weakness caused political dangers. A very public legal case involving the King's intimates exposed murky goings-on at Court. The King's favourite – good-looking young Scots courtier Robert Carr, unworthily elevated to the Earldom of Somerset and loaded with honours – was tried with his new wife (and long-time mistress) Frances Howard over the poisoning of their critic Sir Thomas Overbury in the Tower of London, and both were found guilty (Carr of lesser charges). Ironically, the scandal was ultimately traceable back to Carr and Frances persuading the King to assist in the Countess' divorce from her first husband, the allegedly impotent Robert Devereux, Earl of Essex – son of the executed Elizabethan 'favourite' and later the Parliamentarian commander-in-chief in 1642–6. The details of Essex's incapacities were legally dubious – and Overbury, who probably knew that chicanery had been involved, may have threatened to reveal embarrassing details when he broke with the Carrs. He then had to be silenced, apparently by Frances with some poisoned tarts. Essex, humiliated by the possibly inaccurate details of his private life pored over in court to help his adulterous wife marry her lover, went off to the Continent to fight for the Protestant cause and acquired the reputation and military skills which made him so useful to Parliament after 1640.

After this public relations disaster, the close control of Court morals, codification of rules, and 'clean-up' of standards by a personally dignified and moral new King in 1625 was a strength rather than a weakness to the monarchy's reputation. Even the absence of large numbers of Scots nobles at Court (under a King who left Scotland aged two) had the bonus of avoiding English criticism at their abuses of patronage – Guy Fawkes had boasted that he would 'blow the Scots all the way back to Scotland'. The Scots had monopolised access to the King in the royal Bedchamber, appointments to which they dominated.[73] There was an implicit danger however of the King becoming 'out of touch' with non-Court opinion, which was exacerbated under Charles; the latter decreased the widespread tours of his nobles' estates across England undertaken every summer by Elizabeth. He still went on 'progress' in the summer, but he preferred to stay with a few select 'favourite' aristocrats who shared his cultural interests, above all the Earls of Pembroke at Wilton House.[74] His dislike of public appearances was not however an innovation. James had been irritated enough at popular demands to show himself that on one occasion he threatened to show his bare backside from a window to an importunate crowd.[75] More seriously, it has been reckoned that James spent up to half his post-1603 time in England at hunting-lodges rather than at Court,[76] although until 1612 he had an efficient administrative deputy in Sir Robert Cecil, Lord Salisbury, to 1612. The criticism of Charles was counter to that of James – that he interfered too much rather than being lax.

State interference by royal bureaucrats – annoying, but fully legal and just exaggerated by the victims?
The resistance to petty legal interference by State agencies in local life on dubious grounds was as apparent in secular matters, as seen by the controversies over Royal feudal laws (e.g. wardship) and the rush to abolish all the mechanism of Royal control in Parliament in 1641. The King's officials in the 1630s had a reputation for stretching their legal rights to aid their cause, or resorting to ingenious expedients, as has been catalogued.[77] Opponents were denied a hearing in court or harassed with burdensome legal cases, as when Lord Saye and Sele refused to

pay 'Ship-money', had his goods distrained to the value of the sum due, and was denied a chance to challenge it in court with a prosecution for infringements of antiquated Forest Laws. These and means of raising money were brought back into play, and Council officials trawled through boxes of musty records in the Tower. The dubious new 'monopoly' on making soap in 1631 (granted to a part-Catholic group of projectors) was assisted by banning some of the Royal grantees' rivals in Bristol from operating despite their soap being demonstrably superior, and hampering the remaining independent soapmakers by banning the use of fish-oil in soap. The project still collapsed and the King had to buy the projectors out in 1637.[78] The King's financial projects also encompassed annoying powerful interests in the City of London, by extorting payments from the Vintners' Company for each ton of wine produced; when they resisted their customary auxiliary trade of producing meals was declared illegal and Star Chamber prosecutions followed.[79] An income tax, excise, death-duties, duties on beer, and the sale of offices were all suggested; the frantic search for new fund-raising schemes was noted by the Venetian ambassador in 1634.[80] The inventor of most of these ingenious schemes was the Attorney-General, William Noy; he died in 1634 but the plans continued. As will be examined in the later section on finance, they could have worked financially and kept the Crown solvent – just – but for the Scottish revolt.

But the overall tactic of extending Royal oversight of local matters by money-raising intervention was not new in 1629 – and particularly so in the field of granting monopolistic patents for specific projects. This was not only intended to raise money, but to use Royal power to advance genuine and at times idealistic plans put in writing to the King's Council for schemes of national improvement. This was most notable in the fields of trade and industry – which had the additional bonus of improving mercantile activity and so increasing revenue, plus on occasion helping national defence. Enthusiasm for this and a stream of applications by inventors went back to the era of Edward VI and the improving schemes of the 'Commonwealthmen'. Under Elizabeth such 'projectors' had set up schemes such as developing the mines in the Lake District and establishing a native saltpetre industry to produce top-quality gunpowder, helping to ready the nation's defences for war with Spain. Treasurer Lord Burghley had been particularly keen on them. Under Charles the rash of grants for patents to pursue such schemes was as much about building up trade and 'improvement' as financial gain, and sponsoring such ideas was part of a King's duty to advance his subjects' welfare. There were of course economic 'victims' as well as beneficiaries plus some projectors mainly interested in 'scams', and in a modern note the importation of expert foreign workers to help the major drainage-schemes in the Fenland from 1630 led to complaints that these people would work for lower wages and so put Englishmen out of jobs. The Fenland drainage-schemes to produce productive farmland out of poor-quality marshes ruined commoners with rights to fishing and wildfowling, and led to major riots as in 1637. But this was not a result of ruthless Royal exploitation for financial gain, though the Council urged on progress in drainage, nor was the work carried out by 'monopolist' Court favourites. The 'projectors' who undertook to drain areas of the Fens included the future 'opposition' stalwart, the Earl of Bedford, who drained the 'Great Fen' aka the 'Bedford Level'. Efficiency and action were required, with Wentworth for one eager to denounce the scandal and dishonour to the King shown in examples of incompetence. If the work was not carried out quickly or efficiently enough such patents for 'improvement' could be cancelled later, as was Bedford's; the King took on the work of completing the 'Great Fen' himself to speed it up in 1637 and levied local taxes to pay for it not for his own use. Many of the less successful or remunerative patents were called in by the Council in a 'purge' in 1639.

The extension of 'Ship-Money' – only supposed to be demanded when the nation was threatened by invasion – from the more usual coastal counties to all the country in 1636–7 was justified on the grounds that it was the King's sole right to decide when such an emergency existed. The most famous resistance to Charles' non-Parliamentary taxes was thus in a field – defence – where he could claim 'national interest' and decry his opponents as unpatriotic. To promote this case he had John Selden's book *Mare Clausam* reissued to coincide with the extension of 'Ship-Money' to inland counties, demonstrating that England had the sole right to govern the Channel and North Sea but needed more ships to hold the Dutch at bay there. The King had a better legal and moral case at a time of rampant piracy and a weak Navy. But in the case of the Church this resistance extended from objection to legal interference to religious unease at innovation, and it was apparent that the interfering clergy were taking on a political and administrative role at Court unknown since Mary Tudor's unlamented reign. Clerics, namely Laud (as head of the treasury commission when Treasurer Weston died) and then Bishop Juxon of London, had control of the Treasury from 1635; the last senior cleric in high administrative office had been Mary's Lord Chancellor, Bishop Gardiner of Winchester. The establishment of a clerical Treasurer, who also had a bishopric to supervise, was bad 'spin' for the government, and was probably due to Laud's influence over Charles plus meddling by Henrietta Maria. The latter opposed Laud's own candidate, Wentworth (an anti-Catholic), who would have brought energy and efficiency to the role; but Wentworth had only served a year as Lord Deputy of Ireland and he preferred to stay on there. That cleared the way for the other man talked of for the post, Chancellor of the Exchequer Francis Cottington, and Weston had moved to the Treasurership from this post so it was a good precedent. But Laud did not like Cottington, and managed to block him; Juxon was appointed instead. This was also supposed to have been a defeat for the pro-Spanish faction at Court at the hands of the Queen's pro-French faction.[81] In financial terms, it prevented vigorous action to shake up revenue-collecting and personnel by Wentworth, though there had already been an attempt to regularise and scrutinise procedures and halt abuses via a guidebook issued to officials by Weston and Cottington earlier.[82] There was however confusion over who owed the government what and vice versa by 1635 due to inadequate accounting, as in the case of Philip Burlamachi which a special commission had to sort out.[83] The authoritarian and blunt Wentworth would have put the fear of God (and of himself) into defaulters and embezzlers; Juxon was at least honest.

The reaction: criticism of the monarchy and perceived Royal pro-Catholicism

In the circumstances of current anti-Catholic panics it fuelled popular paranoia about Catholic influence to have a Catholic Queen, and at that one associated with converting courtiers to her own religion and promoting her country's interests in foreign policy. Charles had eventually sent Henrietta Maria's large French entourage – complete with priests – packing after their marriage, but the Queen was an enthusiastic promoter of conversion with a circle of intrigue-prone and proselytizing co-religionists. She was not however a 'French agent' as was glibly assumed;

for one thing she was opposed to her elder brother Louis XIII's reliance on Cardinal Richelieu as chief minister and after their mother Maria de' Medici failed to have the Cardinal sacked and was exiled (1630) Henrietta Maria backed her mother's mischief-making against the current French regime. The anti-Richelieu faction in France included the zealously Catholic *'devots'*, enemies of Protestantism, so this was not conducive to the Queen's good reputation in English politics. A contrast to her urbane and worldly father Henri IV, Henrietta Maria was as politically inept and unaware of the hostility that she generated as a perceived 'foreign agent' and national enemy as the equally disastrous wives of two later European sovereigns who fell to revolution, Marie Antoinette of France and Czarina Alexandra Feodorovna of Russia. In all three cases, a domestically irreproachable foreign-born wife of a well-meaning but stubborn ruler never overcame the handicap of being associated with the national enemy at a time of national and international crisis – though at least Henrietta Maria escaped with her life. Her Court entertainments were perceived by her husband's critics as alien and immoral, with the resulting punishment of the slanderers (e.g. Prynne, Burton, and Bastwick) leading to popular sympathy for them and hatred for her. It was unfortunate for the Queen that the fears for free expression of evangelical Protestantism aroused by the trials of Prynne, Burton, and Bastwick in 1637 coincided with the outbreak of the Scottish crisis and that the collapse of the prospect of an Anglo-French alliance in 1637–8 followed. The revived potential of a Spanish alliance in 1639 was not calculated to soothe Protestant fears, but the Queen made matters worse by proposing a Spanish marriage for her daughter Princess Mary and allowing the pro-'devot' Duchesse de Chevreuse, a militantly pro-Spanish French intriguer thrown out of France by Richelieu, to take the Princess to Mass.[84] Having affected her first patroness Anne of Austria's marriage to Louis XIII by damaging that Queen's relationship with her husband and his ally Richelieu, the Duchesse now further damaged Henrietta Maria's reputation in England. In both cases, the affected Queen could be attacked by nationalist opinion as an agent of extreme Catholicism, however unjustly.

The visit to London of the Queen's mother Marie de Medici in 1638 was a major embarrassment. The Queen Mother of France (Italian by birth) was a pro-Spanish foe of chief minister Cardinal Richelieu, expelled from France after attempting to have the Cardinal sacked by Louis XIII in the 'Day of Dupes' when Louis seemed to give way to this pressure but suddenly changed his mind. The visit provided a reminder of the Queen's anti-Protestant international connections, and in 1638–9 the Queen even became associated with the pro-Spanish faction at Court against her homeland's interests. The Duchesse, having meddled disastrously in French affairs against Louis XIII and the Cardinal in 1624–30, now exercised the same baleful influence on the political reputation of the English Queen as she had in the 1620s on the French Queen, Anne of Austria. Crucially, the pro-Spanish ministers Arundel, Cottington, and Windebank were in favour of a military solution to the Scots problem in 1639 and so were in high repute with the King as he attacked the rebels that year; the pro-Spanish ministers, Catholics, and a tough line on Scotland all became linked in the public mind to their mutual detriment.[85]

Charles collected 'Popish' artworks and was prepared to be courteous towards visiting foreign Catholic envoys and to employ Catholics at his court. He thus saw himself in terms of the cultural 'mainstream' of international European monarchy – though it should be pointed out that Buckingham had seen no incompatibility between collecting Catholic art and acting (temporarily) as a patron of preachers such as John Preston and attacking the French Catholic state on behalf of the Huguenots. Charles' attraction to international Catholic culture was aesthetic, as representing beauty, order, and harmony, rather than political. His patronage of Bernini, as a sculptor based in Rome a potential source of adverse propaganda, was handled very carefully and had no religious element; the King was well aware of the danger of open contact with his fellow arts-patron, Pope Urban VIII.[86] Nor did his warmth towards individual Catholics and refusal to ban converts from Court go beyond good manners and gratitude for loyal service; but he took no notice of the supposedly 'pro-Catholic' Secretary Windebank's request to ban all priests from London (which would have affected his wife's Catholic services).[87] The tactless Queen had to be stopped from staging a public Catholic procession through London to celebrate the birth of her nephew, the later Louis XIV in 1638.[88] Serious political damage was probably done in the capital by the way that formerly secret Catholic courtiers could now throng to the Catholic services at the Queen's chapel at Somerset House (built 1632)[89] and the foreign embassies, which served to 'prove' a growing 'Papist menace' to suspicious Londoners. The number of actual Court conversions was not that large, but the perception of a growing threat centred on the Queen's entourage was more serious than the reality.

A false impression of the rising power of 'Popery' was made worse by Charles' politically disastrous employment of suspect ministers like Secretary of State Windebank – the first targets of the vengeful Commons in winter 1640–1. In fact Windebank was probably still Anglican, though Arminian in sympathies, at this point, and was not in the pay of Spain as was popularly assumed. His preference of a Spanish alliance was more to do with dislike of Dutch and French naval power than 'Popish' sympathies;[90] it was his abilities as a conscientious administrator not Catholic assistance that acquired and kept him his post as Secretary. The Lord Treasurer from 1628 to 1635, Richard Weston (Earl of Portland), seen as the most influential minister in the first years of the 'Personal Rule', was married to a Catholic and converted on his deathbed. He was also a natural object for criticism by men jealous of his rise to power in 1628–9 and his abrupt and (according to Clarendon) haughty manner.[91] But despite contemporary rumours he cannot be characterised as either 'Catholic' or pro-Spanish in orientation; the French ambassadors believed that his sole concerns were national interest and keeping England out of expensive wars. His pre-eminence in Charles' counsels after 1628–9 was believed in throughout his Treasurership by some observers, but was limited compared to Buckingham's, though Laud's sneers at his slowness failed to remove him. His death led to foreign fears of greater rather than less Spanish influence on his successors, which recognised his patriotic priorities.[92] As the man charged with sorting out the kingdom's highly problematic and straitened finances after 1629, he favoured peace with Spain in 1630 for financial reasons; and expert observer Sir Henry Wotton, with no axe to grind, regarded him as a man of integrity and the most competent finance-minister since William Cecil.[93] (Nor was he as powerful as his enemies claimed; Clarendon asserted that he hoped but failed to become 'favourite' in 1628.)[94] The other perceived 'Catholic' in the government, Weston's deputy Lord Cottington (Chancellor of the Exchequer), was also in fact both competent and experienced.[95] His involvement in the 1630 Treaty with Spain and later secret negotiations were enough to blacken his reputation, added to his enthusiasm for Spanish culture and his 1640s exile and conversion to Catholicism in that country. But his papers show that he was the agent of the King rather than the initiator of the Spanish talks, favoured the alliance for pragmatic reasons, and was sceptical that Philip IV would return the Palatinate easily; when the talks failed he turned pro-France in 1635–8 and served on the Council committee negotiating with that country. (He did have a personal reason for this, however; he was seeking the Lord Treasurership and Henrietta Maria's support.)[96]

The evidence for these senior ministers as 'Spanish agents' is thus due to gossip and the 'smears' launched in Parliament in 1640–1 rather than reality, exacerbated by Windebank's and Cottington's actions (e.g. conversion) after 1640 and contemporary pro-Parliamentarian gossip then. Genuine Catholics such as Endymion Porter or Wat Montagu were more marginal, if with powerful friends.[97] In 1638–9 the collapse of Charles' proposed French alliance and the threat of an Anglo-Spanish treaty made public alarm at Windebank's influence particularly acute. The possibility however arises that Windebank was undermined by disappointed rivals who had wanted his office – e.g. Sir Thomas Roe, ex-ambassador to the Mughal court and exponent of a Protestant alliance with the Dutch against Spain in the best Elizabethan tradition. Roe's 1632 'A Discourse Concerning the Allies of England', urging a naval alliance with the Dutch, was presented at Court,[98] but was ignored by the King. This probably had more to do with Royal concern at Dutch naval aggression than malign Catholic influence, but it is possible that the disappointed Roe – whose plans for a colonial war on Spain were backed by 'opposition' peers such as Warwick and Essex – played up Windebank's and Weston's Spanish sympathies to undermine them. The terms 'Spanish', 'French', and 'Dutch' as shorthand for identifying the factions of ministers/courtiers favouring each country in the 1630s were certainly in current use in newsletters[99] – and the 'Spanish' bloc would be cast as villains in Parliament in 1640. The subterranean currents of Court rivalry are a neglected factor in considering which ministers were to be accused of 'Popery' and why.

'Tyranny' and the example of Wentworth in Ireland: a capable minister but a political liability and even dangerous?

Nor did it escape the notice of Court critics that in Ireland the new Lord Lieutenant, the zealous Royal administrator Sir Thomas Wentworth, was carrying out a degree of rapprochement with the King's Catholic subjects of English extraction. Wentworth's over-riding ideals were loyal and effective government, and he had never been comfortable as a Royal critic in the 1625–8 Parliaments though he had been obstinate enough about his 'rights' to refuse to pay the forced loan and be arrested. His rapid 'desertion' of his loudly-expressed enthusiasm for the subjects' liberties once he was a peer (July 1628) and Lord President of the Council of the North (December 1628) was cited as proof of his lack of principle and greed for power.[100] In fact his over-riding concern seems to have been for efficient government with a 'balance' between rights and responsibilities, and he saw no incompatibility between his 'opposition' stance in the 1620s and his role as the leader of 'Thorough' policies – which he saw as restoring ancient traditions of harmony (see below). He supported both the liberties of the subject and the rights of the King as mutually complementary, and was probably angered at the 'hot air' and impractical courses of action urged in the Commons.[101] From 1628 he saw his role as proving his usefulness to the King – and he showed his exasperation at the lack of co-operation shown by the obstructive men he had to deal with.

His brusqueness, blunt promotion of order, and carelessness about causing offence increased natural resentment by his fellow-ex-critics of Buckingham, which his 'desertion' would have stimulated. His zeal for efficiency and trampling on lax administrative practice showed itself when he was a ruthlessly competent Lord President of the 'Council of the North' in 1629–33.[102] He informed Lord Carlisle 'how necessary examples are… to retain licentious spirits within the sober bounds of humility and fear'.[103] Later on he was to say that the best way to deal with the 'Ship-Money' crisis was to have the impertinent Buckinghamshire squire John Hampden, who refused to pay to spark a 'test case' in the courts, given a good flogging. His relentless use of usually dormant Royal powers was made more controversial when he went to Ireland in 1633, as many of his victims were 'New English' noble and gentry Protestant settlers as well as 'Old Irish' and 'Old English' established nobles – men who were more used to little interference from Dublin. But he added to controversy by his careless manner – and stories such as his apparently lying on one aristocrat's best bed without taking his muddy boots off on a visit.

Wentworth showed his ruthlessness and willingness to trample on local elites' sensibilities and the 'special pleading' of entrenched groups in Ireland from 1633, where his main roles as Lord Lieutenant were to revive dormant Royal powers in centralised control, secure increased revenue, and overcome the slipshod and ineffective administration that had been the norm under his predecessors. 'Tightening up' governance to enforce the existing laws and see that local officials obeyed them, seeing that the orders of the Dublin regime were obeyed by the semi-autonomous established Anglo-Irish provincial nobility (of pre- and post-16th century 'Plantations' descent alike, and both Catholic and Protestant) and raising money by all legal means possible were in line with Carolean policy in England as explored above. Given Wentworth's vigour, efficiency, and determination in his home region of Northern England as Lord President of the 'Council of the North' in 1628–33, he was the obvious man to lead similar centralisation and money-raising in Ireland, and he was both blunt-spoken and unafraid to create enemies. There were also some parallels with the situation in Scotland with an administration in the capital (the latter being physically remote from much of the country) distant from and only nominally controlling the proud, wealthy, and feud-prone provincial nobility, and in both cases parts of the latter were Gaelic-speaking and of the Catholic not the Protestant faith. In Ireland, however, there was not a 'union of crowns' with England as with post-1603 Scotland; there had been a partial and later part-reversed conquest of independent Gaelic kingdoms by the Anglo-Norman state in the medieval period which had left some pre-conquest Gaelic dynasties (the 'Old Irish') partially Anglicised, and 'settler' medieval English Catholic dynasties ('the 'Old English') in control of large areas. Given the vast distances involved and the poor roads, the small and poorly-funded Dublin administration had perforce relied on them to rule the localities. Some of these regional 'barons' had turned Protestant after the Reformation arrived from1534, but others had remained Catholic and been left alone as loyal to the Crown; some provincial Gaelic dynasties (e.g. the O'Neills of Ulster, descendants of the medieval High Kings of all Ireland) had revolted in the Tudor era and been expropriated. The resulting 'Plantations' of confiscated areas across Ireland were incomplete and were a mixture of vehemently Protestant (and at that Presbyterian) Scots, especially in Ulster after the suppression of the Tyrone Rebellion of 1598–1603, and Anglican and even Catholic Englishmen elsewhere (especially in the Elizabethan settlements in Munster and Leinster). In some cases the local 'Old English' regional dynasts had co-operated as loyal subjects of the Crown with the incoming settlers, whether or not turning Protestant in the process, and in other cases they as well as the 'Old Irish' were the expropriated victims and Protestant 'New English' settlers had taken over. That added the dilemma for the Dublin regime and its sovereign in London of whether loyal but Catholic 'Old Irish' and 'Old English' nobles should continue to be tolerated as semi-autonomous dynasts in control of their vast estates or be forced to hand some lands over – and as of 1633 Charles had recently 'bought off' much of this nobility by promising to leave their current estates and extensive legal rights alone (in the 'Graces'). This the determined centraliser and coloniser Wentworth was determined to reverse, even to the extent of ignoring his master's previous promises. Of course, he could not know that in eight to nine years' time Charles would need every Irish nobleman who he could lure to his side to fight both Catholic and Calvinist rebels – but even in 1633 his 'bulldozer'-like aggressiveness was risky given the King's lack of a standing army.

The central government in Ireland was more decentralised than in Scotland, given the weak control of a small central administration in Dublin with a small army over a group of far-flung provinces whose entrenched nobility had as much power (and military 'back-up' from their tenantry) as the Gaelic clan chiefs did in the Highlands and Islands of Scotland. James VI of Scotland and I of England had sought to curtail the more autonomous and defiant Scots nobles, both Anglicised (Catholic and Protestant alike) and Gaelic Catholic, with his 'government by pen', so the greater legal interference and aggressive centralism that Wentworth imposed on Ireland from 1633 was in line with this. His use of the established and fully legal but usually somewhat lax 'weapons' of royal courts, administrative orders, and other fund-raising mechanisms to enforce Royal power, raise money, and intimidate defaulters was also in line with the post-1629 activities of the English government, as seen above. This also involved a degree of religious reform in Protestant areas too, to the extent of using the money raised and land secured by secular mechanisms to endow the under-funded and under-staffed Irish (Anglican) Church and make it a desirable career for ambitious clerics – and to change Calvinist, Scots-influenced Church practices to fully up-to-date 'Laudian' English ones. In a similar manner but to an even greater degree than in England, Wentworth presented the new system of government as more honest and smoothly-running than the ramshackle pre-1633 practices, but in doing so rode roughshod over local sensibilities, alienated many of the elites, and was not above legal chicanery himself (e.g. in securing the confiscation of land for the new 'Plantation' in remote, semi-autonomous Connacht by forcing the county juries to invalidate the titles of existing landholders and punishing the jury of County Galway who would not obey him).

The attack on the 'Graces' and thus on the established rights of the regional dynasts was partly about raising money – by making them pay to have these privileges extended – rather than outright central control, as the use of ancient Forest Law and other forgotten legal mechanisms in England was partly about fining offenders to enrich the Treasury. But at the same time as Wentworth was annoying the 'Old English' nobility in Connacht by seeking to confiscate large sections of their lands – which their legal appeals to the King eventually halted – he was also feuding with great nobles in Munster who were traditionally much-needed props of Royal power, especially the Boyles, Earls of Cork. Arguably he was creating too many enemies at once without a thought to the weak military resources available to the Crown in an emergency, albeit with a long-term aim of using the money raised to build up the latter – just as we shall see that the 'reform' of the Scots Church in the mid-1630s was carried out without the necessary 'back-up' to enforce it. One ominous sign of his counter-productive methods and obliviousness to his victims' potential to fight back was indeed his feud in the matter of the Connacht plantation with the local 'Old English' dynasty of the Bourkes, Marquises of Clanricarde, who had valuable personal links at the English Court and so could undermine his reputation there – which was to help his foes in the lack of English noble support for him at home in 1641.

His measures to improve the administration took on sinister meaning to his enemies as an experiment for what was to be tried out later in England too, and his necessary if grudging and delayed acceptance of political toleration of the Catholic 'Old English' lords' hard-won 1620s legal concessions (the 'Graces') could be presented as evidence of pro-Catholicism. His building up of a new army in Ireland was as much for local defence against traditionally restive provincial warlords, mostly Catholic, as for use in England or Scotland. Indeed, his zeal for impartial justice made the ordinary people hail him on his progresses for his refusal to be swayed by the usual vested interests of the higher ranks.[104] His idealism and doggedness were admirable but politically counter-productive, and his usual foes unfortunately had useful contacts among the Parliamentary gentry and peerage in England which undermined his reputation. The most notable target in his restriction of autonomous behaviour by great provincial landowners was the leading Protestant 'New English' settler family in Munster, the Boyles (Earls of Cork), who had close allies in the English nobility.

Wentworth's alleged zeal for crushing resistance across all of Charles' dominions was not that much misrepresented. Indeed, at the time of the legal challenge to 'Ship-Money' by John Hampden (a former supporter of Eliot) and his counsel Oliver St John (who had aided the pilloried 'Puritan' Henry Burton) Wentworth was telling the King that a large navy and army were indispensable to his authority.[105] Implicitly, this meant indispensable in crushing opposition by force. He also tactlessly, though privately, encouraged Charles to use regular requests for 'Ship Money' (even when there was no naval need of new ships) to help raise an army and so earn the greater respect of his fellow-sovereigns – confirming his enemies' allegations that the tax was a political not just a security 'move' and would by-pass Parliament as well as threaten all the King's enemies, domestic ones included. Also, it might seem a useful and efficient innovation to Wentworth to employ demonstrably loyal 'Old English' gentry and nobles in the Irish government and army, but English anti-Catholics feared that this was a rehearsal for the same sort of policy in England. An idealist for the Royal power as the 'keystone which closeth up the arch of Government'[106] (his expression in his first public speech as President of the Council of the North), he was an exponent of the value of intimidation. He was duly regarded by his victims and subsequent critics as the sinister mastermind of 'Thorough', 'Black Tom Tyrant', an unscrupulous agent of autocracy who had to be killed off in 1641 to neutralise him. Wentworth seemed – thanks to his actions in Ireland – ready to use an Irish army to stop Parliament; his prosecution and even his execution became an issue for alarmed MPs. This duly drove a wedge between King and Parliament – and arguably helped to make a civil war likelier. Irish events thus had a major impact from early 1641, not just from the Catholic rebellion there later that year.

Chapter Two

The Scots Crisis: The Tipping-point which Ruined an Otherwise Strong Position in 1637–9?

Ship-Money and the auction of English aid to France and Spain, 1635–9: ruined by the Scots crisis?

The calling and inability to dismiss Parliament in November 1640, which gave the 'political nation' a forum for debating their grievances and the means to legislate to ease them, was due to Royal financial inadequacy. Until the need arose to raise armies to meet the Scots challenge Charles' finances were adequate to the demands of peacetime. The estimates of Royal finances made by the new Treasury Commissioners in May 1641 reckoned that the Royal revenue was nearly half as much again as in 1635; the King's measures had dramatically improved his financial position however unpopular they had made him.

It should be noted that there is a lot of hindsight in seeing the much-publicised 'Ship-Money' legal case as the opening shot in the 'fall' of Carolean 'tyranny', though the fact that a principled and well-respected local Buckinghamshire gentry figure – John Hampden – refused to pay up the tax and challenged it in court was undoubtably a 'publicity coup' for his allies and a blow to the King. It focussed the issue, emboldened resisters – and was a return to the mid-1620s legal challenges to Royal 'knighthood refusal' fines and legal prosecution of refusers to pay the 1626 'Forced Loan' so it was not new for disgruntled elite figures to challenge the King.

The amount of interest in the case showed that Hampden had considerable support – Clarendon reckoned that he had never been heard of outside his home county before it but was a topic of common conversation once he made his stand – and in addition he was a well-respected 'ordinary' (and devout) former MP not a known opponent of the Crown. (His friends, however, had included Charles' arch-critic Eliot, who wrote fifteen letters to him while in the Tower and entrusted his teenage sons to Hampden on occasion, and he was connected to Warwick's 'Providence Island Company' and Lord Saye's Connecticut investor groups.) Hampden lost the case, though, and most people paid up the tax. The indications are that the narrow legal victory of the Royal prerogative to raise special taxes in the 'Ship-Money' case in 1638 induced more county communities to pay up than before the case.

Charles' legal challenger Hampden may have had the moral victory, particularly as seen in retrospect, and his cause had attracted the adherence of an impressive body of gentry, nobles and lawyers; but the State had had the judicial victory. The case was also more complicated than the simple 'Hampden/Parliamentary taxation vs. the Royal Prerogative' nature accorded to it in myth. For a start, there was no question of 'Ship Money' being a deliberate Royal ploy to raise extra-Parliamentary taxation and pretend it was for the fleet; the cause was genuine (though as we have seen Wentworth if not Charles was prepared to use it as an excuse). A writ for 'Ship Money' had been prepared but not used in wartime in 1628, and the issue was revived by ambassador Sir Ralph Hopton's formal written request from Madrid in early 1634 for the King to consider creating a new fleet. The problem Hopton had raised of England's naval weakness leading to rising piracy and general disrespect was duly discussed by the Council in June,[1] and in July some of them began debating the means to be used for 'the King's great business' of funding the new fleet.[2] Clarendon stated that the idea for the tax was Attorney-General Noy's,[3] but it is probable that this refers to the precise means to be used, not the principle of a new fleet which had other, independent originators (including Hopton). Nor was it 'sinister' that the fleet was officially to be raised by English taxation at a time when it was still possible that Spain, a potential ally, might come up with funds. This was not an attempt to 'con' the taxpayers; it was an insurance measure in case Spain did not pay. Hopton shrewdly argued that Spain would be less able to wriggle out of commitments to England if Charles depended on his own money, not theirs, to fund the English fleet for any proposed joint action.[4] The writs were sent out to the corporate towns of the coastal counties (the usual payers by historical precedent) in October 1634 – and the tax was to be paid direct to the

Treasury of the Navy so there was no question of the King seizing the money for non-naval uses.

As is frequent in military matters, the cost of the fleet was found to be greater than envisaged – and the uncertain international military situation of 1635, with France and Spain now at war with each other, made a larger fleet and larger tax seem prudent. The extension of the tax to non-coastal communities thus owed more to the special and dangerous international circumstances of 1635 than to any 'plot' to raise extra-Parliamentary taxation on a mere excuse – though it seems that Noy was envisaging extending the tax in summer 1634, well before the crisis.[5] It was only in July 1635 that Lord Keeper Coventry officially notified JPs that the King intended to extend the tax, due to the Continental wars – 'the dominion of the sea is… the best security of the land'.[6] Laud's explanation of the extension to non-coastal communities, in an August letter to Wentworth, was that 'the navy may be full and yet the charge less as coming from so many hands'.[7]

To make sure of the money, the collectors of 'Ship Money' – now the county sheriffs rather than the mayors and corporations of port towns – were made liable for the shortfall if all the money was not handed in, though this was not unprecedented. This brought the office of sheriff and its local gentry holders into the 'front line' of implementing royal financial policies – necessary in the absence of any local Royal bureaucracy but in the event counter-productive. The sheriffs had no accurate and universal rating-scheme for who was to pay how much, and were bound to be accused of undue partiality in a multitude of lawsuits (some of which were probably launched to delay paying anything). The inevitable use of the sheriffs to collect the tax gave those chosen as sheriffs the unwanted choice of having to defy the King by delay or objection or to annoy their neighbouring gentry by enforcing royal demands, and it seems that attempts to avoid taking on this office increased dramatically. The resultant muddle, ill-will, and lawsuits were due to the failings of the 17th century system of local government and provincial resistance to central government control rather than a 'heroic' and co-ordinated resistance to non-Parliamentary taxation on principle. Moreover, the initial writ for the entire country issued in 1635 brought in over £180,000 in the first year, that is over 90 per cent of the sum demanded;[8] by the end of 1636 95 per cent had come in.[9] The second writ, in autumn 1636, demanded

£196,400 and within eighteen months around 95 per cent of this had been paid too, despite some resistance and delays (and plague).[10] The 1637 writ met more resistance, which was ascribed at the time by some (e.g. William Walter, sheriff of Oxford)[11] and more recently by many historians to people awaiting the outcome of the Hampden case. The (minority) finding of Judge Hutton for Hampden was specifically blamed by some observers as providing legal cover for refusals or delay in paying.[12] But the actual effects were limited. The comparable rate of money paid in by April 1638 compared to that paid in a year earlier was £28,355 down; in June it was nearly £32,000 down; but by December it was only £19,000 down on 1637. Overall, around £90,000 of the tax was paid eventually.[13] The effects of the case were clearly magnified by myth.

Hampden and his counsel Oliver St John did not challenge the King's right to call such extra-Parliamentary taxation in all circumstances, including an emergency – their case rested on the 'Ship-Money' writ illegally leaving out the requisite statement that it was an emergency order.[14] The Royal judges' previous statement in 1636 that the existence of an emergency serious enough to require 'Ship-Money' could only be determined by the King was not at stake either – though it should be noted that the two of these judges who found in Hampden's favour in 1638, Croke and Hutton, had both been dubious enough of the 'emergency determinable only by the King' argument in 1636 to say that they would not be bound by it in all possible legal cases. These two appear to have decided for Hampden on grounds of conscience, with Hutton declaring that there was clearly no danger of invasion so no 'emergency'. That had been the argument of Hampden's assistant counsel, Robert Holborne. Sir John Finch, the Lord Chief Justice who summed up definitively in the King's favour, was clearly a 'place-man' obeying his superiors but was also the ex-Speaker of the Commons assaulted by Eliot's followers in March 1629 so he had a grudge against the 'opposition'. But the charge that senior participants in the case had ulterior political motives could also be applied to Hampden's principal counsel, Oliver St John, who will appear as a leading 'opposition' MP in 1640–2. Cousin and man of business to the Earl of Bedford, close friend of Warwick, and agent for the militantly anti-Spanish 'Providence Isand Company', he had recently had his house raided by State officers looking for evidence that he had assisted the defence of dissident cleric Henry Burton.

In any case, the length of time allowed to raise the tax – six months – showed that there was no emergency need for cash – a Parliament could have been summoned in that time. The Hampden case judges' verdict in February-May 1638 – seven in the King's favour, five against, though this is a simplification – centred on the King's right to interpret the Law as he liked rather than on a simple question of whether his 'prerogative' trumped Parliamentary rights on taxation. Outside observers (e.g. the Venetian ambassador) assumed this 'victory' would be accepted by the public, and there seems to have been a large enough move towards paying up after the court decision to expect Charles to be able to pay for his new fleet. The expanded fleet, after all, was needed to pay for national defence given the recent rash of lawlessness at the western end of the English Channel, including piracy on Lundy Island and raids on the Cornish coast by 'Barbary Coast' privateers. (There was worse raiding of southern Ireland.) It was typical of the local gentry resistance to taxation as late as the Tory attitude to the War of Spanish Succession that government critics extolled a strong navy but were less willing to pay for it.

Foreign policy: a missed chance for Charles to earn popularity by turning against Spain in 1637–9, or common sense?

An alliance with France and/or the Dutch against Spain, involving a naval campaign against the Spanish empire and hopefully forcing Spain to coerce the Emperor into returning the Palatinate, would have been as popular as was such a scheme in Parliament in 1621–4; it was urged on Charles by a section of his Privy Council and their allies like the veteran diplomat Sir Thomas Roe.[15] (Roe was the London agent of Charles' sister Elizabeth the 'Winter Queen', married to the deposed Elector Frederick of the Palatinate.) The death of Frederick in 1632 made restoration seem more plausible, as Cottington pointed out – the Emperor would now hand the occupied lands over to Frederick and Elizabeth's eldest son Charles Louis, untainted by rebellion, instead of a man who had tried to deprive him of Bohemia in 1619 and was thus an untrustworthy rebel.[16] The death in battle in late 1632 of Gustavus Adolphus of Sweden, leader of the recently successful Protestant military assault on the Empire in northern Germany, did not do much to free Spain and the Empire of the Protestant threat (and the need of Charles), as Cardinal Richelieu led France to take over as the Protestants' mainstay in the League of Heilbronn. Hopton's hope was that Spansh fear of the Dutch, 'the thorn that pricks them above all others', would drive them to be more accommodating to England despite the unexpected coolness that chief minister Olivares was now showing to him over promises to help with returning the Palatinate;[17] Spain (via its envoy Nicolaide) sought to woo the King into alliance with Frederick's son Charles Louis to join them in return for his lands' return. The Spanish envoy in Brussels, Abbe Scaglia, added the temptation of invading and dividing up the Dutch 'United Provinces' – whose aggressive fleet was a major reason for Charles' naval needs.[18] To complicate matters further, the Dutch themselves were plotting with Louis XIII of France to divide the Spanish Netherlands between them.

It has also been argued by modern historians (e.g. by L.J. Reeve) that Charles missed out on a major opportunity to help the Palatinate cause by failing to give serious support to Gustavus Adolphus in Germany in 1630–2;[19] though he did permit his senior Scots adviser Hamilton to raise a regiment of 6,000 volunteers for this 'just and honourable' cause and sent an ambassador, Sir Henry Vane senior.[20] For one thing, the excited pamphlet hagiography of Gustavus' victories for the Protestant cause[21] led to public awareness of the English King's lukewarm behaviour and added to suspicion of his sympathies. Indeed, a number of fervent Protestant volunteers for the Swedish cause in Scotland (e.g. Alexander Leslie) were later to use the skills they acquired to fight for the Covenanters against Charles. His inaction would have added to doubt about his sympathies from militant Calvinist peers who feared international Catholic aggression, such as Warwick who in January 1637 urged a Parliament and a French alliance against the Habsburgs on Charles. Also, Charles' inactivity made Spain less nervous of his military potential and so less keen to seek him as an ally. However, it was not a simple matter of him neglecting a useful opportunity; ambassador Sir Henry Vane was amazed at the high-handed demands Gustavus made in his proposed terms for alliance and Charles told Hamilton that the Swedes were as demanding as the Habsburgs.[22] Gustavus, indeed, had his own hopes of luring the Elector of Bavaria, in occupation of the Palatinate for the Emperor, away from his allies – so would he have let Bavaria keep the Palatinate in return and betrayed Charles? Gustavus was playing for higher stakes, the control of Germany, and Charles would have been naïve to trust him to help English plans.

France was not a reliable ally either as shown back in 1625–6, so it was not a simple choice for England of preferring the vague promises of Spain to hand the Palatinate back or forcing its return by military action in support of the Habsburgs' French foe (the main backer of the Protestants after Gustavus' death). Quite apart from the dubious nature of France's dealings with the Dutch, France had its own new fleet and a number of colonial disputes with England in the early 1630s (most notably over Quebec, temporarily seized by England in the war of the late 1620s). Nor was Elizabeth of Bohemia convinced that Louis XIII was committed to Charles Louis' restoration to the Palatinate.[23] France, like Sweden but with an advantage as a fellow-Catholic state, sought to woo Bavaria away from the Habsburgs and in return promised to guarantee its occupation of the Upper Palatinate[24] – and the France-Bavaria alliance against the Emperor was to continue into the 1700s. The French occupation of Lorraine in 1634 also caused alarm. In these circumstances where Charles could not trust any of his principal would-be allies, his caution was sensible rather than weak (quite apart from his lack of money or a viable fleet). As Venetian ambassador Correr warned in 1636, the three main powers who could restore the Palatinate to Charles' nephew (Spain, the Empire, and Bavaria) all had other priorities;[25] and Sir Ralph Hopton gloomily reckoned that the best hope was achieving it as part of a general peace where all parties were prepared to give England this prize, 'which is hard to believe'.[26]

The opening of war between France and Spain in May 1635 made it possible that Louis XIII and Richelieu would pay for Charles to use the new 'Ship-Money' fleet against Spain, whose main English ministerial supporter Weston had just died. The war made Charles hope that he would be courted by all sides,[27] and Roe recommended that England 'look on a while and let these elephants waste their strength'.[28] (The use of the simile reflects Roe's past as ambassador to the Mughal court in India.) The chances of England choosing quickly for France were diminished by Charles acquiring a copy of the secret Franco-Dutch treaty to dismember the Spanish Netherlands, while Spanish dilatoriness in offering any useful terms infuriated Windebank.[29] The Peace of Prague between the Emperor and Saxony meanwhile knocked Protestant Saxony out of the German war and made intervention advisable to revive the Protestant cause. The main theatre of war was now expected to shift to the Low Countries, geographically closer to England and so useful for the new 'Ship Money' fleet or a land-expedition. However, this would probably mean aiding France; and ambassador Sir Ralph Hopton warned that France preferred Charles Louis' confiscated Electoral title to remain with the Bavarian ruler Maximilian rather than return to Charles Louis. Bavaria hoped to use the extra pro-French vote in the Electoral college to take the Imperial title from the Habsburgs at the next vacancy; helping England by returning the Palatinate was of less concern.[30]

Charles did the most possible to put pressure on France in late 1635, sending a new envoy (Sir Walter Aston) to Spain to explore the possibility of Charles Louis marrying a Habsburg princess and another envoy (John Taylor) to Vienna to request that his nephew be invested with the Palatinate now that he was of age (eighteen). He informed his sister that this was to force the French to 'unmask and deal more plainly upon more equal terms'.[31] (Taylor was half-Spanish and hopelessly optimistic – a poor choice?) Alarmed as Charles had intended, Richelieu offered to promise to include the Palatinate in any Franco-Imperial-Spanish peace if Charles would end his Spanish talks and put Charles Louis in charge of the new 'Ship Money' fleet in an alliance. In return Charles tried to lure the French into offering the Emperor their recent conquest, Lorraine, to hand on to the Bavarians in exchange for the Habsburgs handing over the Palatinate.[32] This was playing a weak hand as well as possible, rather than the naivety which some have seen in his approach to France and Spain.

A Protestant (England and the Dutch) league with France against the Habsburgs in 1635–7 thus failed to occur, despite the extra weight given to England's power by the new 'Ship-Money' fleet raised from 1634. Charles instead attempted to negotiate with the Emperor for restitution of the Palatinate by peaceful means in 1636, despite warnings by the visiting Charles Louis, Elizabeth (based in The Hague), and their Court allies Lord Holland (a confidante of Henrietta Maria) and Charles' Scots cousin the Marquis of Hamilton.[33] But he had been told by Taylor that the Emperor – about to hold a Diet at Regensburg to arrange his son's election as his successor so in need of goodwill from war-weary German princes – would be prepared to return the Lower Palatinate at once and the Upper when its occupier, Maximilian of Bavaria, died.[34] The Earl Marshal and head of the Howard clan, the Earl of Arundel – an appropriately prestigious nobleman for the task and a leading cultural patron who had visited Italy

– was sent to Emperor Ferdinand in 1636. His cultural Hispaniophilia did not make him a poor choice to stand up to Habsburgs, as he was fed up with their excuses over the Palatinate.[35] But he only secured a delayed and reluctant offer of the Lower Palatinate without either the Upper or the Electoral title.[36] More to the point, Charles had no means of putting pressure on Ferdinand to carry this out.

After this failure, the idea of war with the Habsburgs was revived in autumn 1636 and the Earl of Leicester's current embassy to Paris was given powers to extend the nature of English assistance. Until the definitive failure with Ferdinand at Linz Charles had only been prepared to let the French hire volunteers in England and loan them ships, without England being tied down to an offensive and defensive treaty – full military engagement – which was what Richelieu wanted. Leicester had warned Secretary Coke that the French were not fools who could be bought off without something concrete: 'they are not children who govern the affairs here and there for will not be fed with shadows ... you must help them or be assured they will do nothing'.[37]

This argues for some naivety in London. But once the Arundel mission had failed England was to offer 6,000 troops and the fleet for the French war-effort, though Leicester still thought that Richelieu would think it inadequate;[38] and the discomfited Arundel told Charles that nothing could be gained by Spanish talks and war was necessary.[39]

The weight of influence at Court thus shifted against Spain, isolating the pacific counsels of Windebank and Laud, and public expectations were of war involving the new English fleet.[40] In February 1637 the Cardinal proposed that England commit 6,000 men and a fleet of 30 vessels to blockade Flanders, and the two nations' representatives started to draw up a treaty in Paris.[41] Yet delays continued, the junior English ambassador in Vienna (Taylor) continued to warn of the folly of trusting an overpowerful Catholic France to assist Charles Louis rather than pursue its own aggrandizement in the Rhineland[42] and the French insisted on consulting their German allies before a treaty.[43] A congress was scheduled for 1638 in Hamburg, but by that date the 'Prayer-Book Rebellion' had broken out in Scotland to distract England – and to weaken its usefulness to Richelieu. Given the previous history of the 'Auld Alliance', there were even dark rumours that the French were encouraging the Scots rebels to weaken England: the Marquis of Hamitlon implied that it was French revenge for Charles aiding the Huguenots in 1627–8 and the French ambassador Bellievre accused Spain of fanning the rumours.[44] Alliance with France thus failed to occur, and Charles continued to be suspected of undue partiality for Spain .

There were always problems inhibiting an Anglo-French alliance as seen above, not least suspicion of what France really intended to do in the Rhineland and the Spanish Netherlands if it destroyed Habsburg influence. The bogey of French occupation of the Netherlands soured relations with France on and off until 1815. As Taylor warned, England's forces needed to be equally strong as France's on land and at sea to induce the old enemy to treat them with respect. France's long-term aims in Germany, working with Catholic Bavaria against the Habsburgs, were different from England's Protestant orientation. But what if the French alliance and a limited expedition to the Continent had succeeded in 1636–7 and the Scots crisis had not intervened?

'Puritan' peers excluded from influence, led by Warwick (nephew of the late Elizabethan favourite the Earl of Essex who had led England's anti-Spanish fleets in 1596–7), were currently funding a private naval campaign against the Spanish empire in the Caribbean through the Providence Island Company. A decision to attack Spain should have led to a rapprochement between them and the King. The war would have been approved by the Queen, whose country was in need of English help against Spain, and led to alliance with England's old Protestant allies the Dutch (a politically advantageous alliance to which Charles turned in 1641–2), together with building bridges to the alienated peers and boosting the King's credentials in the country at large as a defender of Protestantism and his sister's popular cause. But he preferred to avoid costly entanglements in Europe and use 'quiet diplomacy' to urge Spain to restore the Palatinate, with the rising Scots crisis in 1637–9 limiting his possibility of military involvement. The foreign affairs committee concluded in spring 1638 that only diplomacy not war was now possible,[45] and Hopton was sent back to Madrid to treat. But the chief minister of Spain, Count-Duke Olivares, was concerned at the Scots crisis inhibiting English usefulness – he sought ships to help protect Flanders from the Dutch and Irish mercenaries, but the English fleet was now expected to be needed invading Scotland.[46] The ever-optimistic Taylor, back in the Spanish Netherlands agitating for alliance, even thought that the Scots crisis had caused Charles to lose his best chance to regain the Palatinate via a Spanish alliance.⁴⁷ Charles' attempts to auction his aid to Spain and France concurrently in 1638–9 – the price being the return of the Palatinate – would have been more successful had he not been unable to offer his fleet. But was the Scots crisis that decisive for his possible allies in ignoring the chance to help him?

The Spanish politely ignored all attempts to interest them in pressurising the Emperor on Charles Louis' behalf, except when the major Spanish fleet taking aid to Flanders had to take shelter in the Downs off Dover in September 1639. Charles could briefly blackmail the Spanish by threatening to leave their unprotected ships to face the Dutch navy if Spain did not come to a quick accommodation over the Palatinate, and pay him £150,000,⁴⁸ but the Dutch attack which followed (11 October) prevented him using this leverage for long. The English impotence during the major Spanish-Dutch naval battle in the Downs – English waters – which followed was perceived as a sign of England's weak role in international politics and enraged the abandoned Spanish.⁴⁹ A war against Spain, national 'bugbear' in lurid Protestant propaganda since 1588 and subject of the 'Black Legend', would have been as popular as in 1621–5 (though the Government's decision on the necessary level of taxes would still have been resisted). Crucially, it would have brought the King's foreign policy into alignment with the private aims of the most wealthy, militant, and bold 'Puritan' peers – the circle around the Earls of Warwick and Bedford, who were using the Providence Island Company to enact a privateering campaign against Spain in the Caribbean with their base on the eponymous island off the coast of what is now Honduras. The Company's 'contact' within the Privy Council was the Earl of Holland, Essex's more 'court-friendly' brother (despite his Calvinist views a friend of Henrietta Maria), who Lord Conway reckoned in 1640 to be co-leader of the 'Puritan' faction with his brother and to be their 'spiritual' (that is, secret and unobtrusive) commander whereas Warwick was the 'lay' (i.e. open) one.⁵⁰ Given his link to the Queen, Holland could have had a chance of influencing Charles into a less chilly and thus more politically useful attitude to the Company and its 'godly' cause.

The 'Prayer-Book' crisis: Charles' worst miscalculation?

It was his catastrophic ignorance of the mechanics of Scots politics and the fierceness of Scots Lowland adherence to their version of Protestantism which impelled Charles into the unnecessary clash with his northern kingdom and set the stage for him having to call a Parliament. He had only been – briefly – to Scotland once since leaving it at the age of two, unlike his elder brother Henry who had lived there until he was nine and started his education with Calvinist tutors. His only close contacts among the Scots peers, led by his cousins the Duke of Lennox and the Marquis of Hamilton, principally resided at Court. So did his Secretary of State for Scotland, the poet Sir William Alexander – a man more closely involved with 'planting' Nova Scotia than with the intricacies of Lowland politics. The two most senior Royal advisers in Scotland of James' last years, Sir Thomas Hamilton (Earl of Haddington) and Sir George Hay of Kinfauns (Earl of Kinnoul), Lord Chancellor from 1622, were in political eclipse by the early 1630s and seem to have played no part in the rising religious crisis. (It has been suggested that they were 'bought off' from daring to argue with the King by their grants of peerages and estates.) Charles clearly had no concept that the domestic peace and end to open armed aristocratic feuding that James had imposed had been a temporary phenomenon and was reversible, or that his and his father's 'service nobility' was not irrevocably loyal or a strong politico-military bulwark. He misunderstood the current state of the Presbyterian Church which James had taken decades to tame – and which had only reluctantly accepted the restoration of bishops. The Church had lost its ancient landed resources and leading role in local life to the gentry and nobility in the Reformation – as in England, partly a naked land-grab – from 1560, and the resulting alliance of often fiercely independent local Calvinist congregations with their co-religionist lay supporters in Lowland towns and countryside remained intact. Arguably, the new bishops were too dependent on the King and unwilling to stand up to him, as well as unaware of or unintimidated by the potential strength of their enemies; the proponents of the Carolean religious reform had a false sense of security about its success.

James had improved the Royal position and side-lined or silenced the most militant Calvinist clerics, imposing a degree of order and Royal control on their conciliar leadership. The defeat of Andrew Melville's faction of clerics showed that the virtual theocracy established under Knox, where militant Calvinist preachers at the very least had a veto on Royal ecclesiastical policy, was over. After many years' patient work, James had managed to restore an episcopate in the geographical form of the pre-Reformationary one, with a degree of power over its junior clerics. But he was careful, which Charles was not – the episcopal Church structure of the 1610s only superficially resembled that in England and the local presbyters remained a force in the Church; the bishops lacked the weight of long-unchallenged authority or administrative/judicial support that they had in England. They lacked the adminstrative structure and landed resources which aided their power in the English Church, though Charles did his best to remedy this.[51] Nor did Charles appreciate the depth of Scots noble hostility to any revival of ecclesiastical power, the last great Church 'power-broker' in Scotland having been the 'Popish' Catholic chief minister of James V, Cardinal David Beaton (assassinated in 1546). If the King gave lands and office to the bishops, this would be feared as 'targeting' those nobles who had acquired such things from them at the Reformation and requiring restitution. To minimalise chances of an armed uprising by militant Calvinist nobles as had occurred against the Catholic government of Queen-Mother Mary of Guise in 1560 and against her daughter Mary Stuart in 1567, Charles needed to reassure the secular elite of no confiscation of their 'Reformation era loot' lands. But Charles failed to realise that he could not impose the same Church structure on Scotland as on England with the same level of acquiescence, and that secular acceptance of any episcopacy in Scotland rested on shakier foundations.

The furore which had taken place in Scotland by both clerics and laity against the 'Five Articles' desired by James in 1617 (including Anglican-style celebration of Christian feasts, confirmation, and kneeling to receive Communion) should have been an adequate warning that resistance was not over. This had occurred after and despite James' securing Royal control over the Church over bishops and the eclipse of the Melville faction, among men who had gone along with the new order of Royal power.[52] James might have been able to influence or bully enough delegates at the 1618 National (Church) Assembly and the 1621 Scots Parliament to vote for the Articles, but he had to promise on the latter occasion that there would be no more innovations and in 1624 he had to withdraw an order to Edinburgh – centre of the 1637 revolt – to celebrate Communion at Christmas and do so kneeling.[53] He backed down after representations from the clergy and the laity, a wise decision which Charles should have emulated in 1637 – though the fact that he was prepared to 'test the waters' on such a provocative 'Anglican' practice shows that he, like Charles, wished to introduce such English ideas and to attempt to assert his authority if possible.

In secular matters too, the appearance of order was deceptive despite James' erection of a new 'nobility of service', minor lawyers and professional administrators dependent on himself, not on their hereditary rights for patronage (e.g. Sir Thomas Hamilton, 'Tam o' the Cowgate'). Wisely distrustful of the turbulent 'old' nobility, he had long relied on such men to rule Scotland, led by careerist Lowlands lawyers. Since his departure in 1603 those given most power (e.g. Alexander Seton, Earl of Dunfermline and Chancellor 1605–22) had become effective viceroys. These men lacked hereditary power over loyal bodies of tenants in a locality, who could be used as private armies to challenge the Crown – the main threat to the Scots monarchy for centuries. Indeed, they had been granted former Church lands as the basis for their new landed power and social prestige – which meant that Charles' attempt to restore some confiscated lands to the Church (exaggerated in rumour) seemed to threaten their power, thus alienating the backbone of James' support from the Crown. The older, pre-1560 landed nobility were more entrenched in control of the rural hinterland from long-term rights – aided by large bodies of armed retainers and with a more recent tradition of successful defiance of weak monarchs than in England. The main families in this group had backed the Reformation in 1560, most of their numbers becoming Calvinists, and had been rewarded by extensive grants of Church lands. They too felt threatened by the King's resumption of some and perceived threat to resume all of the Church's lands.[54] But Charles clearly regarded his rule of Scotland as a simple matter of his issuing orders and his subjects obeying them in secular and religious matters, and any local disapproval of Episcopacy and any religious innovations as being containable.

Unlike James, he had few senior members of the Scottish nobility in London to advise him, and did not even have experienced close Royal relatives from the junior branches of the Stuart dynasty who had the right under strict protocol to treat him without serious deference in giving advice. Arguably, his personal distaste for and distance from his father's – largely Scots – turbulent and bawdy entourage at Court in the years of his young adulthood meant that he had little concept of the nature and interests of the Scots nobility. James could govern Scotland from afar with his pen, as he boasted, but he had had a lifetime of experience there until he left for London at the age of thirty-six so he knew its personalities and what was politically feasible; Charles did not. James' cousin, contemporary, and close adviser, Ludovick Stuart, Marquis of Lennox (and Duke of Richmond in the English peerage), son of James' first 'favourite' and admired friend Esme Stuart, would have had the political 'weight' to have advised Charles of the true state of Scottish affairs. But this vastly experienced and trusted senior Stuart and his brother Esme both died in 1624, leaving the leadership of the only other branch of the Stuarts with importance at Court to Esme's son, a semi-Anglicised political nullity usually resident in London. Ironically, the latter was being married at Court in London – to the daughter of the late Duke of Buckingham, with Laud officiating – at the time of the first 'Prayer Book' riots in Edinburgh in July 1637. His location, bride, and officiating priest, symbolised all that was politically inept about Charles' planning; and when Charles sent him to Edinburgh to examine the situation in September the warnings the Scottish Council gave him about the seriousness of popular feeling were ignored by the King. Another significant death near the time of Charles' accession was that of the Carolean Marquis of Hamilton's father and predecessor, a long-time adviser to James who could have given Charles expert advice from a more senior position than that of his son, Charles' half-Anglicised contemporary.

There were no other Stuarts with the rank and experience to be chosen for a senior role in Scottish affairs from 1625 and to be listened to by a King very conscious of protocol. Charles' younger brother Robert, a logical choice to govern Scotland and advise him on its politics, had died as an infant. His choices of advisers on Scottish affairs, Lowland noblemen of suitable rank such as the Royal relative James, Marquis of Hamilton, and Lord Traquair, were not noted for their political skill or willingness to tell the King unpalatable truths that might lose them favour. Traquair was a 'new man' peer who was to equivocate between King and Covenanters in 1637–40, though Hamilton was the King's distant cousin, of Royal blood, and less dependent on his patronage. Charles seems to have relied on the Scots bishops as his main advisers on Northern affairs in c.1625–33, and they were granted enhanced influence in civil government (e.g. Archbshop John Spottiswode of St.Andrews, president of the Exchequer from 1626). Dangerously for future competence and leadership on the Privy Council in Scotland, Charles decided to ban the lawyers who also sat in the Court of Session from the Council – an act of administrative tidiness which diminished the 'pool' of competent advisers available on the latter. Many of the most active and ambitious non-noble careerists in Lowland Scotland made their living as lawyers, and they were now unable to take a lead in the administration. The most crucial immediate loss was of Lord Haddington, who had the experience and force of character to have withstood the importunate demands of the most pro-Anglican bishops (e.g. Lindsay) for unwise religious innovations.

At most, it is possible that one capable noble normally resident in Scotland – William Graham, Earl of Menteith – was used as an adviser from 1628–33[55] and temporarily improved relations with the nobility. Graham, from a suitably ancient family, was also useful in that his background gave him more respect from the obsessively proud nobles of ancient family, who looked down on the Jacobean lawyerly 'new men' nobles as parvenus. Crucially, Menteith was politically undermined by malicious stories about his '*lese-majeste*' and claims on the succession due to his pressing his rights as legal heir to the estates of David, Earl of Strathearn, according to one interpretation eldest legitimate son of King Robert II (d. 1390). As this claim entailed treating Robert's first marriage and its offspring, Charles' Stewart ancestors, as illegitimate it could be used to allege that Menteith regarded himself as the rightful King. Undermined as an effective minister, Menteith received lukewarm backing from Charles and was forced out in 1633;[56] no capable political figure succeeded him, leaving the Privy Council weak and quarrelling as of the outbreak of the 1637 crisis. Charles' stiff and hierarchical Court in London added to the problems of visiting Scots nobles gaining access to him, even once the politico-religious crisis erupted in 1637, and arguably any Scots nobles at Court would either not dare to tell him unpalatable truths or would be ignored if they did. James' disrespectful and boozy entourage of Scots nobles at Court in the 1600s and 1610s, much hated by the English, had its advantages in political terms. The story of Charles' personal failure to obtain rapport with the visiting Marquis of Montrose (his future commander-in-chief) on the latter's first visit to London[57] was all too typical. Charles was to commit a similar accidental social blunder at the start of the Civil War in 1642, by a cool and distant reception to Yorkshire 'Puritan' gentry leader Sir Thomas Fairfax as he presented an anti-episcopal petition at a rally – and Fairfax duly ended up commanding the army that defeated him in 1645–6.

Charles did not seek out opinions from his Scots Privy Council or outside the episcopate in the Church before proceeding to impose Anglicised religious reform on the latter, regarding it as a case of him giving his directions which would then be obeyed. He had already sought to re-establish proper funding and landed resources for the Church, which had had much of its wealth looted by the laity in 1560, by revoking all grants made of pre-Reformation Church (and Crown) lands in 1625. In practice this did not lead to large-scale seizures but to negotiated terms of tenancy for the current occupiers, thus raising money without causing disorders by disgruntled evictees, but it brought fears that no legal contracts were safe if the King chose to challenge them. As stated above, both the 'old' nobility (granted Church lands in 1560) and newer creations felt under threat.[58] Arguably, the higher rate of tax which the King forced Edinburgh to pay in 1625, 1629, and 1633 (the latter with added interest) than earlier added to ill-will in his capital and so stoked up trouble, as did his attempts to impose 'efficiency' in corporation office-holding and lengths of being in session.[59]

The tactless but oblivious use of the English Prayer-Book and vestiarian practices on the Royal visit for Charles' belated coronation in Holyrood Abbey in July 1633[60] showed that he regarded Anglican practices as superior and desirable even in his legally separate other realm, and the offence given was noted by contemporary writers.[61] This was followed by evident manipulation of the meeting of the Scots Parliament to obtain agreement – via the Royal prerogative to avoid defeat in a vote – on using Anglican priestly garments in the Scottish Church.[62] Technically, it did no more than reaffirm the 1606 Parliamentary recognition of the Royal prerogative and the 1609 acceptance that the King could prescribe apparel so it was not innovatory; but neither Act had been acted upon before and even the Archbishop, Spottiswoode, had refused to wear an English-style surplice at James' funeral in 1625. The measure was regarded by the annalist Balfour as the first step towards the troubles that erupted in 1637.[63] Those nobles who voted against the King were denied their expected coronation honours in an all too typical mark of Charles' displeasure.

Following the visit to Scotland, Charles required the Dean of the Chapel Royal, Holyrood (Bishop Wedderburn) to 'Anglicanise' the ceremonial of services there[64] and in 1634 required the Lords of Sessions to take the sacrament twice a year and the bishops to draw up a new set of canons and Book of Common Prayer.[65] The subsequent preparation of a new set of canons saw the more resented pro-Anglican innovations in the last set finally implemented, which James had wisely avoided doing, and the planned new liturgy was pronounced as being non-negotiable. The contrast with James' draft liturgy of 1618 was notable – the latter had brought in elements of Anglican practices into morning and evening prayer (based on Matins and Evensong), Communion, and the service for baptism, but had left out potentially inflammatory 'Popish' canticles and using the sign of the Cross and had introduced extra prayers. Anglican deacons were now introduced, and when the Scottish bishops prudently requested that the new liturgy be distinct from that used in England Charles backed Laud's insistence on complete uniformity.[66] Bishop Juxon quipped that the canons would cause more noise than the Edinburgh Castle cannon, but was sure they would be accepted eventually; Clarendon and Laud's biographer Heylyn thought the main problem was not so much the canons' contents but the autocratic way of imposing them.[67] Tidy administrative practice and centralisation came above concessions, and when the Scots bishops were finally allowed to draw up the liturgy they were constrained to follow Royal instructions But the 'guilty parties' in all this Anglicanization were more the Scottish bishops than the usual target cited, Laud – who claimed that his own preference for just using the English Prayer Book was denied by the Scottish bishops who issued their own version.[68] He also accused them (with hindsight, in a 1639 letter to the Bishop of Derry) of ignoring his advice to be very careful about how fast they proceeded.[69] Modern analyist Gordon Donaldson also puts the blame on the Scots bishops in his 1954 study.[70]

Anti-episcopal feeling rose in Scotland in 1635–7 as Charles proceeded to restore the senior clergy to a leading role in civil government for the first time since 1560, with the Archbishop of St Andrews as Chancellor and the Treasurership rumoured to be next in line for an episcopal holder (as in London). Rumour had it that Charles intended to endow the clergy by seizing up to a third of the country's landed wealth for them, or to 'pack' Parliament by restoring an order of 'abbots' to add to the pro-Anglican 'payroll vote'.[71] As with the post-Parliamentary 'supplication' made to him and an earlier protest in 1625, he ignored his critics except to demonstrate his withdrawal of favour. In fact the Prayer-Book had carefully avoided potentially inflammatory language that could be construed as 'Popish' or even English, it was not at all Anglican in theology, and its main author was the orthodox Calvinist Wedderburn; but rumour had it that it was crypto-Catholic.

Contrary to later myth, it seems that the principal fault for the pro-Anglican tone of its language – and thus the violent reaction –lay with an initiative by the Scots bishops, not orders sent from London by an ignorant or provocative Laud. The extent and violence of the Prayer-Book crisis in 1637 thus was not due to a hasty and insensitive imposition of 'centralised' control by a bigoted Charles and/or Laud; and in fact protesters had already walked out of readings of the new Prayer Book at local synods in Scotland in May (presumably not known in London).[72] The chances of avoiding the crisis did not rest on policy-makers in London, but on the bishops in Scotland; though Heylyn later admitted that it would have been better had Charles submitted it to a Church Assembly first to test opinion among the lower clergy.[73] Although Charles had given the bishops clear orders of what was expected with his request for new canons and a Prayer-Book and made sporadic interventions on the contents, the primary responsibility lay with them. It is possible that the deliberate Royal policies since 1603 to draw the new bishops from socially inferior backgrounds in contrast to the pre-Reformation use of aristocratic families, making them more dependent on their King for patronage, meant that there was a greater risk that these men would be too cowed to stand up to an insistent King or to Laud.

From dissent to active resistance: defiance gets out of hand

It is probable that the violent reaction to the first public reading of the controversial new Prayer-Book in St Giles' Cathedral in Edinburgh on 23 July 1637 was 'stage-managed' by leading aristocratic critics as well as by the clergy. Some of the Privy Council who were supposed to be at the service to demonstrate their support for the book mysteriously failed to turn up.[74] As the Earl of Roxburgh pointed out to Hamilton, the riot started when the 'heroine' Jenny Geddes threw a stool at the officiating cleric before the reading had started – implying that the protesters were not spontaneously outraged at the 'Popish' language and that they knew what to do beforehand.[75] Around 2000 of the ordinary people were involved, though believed to have been put up to it by more senior figures. The protest was evidently planned, and there were others at churches across Scotland. Few clergy had the willingness to resist menacing crowds of the Bishop of Brechin, who preached with two loaded pistols in his pulpit.

The co-ordination of resistance was led by the local gentry and nobles – men with a practical reason to resist the resumption of alienated Church lands that Charles was believed to intend, quite apart from questions of conscience. This was the same coalition that had backed the Scots Reformation in arms in 1560, when the 'Lords of the Congregation' had used force to challenge the Catholic regime of Queen-Mother and regent Marie de Guise and her French troops. Some fiercely Calvinist nobles like the Earl of Rothes had been critical of Royal policies since the 1610s; Rothes had annoyed Charles by openly challenging the figures of the vote in Parliament on ecclesiastical apparel in 1633. The most active of the younger aristocrats in the anti-Prayer Book movement, Archibald Campbell, Lord Lorne (soon to be Marquis of Argyll), is likely to have been involved given his immanent emergence as an 'opposition' leader and absence from the contentious St. Giles' service along with Rothes, his fellow-Privy Councillor. His Calvinist father had converted to Catholicism, and whether or not in reaction to this Lorne was violently anti-Papist', and was already known for his expulsion of Catholic clansmen (mainly his Campbells' hereditary Macdonald rivals) from lands in Kintyre. The presence of nine bishops on the Scots Privy Council and the measures taken since 1625 to extend their landed resources both threatened the post-1560 dominance of the nobility, who now used this excuse to use popular feeling for a protest. Apart from Rothes and Campbell, almost all the first leaders of resistance in 1637 were Lowlanders – Lords Balmerino, Loudoun, Lindsay, and Cassilis – and so able to bring armed tenants quickly to Edinburgh.

What occurred was no more than what would have been expected if James had gone ahead with his ecclesiastical plans to have an 'Anglican'-style Christmas service in Edinburgh in 1624. A wiser King aware of the limits of his powers of constraint in Scotland could have ignored the 'insult' and quietly withdrawn the Prayer-Book for 'consultations'. In practice even James' 1618 'Five Articles' had been ignored by many local clerics, and imposing any new orders on an unwilling Church was thus problematic at the height of the supposedly more experienced James' rule. Giving back status, offices, and wealth to the bishops did not lead to due obedience by the junior clergy or laity, whatever the legal position; Charles mistook legal power for real power 'on the ground'. After the riots a few people were arrested, the Privy Council ineffectually ordered the protection of ministers using it, and Archbishop Spottiswoode persuaded them to suspend the use of the Prayer-Book pending a decision by the King.[76] The protesters petitioned the King to withdraw the Prayer-Book, but this seems to have been by no means the only target of the aggrieved – Lord Stirling wrote to Secretary Sir John Coke that the canons and the ecclesiastical Court of High Commission were also complained of.[77] Intimidatory crowds from the local counties assembled in Edinburgh, ignoring Royal orders to disperse, and many members of the nobility and clergy linked up for a formal 'supplication' requesting the withdrawal of the Prayer-Book as containing many points contrary to post-Reformation theology and practices and introduced without the usual consultation.[78]

Lord Treasurer Traquair and the Bishop of Galloway were the targets of the next riots in mid-October, and a new 'supplication' drawn up by Lords Balmerino and Loudoun and the future clerical leader Alexander Henderson on the 18th – and signed by 24 nobles and 2–300 lairds – requested suspension of the bishops from Parliament. At this point the methods chosen for protest were still within the law by petitioning the King, and organiser Rothes assured Lord Balcarres on 2 November that nothing illegal was intended – but the threat of unilateral action if the King did not obey the requests was always there. The whole apparatus of Episcopal control was ultimately at issue, not just one innovation of 1637 and victory would restore the nobility to unchallenged dominance in Scots politics. Balmerino had already been tried for treason for defying Charles' ecclesiastical plans in 1633, and no doubt sought 'safety in numbers' for his latest challenge. Would a quick retreat by Charles have headed this off? But his nature does not suggest that he would have contemplated allowing such open defiance to go unpunished, even had he been better informed about the widespread extent of resistance or appreciated that he was unwise to rely on the timid Traquair (blamed by Spottiswoode for not supporting him in July). There was also the issue of what lay behind the protests even if they were supposedly about just the Prayer Book – Lord Stirling advised Coke that the new canons and the Court of High Commission, i.e. the whole disciplinary apparatus and official theological position, were the real targets.[79] Was the Prayer Book just an excuse, and without it would another issue have been chosen by men determined not to budge an inch from the Calvinism of James' reign (or to reverse its Church centralisation)?

Militant nobles may well have used the opportunity to play up the extent of popular anger to show the King the determination of the Church and its lay members to resist the Prayer Book and restrict the bishops' roles, but their action cannot explain the quick spread of and multiplicity of petitions from across the Lowlands. They may well have fanned lurid rumours and organised petitioning, but they had active co-operation from the lower-class laity. The King and those Councillors in favour of the innovations, led by Hamilton and Traquair, were clearly taken by surprise and had no plans ready to counter the spread of co-ordinated resistance. None of the loyal lords seems to have had the idea of rallying and arming their own rural tenants, unless they had considered it and were uncertain of their devotion to the unpopular cause of the bishops. Ultimately force had been the arbiter of Scots political crises through the 14th to the 16th centuries, with great nobles ever-willing to use private armies to intimidate or even kidnap (or murder) the head of government. This had lapsed since the final threats by armed lords, Highland (e.g. Huntly) and Lowland (e.g. Hepburn) alike, to James in the early 1590s but the recent stability was deceptive and the monarchy still lacked a standing army – which Charles had not considered trying to create as a prudent 'insurance policy'. Having (French) troops had not saved Marie de Guise's equally unpopular ecclesiastical regime in 1560, however.

Possibly Charles' richest and most senior Lowland noble ally, Hamilton, could not have counted on his own Protestant Clydesider tenants to support him in an armed confrontation with the supporters of the defiant lords. (His orders for them to assemble in 1638 were not implemented 'on the ground', probably out of fear of reprisals by militant Covenanter neighbours.) Given his future actions, Hamilton may have been playing a 'double game' already – and been unwilling to risk unpopularity among his countrymen for the sake of a King whose powers he desired to limit for his own benefit or who he expected to lose. Ultimately, deposition of the Stuarts could be to the benefit of their next lineal heir – himself, as senior descendant of James III's sister. A triumphant episcopate threatened his dynasty's hereditary influence on the Scots government. But the Aberdeenshire loyalist magnate Huntly had trustable tenants (many of them Catholics) and in 1644–5 his family could use them as a private army in support of the King. His willingness to run risks and act boldly was not exactly evident in 1639–45, as the frustrated Royal general Montrose was to find out to his cost. But he could have been given explicit orders to intervene which he could not defy; and he was not ordered to bring his tenants into Edinburgh in force in 1637–8 as the King's local officials lost control of events.

From the start, neither the – divided – Privy Council nor Charles acted quickly to bring loyal troops into the Lowlands. In this respect, it is possible that the absence of the ruthlessly realistic Wentworth in Dublin was a major loss to the King as once he was appraised of the need for military action he was quick to offer to send in his own Irishmen to overawe resistance. He failed to raise these troops as hoped, or Charles to use him effectively – but had he been in London in 1637–8 he could have suggested the same military solution using loyal Scots tenants and/or started Continental recruiting (mercenaries or trainers) more efficiently than Charles and Arundel did. Highlanders under Huntly, or Hamilton's tenants, could have been brought into Edinburgh before the rebels could assemble their own tenants. The extent and co-ordination of resistance to the Church reforms in 1637–8 caught the King by surprise, in which his lack of personal experience of Scotland and availability of experienced senior advisers was a factor. However, given his failure to show ability at political manoeuvring or winning over allies by concessions in the 1640s it is probable that he would have dismissed unwelcome advice then as he did later – even from within his family. Giving in over any of the demands meant abandoning his legal right – and his duty as father of the nation – to impose orders on his subjects. Now he failed to realise the extent of opposition and back down on imposing the Prayer Book quickly, firstly ordering obedience in August[80] and when Traquair came to London in December ignoring his advice to abandon both Prayer-Book and canons and ordering him to enforce them instead.[81]

However, giving way could easily have led to more demands, as feared by contemporary observers like Lord Conway in spring 1638; one preacher at St Giles' in July 1638 was already blaming the existence of bishops as the ultimate cause of the innovations. The latter prudently withdrew from the Scots Privy Council at the end of December 1637 (as Lord Loudoun was telling the English Privy Council should be done permanently),[82] reducing potential tension but costing Charles votes in that body. Loudoun was openly encouraging petitions against all ecclesiastical innovations. It was no use the King's envoy from London, the Earl of Roxburgh, angrily ordering the group of leading Covenanters that he met at the Scottish Privy Council in December to obey their King without force to back it up. He ended up losing his temper at their obstinacy, and clerical leader Alexander Henderson told him off for swearing.[83] As with John Knox in 1559–60, the militants could rely on a fearless clerical leadership who saw themselves in the tradition of Moses, standing up for godliness to the authorities; these were not the sort of men that Charles was used to dealing with. The protesters' use of the word 'Covenant' for their protest-document deliberately harked back to that used by Moses' followers in the Biblical Book of Exodus.

Charles did not have a standing army to use in Scotland, relying on his nobles to provide troops from among their tenantry. Nor did he have troops at his call in London, so in any immediate test of naked power over the seething Lowlands he needed to rely on his loyal senior aristocracy (there or in the Catholic Highlands). He ordered his Privy Council to disperse large and intimidatory demonstrations in Edinburgh while lacking the troops to enforce his orders. He recognised that giving in would reduce him to the status of the Doge of Venice[84] and played for time until he could fight. In May Hamilton was sent to Edinburgh as Royal Commissioner, as promised in February, with two conflicting official documents – one order to disband the Covenant as a 'sine qua non' and another just enjoining obedience without specific conditions to this.[85] A proclamation issued on 28 June promised to consider whatever either a Church Assembly or Scots Parliament might propose.[86]

An advocate of armed confrontation by June 1638, Hamilton was thus given the 'hard-line' or softer option to use as he saw fit in his May instructions. Once he was in Scotland he was ordered to keep negotiating with the Covenanter leadership until ships and ammunition could arrive in Scotland,[87] implying coercion was the long-term aim unless they backed down. He was hoping that the Covenanters would commit some blatantly treasonous actions that could be used as an excuse. Charles was reduced to plans to bring in Wentworth and his Irish, which would require co-ordination between London, loyalists in the Lowlands and Highlands, and Dublin, and adequate ships and good weather to succeed, and to buy sufficient ammunition in Holland. Once Hamilton had reported back to the Privy Council on 1 July war was prepared, with Bishop Juxon (Lord Treasurer) saying that the Exchequer could provide £200,000.[88] Charles' limited financial position prevented the recruitment of foreign mercenaries from the Continental wars, a useful source of experienced men – instead the defiant Calvinist noble leadership, under Lorne/Argyll, Rothes, and Montrose, brought in expatriate Scots officers led by Alexander Leslie to join or train their assembling force of volunteers. Leslie returned to Scotland via London in March 1638, probably meeting sympathetic English 'opposition' nobles en route. Notably, officers with foreign experience were scattered across the Covenanter army as lieutenant-colonels (i.e. second-in-command) of the various regiments being formed, thus spreading out their experience usefully across the army. The King was to be less systematic in his appointments. The convenient fact of many restless and ambitious Scots military men having been able to serve the 'Protestant hero' Gustavus Adolphus of Sweden in his German wars from 1631 gave such men invaluable experience with the most up-to-date army of the day – one relying on well-drilled regiments and on the devastating power of an artillery barrage, as was to be used by the Scots at Newburn in 1640. Once they were back in their homeland, drilling their recruits and organising an effective commissariat, they put the King at a military disadvantage as he had fewer experienced officers to call on.

Equally to the point, Charles had a weakness for appointing senior nobles to high command on the basis of birth not experience; it was based on ancient precedent like his financial exactions, but showed his naivety. His chosen commander for 1638 was the hereditary 'Earl Marshal' (i.e. senior-ranking 'feudal' military official), the Earl of Arundel, who had no military experience and naively proposed arming the Borderers with their traditional lances, bows and arrows to resist the Scots. A more up-to-date but socially inferior soldier who had served in Germany, Sir Jacob Astley, was appointed to overhaul the defences of Hull, and correctly warned that Arundel's idea of armaments was useless and muskets were needed.[89] Muskets, cannon, and ammunition were meanwhile ordered from the Low Countries;[90] and the local troop-raiser in the North-East, Sir Thomas Osborne, warned that his recruits lacked adequate arms or trainers.[91] As with the invasion crisis of 1588, English counties' militias' 'military preparedness' only existed on paper; the local gentry organisers had not been kept 'up to speed' by the otherwise occupied Privy Council in London. The Council intended to raise some 24,000 infantry and 6,000 cavalry from the trained bands of each county, keeping the Northern militia as reserves, and letters were sent out to each area's leading nobles and gentry inviting them to attend on the King at York; precedents were searched for the medieval practice of requiring all feudal landholders to join the King for a Scottish campaign.[92] There was no concept of the fact that these untrained soldiers would have to confront military veterans from the Continent. The failings of the 1627 campaign at La Rochelle had not been learnt.

The Covenant and its implications: militant Protestant resistance.
The noble and clerical opponents of the reforms regularised their alliance into an official organisation with the creation of the 'Tables', and Charles' despatch of a stern proclamation ordering their submission as a condition of any pardon met with predictable defiance. It is not clear if Traquair, whose mission to explain the situation to Charles in London had met with this uncompromising response, was so alarmed at the King's lack of realism that he switched sides and tipped off Rothes and Montrose that the proclamation was to be read out first at Stirling not Edinburgh. In any case, as it was read out the assembled 'opposition' leadership and a large crowd turned up and denounced it. A similar demonstration met the proclamation in Edinburgh. Following this, a National Covenant against the religious innovations was drawn up and was signed after a mass-rally at the Greyfriars Kirk (preached to by Henderson) on 23 February 1638. By inviting their supporters to converge on Edinburgh simultaneously the resistance was thus taking a 'revolutionary' step to enforcing its will on

the Council and King by armed intimidation – though it did not so much as anticipate the English opposition's tactics in 1641 London (or that of 1789 Paris) as look back to the popular element in the anti-Marian coup in 1567. The deposition of Queen Mary by a clique of nobles after her 'rescue' from her unpopular new husband Bothwell had been aided by intimidatory crowds thronging Edinburgh denouncing her as a whore; now another large gathering was used to cow the Privy Council and bishops. The Council declared itself powerless to resist, and Archbishop Spottiswoode fled to London. Significanrly, copies of the Covenant soon found their way to London.

The implication of the creation of the Covenant, using the Old Testament analogy, was that the protesters were the united 'chosen people' of the new Israel defending the true religion under the heirs of Moses and Joshua – and that the King and his bishops represented Pharoah. The word 'Covenant' had been used by a previous, anti-Catholic manifesto of 1581 which King James had signed, so it was not entirely new or explicitly anti-monarchical; its association of the Scots with the 'Chosen People' was traceable back to the Declaration of Arbroath in 1320 but this implied that Charles was in the position of the nation's Plantagenet enemies. It did not attack the principle of ecclesisastical government – yet – or claim the right of a Church Assembly to determine the nature of a religious settlement independent of any secular veto, though this may have been a tactic to maximise support. It made its appeal to the Scots by citing recent violations of the Reformation, presenting the 'innovations' as alien and illegal, although probably radicals like Archibald Johnston already had it in mind to seize back that conciliar clerical leadership of the Church which their forebears had lost to King and bishops since James' assertion of Royal power.[93]

The relatively moderate language of the Covenant and its lack of a specific challenge to Royal authority however enabled Charles to respond in kind and maximise his support by a conciliatory attitude. Possibly this was hoped for by Rothes, or even by Henderson. He could have quickly set commissioners to negotiate, granting major concessions and hoping thus to break up the united front of nobles (the men with the main force of arms at their disposal) and turn 'moderates' like Montrose against power-hungry Lorne. Indeed, the latter was one of a group of senior nobles summoned to London by Charles that spring to explain the situation to him; he was so abrasive that the angry King considered arresting him. Had he done so, the Covenanters would have been deprived of a leading 'hawk' (though it would have further incensed them). Alternatively, Charles could have accepted Lorne's uncompromising warnings and been more conciliatory about religion. Instead he eventually conceded the summoning of a Parliament and an Assembly to debate religious matters if the Covenant was abandoned first, which terms his Commissioner Hamilton brought to Edinburgh in May. This was unrealistic in expecting the opposition to throw away one of their main weapons. His suggestion that a Parliament be called was countered by the Covenanters demanding that in that case the bishops should be excluded from it[94] – an intolerable challenge to his authority quite apart from removing a bloc of pro-Royalist votes. It is notable that the King did not send his most senior (and most trustable?) Scots loyalist noble, the Duke of Lennox, as Commissioner – but Lennox was not only inexperienced in Scots politics but had a brother who was a Catholic priest. Lennox was rumoured to have 'Papist' sympathies himself, and could have inflamed the Covenanters. Huntly, another choice and older and more experienced than Lennox, might have been in personal difficulties in Edinburgh as he owed money there.

The Royal reaction: submission, negotiation, or armed force?

Had Hamilton, Traquair, and other loyal nobles been willing – or able? –to raise their Lowland tenants as a loyalist force and to deny the rebel nobles the possession of the only active army of landed retainers, Charles would have had more military potential (though still not enough arms for his men until these arrived from abroad). Bereft of any organised military backing except from the isolated Marquis of Huntly in Buchan, Charles was reduced to sending Hamilton to meet the opposition leadership and in late summer 1638 suspended the Prayer Book, canons, liturgy, and disciplinary machinery – they would be removed permanently if the Scots Parliament so wished it.[95] The requested Church Assembly was summoned to meet in Glasgow, and on Hamilton's advice the King reissued the unequivocally Presbyterian (and non-episcopal) Royal 'Confession' of 1580 as a sign of support for the traditional religion.[96] This was hopefully turned into an 'anti-Covenant' as a rallying-point for the Royal cause and local congregations were encouraged to sign up for it, but this imaginative tactic failed due to a lack of sympathetic local gentry or officials to organise the signatures. The task was left to the local landowners who were mostly Covenanters and so ignored it – as any realistic politician would have expected – and the concession did not satisfy Warriston who attacked Council legal expert Sir Thomas Hope for backing it. (Later the 'trimmer' Hope tried to appease the Covenanters by declaring that the 'Confession' also legalised the abolition of episcopacy, which nullified its use to the King.) When the 'Confession' was read out at the Mercat Cross in Edinburgh both Warriston and Montrose addressed the pro-Covenanter crowds and successfully urged a boycott. Intimidation ruled, with only Huntly in Aberdeen and Buchan able to collect a large number of signatures to the 'Confession' by dint of an armed progress.

When elections were held for the Assembly delegates these were blatantly 'rigged' to secure militants in that body.[97] The question of who were to be eligible for election was extended from the clergy – men including past episcopal nominees who might thus back their patrons – to including the laity, as 'elders', on dubious legal grounds. The more militant Calvinist laity, who dominated the local Church, were thus eligible for election and duly organised their attendance; 17 peers, 9 knights, 25 lairds, and 47 borough representatives were elected. The 142 ministers elected excluded all those who had sat on the Court of High Commission or been JPs (i.e. were Royal protégés) and anyone who had supported the Prayer Book; arguably it was not a fair reflection of the current Church at all but a self-selected assembly of the Covenant's backers. Hamilton called the members all 'most rigid and seditious Puritans' in a letter to Charles on 22 November, warning that disobedience if not outright rebellion was to be expected.[98]

The lack of a mechanism of local support for the King and his loyal Councillors made this outcome inevitable, although organising a campaign of support would have been difficult even had Hamilton or Traquair been willing and able to do it. The open collection of arms for and the drilling of volunteers in the new Covenanter army made it apparent that the opposition were defying Royal authority with the intention of forcing a solution on their own terms. The attempts to stop the provisioning of the few Royal fortresses (e.g. Edinburgh and Dumbarton Castles) was an adequate warning even to Charles that open military defiance was being considered and that the era of armed challenges to Royal authority had returned. Charles may have calculated that his generous offers to the Assembly would meet an appropriate response, or that they would split the moderates from the radicals and expose the latter as a rebellious faction – if so he underestimated his critics' cohesion. He did nothing to help to divide his critics, which a generous use of patronage and flattery might have aided given personal distrust among them; Rothes and Archibald Campbell (Lord Lorne) were contentious figures and the hatred the land-hungry Campbells had aroused among their Argyll neighbours in the early 17th century was a useful weapon against that family.

The weakness of Royal power in the Scots urban and rural areas was a constant of that turbulent realm, which lacked the long-established infrastructure of officialdom in local English politics, but was evidently a surprise to its inexperienced sovereign. Charles (or Hamilton on his orders) did not make personal overtures to some of the nobles involved to try to wean them from their allies – though it is arguable that he was let down by the passive attitude of men like Traquair. He preferred to hope for enemy concessions without the certainty of adequate means to enforce his will if he was defied. Conversely, he did not take the prudent course of abandoning his religious measures immediately in the interest of avoiding the expense of a prolonged war and/or the military occupation of rebellious areas to enforce his authority – which would strain his finances further. If abandonment had been mooted, obviously the Covenanters in the Assembly would press for complete submission to all their demands. This would now include eviction and politico-religious marginalisation of the bishops, restoring the control of militant self-elected local clergy and their lay patrons over the Scottish Church as in the 1560s. Charles would go this far in 1641, but not in 1638–9.

When Hamilton proceeded to Edinburgh in May, and later to the Assembly in Glasgow, he did not bring an adequate military force of his or Huntly's tenants to deal with open defiance from the Covenanters, which avoided bloodshed but gave the opposition heart to press forward on their terms. The fault did not lie with him, as he had ordered his tenants to muster in Haddington to meet him en route to Edinburgh in May,; but local Lowland Covenanter lairds prevented them from assembling; Huntly would have been able to assemble his men without such interference but possibly a move on Glasgow would have caused Archibald Campbell to bring his clansmen South to intercept him en route from Aberdeen.

Hamilton's attempt to get the Privy Council to declare the Covenant illegal had been blocked by its legal expert Sir Thomas Hope, who said that it was legal – though even if Hope had preferred loyalty to his King to his conscience (or fear?) it would have been ignored. (Hope, like Lord Lorne, had been a Council absentee from St Giles' on the day of the 1637 riot.) When Hamilton had a proclamation demanding submission as the price of pardon read out in Edinburgh that spring (a repeat of Charles' failed tactic of December), Warriston equally publicly demanded that Parliament and the Assembly decide the future of the Church and the Council dissociated themselves from Hamilton's action.

In such circumstances Hamilton had little option but to advise the King to accept calling the Assembly to play for time, while Charles put excessive reliance on the current boasts of Ulster Irish Catholic peer Randall Macdonnell, Earl of Antrim, that he could easily bring an army of his tenants to Scotland to offset the armed Covenanters. Antrim – another Buckingham connection favoured at Court, married to the Duke's widow – could not act quickly, and thus aid Charles practically; but the rumours about his intentions alarmed Protestant opinion in three kingdoms about the King's fondness for using Catholic troops against his subjects. Having a claim to Kintyre (Campbell lands) and proposing to land his men there, Antrim added to the alienation of his potential target Lord Lorne from the King; and Wentworth refused to send Antrim's men military supplies as he could not trust them. It is possible that the approach the King made to Antrim indeed raised Catholic Ulster hopes that the Crown would back them militarily against the Covenanters, including the latter's local Ulster Presbyterian supporters, and thus played a part in the planning that led to the outbreak of the Irish rebellion in 1641 – another disaster for Charles' cause.

The Assembly voted themselves the right to decide on the future of episcopacy, and intimidated the presiding Moderator into going along with it. The bishops were indicted by a carefully-organised popular petition listing their alleged crimes so they were unable to sit (and vote) in the Assembly while under investigation. They sent a protest that this exclusion was unlawful, giving Hamilton a legal excuse to dissolve the meeting if he needed; but he would have done better to bring along a large armed force of tenants. (The recent death of the Earl of Argyll now gave Archibald Campbell full control of the clan manpower, another threat.)

Hamilton tried to gain control of procedure by invoking the precedent of using that seen at the last Assembly meeting for which records were extant – that of 1590, when the meeting had been carefully controlled by King James' loyalists. Henderson circumvented this by producing earlier documents, from John Knox's era in the 1560s when the meetings were self-governed. On 28 November Hamilton was reduced to walking out to withdraw Royal recognition of their actions, having produced documentary proof of the intimidation in the elections to show that the meeting's membership had been rigged. Undeterred, as might have been expected, the Assembly stayed in session while he withdrew to Glasgow Castle; they were told by the triumphant Henderson that they were zealous towards their Heavenly master and maintaining the liberties and privileges of His kingdom (i.e. as opposed to obeying an earthly King). This was as much of a revolutionary moment as the 'Tennis Court Oath' in Versailles in 1789, when another self-declared popular assembly defied Royal orders to disperse. The Assembly now voted to abolish the bishops, Prayer Book, canons, and liturgy.[99]

Military confrontation, summer 1639. Bad planning or bad luck?

Charles had failed to even attempt to divide the armed Calvinist Lowlander wing of the nobility and their tenants (which for politico-religious purposes included the technically Highlander Campbells loyal to Argyll). He had allowed the sole resident military power in the country to form and maintain an anti-monarchic alliance with the militant clerics who had insulted his grandmother with impunity and lectured his father as a youth, the most coherent alliance of secular and religious dissidents against Stuart power for generations. He may well have been buoyed up by the welcome news from his Treasurer, Bishop Juxon, in June 1638 that the Exchequer could spare £200,000 for a military campaign.[100] The requisite supplies were being brought over from the Continent, Hull and Newcastle were being fortified, Arundel was (inadequately) arming the Borderers, and volunteers were being trained by the 'Council of the North'. Supposedly Wentworth could supply troops from Ireland in spring 1639, with or without Antrim's Catholics, and land men at Dumbarton to march on Edinburgh. But even if the money and troops were there, would the difficulties of co-ordinating an attack fall into place? And could Charles trust supposed stalwarts like Hamilton, who had once again avoided military action by his tenants by taking no action to disperse the rebellious Assembly? Hamilton continued on apparently cordial terms with its co-leader (behind the scenes) the new Earl of Argyll, formerly Lord Lorne.

Argyll was not deprived of his Council seat for his apparent treason, implying that Charles – usually keen to punish any defiance – had not altogether abandoned hope of winning him over. Possibly Charles was listening to advice from Hamilton, who on the day of the dissolution of the Assembly wrote to him saying that the arrogant bishops were responsible for their own fate and urging an approach to Argyll as the most important Covenanter leader.[101] It was noted that Hamilton had been conferring with Argyll during the Assembly rather than keeping his distance from a known 'hard-liner', though this may have been an effort to win him over as one with influence among the clerics. (Wentworth, by contrast urged Charles to summon Argyll, Rothes, and Montrose to London for arrest and proclaim them traitors if they did not come).[102] It is noticeable that Sir Thomas Hope did not carry out his legal duty and denounce the Assembly; instead he assiduously cold-shouldered the Bishop of Brechin who they had excommunicated, as if accepting their jurisdiction – which his diary suggests was the case.[103] Even if Charles had privately decided on war – and his instructions to the Lords Lieutenant to raise their local militias were issued on the day on which the Assembly was dissolved, before he was aware of this – he was not able to send out a clear message to or be obeyed by his remaining 'loyalists' in Edinburgh.

Sooner than give in to the Covenanters, he chose to undertake the risky course of military coercion from outside Scotland, and had little coherent strategy for mobilising his remaining Scots loyalists like the isolated and often slow-acting Marquis of Huntly. The latter, in Buchan with access to the pro-episcopal port/university city of Aberdeen, needed regular contact and preferably military support once the Assembly had voted to abolish Charles' religious authorities in 1638, preferably with money and instructions to raise other Highlanders. (He did have military experience, albeit only at the French Court as captain of Louis XIII's Scots regiment, and his muddled financial affairs hinted at his lack of competence; he was privately despised by Rothes and others.) Instead the King concentrated on raising his army in England, informing the Privy Council that war would be necessary as early as 1 July 1638 and in September sending the

Tower arsenal north to Hull. On 18 January 1639 he asked Windebank to prepare a letter to all noblemen, gentry and corporations announcing his journey to York and inviting them to aid him, and to look into the Henrician precedents.[104] The main point he should have drawn from the matter was that the last such large-scale attacks on Scotland had indeed been in the 1540s, apart from one march to Edinburgh to evict the pro-French regime of Marie de Guise in 1560; the local militia might well train in peace-time (inadequately) but they had not fought since then. Nor were the gentry used to fighting regularly for their King as they had been in the medieval period. In reality, a great deal of training would be needed to make his army 'battle-ready' – from experts imported from the Continental campaigns, not officers the men were used to serving under. The weapons usually used at the county Trained Bands' musters had not been used in wartime, and were often in poor condition and out of date; as in 1588, the local stocks were in a state of shambles and woefully unready, and had to be replenished from overseas. The nobles and gentry were supposed to supply their own armour and weapons, but even if they possessed them they were unlikely to have used them for generations; many were antiques. The King was relying on a method of provision of men and weapons suited for the 15th, not the 17th, century. The county authorities often endeavoured to spare married men from the district 'call-ups' so that if they were killed their dependants would not be a financial charge on the authorities – meaning the provision of substitutes, who might be infirm, drunkards, or beggars (or convicts). Finding the right numbers and quality of men, then arming and drilling them, was down to local gentry initiative – though some of the latter were diligent and competent, e.g. the diarist Sir Henry Slingsby in Yorkshire and Sir Thomas Jervoise in Hampshire. Nor was there an adequate amount of saltpetre, of adequate quality, stockpiled ready to use for gunpowder. None of these practicalities seem to have been recognised in Whitehall. Was the King, fond of appearing in martial pose on horseback in Van Dyck portraits, confusing image with reality?

There does not seem to have been any notable English enthusiasm for the Scots' cause or feeling that their cause was the Protestant one, unlike in 1640, though it did not help that the Queen and her Catholic courtiers were enthusiastic for war. With her usual lack of concern for political implications, Henrietta Maria even encouraged her co-religionists to fast on Saturdays and send the money saved for the war-effort.[105] It was also noted that some of the most generous aristocratic funders of the war were Catholics, e.g. the Marquis of Winchester, a leading Hampshire magnate and a future arch-Royalist (£1,000) and the Marquis of Worcester, a South Wales magnate and future Royalist army-funder (£1500).[106] Some of the most generous funders were from the City, e.g. the jeweller and arts-patron Sir Paul Pindar (£100,000)[107] but the Inns of Court – hotbed of City lawyers interested in politics – refused to pay up. It is worth noticing that the King did not issue his main public statement of his cause and call for support in a proclamation until 27 February 1639, months after the Scots Church Assembly had started openly defying his orders and dismantling his Church.[108] The same applied to the supportive 'A Large Declaration Concerning the Late Tumults in Scotland', written by Dean Balcanquhall of Durham,[109] which listed the Covenanters' numerous illegalities but which observers thought was three months too late to sway opinion.[110] It was not that he failed to realise the implicit threat of dismantling the Scots episcopate and liturgy to those in England too, as he made clear privately to Hamilton in November 1638.[111] But the Covenanters were able to strike first in the propaganda war – and indeed it has been suspected that earlier in the 1630s their local Scots Presbyterian circles had been publishing refugee English 'Puritans' diatribes against the episcopate.[112] Early in 1638 they published their 'Reasons for which the Service Book ought to be Refused', followed by 'The Confession of Faith of the Kirk of Scotland' and in July 'A Short Relation of the Kirk of Scotland to our Brethren the Kirk of England'.[113] The message was that the struggles of godly Calvinists in both nations against the bishops and their 'popish' practices were identical, and by early 1639 this pamphlet propaganda was flooding into Newcastle and Carlisle en route southwards.[114] The local mayors did what they could to seize this material. Preachers followed, calling for aid to the Covenanters[115] – the local Deputy Lieutenants did what they could to round them up and deport them but sympathisers were clearly helping them. The effects of such propaganda on reluctant soldiers were feared by loyalists as far south as Essex,[116] a region where the leading local landowner was the Presbyterian, pro-Scots Earl of Warwick and he had a network of client clergymen and preachers to help him, and regular newsletters updating events from a 'rebel' point of view – anticipating the propaganda war in 1642–6 – included the 'Scottish Scout'. They were duly found among papers seized by the English authorities,[117] and were reckoned very dangerous to the English monarchy by the French ambassador.[118] Indeed, the contemporary verbal identification of the 1639 and 1640 campaigns as the 'Bishops' Wars' showed that the Scots' stand against episcopacy – and its implications for bishops in England? – were seen as the defining factor. This blow to the King did not mean much in terms of serious politico-military defections yet, but would undermine him as his position continued to weaken (which a victory on the Border in summer 1639 would have abated). The only open defiance was that of Lords Brooke and Saye and Sele, future 1640–2 'opposition' leaders, who when they arrived at Charles' headquarters at York refused to fight the Scots (Saye and Sele alleging that they were fellow-subjects as of 1603 not hostile foreigners) and were arrested.

The King's thorough preparations in 1638–9 ensured an army larger than that which had proved inadequate for foreign expeditions in the 1620s, improving its chances. It included the usual aristocratic volunteers as cavalry officers and/or fund-raisers, some (e.g. the future 'Cavaliers' Lord Carnarvon and George Goring) with experience in the Netherlands. Royal commander-in-chief Arundel's deputy, the Earl of Essex, had also served in Germany. It was backed up by the 'Ship-Money' fleet – though neither most of the army nor the fleet had seen action whereas many of the Covenanter officers had served in the Thirty Years' War. There were problems with deserters and many of those men supplied by the county authorities were 'pressed' riff-raff, drunkards, and gaol inmates;[119] as usual exemptions and excuses for not serving were allowed. Some contemporary commentators (including Hamilton) were pessimistic about their quality, competence, fondness for drink, and lack of fighting spirit – though this seems to refer to the early stages of the muster, before they had had time to train and adjust to discipline. Hamilton's main fear was that they would be forced into action before they were ready.[120] Both Heylyn (Laud's chaplain at the time) and Clarendon reckoned the army to be adequate and even well-equipped.[121] Such problems were however normal for the period; the Elizabethan armies had been no better, as satirised by Shakespeare in his account of Falstaff's recruits. The delay while the Army assembled at York enabled officers to train their men; more serious problems lay in the King's reliance on a naval descent by Hamilton on the Clyde (what about the weather or poor seamanship on new ships?) and on action by Huntly, cut off in the Highlands and noted for his caution. Huntly's first attempt to gather his clansmen at Turriff in February was rudely interrupted when Montrose and armed Covenanter troops arrived, and was abandoned; where were his scouts?

The pessimistic Wentworth, usually a ruthless realist, advised the King on 21 March to delay the war as a lesser risk – too late as Charles had already left London for York.[122] (He then sent the Bishop of Raphoe with a personal appeal to Charles.) Two days later the Covenanters surprised Dumbarton, the crucial port which Wentworth was to have used to invade Scotland – by ambushing the castle governor as he left kirk, a trick that a more vigilant officer would have evaded.[123] Why had Charles not sent an experienced commander there, or asked Wentworth to supply one? The garrison did not resist – but, as Wentworth complained, they could have been stiffened by troops from Dublin.[124] Lord Rothes now took armed men to Dalkeith Castle to seize the Royal arsenal there (and the Crown Jewels) and was not hindered by the occupant, Lord Traquair, who to be fair was heavily outnumbered; and on 21 March Alexander Leslie and a company of musketeers stormed into under-manned Edinburgh Castle.[125] While the King's fortresses were being overwhelmed, Hamilton was still embarking his troops at Great Yarmouth – though the timing of their arrival there was out of his hands. In the event, Hamilton was ordered to head for Leith instead of Aberdeen.

The delay in crossing the Border enabled the Covenanters to take the military initiative when their army was ready, and their general Montrose was able to secure the North-East before Hamilton could land troops from England in the region in June 1639. This was partly the fault of the somnolent Huntly, who typically opened hostilities with an offer to his enemy of a 'gentleman's agreement' not to enter each other's clan territory which Montrose ignored. Although Montrose was younger and a far better general future events would show that the Huntly forces could fight well if led by Huntly's sons. As it was, Montrose could secure potentially disloyal, episcopalian Aberdeen – aided by his superior artillery – and drive the Royalist forces back into the countryside, and Huntly stupidly obeyed a summons to the city to be arrested, sent to Edinburgh, and required to sign the Covenant. His clansmen marched on Aberdeen, but Montrose won the resultant battle over Huntly's son Lord Aboyne at the 'Brig o' Dee' on 17–18 June.[126] The King should have been in closer communication with

Huntly and warning of the need to be vigilant. Leith, where any troops destined for Edinburgh would be landed, was blockaded; meanwhile the slow-moving King arrived at Newcastle on 5 May. He was blandly ordering Wentworth to move his Irish army (most of which was now engaged against a local rising by the O'Byrnes in Wicklow, near Dublin) into Kintyre to fight Argyll, without any indication of where he would land;[127] though at least he had the devious Traquair arrested when he arrived at the Royal camp to excuse his loss of Dalkeith Castle. An ineffective Royal naval blockade had failed to prevent the rebel commander-designate, Alexander Leslie (a Covenant-signing clansman of Rothes' experienced in fighting in Germany), arriving from the Continent, though that was inevitable given the poor state of the English navy. The actions of the pro-Royalist local commander in Ulster, Randall Macdonnell (Marquis of Antrim), against Campbell settlers there gave Argyll an excuse to raise a private Campbell army – supposedly to defend his clansmen against Macdonnell's men but really to play a vital role in the Covenanter forces within Scotland. Wentworth was supposed to attack the Campbells, but was unable to sail. Meanwhile Hamilton – who had complained that only about 200 of his 3,000 men knew how to fire a musket – arrived with his ships off Leith to enforce the blockade, but was afflicted by plague and met militant defiance from on land (including his own Covenanting mother, who threatened to shoot him). He sent the King's proclamation of pardon ashore for all who surrendered – a vain hope – and ended up agreeing to a parley with some of the enemy leadership at night on the dunes near Barnbougall. He did however lend a ship to the refugee Lord Aboyne, Huntly's son, who had been south to report his father's arrest to the King and was now on his way back, so he could rally his clansmen for an attack (the Brig O'Dee campaign).[128]

As Charles finally marched his army north in May-June 1639 he had less than the 6,000 cavalry and 24,000 infantry that he had confidently assumed he could raise, and he gave overall command to the inexperienced Earl of Arundel who had a valid legal claim to lead an army as Earl Marshal but no military background. On 1 June Arundel led the vanguard across the Tweed. But the usual quarrels over precedence afflicted the English nobility – as the English crossed the Border Lord Holland, in charge of the cavalry, refused a position of honour in the van to the Earl of Newcastle's private cavalry troop and the Earl pulled out of the march in a sulk. After the initial agreement to keep both armies ten miles from the border was broken by the Scots, Charles sent Holland over the Tweed with over 300 cavalry and 3,000 infantry in early June. Marching on Kelso, they were confronted by a smaller but probably better-trained Scots cavalry force under Leslie at Duns, Law with the larger Scots infantry visible behind them. The overall size of Leslie's army, infantry included, was larger than the combined forces of the English army – around 8,000. The English cavalry were ahead of their infantry and were taken by surprise, an indication of poor scouting and co-ordination; in any case the usual problem of new recruits being unused to heavy uniforms and weapons and the hot weather would have inhibited the infantry from a good performance had they been in place. Holland claimed he thought there were about 8000 infantry facing him; their 'half-moon' crescent formation was an implicit threat to envelop his force and probably unnerved them. An exchange of formal challenges and requests to withdraw between the rival cavalry led to the Scots charging. Lord Holland, a loyal but militarily inadequate Court favourite close to the Queen (who had secured him his post), retreated without a fight.[129] Holland, indeed, was a Calvinist sympathiser and was to emerge in summer 1639 as an exponent of a negotiated solution to the crisis so he may have been unenthusiastic – or just panicked.

It was only a skirmish without loss of lives but it was a psychological victory for the Scots. Given that the majority of the militarily inexperienced young nobles in Holland's force would have been good horsemen (albeit from hunting not battle) and there had been training at York, they should have had the victory in a clash; apparently the Scots were poorly armed. Possibly the sight of the Scots infantry waiting behind the cavalry inhibited an English attack, as any pursuit of retreating Scots would be dangerous as they took refuge with their foot; and some of the scouts estimated the Scots force at around 10,000 so this would have caused extra fears.[130] The hot afternoon weather may have made the English unwilling to charge. But a disciplined English cavalry force should have been able to restrain themselves from this trap, although Slingsby wrote that without the infantry in close proximity they would not have achieved much had they attacked so retreat was logical.[131] Some English officers present at the abortive skirmish thought they would have won. Instead, the retreat brought inevitable disappointment and a decline in morale, plus criticism in the English camp that intelligence of the Scots' whereabouts had been so poor.[132]

Duns Law: what if the English had won?

Had the English cavalry given an adequate performance and the Scots had to retreat outnumbered, there was a chance that the impressive-looking but inexperienced Scots infantry would have panicked and fled. Leslie and his veterans might not have been able to hold them back if they saw their cavalry fleeing. The Royal army would have been able to move on towards Edinburgh and the Scots leadership would have been tempted to save their men for a prolonged campaign. An English newsletter in August indeed said that public opinion by 'men of good judgement' was that if the large English army had managed to march on to Edinburgh the shock of this and the desertions by ordinary Scots would have forced the Scots nobles to negotiate.[133] The historical Scots response to the invasion of a larger English force was, however, to retreat and wage a war of attrition, usually abandoning Edinburgh as in 1547, and this had the advantage of exposing the invaders to the difficulties of holding onto garrisons in hostile countryside. This was likely to have been followed had Charles continued to advance after winning the cavalry skirmish.

Moreover, if there was a long campaign that brought into action the problem of a military call-up of Charles' own subjects, the opposition would have had a motive to hold out until the English army started to disintegrate as unwilling volunteers started to go home. Calvinist lords in the English ranks, such as Essex, would have been willing recipients for appeals from their Scots counterparts to pressure the King into a settlement that allowed the decisions of the Glasgow Assembly concerning the Scots Church to stand.

After Duns Law – was time running out for Charles?

But as events turned out the English did not press forward into Scotland after the check at Duns Law, the planned naval descent on Aberdeen (to link up with Huntly's son Lord Aboyne) served no useful purpose, and the mood in the English ranks was clearly against further action. The prevailing atmosphere in the King's camp was of listlessness and shame.[134] Quite apart from the inevitable grumbling amidst the disheartened troops (who were not stiffened by zealous clerics to fight for their religion as the Scots were), the senior nobles were against pressing on; Newcastle and

Holland were threatening to fight a duel and Charles' old critic Bristol, who had a long meeting with the King after Duns Law, urged him to call Parliament first. This all argued in favour of playing for time, as the reliable Wentworth had been arguing since March, and on 11 June the King opened negotiations with the Scots after the Covenanter army sent Lord Dunfermline to him to suggest this. Hamilton and Laud talked Charles into agreeing to Dunfermline's idea, though typically Charles insisted that the Scots army leadership read out his proclamation declaring them all traitors in the hope of this sign of his Royal displeasure cowing officers and men alike into a reasonable frame of mind.[135] (They read it out in private instead.) Rothes led the Scots delegation, assisted by Henderson and Warriston; all were zealous Calvinist 'hard-liners', but Charles was not put off and a 'frank and fruitful exchange of views' (as would now be said) took place. Even Argyll was received cordially. A truce followed on 18 June, with royal castles returned and armies to be disbanded.[136] The 'pretended Assembly' (as Charles insisted on calling the Glasgow Church Assembly) failed to have its ecclesiastical reforms ratified, but the King promised to hold a new Assembly and a Scottish parliament in August.[137]

It is possible that the rare personal meeting between Charles and his arch-critics, with circumstances preventing the King from being as uncompromising as usual, helped to induce him (temporarily?) towards genuine confidence in a peaceful solution. Time and again in 1640–8 personal dealings with a cautious but seemingly cordial King were to encourage his critics to hope that he was negotiating in earnest, only to be disappointed by his subsequent secret dealings with their enemies; was this one of these occasions? Or was he genuinely wavering? The overall nature of Charles' character and concept of his role, as will be seen, was that he could be influenced by face-to-face discussion but go back on his goodwill later; and he had no compunction in showing 'bad faith' as he believed his Royal duty was to God not to his subjects, who must respect his choices. Given the extent of disapproval for an aggressive policy towards the Scots among leading peers and anti-recruitment mutinies in the rural areas in 1639–40, Charles might well have faced a backlash even had Holland's cavalry won at Duns Law and the King marched on to Edinburgh. But in the event, the military stalemate of June 1639 acted to undermine his long-term chances by emboldening his critics in both kingdoms.

A truce but no real compromises, 1639–40

Charles' motives for suggesting a new meeting of the Scots Parliament and Assembly did not deceive Warriston, who grumbled – to the King's face – at the talks that no doubt he intended to overturn any unfavourable resolution later by force. Charles indignantly retorted that 'the Devil himself could not make a more uncharitable construction'.[138] Probably Rothes and others were privately as suspicious and Charles had such a motive in mind as a possibility, but the 'Pacification of Berwick' was signed on 18 June nevertheless. Both armies were to disband, and Charles was to come to Scotland for the meetings of Parliament and Assembly in the autumn. As a result of the treaty Hamilton, still officially the King's commissioner, received back the keys of Edinburgh Castle, thus giving the King another chance to dominate the city if he could send troops in, and the arrested Huntly was released and hurried to join his sovereign at Berwick. The brave stand his son Aboyne had made (in vain) against Montrose in Aberdeenshire in June served to stir martial feeling among the King's officers, as did the continuing aggressive preaching of Covenanter ministers which seemed to indicate bad faith. Charles was urged to retaliate by breaking the treaty and marching on Edinburgh now Leslie had pulled his men back, and he harangued those leading Covenanter lords who obeyed a summons to Berwick about the ill-will shown to his Scots supporters. Argyll – who rumour had it Charles now intended to arrest – did not show up.[139] If this rumour was correct, it shows that Charles had swung back towards Wentworth's advice to decapitate the opposition in the hope that a few examples would terrorise the rest of their leadership into giving way (as he was to do in the 'Incident' in Edinburgh in 1641). Typically, he drew back from arresting any of the visitors but was still distrusted – earning the drawbacks of his plan without the benefits. But he had some excuse, in the openly hostile attitude of the crowds in Edinburgh to the arriving Hamilton. When Traquair announced the new Assembly to the crowds on 1 July and added that the bishops would sit in it he had to be rescued from angry rioters.[140] Hamilton was now given private permission by the King to try to win over any of the Covenanting leadership possible by any means he chose – double-dealing no doubt, but no worse than their attitude to the King.[141]

The Scots Kirk Assembly opened in Edinburgh on 12 August, this time presided over by Traquair with Huntly (given immunity from arrest for his debts) accompanying him. There were no bishops – but the King had agreed with Traquair that if they did not turn up it made it easier to declare any anti-Royal votes illegal. As expected, it merely reaffirmed the anti-Anglican and anti-episcopal decisions of the Glasgow meeting – while in London Charles was assuring that even if he had to give way to the bishops' enemies temporarily it would be reversed later. The Assembly declared that episcopacy was – as a matter of theology – incompatible with their religion, thus banning it permanently not allowing the King any room for manoeuvre, and proposed to require the entire adult male population to subscribe to the Covenant.[142] The theological declaration was intended to force the King's hand and justify the abolition of bishops, but also had implications for their position in England if Calvinists there supported it. Crucially, when Rothes and Argyll (accompanied by Henderson) brought these two decisions to the King's representative, Traquair, he failed to refuse his assent although Charles had made it clear that abolition of the bishops was unacceptable – did Traquair fear another riot if he did?

This legislation was then confirmed by the Parliament which met on 31 August, with the agenda firmly in the hands of the Covenanters under Argyll's leadership and no effective pro-Royalist ripostes. The Parliament's 'standing committee', the 'Lords of the Articles' (to propose legislation and to enact it while Parliament was not in session, which was a majority of the time), was controlled by the Covenanter nobles. Of the 'three estates', the nobles, clergy, and lesser citizens (barons and burgesses), the clergy were now without the bishops and so under Covenanter control while the citizens were dominated by the well-organised and intimidatory Lowland Covenanter zealots. Now Argyll secured the right of each Estate to nominate members for the 'Lords of the Articles' in future, so that if the King regained control of a majority of the nobility he would still be unable to control the committee.[143] Monolithic 'one-party' control of the Scots Parliament was thus confirmed in September 1639; it would take military action or a split among the nobility to reverse this. All Charles could do was to order the ineffective Traquair to suspend Parliament on 8 November and send packing two of the Covenanter peers who had come to London to protest at Traquair holding up proceedings by an adjournment.[144] This suspension left the Covenanter 'Lords of the Articles' still sitting as the nation's political leadership with legislative powers. A second military clash was now more likely, and any wavering on Charles' part in June-August was reversed; the recall of Wentworth to London (received by him at Naas on 5 August) showed the King's belated decision to bring his most effective minister into close involvement with the planning. A 'Council of War' was set up to plan the campaign, armaments were manufactured, Arundel was replaced as commander-in-chief by the Earl of Northumberland, and as a gesture towards greater administrative efficiency the elderly co-'Secretary of State' Sir John Coke was retired. This was supposed to have been partly due to his Calvinist sympathies for the Covenanters and the hostility to him of the Queen. Coke's place was not immediately filled despite the Queen's lobbying on behalf of her ally Sir Henry Vane, but many duties went to the effective new clerk of the 'Council of War', Sir Edward Nicholas – who was to remain serving the current Monarch until 1663. Whether the eventual new Secretary of State Sir Henry Vane could be accounted as pro-Spanish or pro-French is unclear, but both Laud and Wentworth opposed his appointment.[145] In that case, this choice shows that even when the two leaders of 'Thorough' were working in tandem in London for the first time since 1633 – with Wentworth briefly back in London on official Irish business – they did not have untrammelled influence and probably the Queen blocked their efforts. Wentworth did not acquire the Lord Treasurership now as was rumoured,[146] though he did gain a peerage. Vane's main backer appears to have been Hamilton, aided by the Queen. It was significant that this moment of greater influence on policy by the Queen was linked both to the arrival of her pro-Spanish mother Marie de Medici in London, which Laud thought inopportune[147] and which caused riots, and by an outbreak of millenarian foreboding among Protestant zealots accompanied by unusual supernatural phenomena.[148] This all implied widespread fears for the future, and uneasiness at the war with fellow-Protestants.

With Wentworth dominating the Council and three meetings a week showing its determination, military planning was far better managed than in spring 1639 – and for once a competent military veteran, Lord Ruthven, was put in charge at Edinburgh Castle. Moves began to hire troops from the Spanish Netherlands and from Denmark – i.e. both Catholics and Protestants – and Berwick was properly fortified, though in typical fashion the arrogant Wentworth managed to upset the eventual new Secretary of State, Sir Henry Vane, by tactlessly lobbying for the title of 'Lord Raby' (Raby Castle, Durham being Vane's residence) for his own son.[149] A more dubious appointment was that of the new Lord Keeper when Coventry died, the aggressively authoritarian Lord Chief Justice and ex-Speaker of the Commons in 1628–9, Sir John Finch. This tactless and self-important Royal servant was the *'bete noire'* of the King's critics.

Chapter Three

1640: Missed Opportunities for Compromise?

Royal failures and miscalculations in 1640: too grandiose plans for poor resources?

Stalemate ensued between the government in London and the militant Covenanters in Scotland until the next military clash, when Charles' new army was ready. Technically Charles' Edinburgh ministers remained in place, but their grip over the country was dubious and the 'parallel structures' of control in the Covenanters' 'Tables' were not suspended. The militant Scots acted in growing co-operation with dissident pro-Calvinist peers in England (led by the Earl of Warwick), with a correspondence to co-ordinate action. Covenanter propaganda, such as the 'Reasons why the Service Book Cannot be Received' and 'Reasons for the Lawfulness of the Subscription of the Confession of Faith', continued to skilfully present their case as that of all Protestants against 'Romish' encroachment, obliquely at first and openly making parallels between the threat to both countries in the 'Short Relation' of July 1638.[1] On the Scots side Baillie believed that this propaganda had some effect on and softened English perceptions of the Covenanters. The 1639 loyalist author Henry Peacham, current official Sir John Maynard, and (in retrospect) lawyer Bulstrode Whitelocke all thought that it was intended to subvert English opinion and might have been successful.[2] Anti-government English stationers who stocked pamphlets by people such as Prynne added Scots pamphlets to their stock, and in 1638 a newsletter suggested that the hopes raised by the Scots rebellion were dissuading previously despairing 'Puritans' from emigrating to America.[3] A few English sympathisers even visited Scotland to subscribe to the Covenant.[4]

This coincided with the defiance to the King's 'new' legal demands in the 'Ship Money' case, and both heightened tension and gave protesters hope that others were standing up to the King so they could do so safely – the City of London, a hotbed of anti-Laudian Calvinists prosecuted by the Church, unusually refused the King a loan for his 1639 campaign.[5] Some confident Scots believed that they had widespread support in England in 1639–40,[6] and 'Puritan' observer Sir Roger Twysden wrote that the example the Scots had shown in standing up for their ancient laws against Royal innovation was seen as parallel with the, less violent resistance to this in England and it was hoped that Charles would take note and moderate his ways.[7] The longer the confrontation went on, the greater the chance of English 'copycat' resistance – and in April 1639 Lords Brooke (later a Parliamentarian general) and Saye and Sele refused to swear an oath of loyalty to the King at the nobility's assembly at York as it had not been approved by Parliament as per custom. Nor were they arrested for this.[8] The fact that relative political moderates not previously associated with Charles' enemies in 1625–9, such as the Earl of Hertford, as well as Warwick and Bedford were to be involved in the peers' campaign against the Scots war in 1640 suggests a slipping-away of Royal support. It was not just the 'usual suspects' who objected to 'High' Anglicanism being imposed and maintained by force of arms in Scotland, and probably the influence over Charles by Laud's and the Queen's Council factions increased a desire by frustrated nobles denied influence to coerce the King. The seeming danger of a Spanish alliance in 1639–40, when fears of 'Popery' and anxiety about impending disaster for Protestantism appear to have revived in England, would have added to desire to take effective measures. This was partly a result of Charles' desire for Spanish Netherlands troops to stiffen his army for the 1640 campaign – not unreasonable given the lack of training, competence, or adequate weaponry shown by his men in 1639. Contemporary anxieties about the situation in the north and what it portended, absent in 1637, are shown in 1638–40 by diaries and accounts of portents. This implied that support for the Scots would grow the longer the crisis lasted. There was also a danger of the Scots undermining English resistance to their 'godly' cause by propaganda claims that the two nations' 'opposition' had similar aims in resisting Popish tyranny; 2000 copies of the 'Information from the Estaits of Scotland' were distributed in England shortly before the April 1640 Parliament met. Charles ordered it burnt by the public hangman for 'tending to raise mutiny and sedition'.[9]

Realistically, to maximise his military effectiveness Charles needed Continental Catholic as well as Protestant support; but his Catholic wife and courtiers made any Catholic aid seem part of a 'plot' to paranoid Calvinists. Indeed, any alliance with the Dutch (politically useful to reassure English Presbyterians and anti-Spanish feeling) was at this point impossible, due to their spectacular naval assault on the Spanish convoy in autumn 1639 and the suspicious presence of Dutch 'observers' at the Glasgow Church Assembly. (The University of Leyden had indeed congratulated the latter.)[10] Ironically, the heightened tension across the Channel had meant that in spring-summer 1639 nervous regional authorities in southern England (e.g. Plymouth) were unwilling to send many militiamen to the north while unknown warships were in the Channel, thus (slightly) undermining Charles' army.[11] Spain now seemed in need of help rather than a threat – but in autumn 1639 Olivares was looking to recruit English troops to fight on the Continent, not to aid Charles, as he told the new English ambassador Hopton (a future Royalist general).[12] France was under suspicion in London, on account of the contacts which visiting Covenanter Commissioner Loudoun had with its ambassador Bellievre.[13] Conversely, the King's difficulties meant that there was even less pressure on the Emperor to hand over the Palatinate to Charles' kin and so give him a much-needed boost to his reputation as a Protestant champion.[14] The most politically useful Continental recruits for Charles would have been Charles' nephews Charles Louis (titular Elector Palatine) and Rupert, who could bring in German Protestant officers from their own followings. But Rupert had been captured in battle in Germany and was awaiting release, and the Elector's visit to Charles in England in late summer 1639 was solely aimed at winning English money to pay for him to recruit new troops (the army of the late Prince Bernhard of Saxe-Weimar) to conquer the Lower Palatinate.[15] Olivares now had to hire English merchant ships to protect his Bay of Biscay coasts against French and Dutch raids.

We must remember that in 1639–40 none of the King's critics, even Warwick and the past leaders of the Commons in 1625–9, had the advantage of foresight to the events of 1640–2 which historians have. In the terms of recent political events in which the 'opposition' would have thought, the King had proved deaf to complaints about Buckingham and 'corruption' in Parliament in his early years in power, and even when an assassin removed the Duke he had refused to come to terms with the Commons – which evidence of his obstinacy argued in favour of coercing him now. Parliamentary protests in 1625–9, without military pressure, had not worked. The normal routes of complaint, and anticipation of a favourable response from the King, were blocked – and in January 1637 Warwick, the leading 'Presbyterian' noble exponent of war with the Habsburgs and a major patron of 'Puritan' clerics in his home area in Essex, had taken the unprecedented step of a (desperate?) haranguing of the unimpressed King in Council about summoning Parliament and fighting the 'Papists'. According to a subsequent account of his speech recalled in 1637, he had urged Charles to recall Parliament and halt 'Ship Money' too.[16] By summer 1640 Lord Conway writing to Laud, regarded Warwick and Holland respectively as the open and secret heads of a 'Puritan' faction, already being called by him a 'cabal' i.e. a seditious conspiracy.[17] This desire to seek allies for a more successful coercion of Charles explains the dissident peers' technically treasonable links to the rebels in Edinburgh, which had first become serious in 1638 through the contacts made by Sir John Clotworthy (brother-in-law of John Pym and currently complaining to the King about Wentworth's rule in Ireland). Militant Presbyterian Clotworthy indeed referred to the Scots cause as the 'new America'[18] – i.e., a worthy cause for 'godly' promotion of their faith against the 'heathen'.

The Scots had been made aware that the dissenting peers sought to pressurise the King to summon Parliament, which from its sturdily pro-Calvinist religious leanings in past meetings could be expected to vote for negotiations with the Scots – and were thus encouraged to hold out and not negotiate with Charles. The King duly became aware of the 'treasonable' links during spring 1640 (though unable to prove it legally in court despite enquiries, with Warwick's London residence raided on 6 May in a search for documentary proof).[19] When he confronted the Earl of Pembroke (February) with a letter that Rothes had sent him asking for help in pro-Covenanter propaganda the Earl denied all knowledge. Local English resistance to fighting Protestants had already extended to a poor turnout for levies for the war among some local gentry. There was now a risk that recalling the English Parliament – which Wentworth thought could be managed into paying up due to the extent of the Scots threat at the Council debate of 5 December 1639[20] – would ignite co-ordinated opposition.

Spanish offers: no need of Parliamentary money if this had worked?

Charles continued to make vain attempts to assert legality in Scotland in the face of overwhelming evidence that it was politically a side-issue. Traquair, as his representative, ordered the prorogued Scots Parliament's self-appointed interim Committee to dissolve itself without effect;[21] all Traquair could do was to hurry off to London to report the defiance indignantly to the King and urge a second war. More usefully, Traquair seems to have got hold of a copy of the leading Covenanter peers' letter to Louis XIII of France asking for his aid, which could be used to indict them for treason. The first Scots delegates who arrived in London in February 1640 (including Loudoun) were received coldly by the King, though the Queen had asked him not to receive them at all and they had been distributing propaganda pamphlets en route to London. They asked Charles to accept the legislation passed by the Scots Parliament, which he had already told Traquair to block, and to accept the 'packed' Committee of Estates run by their faction; in private they compared him to a gullible schoolboy dominated by his sinister pedagogue Laud.[22] The meeting thus inevitably failed, and their supposed Court sympathisers the Earls of Pembroke and Salisbury failed to speak up for them.

At this point the King was more politically confident of not needing to negotiate as Wentworth was promising to manipulate the English Parliament and had summoned an Irish Parliament for March to raise more money. There was also a chance of substantial funds from Spain, whose new embassy under Alonso de Cardenas was negotiating to hire English naval vessels to protect their convoys in the Channel from Dutch privateers. The Spanish desired alliance against the Dutch and were prepared to pay for Charles to do without Parliament in return, with the Spanish heir Prince Balthazar Carlos to marry Princess Mary.[23] Under the terms offered by the Spanish special envoy, Marquis Virgilio Malvezzi, that spring, Spain would also send Charles 8,000 troops to suppress the Scots rebels provided that his fleet attacked the Dutch.[24] Spain would be allowed to hire 3,000 troops in Ireland to fight in Flanders. Cottington (the former negotiator with Spain in 1630), Sir Henry Vane, Windebank, and the Earl of Northumberland were duly appointed to negotiate and were backed by the Queen and Strafford; the talks were widely expected to succeed.[25] The ever-active Duchesse de Chevreuse, exiled by

Louis XIII for plotting against him and now in his sister Henrietta Maria's entourage, also joined in the plans. In May rumours of such talks reached the Venetian ambassador Giustinian, who wrote that it was believed the Spanish were bribing Charles to dissolve the 'Short Parliament' which Charles was summoning to try to fund the war.[26] Apparently Philip IV feared that Parliament would ally with the Scots and depose Charles, threatening his Netherlands dominions, so it was a case of international monarchic solidarity.[27] Philip thus had a distorted view of Parliament's unity and intentions, but was clearly aware of the coercive potential of its leaders in both Houses. Had this Spanish plan succeeded, Charles would not have needed to call a second Parliament when his negotiations with the first one broke down (it was dissolved on 5 May). The timing of the arrival of Spanish troops would have been more dubious, given that Spain was distracted later that year by revolt in Catalonia (June) followed by Portugal; would their expedition have arrived before these disasters distracted Philip IV?

This hope of troops and money proved abortive, although the talks in May produced a draft treaty whereby Spain would pay 1.2 million ducats in return for the loan of the English fleet.[28] Wentworth promised that the King would declare war on the Dutch once the Scots were crushed.[29] Crises in both Spain (revolt in Catalonia) and then England (the second Scots war) intervened. Had a Spanish subsidy been arranged it would have made the King's position stronger, with 6,000 experienced Spanish pikemen (*'tercios'*) likely to make mincemeat of the Scots on the battlefield. Unlike Charles' army the Spaniards would have been used to battle, from the Thirty Years' War, and unlike those Scots who had fought abroad they would have fought together as a body. Charles would have been able to win a confrontation on the Borders and take Edinburgh, though military superiority in the Lowlands against a determined foe had not won Scots wars for Edward I in the 1300s or Lord Protector Somerset in 1547–8. The use of Spanish Catholic troops would have further outraged English opinion about 'Popish' influence at Court, but without Parliament it would have had no means of expressing itself except in already illegal 'libellous' pamphlets.

Charles would not have been able to dispense with an obstinate Parliament permanently as his son did when he received French funds in 1681, particularly if revolt in Spain led to their subsidy being short-term.

However there was potential for at least a short-term financial 'breathing-space', anticipating that which Charles II received from his Catholic ally in 1681–5. A million ducats or so would have funded the immediate campaign of 1640 and prevented the need to call Parliament again, but not provided trained or motivated officers and men to defeat Leslie's heavily-armed force without Spanish troops arriving too. It would not have kept the King's army in the field in Scotland indefinitely, occupying hostile cities with part of his army unwilling to see their co-religionists suppressed at the bidding of Laud's 'Arminian' innovators as paid for by the Catholic enemy Spain.

The 'Short Parliament'

Charles accepted the arguments Wentworth and more moderate Privy Councillors (e.g. Holland and the Earl of Northumberland, the former sporadically and the latter a more resolute Parliamentarian from 1642) to call Parliament in a crucial Council meeting on 5 December 1639. As Wentworth brutally but realistically put it, 'there was no way to bring them (the Scots) to their duty and for His Majesty to re-establish his authority and power ... but by way of an effectual war, and no war to be made effectually but such a one as should grow and be assisted from the high counsel of a parliament'.[30] Laud and Hamilton backed him at the crucial Council meeting. The warrant for issuing writs went out on 12 February, though the Venetian ambassador had heard rumours of a Parliament as early as August 1639.[31] Charles thus faced the first national gathering of his critics since 1629, with the gamble that Parliament would be less patriotic (as he saw it) than Wentworth assumed.

There appears to have been a keener and more confrontational competition than usual for seats, rather than the more traditional gentlemanly 'parcelling out' of who would stand among a borough or county's leading families or factions before the voting. This is the assessment of Mark Kishlansky, comparing the proceedings in spring 1640 to the 1620s.[32] There was also some blatant intimidation, particularly by the militant Earl of Warwick in Essex who sent out his favourite preachers to harangue the voters and instructed the captains of the Trained Bands to threaten violence if the 'godly' candidates for the county seat were not elected.[33] Indeed, the rumours of who had been elected were so alarming that before Parliament met the Venetian ambassador had heard that it could be postponed – in which case the rumours must have come from those 'in the know' at Court.[34] Some surprisingly contested elections, where the initial 'gentlemen's agreement' among the principal gentry over who was to stand was broken, were due to the recent controversies – in the Gloucestershire county election Edward Stephens, an ex-JP sacked for opposing 'Ship-Money', was induced to stand.[35] Some anti-government candidates tried to make sure of victory by starting their campaign early, e.g. Sir Arthur Haselrig in Leicestershire.[36] But in fact only around a quarter of the elections were contested and there were plenty of loyalists chosen, despite the alarming rumours, and it was not a case of a 'takeover' of the Commons by aggrieved victims of the government from 1629–40. Clarendon, even with hindsight, reckoned that it was generally believed that moderate men would be elected and patriotic dislike of the Scots would prevail once it came to voting funds for war.[37]

One possibility was that the King could buy off the discontented by listening to and ostentatiously amending grievances in return for generous funding. But would the pro-Scots Calvinist 'hard-liners' allow him to disentangle the two issues? There was a mass of petitions when Parliament opened on 13 April, on a wider scale than usual due to all the aspects of Government interference in the localities in the economic, financial, judicial, administrative, and religious spheres since 1629.[38] The Irish Parliament of March 1640 – called earlier than the English one by Wentworth in order to set a good example to follow in London – had just voted four subsidies for a Scots war without objection, encouraging Wentworth to believe that the English one would follow suit, and this would provide for around 9,000 Irish soldiers.[39] An idea from Laud of excluding recalcitrant MPs in advance (as in 1614)[40] was not carried out, possibly due to over-confidence from other courtiers that they could manage the discontent. This was in retrospect a major mistake and enabled men like John Pym, MP for Tavistock and thus an electoral client of the Earl of Bedford, Essex's client Sir Harbottle Grimston (MP for Colchester and later Speaker of the Convention Parliament in 1660), and veteran troublemaker Sir Francis Seymour to dominate proceedings.

Charles and Lord Keeper Finch – a judicial 'hard-liner' – therefore made the most of the Scots threat in requesting urgent subsidies at the opening of Parliament on 13 April, while promising that redress of grievances would follow.⁴¹ The Covenanter leadership's letter to the King of France requesting aid (supplied by Traquair) was produced as evidence of their treason and Windebank said that arrested Lord Loudoun had admitted its veracity but this had no effect.⁴² Grimston was elected as chairman of the crucial committee of the whole House to assess grievances on 18 April;⁴³ he could thus influence if not direct proceedings on Warwick's behalf. Charles, Finch, and Secretary Windebank, the latter a provocative choice for spokesman given his rumoured Catholic and Spanish leanings (he opened the government case on 16 April), were taken by surprise by the MPs' priorities. As a client of the leading 'Puritan' peer Warwick, Grimston, duly challenged the government in claiming that the threat to liberty, property, and the Church at home was just as acute.⁴⁴ The veteran 1620s Commons moderate Sir Benjamin Rudyerd advised satisfying the King's just requests and dealing with grievances later rather than jeopardise the future of Parliaments, but the majority of opinion was with the argument of Sir Francis Seymour that the English nation that had elected them needed to be satisfied first.⁴⁵ On the 17th the Earl of Bedford's client John Pym, MP for Tavistock, launched a comprehensive catalogue of offences committed against Parliament, property, and religion, which necessitated redress ahead of granting supply. (Given their past records and their 'Puritan' aristocratic patrons, both Rudyerd and Pym could reasonably have been suspected of hostile intentions and forbidden to take their seats.) The MPs proceeded to form a committee of the whole House to investigate grievances and returned to the contentious issue of the dissolution of Parliament in 1629.⁴⁶ The situation had escaped Court control – though putting the crypto-Catholic Windebank up to speak for the government was not going to ease mistrust. A pointed request for speedy grant of supply to show the MPs' loyalty made in the royal presence by Lord Keeper Finch on 21 April failed to overawe the opposition.⁴⁷ The MPs proceeded to open a lengthy investigation into grievances, and thus blocked any resolution on the King's terms. Seymour warned that though the King needed money MPs had good reason to fear the worst and had to see to grievances first, and future Royalist general Sir Ralph Hopton argued that they were like a servant helping his master by pulling a thorn out of his foot. Secretary Vane warned to no avail of the danger of dissolution if money was not voted for quickly.⁴⁸

The King appealed in person to the Lords on the 24th to reject the Commons' request for both Houses to proceed together on grievances.[49] The Upper House, encouraged by Wentworth and opposed by Lord Saye and Sele, voted to follow the King's request and refuse to join the Commons.[50] The Lords voted for granting supply first and joining the Commons to discuss grievances later, and on the 25th asked the Commons to do similarly and Lord Keeper Finch promised that the Lords would not interefere at the joint sessions in anything pertaining to Commons matters (which would include the legality of the King's treatment of MPs in 1629, still a sore point).[51] As the Commons discussed this on the 27th Rudyerd was conciliatory, but Pym declared it an abuse of Commons privilege to constrain their freedom of action. The more radical MPs won the day in choosing to treat Finch's idea as a breach of privilege in gagging their right to proceed how they wished.[52] Pym and his fellow-'Puritan' zealot Sir Walter Earle, a leading Dorset landowner and future parliamentarian commander, won out over the moderate Rudyerd, and on 29 April the Commons returned to debating the resolution of grievances on Pym's three issues (privilege of Parliament, property, and religion).[53] The signs were that Pym's proposed remedies on the latter, particularly over re-aligning Communion tables, were more contentious and less likely to win a vote than they were on matters like 'Ship-Money'. After the King sent a reminder to the Commons to proceed quickly on 2 May, Sir Francis Seymour proposed that if the King satisfied them on 'Ship-Money' he would be prepared to proceed with supply and would trust the King to deal with the rest later, and was backed by Sir Henry Vane. That day being Saturday, it meant that the Commons would not sit on the 3rd and in the interim Vane could approach the King and the Privy Council for support.[54]

The Privy Council, prompted by Holland and the Earl of Northumberland, duly agreed on 3 May to offer to cancel 'Ship-Money' in return for a promise of twelve 'subsidies' – around £650,000 and thus two-thirds of the cost of the coming campaign. (Wentworth/Strafford had preferred to reduce the demand to six 'subsidies'.) On the 4th Vane put a formal proposal to the Commons for the Royal cancellation of 'Ship-Money' immediately in return for a grant of twelve subsidies, with discussion of the other complaints to be allowed later. This had substantial support, but the immediate vote on it that Charles required was deferred and the MPs started debating the legality of 'Ship-Money' and of military taxes in general. Some wanted other grievances added to the bargain.[55] Either Pym and his supporters managed to side-track the House or the MPs genuinely could not reach a decision, with those obsessed by questions of legality (over military/naval taxation raised solely on prerogative authority) too determined to sort this question out now to grasp the need to satisfy the King. It seems that some MPs were afraid that if they put it to the vote the King would win, and so deferred a decision; and MP Sir Thomas Aston's diary shows that he (so presumably others) was aware that the impatient King might well not tolerate that.[56]

The King lost patience, possibly as hoped for by Pym's group, and dissolution followed on the 5th – with the Speaker called to the Lords so that MPs could not hold him hostage and pass some inflammatory last-minute votes as in 1629.[57] Vane had consulted the King over his proposal beforehand, and if Charles had made a generous gesture on including redress of more grievances in his proxy offer to the Commons on 4 May this might have calmed the suspicious MPs into abandoning the 'ultra' Pym faction. The latter were unlikely to be satisfied without a surrender on religious issues like 'Arminian' ceremonial too, given their strong religious views and co-operation with their patrons in Warwick's group of peers and probable hopes to use the Scots Church reform to attack English bishops. The King's supporters had both a respected 1620s 'opposition' MP in the Commons who was prepared to compromise – Seymour – and a concrete offer to hand, but suspicion won out. Pym made his faction's demands – including religion as well as civil matters like 'Ship-Money' and judicial abuses in the 'Star Chamber' – clear. This requirement for satisfaction of grievances before payment of a subsidy and concentration on matters of religion had been standard practice in the 1620s and could be expected. The extent of grievances across secular and religious matters were such – thanks to the combination of assertion of Royal judicial and financial rights and Anglican innovation – that he carried most MPs with him. Wentworth, isolated in Ireland for seven years, had misjudged his ability to influence or assess them accurately. The majority of MPs seem to have been determined by 4 May to insist on a comprehensive surrender of Royal prerogative powers over military taxes, not just 'Ship-Money'. Charles, prickly about his authority, was unlikely to have accepted this unless he was desperate – he had spent the past decade harassing men like Sir Edward Coke who attacked prerogative rights and trying to stifle debate, even seizing private papers.

The unaccustomed Royal judicial interference in local society in secular and ecclesiastical matters in 1629–40 was an evident source of the backing of some non-Calvinist peers for Warwick, Bedford, and Saye and Sele. 'Thorough', aggressive assertion of Royal prerogative rights, and Church ceremonialism cost vital votes in both chambers; moderates like Rudyerd were unable to prevail over Pym. Charles and his advisers thus paid politically for their efficiency and organizing abilities since 1629 – which they could not have anticipated in advance, though a foreign policy crisis or a rebellion (probably in Ireland) wrecking the King's finances and requiring him to consult a Parliament again at short notice was always a risk. But even if the King was lacking in his father's caution and flexibility, he missed a chance to avoid the Parliament ending in chaos – he could have given way on secular prerogatives to boost Vane's chances on 4 May 1640 and sacrificed his recent constitutional position for financial success. Even if it had not worked, the 'hard core' of resisting MPs would have had a narrower victory and been shown up as disrupters. Instead the Commons majority was adamant on redress of grievances first, deadlock ensued, and the Parliament was dissolved.

According to a pro-Royalist account of 1682/3 Charles had received advance warning that dissident MPs, possibly led by Pym, intended to vote on 7 May on a petition to the King urging reconciliation with the Scots and/or to examine the causes of the Scots war.[58] Some MPs had allegedly been meeting the Scots commissioners, presumably to plan how to assist their cause.[59] Nathaniel Fiennes (son of the 'Puritan' peer Lord Saye and Sele, Warwick's ally in his colonial ventures) would allegedly propose a motion banning the use of Parliamentary funds for the war.[60] This could have thrown a spanner in the works for the King – but would the Pym faction have won this vote?

Summer 1640

Charles now resorted to extending his revival of traditional, perfectly legal but long-disused Royal 'feudal' powers to the military sphere. He sought to assemble a new host for the summer 1640 campaign in Scotland by means of a 'feudal' mechanism, calling on his tenants-in-chief to carry out their legal obligations to him by supplying troops. This had the advantage of meaning that refusal could lead to financially useful fines; this use of dormant laws to raise money had begun with the fines for refusing grants of knighthood in the mid-1620s. Both the measure and the financial 'follow-up' had the political disadvantage of raising local antagonism, which would have adverse consequences were Parliament to be recalled. Indeed, when the first arrangements were made some Deputy Lieutenants in the counties feared to carry out Charles' orders because they feared political consequences – being reported to Parliament – for helping to raise 'non-Parliamentary', illegal troops. The army was supposed to consist of 35,000 men from the counties' Trained Bands; but it was not legally clear that Charles could order these troops – the largest reservoir of extant trained men, c. 79,000 in all – to serve out of their counties.[61] The expectation that a Parliament would soon look into all illegalities both encouraged resistance and alarmed Royal officials who faced being called to account; this crucially affected conditions in raising troops in March-April. Quite apart from that, some crucial local officials – especially county Deputy Lieutenants – were serving in Parliament in April-May so there were delays until their return home. The optimistic orders sent out to the counties in March detailing how many men were to be sent North by what date – aiming at a June rendezvous in York – were thus unrealistic. The rendezvous was soon postponed from 1 June to 1 July, as the first date was impractical – and this meant that those counties (mostly nearest the conflict) where the troops were ready on time had to pay and feed them for another month, annoying the locals. The most sluggish response to the mustering was in those counties in the southwest, furthest from Scotland.

In the meantime, discussion on forthcoming Royal military strategy took place at the Council's 'Committee of War' on 5 May. One drawback for an aggressive strategy was that Charles had made the Earl of Northumberland, not exactly a 'hawk' and lacking in military experience, his commander-in-chief ('Captain-General') in February. As with similar reliance on other inexperienced nobles like Arundel, his family background seems to have appealed to the King more than his capability – the Percies had been the leading English Eastern Borders dynasty for centuries, commanding thousands of loyal tenants and at times virtually viceroys of the county of Northumberland. Also the more belligerent

Wentworth/Strafford was arguably over-confident, as if discounting both the amount of experience that assorted Scots officers had had in the Thirty Years' War and the 'foot-dragging' of English peers. At the 5 May Council meeting Wentworth (Strafford) boldly claimed that 'one summer well employed will do it' to reduce Scotland, the war would not last more than five months, and suggested using the new Irish army on England if needed.[62] The latter idea, noted down by Secretary of State Vane, was to come back to ruin him once it leaked out and would precipitate his elimination and the vital breakdown of relations between Charles and the Parliamentary leadership in May 1641. To complicate matters, both King and Queen were now reported to be furious with Northumberland for opposing the dissolution of Parliament – and any reconciliation with Warwick was unlikely after the 'insult' of the official raid on his house by Royal officials looking for treasonable papers on 6 May.

Lords Brooke and Saye and Sele (who the King had initially refused to summon to the Lords as suspected troublemakers), and MPs Pym, Hampden, and Sir Walter Earle were also temporarily detained and had their lodgings searched for seditious writings. The newsletter-writer Rossingham was explicit that the searchers were looking for evidence of 'treasonous' links to the Scots;[63] the worst that was found was that Lord Saye and Sele had a copy of a letter from Lord Rothes to the Earl of Pembroke justifying the Covenant.[64] In fact Scots lawyer Sir Thomas Hope of Craighall, currently Lord Advocate, wrote in 1639 that Brooke and Lord Saye and Sele were providing information on English matters to the Covenanters, and one of Brooke's servants, Gualter Frost (later Secretary to the Commonwealth's Council of State) had been going to and from Scotland disguised as the employee of a Scots merchant in London, as arranged by Lord Savile.[65] The King's later anger at these peers as incipient rebels was thus correct. In the meantime the King tried threatening the unenthusiastic City of London to acquire money for the war. He summoned Lord Mayor Garraway to announce that he needed £200,000 and that he should provide a list of rich citizens who could provide this and more or it would be raised to £300,000; however the merchants charged with drawing up the list of contributors refused to do so and were duly arrested.[66] This sparked off a massive riot led by the City apprentices, a forerunner of their militancy in 1641 and aimed at Laud whose palace at Lambeth was attacked. Executing some offenders as an example duly made them appear martyrs and assisted propaganda.

Local 'foot-dragging' by unenthusiastic or cautious gentry made the chances of success in raising the hoped-for army of 1640 too optimistic. Charles needed a larger army than in 1639, as shown by his plans, but the immanence of Parliamentary redress for critics and punishment for supporters reduced his chances of securing it. He made no concessions to the probability that using the dormant 'feudal' mechanism of a 'call-up' would cause chaos and delay. Nor were the men entrusted with running the 'call-up' necessarily competent or sympathetic to crushing the Scots, whatever their social eminence. He made little effort to ensure capable commanders, a delay to organise adequate training which would have saved him from a repeat of Duns Law, or conversely a forced march to the Border as soon as his men had assembled to take the Scots by surprise. He seems to have assumed that the Scots would wait for him to be ready to fight, not take advantage of the fact that they had – in defiance of the terms of the June 1639 truce – failed to disband their army. He and his commanders had no strategic ability to consider bold enemy moves like ignoring the fortifications of Berwick (which barred the Border to a direct advance) and marching south across country to the Tyne. Lord Conway, the commander at Newcastle, did not repair the neglected fortifications there, though he did ask the government in London for permission to raise funds from the townsmen to pay for this – his superior Northumberland refused this as it would cause ill-will.[67] The judges did not help by ruling that the officers could not impose martial law unless an army was encamped close to the enemy, which was seen by exasperated experts as undermining discipline and causing desertions.[68] Some observers of the chaos and inefficiency expected disaster if the army had to fight.[69]

The extent and effectiveness of Scots propaganda in making some Protestant Englishmen unwilling to fight their co-religionists is problematic, but government measures to keep out their pamphlets were as inadequate as attempts to silence Prynne. In August the Scots issued 'The Intentions of the Army of the Kingdom of Scotland, Declared to their Brethren of England', assuring that they were fighting for the liberty and religion of both kingdoms; the Venetian ambassador believed it was effective. It tellingly alleged that the peace-loving Covenanters – like

MPs in the Short Parliament – had attempted a peaceful settlement by petition, but had been blocked by evil Papists around the King (led by Laud and Strafford, naturally) so force was the only option.[70]

The issuing of a new and provocative set of ecclesiastical 'Canons' by Laud's archdiocese's Convocation in the early summer was coincidental, apart from the fact that the meeting coincided as normal with the Parliament. The latter had been dissolved before the Canons were voted on so anti-Laudians could claim that Convocation should legally have been dissolved and the Canons were illegal. The document required all holders of listed professional religious/educational posts to swear allegiance to the current rule of the Church by 'Archbishops, Bishops, deans, archdeacons & c.' This so-called 'Etcetera Oath' was thus intended to smoke out sympathisers of the extreme 'Puritans' and the Covenanters. One of Laud's personal critics and targets, the elderly 'High Anglican' pluralist Bishop Goodman of Gloucester, refused to endorse the Canons. He was 'pro' ceremonial like Laud so he was not a natural foe; but his opposition was based on the grounds of the Canons imposing tight State control of the clergy. Laud intolerantly had him suspended from office.[71]

The Canons, an unnecessary new 'provocation', thus added to the sense of Protestantism under 'siege' felt by opponents of the Scots war. The current febrile atmosphere was reflected in a 'Papist scare' in Colchester, where crowds gathered on rumours that Laud and Bishop Wren were meeting a local Catholic in his weaponry-stuffed house with sinister intentions.[72] In Lichfield stories spread of Catholics stockpiling hatchets ready to massacre their neighbours. Nor did the projected Anglo-Spanish treaty proceed quickly as hoped, but the presumption that it would succeed led Spain's rival France, an alternative source of aid, to withdraw its ambassador Bellievre.[73] His deputy Montreuil remained, but did not have full power to negotiate. Charles was being accused of being in the pocket of Spain, who Scots rumours said would be ceded the Cinque Ports, without the benefits that would bring of men and money.

The dangers in a Spanish treaty were also played up by the Dutch ambassador Heenvliet, who warned that it would mean that the United Provinces broke off relations and regarded England as an enemy – Charles could not have good relations with both sides in the Spanish-Dutch war, as he had managed so far.[74] The long royal 'balancing-act' was coming unstuck, but without the compensation of practical help from Spain.

The detention of the arrested Scots envoy Loudoun in the Tower into June and his remaining in England thereafter enabled dissident peers to use him as a conduit to his faction in Edinburgh; the detailed analysis of the personnel involved by John Adamson reveals that Warwick was involved along with his allies Bedford, Saye and Sele, Essex, Savile, Brooke, and Mandeville (heir of the Earl of Manchester and later a senior Parliamentary commander). They wrote a letter to the Scots leadership assuring of their willingness to co-ordinate their actions with the latter, but refused to aid the Scots with an armed force in invading (or even come to their aid before they crossed the frontier) as this was treasonable.[75] Lord Savile then delivered their letter to Loudoun in Yorkshire, apparently with an additional promise that when the Scots crossed the frontier the peers would assemble and press a 'Remonstrance' on the King – and details of the defensive state of Carlisle which were definitely treasonable.[76] Savile's claim that one of the King's regiments would mutiny once the Scots crossed the border, which if genuine was also treason, may be confirmed by a claim about this plan made in a letter by Saye and Sele's son Nathaniel Fiennes in a letter in September.[77] Loudoun passed on their offer of help to his friends. It is notable that Lord Saye and Sele's private advice to the Scots leadership was a quick advance south to seize Newcastle – precisely the tactic followed by them in August – with hopefully no English bloodshed and so no patriotic English rallying to the King.[78]

If not an exact parallel, this letter – by seven leading political figures claiming to be defending Protestantism by assisting a foreign invasion – bears an ironic resemblance to the more famous letter of invitation to William of Orange to challenge James II in 1688. The peers refused to join the Scots army directly, as this could be construed as treason, but the assurance they would come together in a body to pressurise the King and would publish a public 'Remonstrance' against the misdeeds of the King's evil counsellors implied treason in wartime. The excuse was that their petition would be one 'of right' – that is, quoting a breach of law/custom as making the appeal legally justifiable and the King seem in the wrong. Apparently their lawyer ally Oliver St John had discovered a 'Parliamentary' (or 'Great Council'?) statute of 1258 – the occasion of the Oxford meeting of dissident peers to coerce Henry III – allowing twelve disgruntled peers to call a Parliament whether or not the King allowed it.[79] This could be used to provide a legal 'cover' for action in defiance of

Royal orders. The assembly of mutinous armed peers to 'save' the King from his 'evil advisers' had been seen before, in anti-government coups – from De Montfort's activities in 1258 and 1264 to the 'Lords Ordainers' in 1310, the 'Lords Appellant' in 1387, the Yorkists in 1455, and the Seymour regency's foes in 1549. So was there a coup in the making?

Newburn and after: military defeat and a peers' mutiny. The Royal regime starts to unravel – was this the 'tipping-point'?

The situation in England was deteriorating and confidence in the government collapsing, leading to a telling unwillingness to assist it. The refusal of the East India Company leadership to lend money to the King and the unusual aldermanic challenge to the Royal candidate to be elected next Lord Mayor of London[80] showed the seriousness of the King's failure. Striking quickly in the north was essential, but was impeded by the long process of assembling and equipping an army. Delays in providing funds were crucial,[81] and by the end of June Conway was expressing doubts about the defences at Newcastle – a crucial factor which helped to make the disaster at Newburn decisive.[82] He also reckoned some of his men fitter for Bedlam (a well-known lunatic asylum) or Bridewell (a 'house of correction' in London) than for fighting.[83] Despite the blame later cast upon him, then, the commander 'on the spot' near the Border was aware of the problems. The King's authorities in York were aware of the need for speed in preparations, to the point of panic;[84] and the Scots approach to the Border in mid-August was correctly reported, with estimates of their numbers at 30,000 infantry and 3,000 cavalry. At that point, the English army at Newcastle was supposed to be 14,000 infantry and 2,000 cavalry;[85] these numbers were confirmed by the well-connected Sir Thomas Jermyn.[86] The Scots advance was thus not exactly a surprise, and nor was the state of the English army.

Sanguine about facing invasion, Strafford wrote to Hamilton that he saw advantages in fighting the enemy in England – it made them seem the aggressor and could rally national feeling against them – though he also assumed that Newcastle was better-protected than it was in reality.[87] This does not excuse the Council's delay in ordering the Lords Lieutenant of the central and southern counties to call out their Trained Bands (19 August) and in the proclamation requiring all who held their lands of the

King by feudal 'sergeanty' to do their legal duty and appear at Newcastle by 20 September (20 August).[88] Charles did not set out for York until that day, though his personal participation was reckoned to have fired up many half-hearted gentry to rally to him.[89] The excuse for the delays in London is that the authorities assumed that Newcastle was safe and that Conway, as ordered,[90] would hold out until the King arrived.

Charles had just set out for York to take command when the Scots marched quickly south over the Border on 20 August, avoiding Berwick. Northumberland had not arrived to take command, due to illness – genuine or diplomatic? – though his own principal estate, Alnwick Castle, was on the Scots' route. His deputy, Conway, only had around half the promised troops assembled to meet them as the main army was still assembling at York. Strafford, acting commander-in-chief, was following the King a few days behind and sending Conway orders to be more resolute; his gout prevented him proceeding quicker. Caught in an impossible position, Conway gamely led half his army North to meet the Scots so as not to leave Newcastle unprotected. But that only made him more outnumbered, and he nervously abandoned his first stand at Morpeth to move back closer to his base and defend the line of the Tyne – probably outnumbered by around five to one. The Scots forced a crossing at Newburn and routed the small Royal force which met them on 28 August – only a third of Conway's army, as he had left the rest to protect Newcastle. There were around 300 casualties. Conway had riskily moved his troops forward to guard the ford at Newburn to force a battle rather than wait – which might have caused desertions – but his men were shelled by the Scots artillery from across the river and on the village church tower. Crossing to attack the Scots was impracticable, due to the high bank on the north side of the river; the English would have had to scramble up it under fire. Under bombardment (mostly for the first time), the English faced a Scots charge across the river and abandoned their half-completed defence earthwork. More resolute and experienced English cavalry under Lord Wilmot's son Henry attempted to charge the Scots, but were driven back by superior musket-fire. The decisive blows were struck by a mixture of superior Scots artillery and better-trained musketeers.[91] However, it was notable that the danger to the Scots did not end with the clash in Newburn; a high tide in the Tyne subsequently prevented more troops crossing the river for some hours so a counter-attack could have cause major problems for those men already across. None was considered. In fact, Conway was using the high tide to evacuate his ammunition from Newcastle by sea.

The artillery having come from the Royal ordnance seized in Scotland, the fault for its being in rebel hands lay with Charles (or Traquair or Hamilton acting on their own initiative) for not rescuing it and sending it south in time. Charles had had enough ships in 1639 to land men at Leith and march inland to rescue the artillery at Edinburgh, at least if Hamilton had brought armed tenants to assist them; if Huntly had not been so passive he could have still been in possession of a military force to assist this. The failure of the Royal cavalry (as at Duns Law), with the exception of a few capable officers like Wilmot and George Monck (ironically in action in the first English battle of the 'Wars of Three Kingdoms' in 1640 and responsible for the final solution of the crisis by military means in 1660), was apparent. But better infantry firing was always a major threat to even trained cavalry, unless decisively larger.

The English advance-force had now been visibly defeated, a worse situation than that of the ambiguous skirmish at Duns Law in the 1639 campaign, and this time the non-arriving 'back-up' included the King himself. Conway abandoned Newcastle rather than stand a siege, probably a prudent action given low morale among his inexperienced men but not a sign of a forceful commander.[92] The Scots duly occupied the town (30 August), and remained until 1642. The English retired to Darlington. Charles marched belatedly out of York on the 27th to find the war lost, hearing of the disaster when he reached Northallerton. As in 1639 his advance was brought to a halt by a military defeat – this time on English soil. He chose to accept the 'enemy' occupation of his north-eastern counties, an unprecedented military humiliation for a King who put great store on obedience and needed to impress his subjects with evidence that he was as powerful and worthy of obedience as his Court propaganda maintained. Possibly he was constrained by the need for further training of his inexperienced army, which Strafford now organised. Conway blamed the defeat on acting with an ill-prepared army before the Scots artillery was ready and on sending out Hamilton's fleet to attack Scotland in 1639, thus giving the Scots a pretext to invade on land where they had superiority[93] – somewhat disingenuous, as the belligerent Scots had been the aggressors throughout. Nor was the English army unusually small or unusually unprepared; and the army the King had led from York can be estimated by Secretary Vane's administrative records at 17,000 infantry and 2,000 cavalry, well-equipped.[94] There were also plentiful supplies at Newcastle for the Scots to find when they occupied it;[95] by contrast, the Scots army were short of supplies and the English army had eaten up those around Newcastle so they could not forage for food easily if the town held out. Later a Royalist commander Sir John Byron claimed that this could easily have turned the balance even if the gates had remained shut for only twenty-four hours.[96] Did Conway panic unnecessarily and lose the entire war – or was it too sanguine to assume that the Scots would have had to retreat to find food for their horses and men? Or was Conway being realistic about his men's unwillingness to be besieged in poorly walled Newcastle? If the latter was true, he had had time to dig some extra fortifications if he had had the foresight to think of this risk.

Two potential assemblies: the King's 'Great Council' vs a rebel assembly of Warwick's allied peers?

The Scots, holding the military initiative, demanded the summoning of Parliament – no doubt in anticipation that their allies in the peerage would arrange that the latter voted for a settlement on their terms. Using his 'feudal' powers again, Charles resorted to summoning a 'Great Council' of the peers to York which would in practice mean assembling the Lords to vote money without the troublesome Commons.[97] The initiative for this came from the Lord Privy Seal, the Earl of Manchester (who optimistically thought the public would rally behind the aristocracy), backed by Windebank, Cottington, and Arundel.[98] Those Councillors who preferred a full Parliament, such as Holland and Northumberland, were ignored; there were already spontaneous local petitions for this, starting with Yorkshire on 24 August (before the battle).[99] The Warwick-Bedford-Brooke circle and allied ex-MPs were also drawing up a petition for a parliament in London on the day of the battle,[100] and on 2 September sent a letter to their Scottish allies (treasonable correspondence with the national enemy in wartime?) informing them and assuring their support if the Scots also made this request to the King.[101] In fact the idea of a 'Great Council' was not exclusive of a Parliament and it could be 'testing the waters' ahead of calling one; Laud and the Earl of Berkshire believed one would inevitably lead to the other, as did Vane.[102] Windebank believed that only a Parliament could save the government from the rebels, by 'sweetening' the people to fund the war.[103]

Meanwhile Warwick and his ex-MP allies like Pym and the anti-'Ship-Money' litigant Hampden, locked up in the Tower for some weeks after the spring's Parliament for their impertinent obstructionism, were now at liberty and in correspondence with the Scots to co-ordinate policy against their sovereign. Ominous meetings at Warwick's house in Holborn alarmed the Council at the end of August, and it seems that word of the proposed 'Remonstrance' in favour of the invaders had leaked out; Windebank believed the danger of immanent civil war was as serious as at any time since the Norman Conquest.[104] On 30 August the Council retreated from Whitehall to Hampton Court, with Windsor Castle as a further option; while the artillery-positions outside Whitehall Palace were strengthened[105] – apparently a sign of their fears of a military coup by the dissident peers and their (City of London) Honourable Artillery Company allies. This was not mere panic, as Windebank had plenty of intelligence available of what the 'opposition' were talking about and the latter had now sent a secret request to the Scots to have a mobile cavalry force ready to head for London, presumably to join them. (The Scots' correspondent was Nathaniel Fiennes, son of Lord Saye and Sele.)[106] Lord Savile had already written to Lord Loudoun before the invasion stating that when the latter occurred the opposition would draw up a remonstrance demanding a Parliament, showing that the peers' move was part of a well-prepared plan.[107] Lord Howard of Escrick now delivered the peers' petition for a Parliament to the King at York, a first open indication of the coalescing of serious opposition, and according to Gilbert Burnet's later account Strafford suggested that Howard and his co-signatory Lord Wharton (a dissident Yorkshire peer so capable of undermining the local militia) should be shot in front of the army as an example of what to do with rebels.[108] Once again, Strafford swiftly resorted to threats of violence – and was known for this, even if it was just bluster (which events were to show that 'opposition' MPs did not believe).

On 7 September Bedford and the Earl of Hertford met the 'Committee of War' of those Councillors still at Hampton Court not York, to make their case for a Parliament. They had been invited there by Arundel, who Bedford had sounded out (presumably about joining them) on the 6th. They warned that if it was not called they would not be responsible for the disorders which would follow, which amounted to a blatant threat. Windebank, informing the King, noted that though the two denied contacting the Scots they did not refer to the latter as rebels.[109] Different versions of the peers' petition for a Parliament were now circulated through the counties, to put pressure on the King when the 'Great Council' met, and it is estimated that about a quarter of the nobility signed;[110] a separate petition was circulated in the City, apparently co-ordinated by the peers' allies in the Honourable Artillery Company led by the pro-'Puritan' merchants Maurice Thompson, a future mainstay of the Commonwealth (who delivered it to York)[111] and John Venn, deputy commander of the Company militia.

A meeting of 'opposition' peers in London with their City supporters for an assembly of the Honourable Artillery Company in early September 1640 seems to have been designed as an opportunity for arming both bodies of participants – the first use of armed intimidation of this King within England. The choice of organisers among peers and City men seems to have been centred around the Providence Island Company, the militantly Protestant enterprise for private war against Spain in the Caribbean. Warwick, Lord Saye and Sele, and Maurice Thompson (the Artillery Company organiser) were the leaders in both activities. An associated London clerical petition was led by Warwick's protégés, Edmund Calamy and Calibut Downing. In passing, it should be noted that the number of peers who signed the first petition on 28 August – twelve – was the same as those who had signed the first demand for a Parliament to Henry III in the crisis of 1258, the legal precedent cited for their demand by lawyer Oliver St John – it was no coincidence.

The petition was duly taken to the King at York; it coincided with rumours of a plot to stage a pro-Scots mutiny within the 30,000-strong local Trained Bands, whose organiser Henry Darley (a former Deputy Governor of the Providence Island Company) was arrested by Strafford on 20 September and locked in York Castle.[112] His group were supposed to be hampering raising new troops to defend the King at York, if not worse. But the threat would only be effective if the nobility chose to back the dissidents, by appearing in large numbers with armed tenants in London, rather than obeying the King's retaliatory summons of all peers to York for a 'Great Council'. The idea was floated by some Councillors of admitting the 'rebel' peers' leaders to the Council, to engage them in dialogue and break up the dissident assembly in London, but it was not acted upon. Windebank's request to the King to re-employ Warwick's close ally Essex on 31 August[113] presented a formidable irony – the son of the rebel who had led the last London revolt in 1601, the peer humiliated by King James at the request of his favourites the Carrs, was now to be wooed by both sides as the question of another revolt arose. Arundel now asked the King to summon Parliament, so that he would retain the initiative as summoning it freely before he was forced to do so.[114]

Attention now turned to the annual muster of the Honourable Artillery Company in London on 1 September 1640 – a potentially dangerous regiment of trained and enthusiastically Protestant citizens, patronised by Warwick with his ally Essex's friend and fellow-veteran Sir Philip Skippon as the year's commanding officer. (Skippon was to command the Parliamentarian infantry at Edgehill and end up as a councillor to Oliver Cromwell.) An anonymous Royalist, writing in 1643, was to charge the 'Puritan' faction with systematically infiltrating their followers into the Company to use it as an instrument of revolt,[115] and the muster was duly addressed by Warwick's ecclesiastical preacher protégé Calibut Downing with an inflammatory sermon justifying coercion of the King to save the new Israel from his evil counsellors. Quite apart from the usual comparisons of the 'godly' to the Israelites and their 'pro-Catholic' enemies to the Amalekites, a people who the audience would know had been put to the sword by the Lord's Chosen, Downing specifically stated that 'there is… all the justifiable causes of a legal war'. After the sermon, Royalist writer Sir John Birkenhead later noted, Downing took refuge at Warwick's house at Lees in Essex, 'the common resort of all schismatical preachers'.[116] His message was clear enough, and was backed up secretly by the dissident peers writing to the Scots promising that they could seduce the allegiances of around nine of Charles' regimental commanders plus others controlling the Trained Bands. The potential for insurrection thus existed in early September 1640, two years before the 'lead-up' to Edgehill though at the time the 'rebel' leaders were probably thinking in terms of the armed aristocratic coercions of Henry III in 1258 and the Lords Appellant revolt against Richard II in 1387. The latter had indeed come to a battle, with the King's army defeated (at Radcot Bridge) by the rebel peers. The Council ordered Downing's arrest and a search of his house on 18 September, but he openly took the dissident London clerical petition to York without incident.¹¹⁷

Technically, then, there could have been a civil war in autumn 1640 rather than in 1642 had both sides had the will and approximately equal forces. The Council were considering fortifying Portsmouth (the main naval base) as an emergency headquarters and transferring the Tower of London artillery and ammunition there to save it from the rebels. Meanwhile a placarded invitation to the City apprentices to rally in support of the 'reformation of Religion' on 6 September was countermanded by swift action by the Lord Mayor, preventing another source of intimidation.¹¹⁸ This benefit of determined official City support for the Government was to be lost that winter. Luckily, Charles accepted Windebank's urgent written request of 3 September to summon all the nobility to York for a 'Great Council' and pre-empt the 'rebel' attempt to win a monopoly over the campaign for redress of grievances. As the Secretary of State put it bluntly:

> 'The question is whether Your Majesty will not rather give the glory of redress of grievances, and of a Parliament, to your own Lords, or rather to yourself by their common advice, than to the Rebels, if your power and force be inferior to theirs.'¹¹⁹

The assembly in London was thus to be headed off by the King summoning his own, and maintaining some control of affairs rather than having to face the risk of a militarily superior force comprised of his own nobles and the Scots army. Luckily, the gamble worked; the King retained enough residual loyalty from the uncommitted majority of peers to secure the attendance of a larger group than Warwick did. At this stage the King could still call on enough support due to the traditional bonds of authority. Charles assured the two dissident peers (Bedford and Hertford) who made a request for a Parliament to the Privy Council on 7 September that it might follow. Another petition for a new Parliament was circulating in the City of London from 10 September, probably organised by the Honourable Artillery Company; it was Maurice Thompson who duly delivered it to York. About a third of the nobility, led by personal connections of the Warwick-Essex grouping, went so far as to sign copies of the obviously coercive 'Petition of the Twelve' which were sent around the localities to win added support during early-mid September.[120] Meanwhile in Scotland Dumbarton Castle surrendered to the Covenanters on 29 August and Edinburgh Castle on 15 September – both inevitable after the defeat at Newburn.

The Council remained nervous of what proportion of the nobility could be trusted to come to York rather than go to London, with the risk that those peers supporting the calling of Parliament would judge it safer to coerce the King from London than rely on his goodwill. Trusting to their show of numbers or confident of intimidating the King into not arresting them, the twelve petitioner peers had the nerve to turn up at the 'Great Council' themselves (as they were legally entitled to do). The mood in the army was apparently sympathetic to them; the 'Petitioner' peers had support from some regimental commanders and their ally, the later Parliamentarian commander-in-chief Essex, was spoken of favourably as taking over as its commander[121] – making any arrests risky. The petitioner peers all entered the city together in a procession of coaches, in a show of strength. The meeting opened as planned on 24 September, but with the King having already conceded the main point at issue by announcing that he would summon Parliament. The concession was essential with the Scots army at Newcastle and Windebank's latest estimate of the number of peers who would back the 'opposition' at thirty-seven (with around seventy expected to turn up at York, so about a third of the peerage).[122]

The defiance of the summons to York of about a third of the nobility, now with a base in London and with weapons and City support to hand, increased Charles' long-term dislike of those peers involved. When the 'Great Council' met attendance was low enough for the King to accept that he lacked the means to renew the war with the Scots. Luckily for him, he did not face a substantial defection to the peers in London either. He showed the uncertainty of his goodwill by 'cold-shouldering' Strafford who belatedly arrived from Ireland in York. Given the hostility of gentry and nobles alike to the interference in local affairs occasioned by 'Thorough', this was a politically useful sign of goodwill to the people who would shortly have the political and financial initiative in the new Parliament. But it showed rank ingratitude to a loyal and capable minister, and thus reminded Court aspirants of the uncertainty of relying on Charles. From the point that Parliament assembled, the initiative passed to Charles' critics – and the presence of the Scots army in Newcastle made the retaliatory dissolution of Parliament more difficult than it had been in 1625–9.

A note should be made of the way in which the Warwick group now moved to assume control over the crucial negotiations with the Scots, a matter on which a majority of the peers present insisted. The negotiations, and the use of peers sympathetic to the Scots to lead them, were made by the King's long-term critic, the Earl of Bristol – though as the King had no money for a war and dubious public support his proposals were sensible as well as humiliating for Charles. The committee of sixteen set up to negotiate was dominated by the 'rebels', with seven of them being among the twelve 'petitioner peers' (Warwick, Essex, Bedford, Hertford, Mandeville, Howard of Escrick, and Brooke) plus four more who had signed the petition later (Bristol, Savage, Paget, and Wharton). Another member was Warwick's brother Holland, a Royal confidant but a Calvinist and opposed to the war.[123] The crucial question of when and on what terms the Scots army would leave England – removing a major weapon from the King's critics' armoury – was thus left to the decision of the latter. This had serious effects on the King's freedom of manoeuvre.

An inevitable Royal climbdown?

Why did the King not try to pursue the Scots campaign instead? One of his officers, Sir Richard Dyott, under-stated the case when he wrote that 'many do wonder' at Warwick's group hindering the campaign with their peace-petition when the Scots were entrenched in England and the King had 'so great an army' to hand, raised and equipped at great cost. The campaign was 'retarded, discountenanced and indeed overthrown' by this unpatriotic action.[124] Sir Henry Vane certainly thought the army as impressive-looking as any he had seen, as of 16 September.[125] The question is how much the 'petitioner peers' hopes of army support and the extent of mutiny by peers who did not turn up to the Great Council represented serious opposition to the King, and if the latter was unnerved. The opposition's tactics of backing an 'enemy' invasion-force in occupation of Newcastle certainly aroused antagonism in the north which would benefit the King, and by November a (pro-Royal) newsletter was reporting noisy demands that the 'traitors' deserved to be hanged for their actions.[126] This feeling logically fed into the rise of militant 'Cavalier' opinions in the army during 1641, and into events like Henry Percy's plot.

It is possible that the constant reports from Windebank of plots by the nobility and riots by the apprentices in London unnerved the King – if he marched on would he face open revolt behind him? Did the public anger at the Scots only become apparent later? And what of the machinations to spread dissension among his own regiments and the Yorkshire Trained Bands, for which Darley was arrested? Just because nothing actually happened we should not assume that fears of mutiny or revolt were not a factor; was Charles likely to be as demoralised by a restive army as he faced rebels as his son James II was to be at Salisbury in October 1688? His decision to play for time was logical – what was more incompetent was naming many of the suspect peers to the committee to negotiate with the Scots. He may have reasoned that as Warwick, Savile and company had been dealing with them privately the Scots would trust them and so moderate their terms; but he was wrong to place any trust in either group. But a larger 'Royalist' presence on the committee could have led to the talks becoming stalemated and the Scots and Warwick's group being blamed for it – aiding Charles' position if he asked his next Parliament for money to fight them in 1641?

Part II

The Drift to War, 1640–2

When did the War become inevitable, and which side miscalculated most in the power-struggles?

Chapter Four

November 1640–May 1641. Reform, Retribution and Confrontation

Once Parliament had assembled on 3 November 1640, the political initiative lay with the 'opposition' majority in the Commons, led by John Pym, and to a less well-known extent their allies in the Lords led by Warwick, Bedford, and Saye and Sele (only a minority in that House, but boosted by the force of Commons opinion and fear of the City crowds). The dominant faction, if not yet a 'party', had a common fear of what were later to be categorised as 'Popery and arbitrary government', and a common programme – an intention to secure redress for the evils that had been committed under Charles' 'Personal Rule', punishment of the Councillors held most responsible, and prevention of such 'abuses' in future. They agreed on the need to reform the Church by purging it of 'Arminianism', breaking up its judicial machinery, and destroying the rule of Archbishop Laud but not on the extent of reform – only radicals backed the idea of a 'root and branch' removal of all symptoms of Catholic influence to create a full Presbyterian system without bishops (as was now victorious in Scotland). This was the continuation of the long argument over the extent of a 'full' Reformation of the 'Popish' medieval church which had been going on since the 'grass-roots' Presbyterian agitation against Elizabeth's Church in the 1560s – only now the opponents of bishops had stood up for their plans in arms, in Scotland, and successfully defied the King and Laud. The prosecution of the Royal officials responsible for the worst 'abuses' of the law during the eleven years of 'Personal Rule' was agreed 'opposition' policy, leading to the impeachment of the Earl of Strafford and the judges who had legalised extra-Parliamentary taxation in the form of 'Ship-Money'. For the first time since the impeachment of the greedy and corrupt Duke of Suffolk in 1450, unpopular ministers attacked in the Commons had to flee abroad.

'Opposition' to Royal policies in 1639–40: a neglected factor. Peers as well as MPs

One factor in the political situation has often been under-played, thanks to the concentration of historians on the developing drama in the Commons. It was the latter which came to dominate events after 1640, and proved to be the centre of politics and power as the 'opposition' demolished the framework of 'Personal Rule'. It was the nucleus of opposition to the King by January 1642, as shown by Charles' resort to attempting to arrest its leaders, and once he had fled London the latter took over the leadership of the resistance. Most of the Lords' members choosing to leave London in the wake of their sovereign, that House was politically eclipsed as only a rump remained in the rebel-held capital. But are we reading history with the advantage of hindsight to assume that the Pym faction in the Commons was the dominant element of the anti-Royal cause right from November 1640? The work of John Adamson has brought the role of the 'opposition' lords – the faction of 'Puritan' peers centred on the Earls of Warwick, Essex, and Bedford, and Lord Saye and Sele – back into focus.[1] They had political influence in the Commons due to their control of local Parliamentary seats, and thus could select men with known 'opposition' views, critical of the King's secular and religious policies, to sit there in the elections for the 'Short' and 'Long' Parliaments in 1640. Indeed, they had been as prominent as men like Sir John Eliot in criticising the King for his reliance on allegedly corrupt, incompetent, exploitative, and pro-Catholic ministers since the Parliamentary campaign against the Duke of Buckingham in 1625–8.

Given the importance of local aristocratic patrons – as well as the gentry – in selecting MPs, they had a vital role in choosing which Members would sit for their 'pocket' boroughs in any Parliament; the closure of this means of bringing pressure on an unresponsive King by doing without Parliaments threatened their ability to 'lobby' or blackmail their sovereign. Nor should it be claimed that this means of pressure was a 'new' tactic, aimed at aggressively autocratic Stuarts who believed in 'divine right' – Elizabeth had fulminated at Privy Councillors using MPs to pressurise her over her marriage in 1563–6. But, as seen above in the section on the 'Petition of the Twelve Peers' in August 1640, the Warwick group was now openly citing the legal right to resist an uncounselled

Charles I. Far from the oppressive tyrant or an agent of 'Popish' infiltration, the King was (in his own eyes) a conventional monarch operating within historical tradition. He saw himself as the thoughtful and responsible father of his people, though responsible only to God – not the political elite who his predecessors had taken more trouble to conciliate. But his mixture of shyness, formality, lack of tact or imagination towards others, and willingness to try out unexpected methods of governing brought disaster – aided by major bad luck.

Henrietta Maria. 'The youngest daughter of the famed King Henri IV of France, this Bourbon princess was seen as a Catholic proselytiser and a political meddler by much of her husband's elite – and she lacked her father's political skills or realism. Loyal to her husband in often difficult circumstances and his partner in creating a famously civilised and stately court, she emerged to be a major political player – but her stronger will and daring arguably helped to exacerbate the 1640–2 crises,

Sir Thomas Wentworth, Earl of Strafford. A bluff Yorkshire gentry figure whose passion for organization, and a smoothly functioning state made him first a royal opponent and then a valued minister. Chief proponent of boosting royal power and financial solvency, his tactlessness and ability to make enemies gradually negated his positive qualities. Reorganising firstly Northern England and then Ireland, he alienated elites, often needlessly, and ended up urging a ruthless and violent reaction to the King's Scots then English challengers – and became a target of Parliamentary revenge.

William Laud, archbishop of Canterbury. A pro-active new archbishop from 1633 after years of drift, the shrewd and well-organised mastermind of a revitalised Church arguably only continued past Elizabethan practice. Nor was he at all pro-Catholic, though hostile to Calvinist theology professed by much of the elite. But this ministerial ally of Strafford similarly raised hackles by his aggressive attitude, intolerance of dissent, hyper-active supervision of his juniors, and compulsive micro-management. This left him with few defenders when his often inaccurate critics closed in on him in 1641.

James Graham, earl and later marquis of Montrose. The 'Presbyterian Cavalier', a leader of the Covenanter revolt, was opposed to minimalising royal power and was a personal foe of the leadership's main figure, the eighth earl of Argyll. Charles I plotted with him in 1641 to arrest Argyll and secure aid against Parliament – a dry run for his attempt on the Five Members?

Whitehall: the Banqueting House. Built by the age's top Italian-influenced architect Inigo Jones for James VI and I in 1619 as the definitive statement of up-to-date Europeanised royal grandeur. (© *Philip Halling/ Creative Commons*)

The Queen's House, Greenwich. Built as a royal residence for Charles I's French Catholic wife Henrietta Maria in a similar style, divorced from the current English vernacular – as was her court. (© *D S Pugh/ Creative Commons*)

Hatfield House. By contrast, the grand Jacobean mansion of Hatfield House, a former royal palace given by James to his chief minister Robert Cecil, Earl of Salisbury. Had Cecil lived longer and stabilized prodigal James' finances, would Charles have escaped financial confrontation with Parliament? (© *Christine Matthews/ Creative Commons*)

Wilton House and gardens, Wiltshire, home of the courtier Earls of Pembroke. Charles preferred a semi-private holiday here with courtly masques to his predecessors' annual public progresses. (© *Michael Dibb/ Creative Commons*)

The riding school built by Charles' senior courtier and later general the Earl / Marquis of Newcastle, later Royalist commander of Northern England. Another dilletante Royal courtier, this time a major promoter of dressage. (© *Sandy Gerrard/ Creative Commons*)

St. Giles' Cathedral, aka the High Kirk, at Edinburgh. The wheels started to come off Charles' programme to promote centralized Anglican unity in the British Church as the Scots Presbyterians staged a major demonstration against his new Prayer Book here, July 1637. (© *Neil Clifton/ Creative Commons*)

Statue of John Hampden, Aylesbury Market Square, Bucks. The Scots Covenanters' rebellion against Charles' rule was followed by this well-respected Chilterns gentry figure's legal challenge to the King over Ship-Money. He lost in court, narrowly, but this sparked off wider defiance. (© *Richard Croft/ Creative Commons*)

The Covenanters' monument at Duns Law, Lothian, where they set up their standard in their first successful clash with Charles' army in 1639. The Scots' army was full of battle-trained Thirty Years' War veterans, the King's was largely staffed by amateurs led by senior nobles. (© *Russel Wills. Creative Commons*)

The River Tyne at Newburn, Northumberland. Where the Scots invaders crossed the river to successfully attack the King's army in summer 1640, occupying nearby Newcastle and forcing him to call Parliament – where they had a considerable number of sympathisers led by John Pym and the Earl of Warwick. (© *Alan Fearon/ Creative Commons*)

King by force as used by medieval peers. The number of peers involved in that petition was presumably chosen to reflect the cited legal right of any twelve peers to summon a 'Parliament' acknowledged in 1258, with the 'rebels' legal adviser being the defence counsel in the Hampden 'Ship-Money' case, Oliver St John (Warwick's legal adviser and Oliver Cromwell's cousin). The right of resistance was openly proclaimed by preacher Calibut Downing at the muster of the 'opposition'-dominated Honourable Artillery Company on 1 September 1640, as seen above.

Many of the anti-Buckingham MPs (including Eliot) had been seen in 1625–8 as protégés and mouthpieces of noblemen excluded from influence at Court – and lucrative official posts – by the Duke, such as Pembroke and his brother Montgomery (who succeeded to his Earldom in 1630), Warwick, and Arundel. The latter had been won over to the King's service in the 1630s, partly by his divergent religious views from the Warwick group (they were radical Protestants and he was a crypto-Catholic) and partly by his shared love of the arts with Charles. But Warwick and his friends had remained hostile to the 'Personal Rule' and 'Thorough', promoted the sort of 'Puritan' clerics who Laud was trying to drive from the Church, and had shown their attitude to the King's 'pro-Spanish' foreign policy by paying for their own privateering initiative against the Spanish empire in the Caribbean. Their 'Providence Island Company', centred on the colonization of strategically important Providence Island off the 'Mosquito Coast' (modern Honduras/Nicaragua), was designed to arrange naval depredations against the Spanish colonies around the Caribbean and attacks on Spanish shipping in the militantly Protestant tradition of Drake. It is notable that Oliver Cromwell, a friend of Company member Lord Saye and Sele, employed some former Company personnel in his own anti-Spanish colonial venture to the Caribbean in 1655, used the Company's secretary William Jessop, and kept up the Company's private initiative with State money and troops. The Providence Island Company 'network' keeps on reappearing in 'opposition' incidents; one of their deputy governors, Yorkshire gentry 'Puritan' activist Henry Darley was arrested while Charles I was in York in late summer 1640 for trying to undermine recruitment to his army for the Scots campaign.

It is also significant that the leading peers in this critical group were all from an 'Elizabethan' background, older than the King and almost all able to remember the Court of Elizabeth – and the glory of the 'heroic' war with

Spain from 1585–1603. (Given their youth then, they would have been less likely to remember the failures.) The epic Spanish Armada campaign of 1588 had cast a heroic light over the cause of anti-Spanish war as the centrepiece of the struggle against 'Popery', with as many nostalgic myths growing up about it as there were to be later about the 1940 confrontation with Hitler. Spain was seen as the 'evil empire' of its time, the sinister super-power run by Papal agents which had endeavoured to extirpate Protestantism and have Queen Elizabeth assassinated, and there was renewed fear of its reach and aims in the 1610s when its ambassador Count Gondomar had been resident at James I's court. The 'narrative' of a constant Catholic threat and the need for endless vigilance had been reinforced by the 'Gunpowder Plot' in 1605. Among the 'opposition' peers of the 1630s, Warwick had been born in 1587, Bedford in 1591, Essex in 1591, Hertford in 1588, Lord Saye and Sele (founder of an idealistic Protestant colonial experiment at 'Sayebrook' in Massachusetts) in 1582, and the later 'defector' John Digby, Earl of Bristol in 1586; the Earl of Pembroke and Montgomery, a marginal connection in 1640–1 but at odds with Charles I, had been born in 1584. Another contemporary was their favourite, determinedly Calvinist bishop John Williams (in the Tower since 1637 after being 'targeted' legally by his foe Laud for resisting his Church reforms). The only younger member of the group was Lord Mandeville, son of the Earl of Manchester, born in 1602. John Pym, Bedford's client in the Commons in 1640–1, had been born in 1584; Pym's younger half-brother Francis Rous, a distinguished Presbyterian theologian, shared his views and was to stay at the centre of politics (as a minor figure) into the 1650s when he was Speaker of the godly 'Nominated Parliament', Provost of Eton College, and a Cromwellian Councillor.

Their formative years had thus been a time of Spanish and Catholic threat, as opposed to Charles who had grown up at Court in the 1610s with its ambassador a feted guest of his father's, and they could all remember back to the spectacular naval triumphs in and post-1588. Charles' attempts to impose 'distance' from and respect for the King were alien to their experience of Court, and would thus have added to the disgruntled peers' alienation. Some of them came from a family tradition of high politics at Court and little respect for the Crown. Essex was the son and his cousin Warwick the nephew of the Late Elizabethan 'favourite' Robert Devereux, Earl of Essex, executed for rebellion in 1601; Hertford was the great-grandson of Lord Protector Somerset (executed 1552) and had himself been in serious trouble with James I for illegally marrying the potential 'pretender' Lady Arbella Stuart in 1610. Essex – and by female descent Warwick – were indirect descendants (via the Bourchiers and Devereux) of the Plantagenet royal house. Warwick (by male descent), Hertford, and Bedford all came from dynamic and ruthless Tudor dynasties of Henrician 'new men', not the older aristocracy – which mattered to status-conscious nobles, as seen in Arundel's famous dismissal of Lord Spencer as a man whose ancestors had been sheep-farmers while his were barons of royal lineage.[2] They thus expected to be able to use their wits and influence to gain power as their ancestors had done -particularly with Protestantism seemingly under threat – rather than defer to an 'ill-counselled' King. This Elizabethan background and family tradition helps to explain the clique's pursuit of power through pressurising the Court in 1639–41. Indeed, the allegation that Warwick had illegal connections with the rebellious Scots reflected family tradition – his uncle Essex had kept up a secret correspondence with James as King of Scotland concerning the succession in the late 1590s and was accused by his Court rivals of endeavouring to depose the Queen (possibly for James' benefit) in 1601. Essex's father had led the much-lauded sacking of Cadiz in 1596.

Charles turned back to the course of winning Spanish goodwill for a voluntary return of the Palatinate by Spanish mediation in 1639–40, which unfortunately coincided with the rise of anti-Catholic fears in England and disquiet resulting from the Royal clash with the Scots over religion. He did not even have the satisfaction of a Spanish treaty, which at one point in spring 1640 seemed likely to involve a subsidy and the loan of Spanish troops to defeat the Scots. Had the treaty been agreed, he could have used the money to avoid an early Parliament and the experienced Spanish 'tercios' to defeat the Scots – at the cost of popular anger over this use of foreign Catholics to crush Scots Protestants. But the treaty was not finalised, partly due to the revolt against the Spanish state in Catalonia. Autonomist feelings within Spain thus helped autonomist Scots resistance within Great Britain in 1640-1.

The suspension of Parliament from 1629 to 1640 denied excluded peers from making up for their absence from Court by using it to criticise – and hopefully correct – Royal policies. Thus they had a motive for seeking its restoration, to increase their political influence over a King who had ignored them since 1625 in favour of a tight clique of loyalists but also out of fear that the Laudian Church reforms indicated a dangerous move away from the Elizabethan settlement towards semi-Catholic ceremonial and excessive Church administrative interference in secular matters. Laud was perceived to be pro-Catholic, and the number of Catholic ministers (e.g. Lord Treasurer Portland to 1635) and Catholic conversions raised fears of the 'Papists' rising secular influence too. The role of Laud as a minister, controlling the Treasury for a year after Lord Treasurer Portland's death in 1635 and thence with his protégé Bishop Juxon in charge, was unprecedented for an archbishop since 1532 and contentious. His obsessive judicial pursuit of his foes aroused widespread public concern, and the trial and sentence to public whipping and cropping of ears of the militant (and undoubtably viciously libellous) 'Puritan' ministers Prynne, Burton and Bastwick by the 'Court of Star Chamber' (i.e. a committee of delegated Privy Councillors) in summer 1637 was notorious at the time – though perfectly legal. The use of this by the religious 'opposition' for an exhibition of 'martyrdom' of the 'godly' by Laud unfortunately coincided with the Scots 'Prayer Book; 'crisis, adding to the sense of a Britain-wide assault on the 'godly' which a less obstinate Archbishop could have avoided. Wentworth/ Strafford was known for his ruthlessness and willingness to use force, which was reinforced by his role since 1633 as governor in Ireland where the normal niceties of political behaviour were pereceived as not applying and he had armed Catholics to hand. (One of the leading complainers at his use of legal 'short cuts' there in the mid-1630s was Pym's brother-in-law Sir John Clotworthy, who owned lands in Ulster.) But the objectors had no means of pressurising the King as long as a small faction of semi-Catholic courtiers controlled access to the King, who more than James allowed himself to be seen as a partisan of one faction (as in assisting Laud to punish his Calvinist critic Bishop Williams in 1637).

It is now clear that the Warwick faction made the most of the King's difficulties with the Scots from 1637 to actively encourage the latter in their resistance, in the hope that the King's weak military position and inability to crush the revolt would force him to recall Parliament to raise money for war. The 'Puritan' peers' ideological sympathy for a Presbyterian

Church under attack from Laudian reforms should not be treated in too cynical a light, and the lack of enthusiasm among the northern gentry for participating in the Royal army as the King called up volunteers for coercing Scotland in 1640 shows that Warwick's group had much local support. The lynching of Catholic officers indicates that the cause of war was seen as aiding 'Popery' not fighting the traditional national foe, which factor was miscalculated by the King. After all, around twenty-seven peers – a third of the total – did not attend Charles in York for his 'Great Council' in September 1640 and/or were reckoned as hostile to him then. The antagonistic ideological context of 1639–40, namely rising fears over the growth of 'Popery' in England itself, was not restricted to London as rumours spread across the country; contemporary diaries show the extent of popular foreboding in the provinces (e.g. through the reports of ominous natural phenomena). The mixture of Catholic conversions at Court, a Catholic Queen, a rumoured Spanish alliance, and the collapse of the proposed intervention in the Thirty Years' War on the French/Protestant side all added to a belief that Protestantism was under siege. In this context, coercing the King into ridding the nation of Catholic influence via Parliament would have seemed a 'defensive' and morally justified action to the Warwick group. As it happened, the alleged attacks on Protestantism in both England and Scotland coincided with the constitutional argument that the King was abusing his authority over non-Parliamentary taxation and the constant stream of lawsuits brought to assert (or reassert) Royal legal rights over matters as diverse as patents, gentry or Church control of local ecclesiastical patronage, and Fenland reclamation.

The peers' contacts with the defiant Scots leadership in Edinburgh went as far as co-ordinating activities to undermine the King's strategy in 1639–40, and included promises of armed co-ordination with them in invading England and suborning the King's regimental commanders. This technically amounted to treason. The King was well aware of this. It crucially affected his reluctance to come to terms with these powerful nobles – by 'surrendering' to their demands – in 1640 and 1641. The vacancies in senior offices (e.g. Lord Keepership/Chancellorship and Treasury) late in 1640 were not filled by the King's noble critics as was expected at the time. The Earl of Essex at least was courted in honorific rather than politically significant concessions, such as allowing him to carry the King's cap of maintenance in the Royal procession at the opening of the 'Long Parliament' on 3 November. Admitting more of the 'opposition' to office would have helped the King to reach accommodation with the Commons, as the new office-holders would be expected to rein in their MP protégés and rally support for votes of funds. The 'downside' of that hope was that they would not do so, but seek to use their strengthened political power to weaken the King's position further. Their use of the legal precedent of 1258 (Simon de Montfort's coercion of Henry III) in 1640 is one indication that they aimed at permanent 'reform' to Royal policies, not just what would be called in the eighteenth century 'storming the closet' (to gain office for its own sake). In religious terms, these sincere Calvinists seem to have regarded religion – the main issue of Parliamentary concern apart from the 'misuse' of the Royal prerogative – as vital, and the end of the 'threat' from Laud's innovations as a *sine qua non*. Office alone would not satisfy them, though some would have been more amenable to 'moderate' measures on curbing the episcopate than others and promotion of Calvinist bishops would have been vital reassurance to them. Arguably Charles' alienation from the staunchly Calvinist Bishop John Williams, a man theologically acceptable to Warwick's group but still defending episcopacy, was vital – the King had backed Laud in his personal court case against Williams in 1637. Williams had denounced both 'Ship Money' and placing altars at the east end of churches. Williams was a useful 'middle-man' alienated by a King who took on his favourites' personal grudges as his own, as Charles had similarly turned on the Earl of Bristol in 1625–6 for attacking Buckingham.

It was also notable that Charles had endeavoured in summer 1639 to insist that when a truce was called with the invading Scots army his proclamation that their acts amounted to treason was read out to them – a mixture of intimidation and unwise insistence on his legal 'rights'. He was a stubborn and politically unwise character capable of being as intransigent over another issue had the Scots crisis not arisen and he still needed to call Parliament for funds. The noble critics of Buckingham had faced Royal wrath and exclusion from favour in and after 1625–8, the Duke's murder not resolving the issue as Charles clearly felt that the co-ordinators of the Parliamentary abuse had blood on their hands. Eliot was the principal victim then. Now it was Laud who was being abused as a semi-Catholic monopoliser of Royal power, and an attempt to impeach him or Wentworth in the Commons at the first opportunity would have been likely to cause Charles to defend him as obsessively as he had done the Duke.

Could Charles have been more determined to secure support in Parliament in November 1640? Would it have worked?

The potential use of Royal influence to secure a substantial body of complaisant MPs in the next Parliament – and thus block critical votes – was not as easy as Wentworth (hereafter referred to by his new title, the Earl of Strafford) assumed in summer/autumn 1640. Secretary Windebank advised the King to secure the election of as many friendly MPs as possible,[3] and although this was neglected the strength of feeling against recent methods of Royal rule would have made it very difficult to 'fix' elections in Royal-controlled boroughs in practice. Strafford had been able to arrange a complaisant Irish parliament in 1640, but conditions were different there with stronger coercive apparatus and a weaker sense of local autonomy by gentry and corporations. The King's ablest and most ruthless minister had been an active – opposition – MP in the mid-1620s and by birth and upbringing was a member of the Yorkshire gentry, but he had been serving in Ireland for six years and was 'out-of-touch'.

Crucially, if Strafford had been retained in an office in England or brought back earlier he would have been more realistic – though even so he was a potential liability given his increased penchant for violent and intimidatory solutions which Royal resources could not use effectively in England as in Ireland. His attitude to the standard-bearer of legalist constitutional resistance to 'Thorough', the 'Ship-Money' litigant John Hampden, was typical; he thought a good flogging would teach him and his backers a lesson. His optimistic expectations to be able to use an Irish army in England and Scotland in 1639–40 was equally bold but risky, and undertaken without a thought of the long-term consequences for a financially weak and administratively ramshackle state; England was not centralised Spanish Castile. Strafford was also rumoured to be planning to launch legal prosecutions of not only the 'Warwick group' but the Pym/Hampden/Clotworthy group of MPs as the new Parliament opened in November 1640, with military activity at the Tower indiacting that they would be imprisoned there and extra troops would be brought in from York to deal with any City riots.[4] It probably added to the possible victims' desire to strike first and arrest Strafford quickly. Had Charles had a phalanx of senior ministers with the new Earl of Strafford's determination and ability – and a financial bonus of a Spanish subsidy, as seemed possible in spring 1640 – he might have been able to risk taking such drastic actions. But it should not be assumed that Charles did not have any drastic retaliation against his foes in mind when he called Parliament, as some time towards the end of 1640 he asked Sir John Boroughs, his tame antiquarian, to look out precedents for Acts of Attainder in the Tower of London records.[5] A prosecution by attainder needed fewer witnesses and less proof than normal legal procedures, hence the fondness of Tudor regimes for using this method of disposing of their enemies. The possibility also arises that the Scots leadership (or some of them) could be lured by Royal surrender over the bishops into abandoning their English allies. As the first senior Scots delegation arrived at Durham for the peace-talks, Bishop Wren was informed by someone there that a 'great Scott' (presumably a peer) had said that if their allies did not carry out their promises, 'they would quickly make peace with the King, as well as they could, and send him a Roll of those English traitors that sent for them to invade'.[6] The peer involved was probably either Rothes, Montrose, Lindsay, or Cassilis.

Most ministers lacked Strafford's determination, apart from the isolated and hated Laud; he had an unfortunate talent for alienating people and had had no solid backing from ministers while he was in Ireland. The one senior minister of sufficient 'weight' and experience to have aided him usefully in such a policy, Lord Treasurer Weston, had been his rival – mocked in Strafford's correspondence with Laud for his slowness in action – and had died in 1635. Charles had no minister in England with the energy and administrative enthusiasm to have arranged a systematic campaign to influence local boroughs in electing MPs and buy off the gentry or noble families who acted as 'borough-mongers' – and in any case the whole tenor of recent Government policy had been to enforce its rights on and extract money from such men, not to conciliate them. As with Strafford alienating both Protestants and Catholics ('Old English' and Irish alike) in Ireland, the King's chief servants had no fund of goodwill to call on for local support in 1640. It is difficult to see how the King could have counted on local support from his officials, the sheriffs (who ran county elections) in particular. They were men selected from the local communities not sent from London, as there was no seventeenth century 'top-down' bureaucratic structure; they had to be responsive to local pressure from their neighbours and they had their future local careers, social life, and marital arrangements to consider among the county elites. The same applies to the King's mainstay in local affairs, the county Deputy Lieutenants, and beyond them the network of gentry families who ran or at least influenced borough-elections; the extent of influence (and of boroughs being 'closed' and easily controllable) depended on property-qualifications. Indeed, the context of official unwillingness to carry out contentious Royal orders in raising and funding troops in 1639–40 shows that those local leaders of society currently trusted to work for the King in office were more scared of prosecution by the next parliament than of punishment by the King. It was not a simple case of the King 'giving orders' to see that loyal men were elected as MPs in 1640, had he had the political skill or the nerve to do this; the reality of Stuart governance was more messy.

Notably, the payment of 'Ship-Money' (estimated at around 80 per cent after the Hampden case, so still being paid up) collapsed in 1640 once it seemed likely that its legality would soon be challenged successfully in Parliament.[7] Unlike in 1681–4, the King did not have the time to 're-model' borough corporations' charters to secure 'safe' aldermen and electors – even assuming that he could find any such men due to the extent of local grievances across the higher social classes. The multiplicity of petty legal cases of asserting Royal rights in town and countryside had alienated too many people, with Laud's assertion of dormant Church legal powers through the Court of High Commission particularly resented. It should be remembered that the potential electors of 1640 did not have the advantage of foresight, and had no idea that electing the King's critics to the Commons would eventually lead to Civil War; the fear of anarchy and 'the world turned upside down' was not yet a factor in politics. The evidence would suggest that a strong – and politically vital – 'reaction' of feeling in the King's favour was only apparent in 1642. Then anarchy and the dismantling of the entire Episcopal Church apparatus was threatened, and the latter could prove a rallying-point as seen by the extent of loyalist petitions. But the extent of the 'root-and-branch' threat of militant MPs like Pym and their petitioning backers was not yet apparent; loyalist sentiment in 1639–40 seems to have concentrated on indignant nationalist attitudes to the rebellious treachery of the Scots, not to their Presbyterian religion.[8] Stupidly, Charles allowed Laud to impose contentious new canons at the meeting of Convocation in early summer 1640, when that body was unusually kept on after Parliament was dissolved (in order to raise ecclesiastical taxes). The altar-rails were to be firmly placed at the east end of churches, Communion taken kneeling, all ecclesiastical and university personnel required to take a loyalty oath to the current form of the Church, and quarterly sermons preached in the parishes on the legal necessity of obedience. Once again, King and Archbishop were mistaking the imposition of a legal form for the ability to enforce it; the sporadic use of all possible legal rigour to intimidate his opponents also continued by racking rioting apprentices after a May Day attack on Laud's Episcopal palace at Lambeth. Notably, the assembly of Parliament in November 1640 was to be preceded by an open attack on the altar-rails in St Paul's Cathedral by local militant Protestants. A mob then destroyed the records of the Court of High Commission – an echo of the sabotage of the judicial system carried out by the Peasants' Revolt rioters in 1381.[9] The large attendance at the grand public reception for returned militant 'Puritan' 'martyrs' Burton and Prynne on 28 November showed popular feeling – and was an open challenge to the usual stage-managed 'loyalist' parades surrounding the King's entry to London and other places. The 'opposition' peers were in attendance in their coaches as an escort, as grandees usually did for the monarch.[10]

Charles had no answer to or willingness to concede to the extent of discontent, given the ramshackle nature of the State apparatus and its financial constraints. Possibly he may still have been optimistic of Spanish aid. In the event, Charles was forced to summon Parliament again, though he committed one vicarious mistake in allowing the Scots commissioners to come to London (where they were able to meet the 'opposition' once Parliament assembled) rather than keeping them isolated at the first venue for talks, Ripon. The fact that the Scots had successfully demanded a daily payment of £860 for their army as long as it was in occupation of North-East England was, however, burdensome to the locals as well as humiliating, and was good for propaganda.

When the elections were held he could count on probably 64 and at most 80 out of 493 MPs – and the legal mechanisms of Parliament meant that the Commons were able to receive and vote on petitions from unsuccessful candidates, thus giving the majority a mechanism to eject their enemies. The petitions against election-results duly led to the 'opposition', dominating an unusually large Commons committee to hear petitions (forty-seven members), being able to overturn the results in around sixteen more constituencies.[11] The existence of a Commons committee for judging the legality of all elections and hearing defeated candidates' complaints is a riposte to those who might suggest that Charles – or an untrammelled Strafford – could have 'fixed' many more contests had they had the political 'nous' and skill of Charles II's electoral managers like Sir Thomas Osborne, Lord Danby. Strafford and a group of equally determined allies – had such existed – could have managed more constituencies in autumn 1640, especially if Strafford had been brought back to London by then as Lord Treasurer to dole out funds to his allies and Spanish money had been at hand, and Charles should have made the attempt. But the extent of anger among the electors in boroughs and counties alike was such that he would not have had much more success, and the elected 'place-men' would have been ejected on appeal to the majority of the Commons. (The pro-Royal candidates who failed to secure election included Sir Edward Nicholas, future Secretary of State, and Secretary Windebank's nephew Robert Read – the sort of people who could normally count on a seat.) There was less deference by voters in 'open' boroughs to the demands of government ministers for seats for their allies than usual – a sign of provincial rejection of the 1630s demands by State authorities. The most militant anti-Royal MPs, led by Pym who had experience of administrative organisation while working for Bedford, would have been ready and eager to organise their eviction.

The situation as of late 1640: a majority for 'reform' in the Commons, and an uncompromising mood?

Even those critics who wished to retain the English bishops, probably a majority in both Houses at this stage, were alienated by the 'Arminian' ceremonialism and the judicial prosecutions launched by Archbishop Laud in the 1630s and desired to return to a 'purer', pre-1633 order and abolish the Church's judicial mechanism. Future Royalists such as Edward Hyde were opposed to Laud's policies. This sort of reform did not go as far as the Scots were demanding for their own country but shared a common target of the current Church order. Crucially, the veto that the Scots treaty commissioners had on a settlement of the Scots rebellion gave a religio-political weapon to the militants – was a treaty possible without abandoning the bishops, and if not what then? Another war? Noticeably, the Lords quickly ordered the release of Laud's principal Episcopal critic Williams from the Tower (with his conviction in 1637 overturned by a committee 'packed' with Warwick's faction) and his departure on 16 November was turned into a public occasion for the Londoners to celebrate the Archbishop's defeat, the 'opposition' peers escorting Williams through the City.[12] The victimised 'Puritan' pamphleteer Henry Burton and the 'libeller' William Prynne were invited back to London amidst similar political demonstrations of support. The successful petition to the Commons for Burton's release was presented by Pym and seconded by Hampden (7 November), and the 'martyr' Burton's arrival in London on the 28th saw a grand procession of militant Calvinist peers to escort him (very rare for a 'commoner') in a parade. Next day, not coincidentally a Sunday, the atmosphere of public spectacle was continued by a thanksgiving service at Warwick's local church, St Mary Aldermanbury, with the sermon delivered by Lord Brooke's chaplain.[13] The iconography of public spectacle, usually organised by and for the monarchy, was thus usurped by the 'opposition'. The London 'Root and Branch' petition to abolish the bishops, delivered by a large crowd to Parliament on 10 December and sponsored by City MP Alderman Isaac Penington, uncompromisingly condemned episcopacy as an institution as a source of evil and alleged that 'Popish' ceremonial and vestments had led to a debauched and sinful ministry.[14] These demonstrations may not have been 'representative' of majority City opinion, but showed a depth of support for Parliament that an impoverished and politically hamstrung King, without troops to hand, needed to heed.

One of the first preachers to the Commons was the militant Cornelius Burges, who provocatively spoke not only of the need for completing the Reformation but of how Israel had been delivered from Babylon by an army from the north (i.e. Persia in 539 BC). (He was to go further on Gunpowder Plot Day 1641 to compare Charles I to King Rehoboam of Israel, the son of Solomon, overthrown for godlessness – James VI and I often being compared to Solomon).[15] Burges, Edmund Calamy, and other leading Warwick associates were to present a 'Remonstrance' of around 700 clergy denouncing (but not yet proposing to abolish) the bishops on

23 January 1641.[16] This was apparently drawn up at Calamy's house, and was clearly timed to put pressure on Charles – it followed the appointment of 'opposition' legal expert St John as Solicitor-General and was presented by 'godly' Herefordshire MP Robert Harley, later a Parliamentarian leader. But it is important to note that the 'opposition' did not have an automatic majority in the Commons on all matters relating to 'misrule' as of November; matters were a good deal more complex and different MPs had different priorities. Parliament, above all, was a national forum for exposing local grievances, and many (most?) MPs would have been more concerned with their local electors' usual petitions for redress; what was different was the extent and scope of the latter. The scope, significantly, was common to many complainants from across the country and so a 'common cause' would demand a 'common remedy' – but that had been true of monopolies in 1601 and 1621.

The usual flood of county petitions to the Commons began with one from Hertfordshire on 7 November, and had a much wider than usual scope in its list of complaints; typical of what followed, these included the absence of Parliaments since 1629, the 1640 Laudian canons, the inadequate clergy, the oath *'ex officio'* (required of defendants, who had to answer questions without knowing what charges had been made and so ran the risk of falling into verbal traps) excessive military charges and pressing for the army, and the patent of saltpetre. Religious, military, financial, and legal/constitutional abuses were raised.[17] Specific and sensational cases of abuse of legal process and punishment, usually involving the Court of Star Chamber and/or the Church courts, were piled up and no doubt raised the emotional atmosphere (as intended by their sponsors), with the unknown junior MP Oliver Cromwell raising the cases of the imprisoned anti-Arminian pamphleteer Alexander Leighton and the flogged 'seditious books' convict John Lilburne, his future enemy.[18] MPs could be duly outraged by lists of all the 'Popish' ceremonial introduced into churches and University property, usually at the behest of Laud or his minions, as well as attempts to convert people to Catholicism.[19] As abuses were detailed committees were set up to look into general areas of complaint and specific cases; sixty-five were in existence by 16 January 1641, with only about two-thirds of them ever reporting back to the Commons for action to be taken.[20] But this litany of abuses – to be expected after eleven years of contentious governance without an outlet for complaint – was set out by future Royalist leaders, such as Sir Arthur Capel (shot 1648 after the siege of Colchester) and Hyde, as well as future Parliamentarians. It was not an indication of united or even majority support for the plans of people such as Pym, and if the King could address grievances satisfactorily their religious proposals could be side-tracked or out-voted. Many later Royalists, e.g. Sir John Culpepper, had sympathy with part of the 'reformists' complaints, while being uncompromising on episcopacy, and Hyde clearly felt that judicial process had been abused and needed reform; he chaired the committee to investigate the abuses by the Council of the North and was imvolved in attacking Star Chamber and the Earl Marshal's Court too. Personally, Hyde (sitting for Saltash, a Devon naval borough close to Pym's seat) was on good terms with Pym, who told him in an encounter just before Parliament opened of his intention to pull up the causes of all abuses by the roots, and defended both Pym's and Bedford's integrity in his 1668 'History' – though he distrusted Hampden.[21] The lack of a distinct ideological or personal barrier between the two 'factions' in 1640–1 extended to Bedford, who certainly believed in retaining bishops as an institution, shorn of recent accretions of power and ceremonial.

The traditional opening speech by the King on 3 November was uncompromising in referring to the Scots as 'rebels' and demanding an early resumption of the war, not unreasonably pointing out the cost of their occupation to the North-Eastern counties.[22] The King's 'line' was thus to stress his patriotism and stir up anger against the Scots, Warwick's allies – not usually difficult as English dislike of their neighbours was rampant after 1603 and had blocked all James I's attempts to grant equal and inclusive English citizenship to Scots born after 1603. This was followed by an adulatory address to the Commons by Lord Keeper Finch – scheduled to do this by precedent, but an unfortunate choice given his past actions over 'Ship Money' – which was full of laudatory tones about Charles' recent actions and the need to support him against the Scots, stressing the unanimity of all the Council for the Scots war.[23] This implied that Charles would not countenance abandoning the 'hawks' like Strafford (who was now summoned from Yorkshire to take his seat in the Lords, instead of being told to stay away). The tone taken by Finch was not helpful to put it mildly, and was seen as such by expert observers like Lucy, Lady Carlisle (Northumberland's sister). Warwick's group of

MPs proceeded to open an investigation into Irish affairs, implying a move to draw up charges against the Lord Deputy (Strafford); the role here of Pym's brother-in-law Sir John Clotworthy, an 'eye-witness' of events in Ulster and now MP for Warwick's borough of Maldon, would be crucial. It is possible that the original intention was to wait until the Irish Parliament put charges against Strafford and then join in, as the victim expected.[24] Pym was reported to have been drawing up articles of impeachment since September.[25] But on the 6th the House voted (narrowly, 165 to 152) to have the question of investigation into Irish affairs determined by a committee of the whole House, not by a smaller committee which Pym's group could 'pack'. Clotworthy and Sir Henry Mildmay were 'tellers' for the Pym group; though they were defeated they won the Commons' agreement that the House could assert its judicial supremacy over Irish affairs, as advocated by Pym and Sir Harbottle Grimston.[26] The latter was a vehement 'opposition' radical, who was to complain on 7 November that the King's judges had overthrown the Law as in Richard II's time and deserved the fate of the latter's Chief Justice Tresilian (i.e. execution).[27] The cautious Pym did not even mention Strafford in his first major speech listing recent abuses of Parliamentary rights, denials of the subjects' liberties, and attacks on 'godly' religion on the 7th.[28] Presumably intent on building up a head of steam to bind the King's critics together, the Pym faction then proceeded over the next week to organise the Commons' receipt of a mass of local petitions complaining of governmental misrule (administrative, judicial, and financial) through the 1630s.[29] This was normal practice – but in the context of November 1640 implied building up a coherent 'narrative' of what needed to be reformed, ready to propose legal remedies. But remedying the masses of complaints would take time, and the Commons lobby was thronged for months with eager petitioners awaiting their turn to appear. More politically and constitutionally important at this point was the creation of the Lords' 'committee for petitions' on 6 November – a body of thirty-six, led by Warwick and with eighteen of them signatories of his 31 August 1640 petition to the King. This received around one hundred petitions a month in the early months of 1641. Moreover, it reasserted the ancient right of the Lords to exercise judicial power as a court of appeal, and thus served to hear cases of 'abuse of procedure' by the King's prerogative courts in the 1630s; experts have reckoned that the scope and volume of this Lords committee's activities was unparalleled since the crisis of 1450 (another instance of mass-protests at Royal abuses of power).[30]

It should be considered logical that it was fear as much as long-laid grudges which motivated the 'opposition' in the ferocity and urgency of their assault on Strafford in November-December 1640 – the preliminary to the vital crisis over execution which damaged relations with the King in May 1641. The raids on the Warwick group's residences in search of incriminating material on their Scots contacts in May 1640 had not produced evidence of treason, but Strafford was supposed to be boasting of access to incriminating documents and immanent arrests.[31] This may have included the peers' indiscreet if cautious June letter to Loudoun. If true, his arrival in London to take his seat in the Lords on 9 November might precede his laying charges against the 'Petitioner Peers' and their removal to the Tower (which was being strengthened and had councillor Lord Cottington as governor), vitally weakening opposition. He could still use the Royal troops in York (around 22,000) against Parliament, or bring in his Irish army. Accordingly, there were alarmed rumours that the King's visit to the Tower – where defences were being reinforced as Strafford was due to take his seat on 11 November – was connected to an immanent military 'strike' and/or arrests, centred as usual on ill-affected 'Papists' at Court. The Commons' principal City informant was 'Puritan' merchant Matthew Craddock, a long-term Warwick ally and former Governor of the Earl's New England Company – did he exaggerate deliberately? There appears to have been panic in the Commons, stoked by lurid and possibly deliberately exaggerated reports, and the doors were locked.[32] Laud accused the alleged victims of Strafford's plan of indicting him to save themselves.[33] However, there were no quick arrests of troublesome peers and MPs – but neither was there a quick 'opposition' motion to impeach Strafford before he could strike, so did the potential victims lack the confidence that they would win a vote?

The first major analyst of the documentary Parliamentary evidence, S.R. Gardiner, believed Charles lost his nerve and fatally dallied, letting the more determined Strafford down and losing his best chance to decapitate the opposition. John Adamson believes that neither side had its evidence to hand and even Pym was not ready for action.[34] Instead of a showdown, 11 November saw only a tentative move by Pym to implicate the Secretary of State, Windebank – a Catholic but also in charge of intelligence and thus incriminating documents – in a plot for a 'St Bartholomew's Day'-style massacre by an Irish priest in Marie de Medici's service at St James' Palace.[35] The speech by Pym which Gardiner presumed as the first great attack on Strafford did not even mention him,[36] according to assorted Commons diaries;[37] Clotworthy then attacked not Strafford himself but his legal adviser Sir George Radcliffe, who had supposedly admitted that the Irish army was for use in England as well as Scotland.

The small Commons committee set up to prepare matters for a conference with the Lords on matters touching a threat to Church and State on 11 November was, Adamson believes, not intended by most MPs to be specifically aimed at Strafford alone – this effect was produced by its members, led by Pym, Clotworthy, and Bedford's cousin and protégé Oliver St John, directing its agenda to that end.[38] Other members included Denzel Holles and William Strode, two of the future 'Five Members'. The 'attack on Strafford' and preparation of charges against him was thus the action of a small, 'activist' group not of majority opinion, and at this stage Pym was not in possession of as secure a majority on the issue as earlier reckoned. According to Hyde's recollection years later, Pym now warned MPs that if Strafford was not arrested and thus neutralised he had the credit with the King to secure the dissolution of Parliament.[39] The original instructions for the committee, however, had not referred to Strafford by name,[40] and it was thus deflected into serving the Pym group's ends. The move was made to have Strafford placed in custody. In a mood of panic over the King's visit to the Tower, Pym led a delegation to the Lords to deliver a charge of treason, and by the time the crucially absent Strafford arrived to answer it he was too late. Had he been in his seat, could he have levelled a counter-charge of communicating with the Scots rebels against his foes with any success in winning over the majority of peers? The 11th ended with him in custody (in Westminster)[41] and a major first blow in favour of the Warwick-Pym grouping, with the resultant psychological advantage of unbalancing their opponents. With the King's most visible and vociferous ally in custody amidst the attendant public humiliation of his arrest, it was clear who had physical power – the King's challengers, not his most feared minister. After the arrest, on 3 December Windebank fled London to evade being summoned before the Commons.[42] A purge was set in motion – but partly defensively.

John Adamson sees the membership of the Lords' newly-elected Committee of Privileges that December – the body responsible for nominating and investigating the principal targets of 'opposition' attacks on Royal misrule – as a cabal of the Warwick group, co-ordinating their judicial assault on 'Thorough'. Thus the assault on Strafford could be followed by further 'targeting'. He also argues that a relatively co-operative speech by Pym about the need to settle the King's finances provided that grievances were answered, and the delay in the legislative assault on the apparatus of 'Personal Rule' into the New Year of 1641, were a deliberate political strategy by the 'Puritan' peers and their MP allies, intended to give the King time to show his willingness to listen to his critics by appointing some of them to recently-vacated senior offices.[43] But behind the pressure lay the implicit threat of judicial prosecution for obstructors, particularly once the Lords 'committee for petitions' was in existence and Strafford was in custody – and some cases might well proceed even if the King gave way, thus precipitating further crisis. Could the hot-heads be reined in? The case of the Commons 'committee of twenty-four', set up on 10 November to look into the 'estate of the kingdom', was instructive, although a third of its members were future Royalists and so would probably try to block extreme votes. Warwick's ally Sir Harbottle Grimston's reference on 7 November to the execution of Richard II's Chief Justice Tresilian – beheaded by Parliament in 1387 for upholding the Royal prerogative against subjects' rights – implied that modern instruments of Royal tyranny should go the same way.[44] The effective 'lynch law' of the anti-Ricardian purge could thus be repeated, and the obvious target was ex-Lord Chief Justice, now Lord Keeper, Sir John Finch for his defence of 'Ship Money' in the Hampden case. The effect of this sort of threat would have been to intimidate the King's senior officials further.

But there was some sign of 'opposition' putting forward constructive suggestions of meeting the King's needs. Oliver St John, the opposition's chief legal spokesman now closing in on his ex-nemesis Finch, spoke in favour of settling the revenue on 14 December.[45] The King would thus be able to make up for his loss of 'Ship-Money' and other 'illegal' non-Parliamentary taxes, but only on Parliament's terms and explicitly by the latter's authority. This 'carrot', seconded by Pym, went in tandem with St John's use of the 'stick' against the government, in his 27 November speech

Reform, Retribution and Confrontation   169

against 'Ship Money' which he argued had to be declared illegal or there would be 'no use of Parliaments'. (He was followed on that occasion by Sir Simonds d'Ewes demanding a similar fate for tonnage and poundage.)[46] St John's 14 December speech included a motion to look into the future Royal revenues to make compensation for the banned 1630s measures, and was followed by a conciliatory intervention by Pym, asking (Treasurer of the Household and) MP Sir Henry Vane senior to convey the House's goodwill to the King and to ask his permission to look into the matter of his future revenues.[47] Vane was known to be sympathetic to a measure of reform[48] and could be a conduit to the King. The King duly gave the Commons permission to discuss his revenues (17 December).[49] Indeed, the Earl of Northumberland wrote to his brother-in-law Leicester (Sir Philip Sidney's nephew, a former ambassador to Vienna and Paris) that there was to be a general admission of these marginalised peers to office and Leicester should stake his claim; Bedford was supposed to be intended for the Lord Treasurership.[50] A similar story was reported by Northumberland's sister, Lady Carlisle,[51] a well-connected intriguer later to be claimed as Pym's mistress. Among recent historians' interpretations of this possible reconciliation, Brian Manning and Conrad Russell consider it plausible and a missed opportunity by the King.[52] The apparatus of Royal prerogative rule had been dismantled without resistance and the leading perpetrators of it arrested or forced to flee the country. It should be noted that on the day of Lady Carlisle's letter St John (who Bedford wanted to be made Solicitor-General, a key legal appointment) was abusing the excesses of past Royal prerogative judges, led by Finch, with ominous reminders of the 1387 prosecutions but his main choice for punishment, Finch, had just left the country.[53] There had not been such an exodus of terrified ministers since Parliament turned on Henry VI's ministers in 1450 – and Henry had later been deposed and murdered, as had recently-cited Chief Justice Tresilian's sovereign Richard II. The principle of banning 'abuses' and prosecuting the guilty need not lead to executions if the accused were out of harm's way – though Strafford was not. Trials thus might not wreck accommodation with the King. Could a generous Royal gesture of admission of Charles' leading critics to office have worked?

But this prospect, rumoured in December-January, did not come to fruition; the King evidently baulked at admitting the Scots' 'treasonous' allies to his favour. Instead, the assault on Royal prerogative powers and the judicial investigation of Laud and Strafford commenced. Adamson argues that the political strategy of demolishing the King's remaining non-Parliamentary powers of raising taxes, thus forcing him to rely from henceforward on meetings with his subjects to obtain funds, was primarily the work of Warwick and Bedford. They were the main leaders, and Bedford the principal theorist, of the peers involved in the abortive plan for a military rally in London in late summer 1640, and were now seeking to force the untrustworthy King into dependence on Parliament. This time, nothing would be left to chance; Royal legal powers would be strictly defined, sources of money subject to 'opposition' control, and dangerous ministers destroyed. Warwick's group would even take charge of the financial side of dealing with the Scots occupation. Unlike in 1629 and April 1640, the King would no longer be able to neutralise his critics by shutting down Parliament and finding his funds from elsewhere. Crucially, a bill to require regular Parliaments (the Triennial Bill) was first proposed by radical Devon MP William Strode on 24 December and was passed to a committee run by opposition MPs. When the Commons passed it on 16 January, it was taken to the Lords by Bedford's son-in-law George Digby;[54] and once it was passed by both Houses Bedford would lead the delegation taking it to the King. Parliament, crucially, would sit annually whether the King called it or not and if he did not summon it twelve peers would do so.[55] The intent, i.e. legislative coercion of an untrustable sovereign and avoidance of his vetos, anticipated the ideas of the 'Whigs' in the 'Exclusion Crisis'; but the leadership of the coercers by peers looked back to the late medieval factions of nobles who had coerced Richard II and Henry VI.

But it should also be noted that the torrent of county petitions in November–December 1640 against governmental abuses of power and Laudian religious 'innovation' did not lead to a mass of legislation to remedy this. The 1624 Parliament, which had also sat at a time of crisis and 'Papist' threat, impeaching a senior minister (Lord Treasurer Cranfield) and demanding war on the international Catholic menace with assorted peers (including Buckingham) encouraging client MPs, had passed thirty-eight public and thirty-five private bills in fifteen weeks; the 1640–1 Parliament only passed eight in six months.[56] The diversion of time and energy to prosecuting Strafford and the contentious nature of religious reform are not adequate excuses; the majority of MPs seem to have been prepared to see 'reform of abuses' on legal, constitutional, and financial matters and the demolition of the structure of 'prerogative rule'. Most notably, the issue of 'Ship-Money' was under investigation by a committee from December but the latter's leader St John – who had taken the dangerous step of defending Hampden in 1638 and was personally committed to reform – did not introduce a bill on it until 12 June. Instead, the various Commons committees proceeded to pile up the evidence of Royal and Laudian misdeeds more than was strictly needed as a basis for reform – most notably the committee for religious abuses, a.k.a. 'scandalous ministers', which advertised publicly for complaints against ministers across the nation (with the relevant handbills being printed by an ex-Artillery Company man, Henry Overton). There were possibly up to 900 religious petitions (all destroyed in the Westminster fire of 1834). The impression is that this Commons was as intent on compiling a massive collection of anti-governmental and anti-Laudian propaganda as on taking swift action. This in turn poses a problem for those who believe that a compromise could have been reached between King and 'opposition' in winter-spring 1641 with opponents admitted to office – the self-generating activity of these committees was a permanent irritation and insult to the ever-touchy King. Also, John Adamson points out that the often-overlooked House of Lords activity in winter 1640–1 saw their 'Committee for Petitions' (led by Warwick and including Essex, Saye and Sele, and Bedford) asserting legal dominance over not only the regular Common Law courts but over the King's prerogative courts, especially Star Chamber. Complainants thus brought their petitions to this militantly anti-prerogative body, and were assured of a warm welcome. This amounted to a potential legal coup against Royal power.

The danger arose of the Scots, whose commissioners were now in London watching the proceedings of Parliament with hope of co-ordinated coercion of the King, pressing their demands for a Presbyterian form of government on the English Church too in alliance with the most extreme MPs – which would lose the latter the necessary votes of the moderate majority of the Commons. To add to the Scots problem, the Commons had voted on 24 December to place the administration of the £30,000 allocated for relieving distress in occupied north-east England with the treaty commissioners, a body dominated by Warwick's group, not the usual Royal officials.[57] Could they be trusted to use the money properly? The motion was successfully proposed by young Devon 'hard-liner' William Strode's brother-in-law Sir Walter Earle, the main gentry 'Puritan' patron of central-eastern Dorset and later a senior Parliamentarian commander. One injudicious memorandum about future Presbyterian Church governance in England by the leading Scots delegate Alexander Henderson gave the game away and caused English 'moderate' alarm – but anti-Scots speakers in the Commons such as Gervase Holles (who called the Scots army 'vipers') were silenced. The 21 January debate saw an anti-Scots protest from the usually 'opposition' and 'pro-Pym' MP Sir Benjamin Rudyerd.[58]

At this stage, despite the provocative public welcome of 'martyrs' Burton and Prynne back to London (28 November), rowdy pro-'root and branch' demonstrations in London and impressive and insistent petitions, the radicals who wanted to abolish English episcopacy lacked the votes and had to conciliate the more cautious pro-episcopal MPs whose support was needed to punish the King's ministers. John Pym, the leading co-ordinator of the 'opposition' programme in the Commons, was too realistic to press this part of the programme this early, concentrating on compiling a massive dossier of 'Papist' misdeeds by Laudian clergy, abolishing the judicial apparatus of Church power, and prosecuting the leading exponents of Royal 'misrule' in 1629–40. Even the arrested Laud was informed unofficially by a well-connected MP on 21 January – the date of another rumour of immanent appointments of Bedford's group to the Council, by Leicester's protégé Sir John Temple – that his prosecutors would be satisfied with sacking him from the Council and the archbishopric. The conciliatory tone of the King's speech of 23 January – Church reform, and abandoning non-Parliamentary sources of taxation – suggests that he was playing along with this. His public support for reform had limits, however – he said in this speech that he was in favour of the 'reformation' of government but not the 'alteration', and that he would not tolerate curbs on his right to summon Parliament as he wished (i.e. the current form of the Triennial Bill).[59] The King's protests that allowing unknown local officials not him to call Parliaments impugned his honour was however reasonable and was calculated to win him sympathy, and despite the dismay of religious zealot Sir Simond D'Ewes at the King standing firm on religion[60] the speech was a sign of openness to negotiation. Next day the King's and Laud's opponent, Bishop Williams, was allowed to preach at Court, as another conciliatory gesture. As far as religion went, was using Williams a hint that 'reliable' Calvinist bishops could replace Laudians but the King would not have 'Root and Branch' abolition? But Pym's willingness to compromise on any matters was limited – he announced on 29 December that any taxes (and the customs) should only be collected once Parliament had approved them.[61] This implied that the King's current taxes should not be paid in until Parliament had 'cleared' their legality, and was effectively blackmail.

There was no unanimity of the religious reformers over episcopacy; arguably the King stood a chance of saving the institution from 'Root and Branch' if he could exploit this and show himself reasonable on secular matters, and his speech on 23 January showed that he was using this tactic. An important factor here was the acceptability of 'moderate', doctrinally ultra-Calvinist bishops to all but the most radical MPs. Could such men be accepted by the majority of MPs as returning the Church to 'safe' doctrines? John Williams was one such man, and Irish Archbishop James Ussher another. Ussher, who had stayed at Warwick's London house in 1640 and was a personal friend of his, was a 'safe' Calvinist and was in favour of retaining bishops subject to their being guided by the counsel of their clergy; and on 21 January Charles summoned him for a discussion on religious matters[62] Could he spearhead a compromise? During the third week of January Charles agreed to reform the Church to its condition under Queen Elizabeth, the alleged pre-'Arminian' 'golden age' of Calvinist theological dominance for 'Puritans' but one with a disciplinarian episcopate.[63] This was then backed up by Charles' conciliatory tone in his speech to Parliament on 23 January; and on the 18th St John was named Solicitor-General despite his recent attacks on prerogative judges. The ex-judge Sir Robert Heath, sacked from office in 1634 apparently on religious grounds and now a work-colleague of St John, was reinstated.

It should be noted that in the vital 8–9 February 'Root and Branch' debates Pym and St John, allegedly leading 'militants' in favour of radical reform, did not speak. The Commons had to consider whether to use the 'Root and Branch' London petition of 10 December or a more moderate ministers' 'Remonstrance' (presented and sponsored by Edmund Calamy), which spoke of retaining bishops, as a basis for discussions. Alleged 'ultra' radical Sir Harbottle Grimston was in favour of using either, and spoke about reforming not abolishing episcopacy; and future Royalist leaders Lord Falkland and Sir Ralph Hopton were both prepared to accept abolition if necessary. The first speaker, Sir Benjamin Rudyerd, a Royal office-holder (at the hated Court of Wards), advocated trimming the undesirable secular power and ceremonial of 'prelacy' but not destroying episcopacy which would lead to an entirely new and foreign Church, and pro-Royalist Lord Digby, who was also Bedford's son-in-law, desired 'reformation' but demanded immediate rejection of the ministers' petition.[64] There was no clear 'line-up' of 'radicals' from the 'Pym faction', enemies of episcopacy 'per se', against everyone else yet; Gardiner's estimation of this debate as delineating future Royalists and Parliamentarians was premature.[65] The chance of winning a majority of votes to retention of bishops was there.

Miscalculation or panic in the Strafford prosecution and trial. Did the 'opposition' press matters too far, or were they genuinely afraid of a counter-coup?

Charles was momentarily weak, unable to close down the meeting as in winter 1640–1 with the Scots militarily triumphant and needing Parliamentary funds to pay and enlarge his own demoralised army. His Catholic officers had largely fled their posts in fear of Parliamentary prosecution, as had Catholic ministers such as Windebank, though Strafford was presumably caught unawares by the quick vote for his impeachment – or arrogantly confident that he could handle it – as he did not refuse to come to or withdraw from London in time. Lord Keeper Finch and Secretary Windebank, who were more realistic and had the fate of Strafford to warn them of their critics' intentions, fled London as soon as legal proceedings began – so did Strafford's arrogance and lack of realism cost him his life, infuriate the King, and hence make the attempts to reach a compromise in late spring 1641 less likely to work? On Sunday 24 January the pro-'opposition' peer Lord Pembroke, as Steward of the Household, arranged for the Laudian victim Bishop Williams – welcomed back to freedom by the City crowds weeks earlier – to denounce any abolition of episcopacy in his Court sermon to the King.[66] The tone of the speech was presumably accepted by Calvinist and anti-Laudian 'martyr' Williams' political backers beforehand, and thus reassured the King about their attitude to 'Root and Branch'. The use of Royal 'bugbear' Williams, and his pro-episcopacy language, would indicate a tentative move towards backing a purged episcopacy on the part of both King and 'Warwick group'. The Williams sermon, a substantial indication of senior 'opposition' figures' moves towards moderation, was balanced by the anger roused in the Commons and Lords over the King reprieving condemned Catholic priest Father Goodman, which unfortunately leaked out on the day of the King's speech, 23 January, and so undid the latter's good work. The Earl of Pembroke's lawyer protégé John Glynne (later the Commonwealth's Chief Justice) argued tellingly that the King was using precisely that Royal prerogative which his subjects were now seeking to declare illegal, showing his true colours – and doing so for a Papist.[67] The Goodman case thus had a legal dimension as well as stirring up the inevitable anti-Catholic paranoia; the King's critics were not just religious fanatics who loathed Catholics. The Papal representative thought that the Goodman case, with its implications of Royal or Parliamentary judicial supremacy, was a crucial test. In response the King eventually summoned the Houses to an audience and publicly withdrew his reprieve of the priest, plus promising to order all priests and Jesuits exiled within a month – though not until the Lords had postponed Strafford's trial for a fortnight to let the accused prepare his papers, possibly as a *'quid pro quo'*.[68]

Appointing Bedford, Saye and Sele, Hertford, the Earl of Essex, and a few more 'opposition' figures to the Privy Council (19 February)[69] was symbolically useful and followed the King's public ratification of the now-passed Triennial Act on the 16th.[70] The 16th also saw the Commons presenting the King with their first financial present, the four 'subsidies' (amounting to some £240,000), which had been voted for on 23 December but had been ordered to be paid to their commissioners, not the Exchequer as usual. This ended their legal 'block' on funding the government since December. The tentative steps towards agreement extended to foreign policy, as the King now announced to the Lords (10 February) that the Dutch treaty negotiations begun in December were nearly complete, an offensive and defensive alliance would be made, and his daughter Princess Mary would marry Stadtholder Frederick Henry's son and heir William. This should be a major step towards the restoration of the Palatinate to the King's nephew Charles Louis.[71] The Court backers of this plan were Northumberland and Hamilton, and it explicitly reversed the spring 1640 plans for a Spanish alliance – though thanks to the Catalan and Portuguese rebellions Spain was no military or financial use to Charles anyway.

Notably, Warwick was not added to the Council until April, but Charles sought to allay his critics' fears by appointing an 'opposition' peer, Essex, as commander-in-chief to succeed Strafford. This was probably for his Continental military experience rather than his symbolic status as a friend of Charles' late brother Prince Henry and as a Royal 'victim' through his scandalous treatment by James I (who had virtually forced him to divorce Frances Howard to enable her to marry James' favourite Robert Carr with his alleged impotence being paraded in court). Essex had also been popular with the troops at York when he visited the army there in 1640, as an unimpeachable Protestant war-hero. The appointments to the Privy Council were unlikely to suffice in assuaging Charles' belligerent critics' fear of and desire to control his policies, though he may have hoped Essex could be 'bought off' more easily than Warwick or Bedford. In the meantime, the centrepiece of the 'rebel' peers' success – the Scots army on English soil – was still a target of Royal military hostility, with determined if probably over-hopeful plans for a counter-offensive by the Royal army at York (under Sir John Conyers) to attack Berwick or Leith that spring.[72]

The evidence of Hyde, a principal player in events for the next two-and-a-half decades, is crucial if written with hindsight. He named the leadership of the dominant 'opposition' faction in Parliament as of early 1641, already referred to as a 'junto' (the first use of that word, the Spanish for 'council') as six men. There were three peers – Bedford, Saye and Sele, and Mandeville – and three MPs – Pym, Hampden, and Oliver St John. In their full confidence were Nathaniel Fiennes, younger son of Saye and Sele, and the new Secretary of State Vane's son Sir Henry Vane. Dominating the Lords were Essex, Bedford, Saye and Sele, and Mandeville, supported by Broooke, Wharton, and Paget (all involved in the summer 1640 'plot' in London); dominating the Commons were Pym, Hampden, St John, Denzel Holles, and Nathaniel Fiennes. Allegedly Essex and Warwick were not fully in the confidence of Bedford and Saye and Sele about the latter's plans, nor were radicals like Strode in Pym's full confidence unlike St John and Fiennes.[73] Adamson sees Bedford – a 'projector', as seen in his Fenland drainage – as the key theorist, not least in the novel and revolutionary use of proposals to organise the future meeting of Parliaments whether the King summoned them or not; as early as late December 1640 the radical Devon MP William Strode was introducing a motion for an automatic annual summoning of Parliament. The leader of the legal assault on prerogative rule and the resultant illegalisation of all laws not created by the 'High Court' of Parliament, Oliver St John, was Bedford's cousin and confidant – though it is unclear which of the pair was the originator of this idea. St John had even been briefly sent to the Tower in 1629 for his seeking legal justification for Parliament's resistance, and was to be the 'opposition's legal expert.

Already, religion was the crucial issue of mutual incomprehension between Charles and the dissidents. He made it clear to the summoned Houses at the audience at Whitehall on 23 January that he would only return to the Elizabethan settlement of the Church – which implicitly admitted the allegations of his critics that there had been innovations – and surrender those tax-raising powers which had been found 'illegal or grievous to the public'. The two most objectionable bishops, Laud and Wren, were already in the Tower without Royal interference in the Houses' legal right to prosecute, but the King would not remove the bishops' right to vote in the Lords and the most he would do was to reverse any Episcopal over-stepping of their bounds into temporal power.[74] On 25 January he made it clear that he would not accept the large-scale petitions from London (allegedly signed by over 11,500 people) and eleven counties to abolish the bishops. But the popular campaign pressed on, with thirteen county petitions for 'Root and Branch' during 1641; the Commons debated the subject on 8 February (for eight hours with 60 speakers) and 9 February. This debate has often been seen (following S. R. Gardiner) as 'the' major indication of future Royalist or Parliamentarian allegiance, with those who spoke up for committing the petitions to a committee for consideration being in favour of action – i.e. abolishing the bishops, a sign of Parliamentary sympathies in 1642.[75] In fact, some future Royalists who favoured retaining bishops but were in favour of some measure of reform – e.g. Hopton and Falkland – spoke up for the 'consideration by committee' plan, as well as known Bedford allies like Digby doing so, and Digby did not want bishops abolished, only curtailing their power and revenues.[76] An episcopal system of carefully limited powers, supposedly returning to ancient precedent, was backed not only by moderate reformist

Rudyerd but even by radical Grimston.[77] This would suggest a concerted 'line-up' by moderates on both 'sides' in favour of reforming bishops but not abolishing them, rather than a 'Royalist vs Parliamentarian' split; and Adamson suggests that sending the proposals/the petitions to a committee (and the very busy 'committee of twenty-four' at that) was a measure to 'sit on' the contentious issue until a more propitious moment.[78] Most of this committee were not 'Root and Branch' supporters, though the radicals now hastily had their allies Fiennes and Sir Henry Vane junior added to the list. Was this a hopeful sign of moderates coming together and Pym being side-lined? The issue of large public demonstrations to accompany the arrival of 'Root and Branch' petitions at Westminster[79] could be used usefully to accuse the enthusiasts for radical reform of intimidation, however Nathaniel Fiennes (MP son of Lord Saye and Sele) defended them as showing that the impressive numbers of signatures were genuine and reminding the Commons of popular wishes.

A conciliatory initiative which failed? The case of St. John taking control of prosecutions.
A more risky appointment for the King was that of the lawyer who had attacked the lawfulness of 'Ship Money', Oliver St.John, as the new Solicitor-General. The latter, a key figure among the Commons leadership and a relative of Bedford, was the lynchpin and probably the originator of the systematic demolition of the legal apparatus of 'Personal Rule', namely prerogative powers – which entailed reversing over 30 years of legal decisions from the approval of 'impositions' in 1606 (Bates' Case). A younger son of a junior line of the aristocratic St. Johns (Lords Bletsho), educated at Cambridge and ironically tutored by King Charles' only 'Puritan' chaplain, John Preston, he was married into the prominent Essex 'Puritan' family of Barrington and was financially dependent on Bedford. He made the most detailed and well-argued Commons legal attack on the whole concept of 'prerogative' law on 14 January, citing the punishment of Richard II's judges for similar abuse of the subjects' rights in 1388 as a pattern to follow, and then launched the prosecution of his main target Finch. The King duly appointed a conciliatory figure, Sir Edward Littleton, as the new Lord Keeper; he was noted by Clarendon for his eagerness to satisfy the Commons[80] and (in return?) nobody mentioned his dubious past as the Solicitor-General who had backed 'Ship Money'

in 1637. 'Moderate' peer Northumberland's friend Sir John Bankes was made Lord Chief Justice of the Common Pleas on 19 January and at his arrival to take up office thanked his sponsors Northumberland and Bedford.[81] The prime mover in all this was probably Bedford given his interests in law and the constitution. Bedford presumably saw St.John as a dedicated 'reformer' who had proved his priorities by defending Hampden in the 'Ship-Money' controversy and would make the right legal decisions (and prosecute the right people, i.e. the prerogative judges and ministers guilty of 'illegal' exaggeration of royal powers). The go-between with the King was named as Hamilton, who was now moving towards the 'opposition' in an apparent 'quid pro quo' concerning his own safeguarding from prosecution.

If there was an attempt by the King to buy St. John off from backing further prosecutions it failed; through his office he could assist Pym's faction in organising the prosecution of Strafford, accused of abuse of power as Lord Deputy of Ireland and believed to have the power and the ruthlessness to use Catholic Irish troops against the King's critics in England, and the 'Ship-Money' judges. The King did not endeavour to refuse or interfere with the judicial proceedings, being in a weaker position than in 1626–8 when he had angrily countered Commons endeavours to prosecute the equally hated Buckingham. The likeliest explanation is that Charles had abandoned Strafford, who current rumours collected by Court poet William Davenant (19 January) said would have to fight his own way out of trouble as would Finch,[82] but he did not think the Earl would be executed due to the insubstantial nature of the evidence making conviction doubtful. Was Charles thinking of the way Cranfield had been thrown to the wolves and the late King had escaped unscathed in 1624?

However if so Charles' gamble failed. His grant of a key legal appointment crucial to the trial to an 'opposition' figure was a miscalculation, enabling the prosecution to proceed as the Earl's enemies planned rather than retaining a degree of control of the trial. Any reduction in the charges or arrangement for a pardon (or imposing banishment instead of execution) would have led to angry complaints in both Lords and Commons, but the King should have had the legal power to defy them. Evidently he was confident that the legal case would not stand up and could be satisfactorily managed, even with St.John, not a more neutral lawyer, in charge. The whole issue of allowing the 'opposition' control of the levers of legal prosecution in 1640–1 was such as to sap the will of Royal servants to resist the orders of Parliament, and to inhibit raising troops for the King early in 1642. It was probably inevitable given the numerical majority held by Charles' critics in the Commons, if not the Lords – they would have challenged any unacceptable appointments. Possibly Bedford insisted on it as his price for entering the Council – though it would have been more of a gain for the King to lure Warwick and Pym into office too. Charles showed no sign of the political need to encourage crucial figures such as St. John to work with and not against him, which – as with the 'opposition' peers – would have been evident had he showed more signs of personal favour to them and made symbolic grants of perquisites. Whether men such as St. John would have accepted his assurances without submission to their requirements (e.g. on 'Root and Branch') is more problematic.

Adamson argues that the lack of speeches by Pym's 'leadership' group in the debate on the London 'Root and Branch' petition on 8/9 February and the decision to refer the question to the 'Committee of the State of the Kingdom', dominated by men prepared to accept bishops, shows that the 'moderates' had the upper hand at this point. The 'quid pro quo' from the King's side for this compromise was clearly his consent to the Triennial Bill, granted in person on a visit to Parliament on 16 February – when he said that in return for yielding up 'one of the fairest flowers in his garland', he hoped they would not press him too hard on a second – i.e. religion. But his reluctance to do this much had been shown by a burst of rage on hearing that the Triennial Bill empowered twelve peers to summon Parliament if he did not (legal under the 1258 precedent used against Henry III, according to St.John), and he grumbled that Parliament 'had proceeded to the disjointing almost of all parts of his government'. He hoped that, like a watchmaker disassembling a watch, they would now put it back together.[83]

The question remains of whether a potential defusing of the religious crisis was apparent in Pym's inaction in the 8 February debate, and was sabotaged by the confrontation over Strafford. Or would confrontation have occurred anyway over another issue, most notably the continuing existence of a part-Catholic standing army in Ireland?

The Strafford trial

Strafford's meek surrender to be tried and tactics during his defence indicate that he – presumably by co-ordination with the King – intended to argue that he had not committed capital crimes. His defence was aimed at showing that his actions as a servant of the Royal prerogative were fully legal, thus defeating the attacks on Royal prerogative powers by pro-'opposition' jurists (who were following the arguments of James I's critic Sir Edward Coke). By a legal victory in court, he could blunt the legal basis of current attempts to curtail Royal powers. Charles and Strafford crucially miscalculated – for a start by surrendering the initiative. The appointment of a friendly lawyer as Solicitor-General would have blunted the 'opposition' attack, and if the official strategy was to allow the question of Strafford's supposed treason to be argued out reasonably in open court it was politically naïve. It did not allow for the fierceness and 'political' basis of his enemies' endeavours to destroy him as a means of intimidating Royal servants and preventing any repeat of the 'Personal Rule'. He and Charles clearly did not anticipate that Pym's group intended to have him executed rather than merely fined or imprisoned, a punishment more normal for the violent attacks on Royal 'favourites' by powerful factions of peers in the fourteenth and fifteenth centuries than recent trials. Executed Tudor ministers like Sir Thomas More (1535) and Thomas Cromwell (1540) had been victims of the Crown, not primarily of non-royal enemies; the last destruction of Royal ministers who still possessed the King's confidence had been in 1450. If Strafford had been more circumspect and less confident and had fled the country it would have led to fury in the Commons, self-righteous claims that this showed his contempt for the Law, and no doubt to a death-sentence 'in absentia'. But this could be reversed once the King had regained the political initiative; this outcome would not have poisoned relations between Charles – who abandoned Strafford to his enemies' vengeance and regretted it ever after – and the 'opposition'.

In the meantime Charles was giving way over issues such as the vote for a 'Triennial Bill' – making Parliament now a permanent part of the government to constrain him, though with no machinery for calling it if he refused to carry out his legal duty – and the steady demolition of his Church legal machinery and lay 'prerogative' courts. The constitutional demolition of Royal power was going according to plan in reversing the policies of the 1630s and their legal basis; and from now on Charles would need Parliament regularly in order to raise money. There would be no more long gaps between meetings when his subjects had no way of seeing that grievances were addressed – unless he could raise money from foreign allies. There are signs that he had not abandoned hope of being able to fight the Scots later in 1641 either, as the army stationed at York was kept in being and supplied with ammunition. Charles now sought to demonstrate a more 'Protestant' foreign policy than he had in the late 1630s. The arrival of a high-powered Spanish delegation to negotiate a military alliance in Spring 1640 had been a bonus to his critics, though the outbreak of revolt in Catalonia (followed by Portugal) had reduced Spanish effectiveness as an ally. He had seemed to abandon the popular Protestant cause of his nephew Charles Louis after initially considering an alliance with France and the German Protestants to restore him to the Palatinate by force, though reality had been more complicated. Hoping that evidence of his goodwill would induce the Spanish to persuade the Emperor to restore the Palatinate voluntarily was optimistic, though the existence of a strong English fleet (due to 'Ship-Money') added to his attractiveness as an ally – and the Scots revolt proved him to be militarily weak and thus diplomatically unattractive. Now he reverted to a Protestant orientation, betrothing his daughter Mary (intended for a Spanish prince in 1639–40) to the son of the Prince of Orange, the Dutch 'Stadtholder'. The Dutch had been England's long-term ally against Spain from 1584. Charles duly played up the usefulness of this alliance, telling the Lords on 10 February that it might regain the Palatinate,[84] and it ended the chance of Dutch Calvinists assisting their Scots co-religionists. In the long term, the treaty could enable foreign – Protestant – troops to be hired to attack the Scots now that the English nobility had proved unreliable. The Dutch troops would be Calvinist in religion, so more acceptable to English local levies than the Catholic officers who had been lynched in 1640 or the much-feared Catholic Irish loyalists who could be used instead.

Strafford had been granted one delay of a fortnight in the trial to enable him to prepare his case, supported by Bedford who throughout seems to have been less keen on revenge than Warwick. The ever-vigilant Clotworthy, either aware of or exaggerating Strafford's belligerent plans in prison, was now alleging that the Irish army was to be brought over to England to link up with the Catholic tenants of the greatest feudal magnate in south Wales, the Marquis of Worcester, at Raglan Castle.[85] Clotworthy had his own personal ends in mind, as Lord Holland was said to have offered him a senior post in the Irish Army if he succeeded Strafford as Lord Lieutenant and he duly petitioned the King for Holland's appointment.[86] A further, shorter delay was granted so Strafford could send to Ireland for more papers and one spectator (Daniel O'Neill) heard that the Lords would duly acquit him,[87] but the Scots treaty-commissioners now in London made an uncompromising request for his swift trial and execution, citing the Israelites' punishment of the Amalekites.[88] The latter was to become a favourite aphorism of Cromwell and other 'hard-liners' – God had abandoned King Saul because he had pardoned not killed the sinful. The threat posed by their army added to their political weight, and they were possibly prompted by 'die-hard' English politicians like Warwick and Pym. Indeed the 'opposition' peers, some of them now on the Privy Council as of mid-February (led by Bedford), were reported to be quarrelling over who should have the Lord Lieutenancy of Ireland after Strafford – Northumberland led one group favouring his brother-in-law, the Earl of Leicester, and Warwick preferred his own brother Holland.[89] Holland, significantly, had organised the public printing of the Scots' proposals to punish Strafford, a blatant bid for popular support for execution by alerted Londoners which tactic was to lead to rowdy demonstrations during the trial. The tactic infuriated the King, and diminished the chances of him granting the Lord Lieutenancy to Holland – or of any 'pay-off' to his brother, Warwick.

Pym now moved that the committee considering charges against Laud make its report, and on 24 February the Archbishop was indicted for treason, Pym delivering the Commons' articles to the Lords where Warwick proposed their adoption.[90] The 'opposition' could unite against this target if not against Strafford. But even as Strafford's impeachment opened with the first hearing on the 24th, his acquittal remained possible despite the anti-Royal action of Bishop Williams, Laud's leading critic among the episcopate. He persuaded the bishops to withdraw from voting on this capital case in the Lords – thus denying Strafford crucial votes for an acquittal. But was the treason-charge watertight? The case against Strafford for treasonable actions in England depended on Article 23, namely his alleged statement in Council in 1640 that the King should use his Irish army in England, and this rested for proof on the words of Secretary of State Sir Henry Vane (father of a junior 'opposition' MP) and his son's written reconstruction of his father's notes on the Council proceedings. This was not strong enough legally for conviction, and Strafford's strong defence of his activities and mocking of his opponents' claims on the 24th showed them up. The King attended the hearing, raised his hat as Strafford entered the Lords, and openly declared his disbelief of the charges; and Strafford launched a counter-accusation against Vane for misleading the Commons about the King's intentions and 'vice versa' in April 1640, leading to the dissolution of the 'Short Parliament'.[91] This would not move implacable opponents like Warwick and Pym, but it might win over waverers.

The use of the 'Scots Army weapon' to back execution was also counter-productive, as national patriotic opinion might rise against the arrogant proceedings of a foreign army on English soil. Most immediately the Scots Army had to be paid another £25,000 to stop them starting to take free quarter from the occupied northern counties or advancing Southwards, and Warwick made an emergency appeal to Parliament for this on 6 March; Vane assisted in taking the money to them.[92] The 'opposition'-Scots link was a valuable propaganda weapon for the King and could sway votes in both Houses, if activated at the right time. For the moment, the fact that money was paid first to the Scots Army not the English Army served to embolden anti-Parliamentary feeling in the latter, with a petition organised among the officers (some of them MPs) in early-mid March threatening action if the Irish army was disbanded before the Scots left England, if the bishops were abolished, or if the King's revenues were not returned (from Warwick's commissioners) to him.[93] The main organiser was Sir Henry Percy, captain of the King's Bodyguard, aided by Sussex landowner and Royal aide John Ashburnham (who was to remain in Charles' service until the flight to the Isle of Wight in November 1647). Ashburnham sought to win over the Earl of Essex by suggesting inviting him to take over as commander-in-chief.

The first rumblings also emerged of a separate, more dangerous plot for action in London by officers now at Court, led by the Queen's 'Master of the Horse' Henry Jermyn – the 'Army Plot' which was to inflame proceedings later that spring. Percy duly visited Court to consult wth Charles, and this evidence of a useful 'loyalist' backlash would encourage

Charles to hold out on more concessions. The army could indeed aid Charles physically, and plans were made – and allowed to leak out – for them to march South to London if Strafford was either convicted and sentenced to death or acquitted and kept in custody. Colonel George Goring, the belligerent governor of Portsmouth, was to become second-in-command of the army in York, with the loyal Earl of Newcastle (greatest magnate in the north-east midlands) as his superior[94] – two men who would never back Parliament against Charles, unlike the Army's 1640 commander Northumberland would. The fact that Goring openly informed Warwick's half-brother Lord Newport of the plan shows that he had had 'the nod' from superiors at Court and that the 'opposition' were being warned not to press the King too hard.

The case against Strafford was far from clear legally, quite apart from the danger of a majority of peers resenting a blatant attempt to coerce the unwilling King to execute him. The proceedings on it, from 22 March, proving this as the usual drama of a 'show trial' was carried out in the public arena of Westminster Hall. The procedure of an impeachment was for the Commons to lay formal charges, and the Lords then to try and to judge; but the previous such trials had all had 'hidden hands' behind them quite apart from the MPs who launched the process – back in 1386 and 1449–50 the impeachments against the favourite ministers of Richard II and Henry VI, Michael and William de la Pole (grandfather and grandson), had been started by the Commons but backed by assorted peers. As in 1641, the intention of the latter had been to forcibly remove a powerful rival who the King would not sack. In 1621 and 1624, rivals had moved thus against Bacon and Cranfield, using allegations of fiscal corruption but for a political purpose. The possibility was open that the prosecution, again launched by a political faction not by men within the government, would be amenable to calling off the worst charges if they were admitted to senior office. The lawyer Bulstrode Whitelocke, now deputy counsel for the impeachers and later a senior Cromwellian in the 1650s, considered this possible; Sir Thomas Woodhouse considered that the prosecutors would be satisfied with the senior State offices for themselves, junior ones for their allied MPs, the King's reduction to a figurehead, and Strafford's debarring from office.[95] But Essex was apparently determined to have Strafford permanently ruined and probably executed, as were Warwick and Brooke.[96]

Alternatively the case could collapse; the possibility of Strafford or his backers outwitting the prosecution was aided by the unusual staging of the impeachment in Westminster Hall (more usual for State judicial trials than for a procedure which was technically a Parliamentary trial by the Lords). The public were admitted, with plenty of space left in the Hall for them – though they were more likely to be against than in favour of 'Black Tom Tyrant' the agent of 'Popery'. Significantly, no arrangement was made for the King – unprecedently a partisan of the accused – to sit on his throne; he had to make do with a private 'box' like an ordinary well-to-do citizen. On legal grounds, the multiplicity of (28) charges hid the fact that not one of the instances of alleged misgovernment and tyranny was definitively treasonous in the sense of levying war against the King and Kingdom. Apart from the alleged intention to bring in the Irish army to use in England, which relied on Vane's word and a subsequent written summary of a Council meeting, the worst charge was that Strafford had used the Irish army to enforce Irish Privy Council decisions, thus waging 'war' on one of the King's realms. The case was clearly 'political', and for once not presented by the undoubted authority of the Head of Government or by a coherent body of senior figures controlling political power; the most recent cases of impeachment, against Bacon (1621) and Cranfield (1624), had been launched by the will or connivance of the dominant Duke of Buckingham with the King's acquiescence. Political trials for treason were usually spearheaded by the Attorney-General or his deputy. Would an impeachment explicitly not backed by the Sovereign have the same success as the usual legal procedures which the government backed? From 5 April the 'opposition' case switched tactics from a cumulative account of Strafford's misdeeds in Ireland. Bulstrode Whitelocke (formerly junior counsel to St John in the 'Ship-Money' case) and Sir Walter Erle presented the charge that Strafford had intended to use the Irish army to wage war in England, and Vane delivered his memories of the crucial Council meeting. However, the unnamed 'kingdom' which Vane said Strafford had offered to reduce with the Irish army could have been Scotland, not England – and his backers argued this version of events. The prosecution resorted (8 April) to using Earle, untrained in court but expert on Irish affairs, to produce evidence that Strafford's commission in command of the Irish army had empowered him to use it in England. Strafford, however, could show that that was standard procedure for military warrants, and the wording was the same in the Earle of Northumberland's commission of command in 1640.[97] The attack was blunted, and disaster followed their attempt to land a crushing blow for conviction on 10 April. As 'opposition' counsel Sir John Glynne tried to seek permission to introduce damning 'new' evidence (the notes of the Council meeting made by Vane's son) Strafford countered with a request to produce more evidence also. The Lords voted to allow this despite protests from the Warwick group, showing a clear willingness to be fair to the accused. Uproar resulted amidst clear Royal appreciation of the prosecution's embarrassment by the watching King.[98] The trial was adjourned, and the prosecution contemplated the drastic solution of reverting to conviction by attainder – an easier process for them legally, but at risk of alienating votes in the jury (the Lords) by its curtailment of defence rights.

As the case stood on 10 April, it looked as Strafford would be acquitted – although it was also possible that if he was convicted he would escape with his life. Impeachment more usually ended with fines or imprisonment than execution, and this would neutralise the supposed mastermind of 'Thorough' but avoid enraging the King by execution. It seems that this compromise – conviction but not a capital sentence – was favoured by Bedford, who was still rumoured to be lined up for the Lord Treasurership. The Commons hastily returned from Westminster Hall to their chamber, locked the doors, and considered what to do. Now Pym introduced a 'Bill of Attainder' in the Commons, a draft proposal having been produced by his ally Sir Arthur Haselrig casually from his pocket during a debate after the idea had been raised by Sir Philip Stapleton (a leading Presbyterian MP through the 1640s).[99] The precise details of who said what in what order is unclear, but the identity of the idea's proposers shows the influence of the Warwick group. Haselrig, brother-in-law of the 'Puritan' peer and Warwick ally Lord Brooke, was presumably acting for the more determined members of that group – who were sidelining Bedford. Their seeming vindictiveness did have a serious political 'point', as allowing Strafford to escape with his life (if not his offices) ran the risk of him using his Irish army clients in co-ordination with the Jermyn-Goring 'Army Plotters' in England. Contrarily, the non-disclosure of the vital evidence of Vane senior's account of Strafford's boast to the Privy Council about using the Irish army in England earlier by Pym has been suggested by Adamson as implying that he – and Bedford – did not want to press matters to the point of execution until the problems of 10 April occurred, and so avoided using this evidence until they had to do so.[100]

A conviction by attainder would only require proof that Strafford's death was necessary for the good of the state, not legal proof assessed by judges, and securing it was a matter of the right number of votes. It would counter Strafford's clever legal defence of his case, and make a death-sentence mandatory if carried. Being mandatory, the King could not revoke it without an uproar; it closed off the option of pardon which lay with any sentence passed for a 'normal' conviction. As Strafford was seen as the lynch-pin of attempts to bring in military force to coerce Parliament, his elimination could be plausibly presented as essential. Clearly the idea of an attainder, usually used by Tudor sovereigns to destroy their political enemies without need for full judicial proof, had been thought out beforehand to prevent acquittal or a non-capital sentence, and was a sign of a rift among the 'opposition'. The proposal was probably a measure by Warwick and Brooke to prevent an agreement between their more moderate allies, such as Bedford, and the King which left Strafford alive to coerce Parliament later. Killing Strafford should also embitter the King to the point where he would not offer office to any of the 'opposition'; thus Bedford and anyone else interested in a political accommodation that left the Church intact would be disappointed. Was the 'attainder' strategy aimed by the backers of a Calvinist reform of the Church at preserving the unity of the King's enemies, by keeping all of them out of office, as well as preventing Strafford rallying troops for his master later? Did it show Warwick as prepared to alienate or politically undermine his ally Bedford? A charitable explanation would be that Warwick thought Strafford too dangerous to live and Bedford too naïve about him; an uncharitable one that Warwick was sabotaging compromise over the retention of bishops. In 17th-century terms, it had an important psychological 'turning-point' in forcibly constraining the King.

It is evident that Warwick and Brooke – unlike the more humane and conciliatory Bedford – were prepared to risk alienating the King over the execution of Strafford, confident that they could coerce him at need. Their apparent belief that Charles could not be trusted to keep to any agreement was an accurate reading of his character, as he was to show himself equally

Reform, Retribution and Confrontation 189

unreliable in far more desperate circumstances in 1647–8, and removing Strafford permanently duly weakened Charles' ability to fight back. His stated support for episcopacy was one matter on which they could never agree. But if that was their strategy it argues that any putative political alliance between King and peers in summer 1641, centred on Bedford still being alive and taking office, would have been highly problematic. If they had not been constraining him over this issue, would they have expressed this distrust in some other way – e.g. insisting that their allies, the Scots Army, remained in England until they had carried through all their politico-religious programme? Logically, the Scots could refuse to accept any treaty until the English abolished bishops.

The peers' strategy had its problems, given that the unusual expedient of executing a recalcitrant minister would give him support. The vote in the Lords was particularly problematic, given the fear of many peers about the wisdom of sacrificing a Royal minister to an unprecedented and legally dubious attack, and Strafford's defence on 13 April judiciously based his appeal on the requirements of the law, the need for balance between Royal and subjects' rights, and the malice and inaccuracy of the charges. He pointed out that two pro-'opposition' peers present at the vital Council meeting of 5 May 1640, Northumberland and Holland, had said that the Irish army was intended to be used in Scotland. The prosecution 'team', perhaps on the 'moderates' request not to antagonise Charles, politely maintained the line that Charles too had probably intended it for Scotland.[101] Glynne, temporising, said the King probably meant it for Scotland but Strafford for England.[102]

The Bill of Attainder's consideration by the Commons had been put off until their next session rather than being rushed through, without any attempt to speed it up by the Pym-Haselrig zealots. Apparently the impeachment option was still being considered seriously by these men, as Hampden and then Pym now argued that abandoning it would dishonour the House (16 April).[103] A poor speech by Pym at the trial on the 13th may indicate loss of nerve, and the Commons could only agree that Strafford had intended to 'subvert the ancient and fundamental laws of these realms and to introduce an arbitrary and tyrannical government, against law' without defining which law had been broken and if this was treason.[104] Possibly Bedford was working behind the scenes to keep open the way to letting the King pardon Strafford or mitigate the sentence, impossible in an attainder case. The use of attainder would require a decisive legal case that Strafford's actions amounted to treason, which the Commons seemed confused about. St John now put forward a motion that the accused's intended use of the Irish army in England amounted to treason; it had to be withdrawn on its first 'outing' (17 April) but had much better success two days later. It passed the Commons with a vote of around four to one in favour on the afternoon of the 19th.[105]

Was this the 'tipping-point' to the showdown over Strafford's execution and the resultant damage to relations between the King and the Warwick-Bedford group? Evidently the mood of the Commons had changed, tilting opinion against impeachment (with its possibility of pardon) towards attainder (which would tie down and alienate the King). The key factor may have been the King's orders to all army officers (including MPs) to return to their commands, issued on the weekend of the 17th–18th. April. Adamson believes that this re-inflamed fears of the possible march on London by the Army at York, believed to be intended as a 'link-up' with the Jermyn 'Army Plotters' in London.[106] This was coupled with the news of the arrival in England of the fiancé of Princess Mary, Prince William of the Dutch United Provinces (son of Stadtholder Frederick Henry), with his entourage – and possibly with large funds for the King.[107] Could this dowry be used to fund an army march on London? As the concerned MPs saw it, a military occupation of London could back up the forcible dissolution of Parliament to save Strafford. This may have caused panic among MPs and a desire to execute Strafford so he could not be released and take over the army (and money) to confront them.

The Commons' speedy proceedings with the Bill of Attainder led to fears of a Royal riposte. When their Scots ally Archibald Johnston of Warriston called on Charles on 21 April (at Hamilton's suggestion) he reported the King to be looking uneasy – or shifty – with some 'project' being considered. This was possibly a Parliamentary adjournment for a fortnight on the excuse of the forthcoming Mary-William wedding, with dissolution to follow.[108] The delay caused by the wedding would allow time to bring troops into London to stop resistance when Strafford's attainder was halted. Accordingly, it would seem logical that the speed with which the 'opposition' proceeded with the attainder was as much defensive – hastening to complete proceedings before Charles was ready to react – than vindictive. Later on the 21st, a crowd of Londoners led by part of the Trained Bands marched into Westminster to present and noisily support a petition for Strafford's execution; Johnston of Warriston, one of the Scots commissioners, had heard that it was collected by the City authorities at the request of Parliament to block the approaches to their meeting-place against an expected Royal attempt to dissolve it. D'Ewes estimated its size at around 10,000; the principal spokesman as the crowd delivered a petition for Stafford's execution was the Artillery Company's Captain Sergeant-Major, John Venn.[109] The assembly can be presented as being 'defensive' as much as intimidatory; a large crowd would physically prevent the King from proceeding from Whitehall to Westminster to dissolve Parliament (by land anyway; he could go by barge). The petition referred to fears of 'dangerous matters in hatching', not to Strafford's past crimes.[110] But the usefulness of the crowds, who were to return regularly throughout the final days of proceedings, was also apparent in intimidating MPs and peers into voting for execution. A parallel exists with Danton's use of the Paris crowds to intimidate the jurors at Louis XVI's trial in 1792–3 or the Iranian revolution's 'hard-liners' use of the Tehran crowds to intimidate the Majlis at the impeachment of President Bani Sadr in 1981.

204 MPs duly voted for the attainder late on 21 April and only 59 against, though many seem to have been absent – either in protest against the intimidation or, as with Charles I's judges in 1649, out of fear of later Royal revenge. The Earl of Bristol's son George Digby, allied to the 'opposition', bravely spoke up against the attainder and was denounced by Pym and Strode, and Hampden failed to vote for it. Around 50 MPs walked out before the vote.[111] The Bill now proceeded to the Lords, and had an uneasy reception from those concerned for justice for the accused. Two leading Royal noble critics, the Earls of Bristol and Bedford, were opposed to the death-sentence more than they were to Strafford. The expected Royal grant of the Lord Lieutenancy of Ireland to Essex, a keen backer of Strafford's execution, and the actual grants of the Lord Generalship North of the Trent to Holland and (25 April) a Council seat to Warwick were evidently intended to buy them off. Essex appears to have believed that the King should be legally obliged to obey Parliament's instructions, which Adamson attributes to his enthusiasm for the system of government in the United Provinces where he had fought.[112] Notably, the Commons 'leadership' allowed Strafford's ex-client Sir Thomas

Widdrington and Denzel Holles, who opposed execution, to join Pym and Strode in representing the House at conferences with the Lords about the bill – a sign of Pym being keen to steer the result away from execution, at Bedford's request? On the 25th Bedford met Hyde on the Whitehall bowling-green and told him that the King, who he had just seen, was prepared to accept Strafford being banished or imprisoned for life.[113] A vote for conviction could still lead to exile rather than execution, which Charles had been brought round to accept – but it relied on the Lords majority co-operating with Charles and was less safe than acquittal. Arguably, given the radical nature of the proposed remedy for Strafford's crimes – execution – and the blatantly political nature of the prosecution, unease in the Lords could have translated into a majority of votes for acquittal and in the crucial debates every speech was vital. The role of the respected and 'moderate' Lord Falkland, a future Royalist, in speaking against Strafford and arguing that the case did not require precise legal proof was likely to have swayed some uncertain peers.

Crucially, the supporters of execution were unexpectedly and vehemently backed on the 29th by St John. His legal opinion would carry weight, as he was the lawyer who had heroically defended Hampden over Ship-Money; probably he was so alarmed at the rumours that an acquitted Strafford would lead a military coup that he judged his execution politically essential. He argued that it was necessary to kill Strafford just as it was never counted cruelty to 'knock foxes and wolves on the head', the ex-minister thus being equivalent to a dangerous and uncontrollable predator. Equally significantly, he argued that the phrase 'levying war against the King' did not mean against the 'mere person' of the King but against the Commonwealth, which the King personified – the implications of which new interpretation were to be shown when Charles himself was charged with the same offence in 1649. Subverting the laws, in St. John's opinion, was equivalent to waging war on the King and was thus treasonous.[114] One constitutional innovation of the 'British Revolution' was thus present in the thinking of a crucial 'Parliamentary' figure – Cromwell's cousin and at this point political senior – as early as 1641. It was already implicit in his arguments in Hampden's defence in 1637 that the accused's alleged offences could only be proven if they were against the State, i.e. Parliament which had not then been sitting, rather than against the King.

The political atmosphere now worsened. Could Bedford have carried Warwick or Pym with him? St John's speech on the 29th showed that Bedford could not carry the new Solicitor-General, his own protégé, with him. To make matters worse, an evidently annoyed Charles addressed Parliament in person on 1 May to warn them that in such matters of conscience as Strafford's proposed execution 'neither fear nor respect whatsoever shall make me go against it'. He did not think Strafford fit for any employment in future, even as a parish constable, but he would not disband the Irish Army – and thus reassure those who feared its intervention – until all the armies in his kingdoms, i.e the Scots too, could be disbanded together.[115] This stimulated rather than intimidated resistance to sparing Strafford, showing Charles at his most arrogant and inflexible and adding to the Warwick-Pym group's arguments that he could not be trusted – what if he re-employed an exiled Strafford? The last 'tyrannical' Royal minister to be forcibly exiled (by impeachment) by an insurgent Parliament, the Duke of Suffolk in January 1450, had been a similar threat – and had been intercepted *en route* to exile by pro-'opposition' vigilantes and executed to make sure he could not return to power. To add to the disarray of the 'moderates', at this point (the beginning of May) Bedford was taken ill with what would turn out to be a fatal bout of smallpox, thus removing him from the 'opposition's counsels. At this point, he was trying unsuccessfully to persuade Essex to agree to support keeping Strafford alive, via an approach by moderates Hertford and Hyde,[116] and someone had persuaded Charles to accept Warwick on the Privy Council (25 April). The fact that neither Essex nor Warwick budged an inch on killing Strafford would argue that Bedford's attempt to mediate was doomed, even had he not fallen ill.

The 'Army Plot' and attempt to rescue Strafford – a Royal counter-attack goes awry.

At this crucial juncture the rumours of a plot in the army to seize the Tower and turn on Parliament broke. The apparent plan was for a force of around 100 men recruited by the rakish courtier poet Sir John Suckling, allegedly intended for service with the Portuguese rebellion against Spain, to be admitted to the Tower, overcome any resistance, and secure Strafford's person to facilitate an escape. What the peers decided in their vote about his sentence would thus be irrelevant, the Tower guns would overawe the City, and either then or when the York troops arrived in London Charles would dissolve Parliament. It is unclear what Charles knew about this plan or if he gave specific orders, though the proposed commander of the Suckling 'infiltrators', Captain William Billingsley, was at the Royal apartments in Whitehall on 1 May. An ex-page of Strafford's and formerly his land-agent in Ireland, Billingsley apparently believed that he had Royal sanction to seize the Tower on 2 May.[117] Suckling's motive appears to have been loyalist indignation at the affronts that the disloyal and power-hungry Warwick group were forcing on the King; this young Court officer, son of a senior Household official, was a veteran of the Swedish army and had fought at Newburn. Jermyn, the Queen's senior adviser, was probably the Court co-ordinator; the King received and had thus requested a complete Ordnance Office listing of all his ammunition available in strategic places (including the Tower).[118]

On Sunday 2 May Suckling assembled his men at a tavern near St Paul's while public attention was distracted by the State entry of the Dutch Prince William, en route to his wedding to Princess Mary – but not enough men showed up for him to proceed to the Tower as planned. He lost his nerve and postponed the infiltration until next day, and that evening rumours seeped out and a large crowd of Londoners – possibly co-ordinated by the militant Alderman Pennington – assembled on Tower Hill to block any movement on the Tower.[119] The coup had to be postponed indefinitely, and the chance of physically rescuing Strafford and making the vote irrelevant passed. The London crowds' action is parallel with their move on the Bastille in Paris in July 1789, physically massing in defence of the threatened legislature and to threaten the monarch's expected coup.

Had enough men turned up at the tavern and Billingsley taken them to the Tower in time as planned, it is probable that they would have had little if any resistance – Governor Balfour had apparently been ordered (verbally by the King?) to admit them.[120] The implicit defiance of the will of Parliament would have probably rallied indignant MPs to the Pym faction, as the attempted seizure of the 'Five Members' was to do in January 1642, though most peers were more likely to have accepted that Charles had had to act to save his 'honour' in rescuing a loyal minister from execution. The probability must be in favour of a resultant dissolution of

Parliament, possibly with angry demonstrations in Whitehall which the small number of Royal guards would have had difficulty containing until York troops arrived. As it was, the City was alerted and on Monday 3 May crowds turned up at Westminster too to lobby and 'protect' Parliament. Seizing the initiative, the 'opposition' peers secured a Lords vote that Lord Newport, Warwick's half-brother and Master of the Ordnance, should take control of the Tower from Balfour – which he had some excuse to do, as the official in charge of the King's ammunition, but not without Royal orders. The King's permission was not asked; and Charles was for once too disheartened by the reverse to object to this blatant usurpation of his privileges. A delegation of peers (including the militant Brooke) proceeded to the Tower to question Balfour about the plot, scaring him out of any further dalliance with Parliament's enemies, and Holland, Essex, and Hamilton proceeded to Whitehall to question the King (who denied all knowledge).[121] This crisis seems to have persuaded the notoriously fickle Hamilton either that Charles was untrustworthy or that he was politically doomed; soon Hamilton was acing as the Warwick group's liaison with Argyll in Scotland. During the afternoon the peers sent Pembroke out to reassure the angry demonstrators that justice would be done on Strafford shortly, a blatant act of courting popularity and pressurising the beleaguered peers resisting execution to vote for it or face the people's wrath. The King was furious and was soon to sack Pembroke as Lord Chamberlain,[122] alienating another potential mediator who ended up a Parliamentarian in 1642. In an act of illegal assertion of power, the Lords voted to send Essex and Brooke – who had no legal office excusing their presence – to help Newport guard the Tower with a force from the reliable Tower Hamlets Trained Bands.[123] The fact that the Lords were prepared to usurp Royal powers testifies to their panic, no doubt encouraged by Warwick and Essex.

By the time that the Lords had to vote there were angry and alarmed Londoners available en masse to intimidate them, an unexpected but clearly exploited bonus for the Warwick group. Pym told the Commons on 3 May that he was sure there was 'a great design in hand by the Papists to subvert the Kingdom,[124] thus linking the defeat of the plot with other 'miraculous deliverances' like the Gunpowder Plot and branding Strafford with Guy Fawkes and Philip II of Spain as a villainous Catholic agent. Proposing a motion of thanks for deliverance from the plot on 4

May, Warwick's ally Lord Stamford (a future Parliamentarian general) specifically mentioned the 'Gunpowder Treason' as their precedent.[125] In practical political terms, the effective seizure of vital powers from the King saw both Houses voting that this Parliament could not be dissolved without its own consent (6 May) and the Lords deciding that, as St John maintained, it could decide what constituted treason.[126] This meant that Strafford's crimes did not have to be fitted into the existing legal definition of what had constituted treason in the past; the Lords could vote that his meddling with the Irish army to invade England constituted treason without having to find an exact precedent. In another blatant act of constitutional defiance, a delegation of Lords (led by Warwick) required the King to accept their choice – of Essex – as the new Lord Lieutenant of Yorkshire, replacing Strafford, instead of the Royal candidate, the less militant Lord Savile.[127] Strafford was duly convicted by the Lords by 51 votes to 9 on Friday 7 May – the numbers present, down from c.80 to 60 in days, is significant evidence of fear of both the crowds and of the King's fury.[128] On the 8th a joint delegation of Lords and Commons duly carried the verdict to Whitehall to present the King with two equally unpalatable bills, one for Strafford's execution and one for Parliament to be allowed to dissolve only with its own consent.[129] The despatch of a delegation of 'hard-liners', including Clotworthy and Lord Mandeville, to take over the command of the crucial port at Portsmouth[130] shows that the 'opposition' intended to make sure that the 'Papist' Queen did not invite any French troops to land to help her husband defy them.

Moreover, the Warwick group had now apparently decided to implement a plan laid out earlier for creating a legal/administrative basis for an 'emergency government' of their own (in modern terminology) should Strafford escape or be released and head off to York to collect the army. This was an updating of the Elizabethan 'Bond of Association', the oath of 1584 whereby the political elite and their supporters pledged to carry on the government and assume Royal powers should Queen Elizabeth be assassinated by evil 'Papists'. In either case the absence of a monarch would lead to the Privy Councillors and Parliament assuming power and taking an oath of allegiance to the new government – but in this case the King would still be alive, only untrustworthy. As Strode claimed in putting the plan and its oath to the Commons, 'the King understandeth not what treason is'; in other words, he was incompetent and his powers could be usurped for the nation's safety. The proposal was backed by 'usual suspects' Sir Thomas Barrington, Sir Philip Stapleton (a leading Presbyterian MP into 1647), and Clotworthy, plus Oliver Cromwell and future republican Henry Marten. A committee dominated by the radicals was set up to form and administer this oath, to 'defend church and commonwealth'. All the MPs present now swore to it in a hurried session the same day, presumably to give legal justification to resisting any dissolution.[131] Was this the English equivalent of the French Revolution's 'Tennis Court Oath', the first explicit legal defiance of their King? It had an Elizabethan precedent, but this time the monarch was implicitly the villain, not the symbol of unity.

The attainder bill was accompanied up Whitehall to the Palace on 6 May by a large and menacing crowd, thus placing the King under audible pressure to sign it from his subjects – as no doubt intended by its sponsors.[132] Among the bishops he consulted, Williams apparently advised sacrificing Strafford[133] – which possibly led to greater Royal hostility to him in the crucial coming months, as the King felt guilt for giving in to the demands. The Queen apparently considered fleeing to Portsmouth, and decided against it as there was a risk of pro-'opposition' militiamen arresting her en route.[134] Warwick assured the Lords that he had asked Northumberland (Lord Admiral) to check that all the Navy's ships were in the hands of 'religious', i.e. reliable officers, and the King apparently intercepted a letter from the Earl of Essex asking Alexander Leslie to send fifty Scots officers to London.[135] Essex had told the Commons on 22 April that in the event of a confrontation they had enough men, but not good officers.[136] Charitably, this might be put down to fear of a coup by the King and the Army officers in York, aided by rash courtiers and the French; uncharitably to a desire to use the crisis to gain military control over King and capital, anticipating the unilateral army-raising of spring 1642. The King gave in and signed the attainder (10 May), but issued no date for the execution; the Lords proceeded to set one themselves[137] to make sure that they were not cheated of their victim. When the King still delayed announcing the date, they sent him a delegation warning that they could not answer for the safety of the Royal Family if the sentence was not carried out.[138] All this argues for sustained and deliberate intimidation of the King, albeit out of fear of Strafford's capacity for further threat, and was to rebound on the perpetrators in the form of rising Royal intransigence – which the discourteous rejection of a personal appeal by the Prince of Wales would have assisted.

Bedford's sudden death on 8 May robbed the 'moderates', reconsidering the need for execution, of a leader. Had Bedford still been alive and made a speech arguing against execution, or the 'Army Plot' not stirred up panic about the forced dissolution of Parliament with its work incomplete, the Strafford vote could well have been lost. It was unfortunate for Strafford that the very nature of the alleged plot was such as to remind waverers of one of the charges against him – that he had argued in favour of military action to coerce Parliament. Executing him would show that the King's subjects were not to be intimidated – and prevent an acquitted (or even exiled) Strafford being in a position to coerce them in future. As St John warned, Strafford was like a baited bull, maddened by the darts stuck into him, who would wreak havoc if let loose; Strafford's known character and past boasts about using violence made this interpretation seem plausible.

The vote in the Lords on Strafford's fate duly favoured conviction, with Charles having foolishly based his own appeal for acquittal on the grounds that he – as the fount of the laws – was not convinced of Strafford's guilt rather than a judicious summarising of the dubious evidence. If the political 'storm' had not broken at this point, enough peers could well have voted in favour of acquittal to see the prosecution fail and give a major boost to the King's supporters – though Pym would have gone on to attack episcopacy and could expect popular demonstrations in support of that cause. He and Warwick would also have continued to have the backing of the Scots for a non-episcopal religious settlement in England. The 'showdown' would probably have occurred over the nature of a Church settlement even if some compromise had been reached – by the mediation of Bedford? – over Strafford and the King not been furious at the Earl's accusers for forcing him into accepting execution.

It is noticeable that on 27 May, with Strafford and Bedford both dead, the controversial 'Root and Branch' bill to abolish episcopacy was introduced into the Commons – introduced by the Kent MP Sir Edward Dering after apparent lobbying of him by Haselrig and Oliver Cromwell.[139] Was Haselrig acting as a conduit from the Presbyterian zealot Lord Brooke, his brother-in-law? Coincidentally or not, Brooke (who shared lodgings with Haselrig) had recently entertained the Scots commissioners, Lords Loudoun and Rothes in his rooms in Holborn[140] and the latter were pressing the English at their treaty talks for Church reformation. The bill's promoters were clearly keen to sabotage the chances of Archbishop Williams' committee which was looking into the future structure of the Church. The first MP to speak in favour of the necessity of completing the current campaign of 'reform' by abolishing episcopacy – a link which had not won majority support in the religious debate of 8 February – was Denzel Holles, a 'hard-line' ally of Warwick and Brooke. John Adamson also thinks that the move was designed to reassure the Covenanters about MPs' religious zeal, with the King having just announced to the Scots Commissioners on the day of Strafford's execution (12 May) that he was to visit Scotland to open their Parliament – and thus possibly flatter the Covenanters into abandoning their English allies?

There was a major problem for the 'opposition' at this point over the inadequacy of their financial 'pay-off' to the Scots army. The four 'subsidies' granted to fund it, plus other current taxation, would only raise around £300,000, leaving a shortfall of some £700,000 for the sum currently owed to them, as reported on 17 June by 'opposition' MPs Sir Thomas Barrington ('teller' for the Strafford attainder on 21 April and a friend of St John since the 1620s), Sir Henry Mildmay ('teller' for submitting the Strafford investigation to a controllable select committee, and to be promised the Treasurership of the Household in August), and Sir John Hotham (later Parliamentary governor of Hull, where he shut the gates in the King's face).[141] The choice of these three 'hard-liners' to deal with finance shows the 'opposition' determination to control the matter, to their Scots' allies' satisfaction. If the Scots army was not paid off, would this enrage its leaders and lead them to withdraw to Scotland to find much-needed supplies – or to deal with the King instead? The proposed remedy, put forward by the unusual duo of City militant MP Isaac Penington and temporising Secretary of State Vane, was for a 'poll tax' on all citizens – graded so as not to cause anger at injustice[142] – but this could still be used by Royal supporters to raise anger at the Commons sacrificing the national interest to pay off its invading 'traitor' allies. £80,000 was to be paid over in August and the rest of the money later – but the overall sum was twice that of the King's supposedly 'extortionate' annual 'Ship Money' demands in 1635–7 and was a potential coup for a Royalist 'backlash'

The possibilities of a pro-Royal backlash aiding Charles – and the capital's crowds as a weapon for the radicals

Many of the MPs who had been elected as critical of Charles' government, wanted a major overhaul of the administration, and voted or spoke up for Pym's group at first were to rally to the King by late 1641. Among them were such later 'Royalist' figures as Sir Edward Hyde and George Digby, and without them the King would not have had political backing ouside his Court and been able to attempt to seize the initiative that winter. Lord Falkland, later to fall in the Royalist ranks at Newbury in 1643, was prepared to consider the abolition of bishops in February 1641, as was Hopton. Hyde was not, but saw the destruction of the apparatus of 'Personal Rule' as necessary and the imposition of 'Ship Money' as a mistake which coalesced an alliance of men justly alarmed at its implications of arbitrary Royal legal decisions. They saw the destruction of Royal prerogative powers by the legislative acts of spring 1641 as satisfying the need to politically curb the King and remedy current abuses of power, and the removal of Strafford and the imprisoned Laud as having neutralised his most dangerous and abusive ministers. Grievances had now been satisfied, as was the duty of the Houses to enact and the King to accept; was there any need for further action? But this reversal of fortunes was only possible for the King once the most pressing grievances had been settled and his most 'dangerous' ministers removed; his future 'political party' could only emerge at this point. This breach in Commons unity widened as the demands of their militant colleagues, led by Pym, Haselrig, and St John, seemed to spiral out of control and go beyond necessary reform or protecting the subjects' liberties and religion to infringing on the King's prerogative and dignity.

For some radicals, as for Brooke and Warwick, the permanent political emasculation of the monarchy and abolition of the bishops – major innovation in State and Church – seems to have been the objective. The abolition of the bishops was also desired by their Scots allies, who could desert them if not satisfied, sign up to the King's treaty, and take their army home leaving Parliament to face their angry monarch and his troops. But the passion and obstinacy the radicals showed for abolition shows that this 'Root and Branch' plan, renewed in May, was sincere. For some moderates the execution rather than imprisonment or exile of Strafford, generally regarded as the architect of arbitrary rule and desirous of bringing in his Irish troops to coerce Parliament, was the turning-point in defecting to the King; for others it was the continuing demands for further religious reform into autumn 1641 as the Irish revolt seemed to require a move towards agreement with the King in the national interest. But the introduction of the 'Root and Branch' bill in mid-May shows that the religious 'showdown' was from then on inevitable. The bill passed its second reading then by only 21 votes, so it was self-evidently risky[143] but that did not halt its backers.

There were two points at which the political situation could have altered radically in the 'slide' towards civil war between November 1640, when the Long Parliament assembled, and the final collapse in relations with the King after the attempt to arrest the 'Five Members'. One crucial period was May 1641, as the Commons majority pressed the King to execute Strafford with the aid of intimidatory demonstrations by Londoners. The other was the late autumn and early winter of 1641, the weeks leading up to the King's march on the Commons on 6 January 1642. On either occasion, there was a chance for the political 'centre' to take the initiative and/or the King to stand firm without acting as provocatively as he did in reality. A mixture of bad luck, bad judgement, and the King's all too frequent political blunders ruined both opportunities. But in May 1641 Warwick was to blame as much as the King and it is questionable if a surviving Bedford could have reined him in. Even Bedford's cousin and client, St John, had started acting independently of him by pressing for Strafford's execution; and the moves to assert military control of the capital and Portsmouth (led by Essex, who had relevant experience) occurred while Bedford was still alive. Was Bedford being outmanoeuvred anyway? In addition, it was crucial that the King's sympathisers in the City of London had lost control of the Lord Mayorship and Common Council in the late 1640 elections to a faction of pro-reform aldermen who were willing to tolerate or support the frequent demonstrations of rowdy citizens (especially apprentices) in favour of Pym's group in Westminster. Most of the remaining army was still at York, watching the Scots; the King now only had a small body of troops at Whitehall and another at the Tower to counter the control of his capital by his critics.

Had Balfour handed over the Tower to the King's supporters as planned it would have led to furious Parliamentary censure and a trial of strength between King and Houses over who was to control the fortress to add to the tension over what to do with Strafford, whose execution would have been even more certain from a Commons reminded of the military threat which he symbolised. At best, the extra armed manpower in London could have given Charles the confidence to risk dissolving Parliament – to stop Strafford's execution if the Earl had not escaped in the chaos. Had that happened, Charles would still have needed money and men to take on the Scots (who Warwick's group would logically have encouraged to advance on London). His new Dutch allies were one potential source of both, but were to prove disappointing to his cause once war broke out in 1642. The Stadtholder was not an absolute ruler – could Frederick Henry have managed to send aid without a veto in the States-General, even if he had wanted to? If Parliament had been dissolved, as in 1626 and 1629, MPs and peers would have had to decide whether to back the King – who had already agreed to the abolition of his contentious prerogative powers so there would be no early return to the 'misrule' of the 1630s – as the source of stability against a faction of 'rebel' lords and Scots. Charles would have been wise to give in quickly to the Scots' politico-religious demands to neutralise their threat; this need not have been sincerely meant. (He did sign up to these terms in Edinburgh on 25 August in real life.) The potential of a Royal link with the 'moderate' Covenanter general Montrose, a signatory of the Covenant but against coercing the King by 1641 and possibly capable of staging a coup, was created by his establishment of a secret group, including his kinsmen Lord Napier and Sir George Stirling, to resist the Argyll/Loudoun faction's dominance of the Scots regime in winter 1640–1;[144] the crucial point for them would be the meeting of the next Scots Parliament in May 1641. Montrose agreed to send Colonel Walter Stewart, a Covenanter officer and cousin of Lord Traquair, to London on the excuse of arranging a commission for Montrose in the exiled Palatine court's army; he would then urge the King to come north for the Scots Parliament meeting and help to overthrow Argyll.[145] Montrose could also provide written depositions from contacts that Argyll had talked of the circumstances when deposing Charles might be viable, so the King could have him convicted for treason if he was arrested.[146] Stewart was in London in March and later in April, and it is clear that Montrose required the King to make his task of winning over Covenanter support easier by sacrificing the Scottish bishops and accepting the Covenanter Church

Assembly's decisions of 1638. In Montrose's instructions to his envoy, 'R(eligion) and L(iberty) being granted, he (Charles) will be powerful to crush the Elephant (ie Argyll)'.[147] Graham dealt with Traquair and the King's young cousin the Duke of Lennox, not the dubiously reliable Hamilton, and the King's decision to go north (announced on 12 May) was clearly a result of it.[148] We cannot know what precisely Charles intended – but Montrose had left him in no doubt that abandoning episcopacy in Scotland was necessary.

The 'Army Plot' and the Commons committee set up to investigate it in May provided another impetus for Commons fear of the King's and courtiers' intentions. As seen above, the timing of the revelations came at a vital moment for the Warwick group, as the Lords were about to vote on Strafford's attainder, and thus aided their cause; demonstrations pressurised the Lords. But the lack of a large Royal military presence in London or Westminster throughout the crucial months of 1641 gave the initiative in intimidation to Pym's group, and the uncontrolled demonstrations during crucial votes must have resulted in more timid peers voting for measures that would normally have been rejected such as Strafford's attainder. As in Paris in 1789 and 1792, St Petersburg in 1917, and Tehran in 1979, the regime's foundering was aided by its loss of control of the streets of the capital. In turn, the prosecutions of the 'Junto's enemy Strafford was as subject to the threat of 'mob' force by the prosecutors as were Louis XVI's trial in 1792 or the impeachment of Iranian President Bani-Sadr in 1981 – though there was legitimate fear of an avowedly brutal Strafford. The King lacked either troops or level-headed officers, and his stalwarts' bold plans for a counter-coup relied on uncontrollable factors like the activating of enough volunteers to seize the Tower.

Was a settlement possible in May-June 1641?

What if a political settlement could have been reached in 1641 and the 'centre ground' had held? That would have meant leaving those MPs and (far fewer) peers in favour of 'root and branch' religious reform isolated, or at least forced to put off their aims until a later date. The comparative unity of the Commons for whatever measures the Pym group proposed had changed since Parliament first met in November 1640, when the

King's main critics in the Lords (the Earl of Warwick's group, including Bedford, Brooke, Essex, and Saye and Sele) and in the Commons had been able to organise majorities for their programme of 'reform' of abuses that had crept into Church and State since 1629. The main legislative goals of the 'opposition' peers and MPs who held a majority in Parliament and the political initiative – the demolition of the legal and administrative apparatus of 'Personal Rule' and the punishment of its leadership – had been met by May/June 1641. The King's expedients for raising money without Parliamentary grant had been declared illegal, his prerogative courts had been abolished, and the judges who had given verdicts in favour of the King's dubious practices in the 1630s (especially Ship-Money) had been impeached and/or banned from office – Lord Keeper Finch, their leader but also father-in-law to the senior MP Sir William Waller, had been allowed to flee the country. The leading Catholic ministers at Court – especially the Secretary, Francis Windebank – had fled so that 'Popish' threat had been neutralised. The most dangerous Royal minister, Strafford, alias 'Black Tom Tyrant', had been executed in May 1641 despite all the King's pleas and protests. This in itself was an unprecedented incident of direct political pressure from the Commons rather than cliques of aristocrats eliminating a major Crown servant: it mixed up 'medieval' noble coercion of a King with 'modern' popular pressure.

Subsidies had been abolished, tonnage and poundage placed under Parliamentary control, the proceedings against opponents of Ship-Money nullified, and a bill brought in to ban bishops from administrative or legislative functions (including the Lords). On 5 July the Courts of Star Chamber and High Commission were to be abolished. The process of passing a 'Triennial Bill' to ensure the regular future meeting of Parliament had proceeded, providing a potential clash over whether or not to arrange for it to meet whether the King summoned it or not. At the crucial moment of the Strafford attainder crisis in May 1641, the King had given way on abolishing the hated and extortionate Court of Wards and so abandoned a major non-Parliamentary source of revenue. He was thus keeping to his promises in January of abolishing extra-Parliamentary and/or disliked sources of revenue. Despite the continuing crisis, Charles was to give Royal Assent to all outstanding measures restricting his powers in the early summer. Parliament had now done its duty in answering the pressing grievances of the nation, and the King had been unable to block it as he had done repeatedly in 1625–9. There was no precedent for proceeding further in contentious legislative measures, particularly on abolishing episcopacy – though the enemies of the latter clearly regarded the existence of 'Romish' and coercive institutions within the Church as being as dangerous as the secular Royal prerogative powers now desroyed. Could Bedford have talked the radical 'Root and Branch' supporters out of putting their bill forward, perhaps aided by Archbishop Williams? This was unlikely despite some modern historians talking of this as a missed chance for settlement.

Charles now had neither the men or the means to restore his position once Parliament was no longer sitting, even when the Irish and Scottish crises had been solved. He had been driven into considering recruiting former critics to ministerial office; Bedford, Essex, and Bristol and Lords Saye and Sele and Mandeville (the latter an MP as the son of the Earl of Manchester) had been made Privy Councillors in February and Oliver St John, lately counsel for Hampden over the Ship-Money case, made Solicitor-General. Essex became Lord Chamberlain (in place of Pembroke) and 'Lord General'; Warwick's close relative Mountjoy Blount, Lord Newport, became Master of the Ordnance; the Earl of Leicester became Lord Lieutenant of Ireland; the 'moderate' courtiers Northumberland and Holland became Lord Admiral and Groom of the Stool (a Court office in close attendance on the King); and Essex's brother-in-law the Earl of Hertford became governor of the Prince of Wales, giving an assurance of the heir's freedom from ultra-royalist guidance. The fact that these 'opposition' peers held the senior offices in charge of the army and navy was of crucial importance in giving their faction confidence that they could prevent a Strafford-type attempt to use the armed forces against them. Northumberland was the Calvinists' choice for the 'regency' post (*'custos regni'*) controlling the King's administration when Charles was due to go to Edinburgh in August, though the King backed out of it and as he left on the 10th appointed an unwieldy regency council of twenty-two men instead. This included one of Strafford's allies, the Earl of Newcastle,[149] a leading loyalist and future Royalist commander of the north. But the fact that all these men held senior office did not mean that they trusted the King, or that they would halt their assault on Royal powers and episcopacy. (The Earl of Northumberland, commander of the fleet, was prepared to 'shop' his brother Henry Percy to the Commons for his part in the 'Army Plot'.)

The 'opposition' peers, men excluded from senior office or any influence on policy in the 1630s, had been endeavouring to coerce their sovereign into calling and then following the dictates of Parliament – including through links to rebel Scots in 1639–40 – in the tradition of their ancestors' coercion of mediaeval rulers such as Henry III, Edward II, Richard II, and Henry VI. The precedent for their action, in the traditionalist terms of political thought, lay with the 'Lords Ordainer' (1310) and 'Lords Appellant' (1388). John Adamson also thinks there could have been a contemporary political model as mentioned in Bedford's papers, namely the oligarchic government of Venice with its 'figurehead' Doge and powerful Council of Ten; Venice was admired for its anti-Papal foreign policy.[150] The indications from Bedford's papers are that he favoured a resticted monarchy; Warwick's preacher ally Jeremiah Burroughs had been talking approvingly of the elective Venetian and Polish monarchies. (This was what the Venetian ambassador heard too; but were his informants mainly flattering him?)[151] The gaining of office and control over policy – long-term – had been their aims, and Warwick's group had every reason to preserve the existing order. Was Bedford their main theorist, or did his death make no difference to their desire to permanently coerce an unreliable King? The crucial point of division among them was episcopacy; the most irreconcilable 'Puritan' radicals like Lords Brooke and Saye and Sele (and Warwick too) differed from the others. The question remains of which peers in the 'rebel' group would have accepted office, or if they had taken it stayed in post, had Charles endeavoured to save the episcopate. The militant Calvinism and support for abolishing episcopacy shown by Warwick, Saye and Sele, Brooke, and Mandeville in 1640–4 indicate that they were likeliest to have held out for 'Root and Branch'. They had a useful ally in the Scots army, still in Newcastle, and the Scots commissioners negotiating with Charles for a settlement of the 'Prayer-Book' rebellion. Conrad Russell believes that this issue would have wrecked any attempt at a politico-religious settlement in England that involved Bedford and his allies taking office and being allowed to initiate government policy in May/June 1641. The Scots' obduracy, which enraged the King at the time, would have meant that a Scots treaty could only be agreed on the Calvinist religious terms which Warwick, Brooke, and Saye and Sele wanted but the King rejected.

If Strafford had been acquitted by the Lords – or even the Commons, given the defection of a few more vital MPs after George Digby – or had fled the country back in January the King would not have been haunted by guilt at his weakness over the execution, and potentially been more open to conciliation in the following months. On the other hand, would he have asked Charles to let him go to York and lead the army on London, precipitating a civil war or at least the Warwick group's flight from London?

Even if the King was reluctant to make serious changes in government to admit Warwick's group and did not show any desire for advice from those 'opposition' figures who did gain some appointments – the influence of 'opposition' MP Vane's father as Secretary of State could have been crucial but was a missed opportunity – a series of offers of significant posts to his most determined critics this summer could have made a difference to later events. The adherence of the peers was vital, even with Bedford – the main conduit to Pym, so possibly able to win him over – dead. Even had someone such as Hampden or Holles – Pym was more abrasive – been given a Secretaryship and allowed to draw up policies, they would still have been insistent on some major reform of religion and using Commons and extra-Parliamentary popular pressure on the King. The chances are heavily in favour of their suspicious attitude to the proto-Catholic Court causing some clash with the King or Queen, and his being sufficiently offended to dismiss them. A monarch keen on his dignity such as Charles was unlikely to put political necessity above perceived impertinence, unlike his father James had had to do with regard to Scots nobles and clerics. A settlement could have collapsed within months, as the incoming ministers were made aware of their lack of influence and were snubbed by the furious 'ultra' coterie around the Queen. The probabilities of Court contacts with anti-Covenanter lords in Scotland were a problem, Montrose's envoy Colonel Walter Stewart being in London that spring, and ran a major risk of reviving the suspicions of any co-opted 'opposition' ministers of what Charles really intended.

Nor did the King show enthusiasm for peers who had proved their alleged disloyalty in the past; Pembroke, a potential 'bridge' to the Calvinist group, was 'frozen out' at Court through 1641 despite his political usefulness and later that autumn was to receive a major snub by not receiving the expected Lord Stewardship (which went to the loyalist Duke of Richmond and Lennox). Probably his appeasing address to the anti-Strafford protesters outside Parliament in early May irrevocably offended Charles. Jermyn, Henry Percy, and the courtiers around the Queen would have continued to urge a show of strength, with every chance of the King preferring their counsels – and a crisis like the Irish rebellion or proof of Charles' dealings with Catholic Irish lords caused the critics' resignations. But peers had more opportunities to approach the King at court, and Essex, Warwick, and Saye and Sele (or Bedford had he lived) might have been able to persuade the King to avoid blunders such as the arrests of the 'Five Members' – if Charles had suspended his petulant annoyance at their past behaviour. Again, the danger is of the King's lack of rapport with or trust in them; to Charles they would still have been the men who had dabbled in treasonous relations with the rebel Scots in 1639–40.

But it is arguable that as the Irish crisis polarised feelings from that October Parliament would have been more tractable if it had not occurred. It should be realised that the revolt could have broken out if the King had admitted his senior critics to office, precisely because of their 'Puritan' and anti-Catholic reputation. Charles using the office of Lord Deputy of Ireland as a useful bait to entice a prominent 'opposition' peer (Warwick? Essex?) to his service during spring/summer 1641 could have sparked off revolt from Catholics alarmed that such a 'Puritan' zealot would start confiscating more land. In fact he chose the less senior, but 'opposition'-linked, Leicester as Lord Deputy and the rabid anti-Catholic talk in Parliament was enough to spark off revolt anyway with rumours that the King's critics intended to depose him and/or carry out another major 'plantation'. Ironically, given Strafford's reputation in England for being an ally of Catholicism intending to use an Irish Catholic army on Protestant Englishmen as well as Scots, the Earl had laid the fuse for the Irish revolt by his Protestant vigour (e.g. in proposing to 'plant' Connacht). Strafford's enemies included both Catholics, in danger of 'planting', and militant Calvinist 'planters' such as Clotworthy in Ulster. The Scots element of the crisis could also have caused similar Irish Catholic fears, given that the King had to go to Edinburgh in summer/autumn 1641 to sign a treaty which accepted a similar ascendancy of anti-Catholic elements in that country. The Scots Presbyterians were already colonising the O'Neill lands in Ulster (e.g. Londonderry) where the revolt was to break out, and the terms of the King's 'surrender' to Argyll's party that August were such as to make him powerless to protect his Irish subjects against a new 'land-grab' by the Scots. Thus a tentative settlement between King and 'opposition' in London in summer 1641 would not have avoided a major risk of an Irish revolt, either against the predatory threat from the 'Puritan' element in the London government or from the triumphant Covenanters.

Proclaimed Royal willingness to subject the current nature of the Anglican Church to review by an independent commission of senior figures (Bedford's suggestion of relying on Archbishop Williams would have been useful to rally Anglican moderates), would encourage 'opposition' peers to rally client MPs in favour of a halt to controversial new measures – once the Triennial Bill (which was essential for Parliament's future safety) had received Royal assent. The problem here was that Williams, like Warwick but on less creditable grounds, was distrusted by the King. Charles had taken on Laud's opinions of the latter's enemies, and thus disliked his rival Williams. The chances of Charles being prepared to declare his support for Williams as a reformer of Church doctrine and structures were small – particularly once he was embittered by Strafford's execution.

There was an intensely disturbed and excited atmosphere at Westminster in May-June 1641, with no greater calm than when Parliament had first met. MPs, peers, and the militant City public that thronged to the House did not think that the King's political and administrative concessions had ended the crisis (he gave Royal Assent to the final tranche of abolitions of his old powers and administrative machinery in June-July). There was panic after a noise like a gunshot echoed around the Commons one day, and it was immediately assumed that Papist assassins were to blame. In fact it was only a railing breaking under an MP's weight as he leaned over to retrieve a paper.[152] The agitation for abolition of the bishops and further reform of the Church on rigorously Calvinist lines was continuing, and the King's attempts to deny 'justice' by saving Strafford's life could be interpreted as a sign of untrustworthiness. He had based his initial refusal to execute Strafford on his prerogative rights not the legal weaknesses in the case alienating potential allies among MPs. As we have seen, fear of the King's intentions was at this point so acute that MPs voted for the Warwick group's plan to revive the 1584 'Association' and create a temporary but legal non-monarchic executive if the King turned on them and attempted a dissolution. This is not the atmosphere of compromise and potential agreement, but of fundamental differences.

The King subsequently regarded his failure to save Strafford's life as his worst mistake, a sign of weakness that he should not repeat as well as a sin for which his misfortunes were punishment. Arguably, it encouraged him to be firm – or rash – on later occasions when greater flexibility would have been more advisable. It was condemned by others too, among them Archbishop Laud in his diary. The political atmosphere at Westminster that spring meant that the minister's enemies were determined to destroy him as the architect of 'Thorough' and the supposed organiser of a plan to bring in the Irish army to coerce them. It is possible, as argued above, that the Lords or Commons votes on impeachment or attainder could have gone the other way. But once the 'Army Plot' crisis had broken out the King's lack of armed forces to oppose the intimidation of the Lords by large crowds was crucial in securing a 'guilty' verdict, and Charles' appeal for mercy on account of his conscience rather than legal justice was a mistake. He could not have refused to sign the death-sentence without a breach with Parliament, though the deadlock could have been temporary had Bedford (opposed to execution) been alive in June or July to rally moderates. If the plan for Strafford to escape the Tower in April had succeeded there would have been no victim to execute, though that occurrence would have led to fulminations in Parliament about sinister Papist courtiers aiding his escape and demands for Parliamentary control of the Tower garrison. If Strafford was allowed by Charles to lead an army on London, a military confrontation was possible – and if he was sent abroad it would still have heightened 'opposition' desire to turn the untrustworthy King into a political figurehead.

Chapter Five

May 1641 to January 1642.
Missed Chances or Inevitable Showdown?

After May 1641: was Charles irreconcilably alienated from the 'opposition'?

The death of Bedford (8 May), execution of Strafford (12 May), and failure to open major offices to 'opposition' figures prevented various alternative routes to a resolution of the ongoing crisis that summer. But the situation as the Houses adjourned was not as secure for the 'opposition' as it had been earlier that year. To the King's benefit, there was no consensus in either House in favour of the main outstanding religious measure that the leading religiously 'radical' MPs – the clique based around Pym and his ally John Hampden – and some Lords allies (e.g. Lords Brooke and Saye and Sele) wanted to impose. The total 'Root and Branch' abolition of the bishops and reform of the Church on 'purified' lines, if in one argument completing the Reformation from where it had wrongly halted in 1559, went too far for many political leaders who had been critical of the abuses of power by the ecclesiastical courts (now abolished) or even sympathetic to reducing clerical power. The bill to abolish episcopacy introduced by Oliver Cromwell and the younger Sir Henry Vane on 27 May barely passed its second reading (139 to 108 votes), and the Lords voted against excluding the bishops from their House.[1] Would the bill ever pass a House of Lords containing over a dozen bishops? Royal official Edward Nicholas reckoned it would never be enacted; only about twenty-five out of sixty-eight peers (ignoring the dozen or so active bishops) would support it in the Lords.[2]

This heralded a revival of support for the King from those alarmed at a threat to the institution of episcopacy, and in practical terms the retention of a powerful bloc of votes for Charles in the Lords. To these people, reform had gone far enough. It is possible that the sudden revival of 'opposition' enthusiasm for 'Root and Branch' reform after a hiatus of several months was mainly due to a desire to reassure the Covenanter leadership in Scotland, as suggested by John Adamson;³ or it may have been a move by Pym to reassert his leadership and credentials after a 'threat' of a moderate/Royalist reconciliation. The end of the Strafford trial may just have removed a practical obstacle to spending time on this issue, which the Warwick-Pym group always intended to consider next; or the militants in the Commons (e.g. Pym, Haselrig, and Denzel Holles) may have forced the issue, emboldened by Bedford's removal. But Charles had just announced his intention to go to Edinburgh for the next session of the Scots Parliament in July, raising the prospect that he could 'surrender' to the Covenanters on religion to have their army removed from England. Once that happened, he could easily send his own army from York to London and close Parliament down. Pressing ahead with English religious reform should secure Parliamentary legislation for abolishing the bishops before this eventuality occurred, and remind the Covenanters' Commissioners in London that the anti-episcopalians in both kingdoms needed to act together. One thing the radicals did not want was Charles being freed from the menace of a hostile Scots army before 'Root and Branch' was passed. The need to preserve military security from a treacherous King was shown in the radical success in having the Commons 'Committee of Seven' (set up in early May to investigate the King's attempts to win over the army) authorised to draw up special measures in late June. These 'Ten Propositions', reported to the Commons by Pym, included purging the King's and Queen's households of 'Papists' and requiring all military officers, including the county Lord Lieutenants and their deputies (as commanders of the militia), to swear an oath to be loyal to the 'commonwealth'. The Venetian ambassador Giustinian reported the word as 'republic', but Adamson thinks this was a mistranslation and so not a direct republican threat to the King – though in any case it envisaged loyalty to the State not to its untrustworthy monarch. In either case, this was a sign of Parliament being prepared to take over the armed forces for its own defence six months before the 'Arrest of the Five Members' crisis.⁴

Reforming 'semi-Catholic' religious vestments and ceremonies, or replacing the altars (re-aligned in a 'Catholic' direction by Laud) by simple, undecorated Communion tables and replacing church decorations with something more austere and less 'idolatrous', was supported by local petitions to the Commons from certain areas, mainly in the south-east. The amount of petitioning in 1641 and the outbursts of enthusiastic iconoclasm in East Anglia in 1644 showed that there was popular support among congregations for further reform, though more 'conservative' areas such as Cheshire petitioned against them. Broadly speaking, as illustrated by the 'grass-roots' religious feeling (either pro- or anti-bishops) shown in local petitions, the south-eastern counties that were to form the heartland of the Parliamentary cause in 1642–4 were the most radical areas and the 'Royalist' areas strongest in support of the existing state of the Church.[5] It is probable that the petitions exaggerated the depth of support for abolishing the bishops, being (as is usually the way) organised by the most vocal militants and having extra assistance from networks of sympathetic 'godly' gentry. The existence of zealously 'reformist' local ministers ready to organise the petitions and lead the delegations depended on control of patronage of parish appointments by their secular backers – and Warwick, based at Leez Priory in Essex, was a major patron in East Anglia aided by the local Barrington family. However, there was no noticeable 'backlash' to overthrow this militant monopoly from within the local gentry once there was an opportunity to do so militarily in 1642–3; probably the officious interference in local Church matters by the 'High Anglican' Laudian ally Bishop Wren of Norwich had strengthened anti-episcopal feelings.

The destruction of the oppressive apparatus of State/Church control of religious practice in 1641 had led to substantial 'grass-roots' initiatives, with the formation of semi-autonomous local congregations in London and towns in the south-east. These people, some Presbyterians but others the nucleus of the later 'Independent' sects, had a stake in ensuring that the new religious order agreed by Parliament and King did not impose a new disciplinarian network to their detriment – though the Presbyterians feared having no such discipline at all as fostering anarchy. The collapse of official censorship enabled a boom in pamphleteering, newsletters, and petitioning of Parliament on the preferred religious settlement. The resultant ferment, particularly in and around London, was useful to Pym's group in keeping up the pressure on Parliament to reach a solution that destroyed episcopacy. The amount of pamphlets available to London collector George Thomason, whose collection is our main 'grass-roots' source for early 1640s events, increased rapidly during 1641, showing that many more were being printed. It provided a continuing tumult in favour of the Commons zealots, giving them the initiative in pressurising the regime whenever they wished. Demonstrations by zealots in Westminster, organised in the City, intimidated the waiverers. But the 'root and branch' solution that Pym's group wanted amounted to imposition of full Presbyterianism on the Scottish model, which was not desirable to many MPs who had rallied against Laudian Anglican discipline and 'innovation'. They wanted to return to the supposedly Calvinist, pre-Laudian Church of Elizabeth and James, not follow Scotland's lead.

The fate of the next religious votes is significant. The Commons duly agreed on 1 September to remove the contentious Laudian altar-rails and other 'Popish' innovations and to return the Communion tables to the centre of the church buildings, but the pro-Royalist MP Sir John Colepeper failed to get enough votes for his 'moderate' proposal that they should specifically defend the Prayer Book as established by law (6 September). The radical speakers who led his defeat were a nexus of Essex deputy lieutenants, headed by Barrington, his relative Sir William Masham, and proposed Treasurer of the Household Sir Henry Mildmay, plus the still marginal Fenlands MP Oliver Cromwell.[6] At this point, Cromwell's main role seems to have been as a 'godly' hard-liner, as was to be shown by his enthusiasm for the Petition of Right in late 1641; he clearly believed that the King and his bishops were a menace to reformed Protestantism and was averse to any compromises. His financially and socially precarious position, as a junior member of a prominent Huntingdonshire dynasty with court connections (and future Royalist cousins) but himself reduced to farming rather than living off his rents, and his experience of hard-nosed Royal drainage contractors in the Fens probably spurred on his distaste for the government – but as yet his political contribution was minimal. The Prayer Book referred to was the 1559 version, the theological basis of Elizabethan Anglicanism – which had Calvinist overtones from its Edwardian predecessor but had been acceptable to all Anglican thinkers, Hooker and Laud included. It was at variance with the more 'hard-line' Geneva Prayer Book, used in Scotland since 1560 and favoured by the Covenanters and their English 'Junto'/'Root and Branch' allies. Those MPs who voted against defending the lawful Prayer Book could thus be 'smoked out' as favouring innovation and the Scots model of a Church. The Lords voted in favour of Colepeper's 'line' (by 12 to 11, showing the small number of members present), and proposed that the ordinance – ie a temporary 'Act' pending Royal approval – to be issued by Parliament on removing superstitious innovations should specifically mention carrying out services according to the 1559 Prayer Book.[7] The Commons majority refused to join with their declaration, the 'hard-line' case being put by the notedly 'godly' pro-Warwick diarist Sir Simonds D'Ewes after consultation with the Earl, and put it on record that only eleven peers of those present during the vote had backed that decision.[8] In other words, the vote could be ignored as it was not 'democratic'- an argument not used for any unwanted vote that went the 'reformists' way. Indeed, the belligerent and non-consensual attitude of the 'Root and Branch' backers showed that they were more concerned for a 'pure' revision of the Church than for one that would more easily be passed by both Houses. It cannot be written off as merely a desire to satisfy the Scots. Worse, after the 9 September debate the Lords minority published the names of those who had voted on both sides and the 'Warwick' group's rebuttal of the majority's decision, as if inviting the public to turn on the identified pro-'Arminian' 'traitors'.[9]

It is arguable that the Pym faction's tactic of sending the bill for the abolition of the bishops to the 'Committee of the Whole House', where it would obviously become tied down in prolonged speeches and arguments, meant that they were intending to 'grandstand' with noisy public attacks on the bishops rather than being concerned for a quick solution. Their opponents accused them of seeking to do this to please their Scottish allies with their public zeal for 'reform'. Similarly, the 'religious censorship' committee deciding which proposed sermons should be licensed and which banned was put under the leadership of the contentious Kent 'Root and Branch' supporter Sir Edward Dering, a Pym ally who had introduced the bill to abolish the bishops on 27 May at Haselrig's and Cromwell's request.[10] None of this augured well for agreement or compromise, particularly by the 'godly' zealots. Though concerned 'opposition' figures – led by peers such as Warwick – had been ready to use the Scots' victories of 1639–40 to pressurise and corner the King into allowing free rein to Parliament this did not mean adopting the Covenant. In their minds it would have had more to do with a 'traditional' political campaign to remove Court opponents, as practised by the enemies of unpopular Royal favourites in the 14th and 15th centuries. What was new was the extension of this tactic to imposing religious reform as well as clearing out 'evil ministers' from Court and compelling the King to accept 'good' advice – and now St John's and Bedford's constitutional vision (shared by Essex?) justified legal constraints on the King to accept Parliamentary votes and act as what would later be called a 'rubber stamp'.

There was thus the prospect of a breach in 'opposition' ranks once their main aims were achieved, and a loss of momentum in Parliament after Strafford's execution which coincided with the early autumn harvest and then the King's absence from 12 August on his visit to Scotland. It was unfortunate that the King chose to show a lack of politically advisable goodwill to the crucial group of 'Puritan' peers at this juncture, by dismissing the important Earl of Pembroke from his role as Lord Chamberlain (albeit in Essex's favour). The Earl of Pembroke, Chancellor of Oxford, was not a leading member of Warwick's 'political' group bent on coercing Charles, but he had been associated with the resistance to 'pro-Catholic' favourites since the time of Buckingham – when he had activated a group of MPs under his patronage against the Duke. As a 'reformist', he had joined Arundel and Holland in escorting the Triennial Act to Whitehall for its Royal signing-ceremony in February. He had tried to save Strafford, a Court rival, from trial and later from a condemnation that would necessitate execution, only to change his mind (partly to save his reputation with the angry City public, as High Steward of Westminster) and assure the crowds that justice would be done. This courting favour at the cost of Strafford's life is supposed to have won him Charles' contempt, and his dismissal followed at the end of July. Once again, Charles let his personal loyalties affect his political judgement. Excluding him from Court office meant that Charles had lost personal contact with a 'moderate' opponent of 'Thorough' who had no interest in letting Pym's faction loose to abolish episcopacy, making the King more easily influenced by the 'ultra'-Royalists around the Queen (e.g. Jermyn) and Lord Goring. This all added to the risk of Charles acting rashly and ruining the possibility of a political compromise, as was to be seen the following January.

The Scots factor – could the 'opposition's allies in Edinburgh have been overthrown in autumn 1641?

While Parliament was in recess in the late summer for the harvest, the King journeyed to Edinburgh to meet with the Covenanter leadership.

This time there was no repeat of the arrogant insistence on using Anglican religious ceremonial of 1633, or any Royal protests that the meetings of Scots Parliament and Church Assembly since 1639 had been illegal as the King had not sanctioned them. If the King had kept to his earlier line, he would not even have met with their 'illegal' representatives. Instead there was a Royal charm offensive as Charles set up his residence at Holyrood. It should also be remembered that there were strong enmities within the Covenanter leadership which he could exploit, particularly between Argyll and Montrose. The latter, the 'Presbyterian Cavalier' of John Buchan's terminology, was uncompromisingly loyal to the 1638 programme of a Church free of Anglican 'innovations' (bishops included) and a King listening to wise advice not imposing his will regardless. This much was made clear in Montrose's undercover negotiations with the English Court in spring 1641; he would only back the King if these points were guaranteed. In return for that, he would provide evidence to have Argyll tried for treason. His position was different from that of men who were prepared to back the King in virtually any circumstances, e.g. Traquair, but he did not seek to subject the King to permanent control as did the distrustful Argyll. 'King Campbell' was already being accused of aiming at a virtual dictatorship with the King as his puppet, and had taken the lead in the 1640 Scots Parliament as it reduced Royal powers and set up a Committee of Estates to run the administration when it was not sitting; there was talk of him being appointed 'dictator' on the Roman model as an interim emergency ruler with full powers.[11] Rumour said that he had discussed deposing the King for desertion or treachery.[12] In Scotland, this could rally alarmed peers to Montrose's side in the defence of collegiality – though even if true, Scots monarchs had been deposed before (including Charles' Catholic grandmother Mary Stuart, technically by abdication, in 1567). In England it appears that when Colonel Stewart informed Traquair of it, specifying that Argyll had even stated which articles of deposition-worthy treason the King had committed (tyranny and waging war on his subjects), he asked Montrose to collect written testimonies of Argyll having committed treason. Charles was clearly behind this. Was this the Scottish equivalent of Charles' threats to have Warwick and his friends impeached in England in early 1641? Just because neither prosecution actually happened should not mean that they were not important, at least in the eyes of the potential accused – driving them further into 'opposition' out of fear of Royal revenge?

The King did not embrace the prospect of abandoning the Scots episcopate to secure Montrose's allegiance with alacrity; the talks which Montrose's emissary Stewart conducted in London in the early spring did not reach early agreement despite the backing of the Duke of Lennox and Traquair. Charles' acceptance of the plan only followed Stewart's second visit, this time with written proof of Argyll's treason.[13] Charles had promised Argyll that he would meet all the Covenanters' demands in return for their army's military support in England – though he was naïve if he imagined that Argyll would be prepared to use the Scots army to save English episcopacy. The threat of Charles buying off the Scots with religious submission then using their army against Parliament was rumoured plausible in Westminster in early July, according to the Venetian ambassador.[14] In the meantime, the Scots Army in England continued to pose a major financial problem to Parliament – and potential propaganda bonus to Charles. Its passivity in English politics was not to be relied on – and had been unpaid by the English since January and was still owed the 'ex gratia' sum of £300,000 (termed 'Brotherly Assistance') granted by Parliament.

The eventual outcome of events should not blind us to the probabilities of the situation as it seemed in summer 1641. There was if anything less threat of immanent confrontation between the King and Parliament than there had been at the time of his attempts to save Strafford's life; that issue was now resolved and the current 'knife-edge' votes on 'Root and Branch' showed that religious reform was much less well supported in the Commons. The military presence and financial demands of the Scots army were a current bonus but future threat to Warwick and Pym's faction, with the danger that a backlash against them would aid the King to raise a larger army and defeat his challengers. There was also the possibility that he could wrest control of the Scots army from Argyll's faction by a coup on the part of discontented Scots nobles, particularly Montrose – which made his journey to Edinburgh to show himself to his Scots subjects particularly important. Once in Edinburgh he could charm and make offers to potential Montrose allies 'face-to-face', as he had endeavoured to do to the English 'opposition' peers with his offers of posts and honours in spring 1641. Alternatively, he could rely on the current, Argyll-led regime to accept his recognition of their control of Church and political life in return for their abandoning their English allies – which prospect made it vital to the English 'Junto' lords to keep Argyll on their side. Warwick appealed to the King in person not to go to Scotland, evidently fearing his intentions to break up the 'Junto'/Argyll alliance. Just before Charles left, on 8 August the King admitted his politically reliable cousin, the Duke of Lennox, to the Lords by creating him Duke of Richmond – to rally support against Warwick, with whom Lennox was already publicly at odds?[15]

There was however a problem for Charles' Scottish plans in August which had not existed during Colonel Stewart's visits to London in the spring. Not for the last time, Montrose acted rashly, bringing the anti-Argyll witness John Stewart of Ladywell to Edinburgh to testify before the Committee of Estates in May. Stewart was duly locked up in Edinburgh Castle and questioned[16] – but this served to tip off Argyll, though he no doubt had other sources of information as to what Montrose was up to. Colonel Stewart's visits to London had been noted and on his return in early June he was arrested and his secret cache of papers read. One of them confirmed harmlessly that Charles would guarantee the Covenanter legislation in return for Montrose's support, but there were also instructions (from Traquair?) to collect evidence ready for Argyll's arrest and trial for treason during the Royal visit.[17] As a result, on 11 June the Committee of Estates arrested Montrose, Lord Napier, and their allies,[18] and on the 19th the news of the 'plot' was announced to the 'opposition' leadership at Warwick House, London by treaty-commissioner Lord Loudoun. It was then given to the Commons on the 22nd by 'hard-liner' Haselrig, implicating the King in Montrose's actions.[19] The use of indiscreet written evidence of the King's deviousness – this time via Traquair – was to be repeated in 1645 when his papers were seized after the battle of Naseby, and no doubt the 'opposition' hoped to use it to bind wavering MPs to the course of legally and financially constraining their devious sovereign. So when Charles went to Edinburgh his potential partner Montrose was in prison – albeit usefully close to his residence in Holyrood – not at liberty to present evidence of Argyll's activities, and Charles had to deal with the suspicious Scots Parliament at a disadvantage. One of Montrose's assistants and a 'witness' to Argyll's talking treason, John Stewart of Ladywell, was condemned to death by a court headed by a Covenanter Army official and was beheaded by the 'Maiden' (the Scots proto-guillotine) on 28 July, implicitly a cold-blooded warning to the King. Had Montrose not been detected, would Argyll have suddenly faced a charge of treason in the manner that Charles was to plan for the 'Five Members' in England in January 1642?

For the moment, it seemed that Charles would go along with the terms demanded by the Argyll-clergy Covenanter leadership in Edinburgh in order to keep their goodwill. The recent arrest of Montrose and a band of his alleged allies by Argyll enabled the Campbell leader to present a 'united front' to the King, free from threat of an immanent coup, and indeed the Covenanter government sentenced Traquair to death *'in absentia'* just before the King's arrival.[20] Charles had to put up with snubs like having Lord Balmerino, sentenced to death for treason in 1633, imposed on him as Lord President of the Parliament, and provocative sermons denouncing the bishops;[21] but his public graciousness extended to inviting 'rebel' commander Alexander Leslie, victor of Newburn, to ride in his coach as he entered Edinburgh on 14 August. The Scots army, which Charles reviewed *en route* to the Border, now moved back from Northumberland to Leith and was partially disbanded. Charles' willingness to accept the abolition of bishops and drastic curtailing of his political powers in Scotland in 1641 arguably encouraged the preparedness of many Covenanter leaders to continue negotiating with him as late as autumn 1648. Had he not been so accommodating in summer 1641, would he have had this level of support – which enabled him to play the Covenanters off against the Englsh Parliament – for years to come? On 25 August he signed the politico-religious terms demanded by the Scots negotiators for an Anglo-Scots settlement, the 'Treaty of Edinburgh'. This was a major concession, as it accepted all the religious reforms initiated by the rebels since 1637 – including the abolition of episcopacy – and returned the Scots Church to its fully Calvinist state of the 1560s with power handed over to the militant junior clergy. The treaty also confirmed Charles' acceptance of all the political measures enacted by Parliament since November 1640, principally the demolition of his prerogative powers and reduction to dependence on Parliament for funds. Crucially, it ruled that he could not use his English army in Scotland or Ireland without the permission of Parliament, which ended his right to use the armed forces as he saw fit. It thus seemed to ratify his agreement to being a politically neutralised constitutional monarch in return for peace and his acceptance of the power of Argyll and the Kirk elders in Scotland;[22] the treaty was duly celebrated by the English 'opposition' in London on 7 September (appropriately for a Protestant triumph, Queen Elizabeth's birthday). The celebratory sermons were preached to them at Lincoln's Inn chapel by well-known radicals Stephen Marshall, who proclaimed that Parliament should carry on its good work until the reformation of both Church and State was complete, and (Warwick's ex-chaplain) Jeremiah Burroughs.[23]

But the treaty, as was to be seen with other later concessions by Charles, was only a temporary political tactic. He remained insistent on defending the Church and its bishops in England, as was implied by the seemingly innocuous recent proposal by pro-Royalist MP Sir John Colepeper to punish any insulters of the (Anglican and pro-episcopal) English Prayer Book. This was aimed at both 'Root and Branch' reformers and their Scots allies. Warwick and his allies, confident in their influence on military policy with Essex as Lord General and Northumberland as Lord Admiral, began to plan for a 1642 expedition to the Continent to restore the Elector Palatine to his lands and a naval expedition to raid the Spanish empire in the Caribbean. The latter was intended as an extension of the private initiatives of the Providence Island Company in the 1630s, now with half the profits going to the Elector Palatine to fund his army; and it was announced by new Essex MP Sir Richard Cave, London agent for the Elector and sitting for a family 'rotten borough' of Warwick's.[24] Spain had recently retaken Providence to halt that venture, but in 1639 Warwick had obtained a Royal licence for privateering attacks in the Caribbean; and the new plan rehashed one thought up in 1626 by Warwick's cousin Sir Nathaniel Rich, Pym, and Sir Benjamin Rudyerd.[25] Both campaigns implied that the 'Junto' intended to direct foreign policy – and to do it on the militant Protestant lines supported by Parliament in the 1620s, to which Saye and Sele's protégé Cromwell was to return in 1654. Warwick, Pym and Mildmay now took over financial direction of the Admiralty;[26] a practical step towards the unshakeable Parliamentary control there to be exercised in the Civil War. The probable commander of any land expedition in Europe was the current English commander-in-chief, Essex – who would thus have an excuse for taking over Charles' army at York and sacking any 'suspect' officers.

There was a potential bonus for Charles too, as such campaigns would surely need the attention of experienced officers who had already fought in Germany, e.g. the current Scots commander Alexander Leslie – thus removing them from British politics. The Elector Palatine duly accompanied Charles to Edinburgh in August to lobby the Scots Parliament for troops. Luckily for the belligerent peers' and MPs' hopes, the current German negotiations at Regensburg to restore the Elector to his dominions by Imperial order rather than by Protestant warfare collapsed. (Sir Thomas Roe, veteran exponent of a 'Protestant' foreign policy aimed at an international anti-Habsburg alliance, was representing England there.) Charles duly issued a belligerent statement from Edinburgh anticipating collapse and a new war to regain the Palatinate.[27] Would this war have taken place but for the Irish rebellion of October 1641 diverting Parliamentary military interest to Ireland, or would the 'King vs Commons' clash of December 1641 – January 1642 doomed it anyway?

The King's agreement with the Covenanters, 25 August 1641: a model for his deviousness in England in 1646–8?

In Scotland the King seems to have been as untrustworthy an ally for Argyll in 1641 as he was to be for Parliament in 1647–8. His involvement with plans to overthrow the dominant politico-military leadership whatever he said to their faces did not commence in 1646 with his defeat; it was already evident in Scotland in 1641. Any earlier Montrose plot to deal with Argyll had not been implemented, and at the time that Charles was in Edinburgh Montrose was a prisoner in the Castle as a result of his enemy's suspicions. But now Charles had signed the Treaty he had publicly accepted the Covenanter takeover of the Church and State, thus removing the 'casus belli' between him and the rebels of 1637–9, and Argyll did his best to secure the Lord Chancellorship of Scotland for himself and the Lord Treasurership for his cousin Loudoun, refusing Charles' attempt to give the former to his father-in-law Morton. In the end Loudoun became Lord Chancellor instead.[28] The King was also constrained by the arrival of a group of English Parliamentary commissioners in Edinburgh to liaise with the Scots Parliament – as was to be expected, dominated by 'oppositionists' (Lord Howard of Escrick, Nathaniel Fiennes, Hampden, and Sir Philip Stapleton);[29] Edward Nicholas advised his Royal master to regard them as spies for his English enemies.[30] The loyalty of Hamilton, now with the King in Edinburgh but on good terms with Argyll and corresponding with the Warwick group via Lord Mandeville (the Earl of Manchester's son and a future Parliamentarian general) was suspect.[31] It appears that Charles sought to use the revival in his local support in Scotland for his acquiescence to political/religious reforms to plot a coup against the obdurate Argyll. Details of 'The Incident' are unclear, but the influential junior Royal Bedchamber official Will Murray – a Scot normally domiciled in London – was involved with Montrose's allies, particularly the Earl of Roxburgh, in a plan to entrap Argyll and his current ally Hamilton (who had evidently decided that Argyll was a better master than Charles at the moment). This followed indiscreet verbal abuse of and a threat to fight a duel with Hamilton's kinsman Sir James Hamilton by Roxburgh's son Walter Kerr, who called the Marquis of Hamilton a traitor at a party at Murray's lodgings – a sign of high feelings in the Royal entourage. The recent Scots Parliamentary vote to have the right to veto any Royal appointments of councillors, officers of state, or judges (16 September) and the appointment of Loudoun as Lord Chancellor and Argyll's block on the King's nomination of Lord Almond as Lord Treasurer (30 September)[32] were probably to blame for the strength of feeling; Almond joined the plot. (The King now made him Earl of Callendar, showing his feelings.) Seemingly the two Marquises and Hamilton's brother Lanark were to have been invited to a secret Royal audience in Holyrood and arrested – and possibly murdered, as the Earl of Crawford apparently suggested at a planning-meeting with Murray – in October. A Colonel Cochrane, based at Musselburgh, was sounded out by Murray and agreed to lead his men to arrest the two peers when they obeyed a summons to Charles' apartments at Holyrood Palace (where they were currently staying), probably on Monday 11 October; the armed affinities of Lords Roxburgh and Home would then reinforce the Palace and remove the two accused.[33] The plot leaked out, apparently thanks to Cochrane's junior Captain Hurry (later a Covenanter general routed by Montrose in 1645), and the King denied all knowledge.[34] The tension would have been heightened by the presence of large numbers of armed retainers in the capital, which could spill over into a bloody confrontation; Argyll and Hamilton were supposed to have 5,000 men in the city, and Walter Kerr was to parade with 600 retainers to Parliament to defend his accusations against Hamilton.[35] The last such serious episodes in Edinburgh had been in the aftermath of Lord Darnley's assassination and Queen Mary's capture in 1567.

Nothing could be proved against Charles, but relations with the Scots leadership soured and once their Parliament had refused to loan Charles troops to fight the Irish rebellion he decided to return to London in November. Had the coup been successful, and Argyll been removed from power in favour of the militarily capable and determinedly Covenanter Montrose, Charles would have been unable to go back on the Treaty for fear of losing Scots support. The Royal loss of political and ecclesiastical authority in Scotland would have had to be maintained to secure noble and clerical support. But with the potential for a Scots army under Montrose at his back in 1642, he would have been likely to have taken a harder line in London even sooner than he did over the 'Five Members'. As it was, he was left with having to surrender all the demanded official posts to Argyll's nominees to secure his goodwill, and accept Scots Parliament control of nominations to the Privy Council. This had an effect on the crisis in London, by encouraging Warwick's group of equally mistrustful English peers into considering forcing a similar measure on him in England. But, as seen above, they had already drawn up legal measures to assume control of the armed forces back in June – they already distrusted Charles then.

It should not be assumed that Charles' efforts to turn Scotland into his weapon and/or resume the political offensive in London were unsuspected by the 'opposition' there. During the English Parliamentary recess the Warwick group of peers were reported by Venetian ambassador Giustinian as holding secret conclaves to try to anticipate what measures the King might use against them on his return home. As he now no longer had the legal right to shut down this Parliament without its consent, this meant extra-legal means.[36] In the meantime, the Lords voted before their recess to extend their Petitions Committee's right of receiving appeals from across England to Ireland too.[37] Based on the principle of Poynings' Act (1494), its practical implication was to subject all Irish legal decisions (e.g. in landholdership cases) to the veto of a committee dominated by Warwick's party of 'godly' Protestants who could be guaranteed to decide against any Catholic appellants. This, coupled with rumours of a new 'plantation', would encourage Catholic landholders living in areas under threat of confiscation to revolt rather than accept unfair rulings, with the King no longer able to protect them. The personnel who might lead such a revolt, namely militarily ambitious or experienced younger Catholic men, had just been denied their traditional 'escape-route' of service with a Catholic army on the Continent; Parliament had banned this so the Habsburgs could not use Irish troops against the projected Anglo-Scottish campaign on behalf of restoring the Palatinate.[38] Did these two seemingly minor decisions play a crucial role in inspiring determined young landed Catholics to stage a revolt that autumn? Significantly, rumours in Ireland had it that Charles was to be deposed by his English and Scots Parliaments in favour of his nephew the Elector Palatine, a 'safe' Protestant ruler.[39] Possibly gossip to this effect was circulating in London and was transmitted to Dublin – and Charles Louis was suggested as a new King of England by radicals in 1645.

A rising arc of disaffection in Ireland tips over into revolt, autumn 1641: 'anti-centralism' in Ireland as in Scotland in 1637, but this time by Catholics

The question of an 'invasive' central government in London imposing their (religious) 'norms' on a normally autonomous 'Celtic' nation with a distinct administration and culture had sparked off disaster in Scotland in 1637. Now the same happened in the third part of the British 'multi-state', Ireland – but this time the threat came not from the King but from his critics in Parliament. Arguably, both monarchs and the political elite in Parliament were equally culpable over the issue of Protestant settlers from England occupying large chunks of land in 'barbarous' and 'Papist' regions of Ireland, and had been since Elizabeth's time. She and her ultra-Protestant ministers had sought to solve the security problem of proudly autonomous, often rebellious Catholic magnates such as the 1570s Earl of Desmond in Munster by replacing them with loyal Protestant English colonists. On a legal plane, the documents by which these magnates held title to their lands were often 'defective' (in English terms). This 'planting' of the English far from Dublin had been commenced by the Catholics Philip and Mary I in Offaly and Laois in the 1550s. The early 'projectors' in clearing out local Catholics by dubious means had included Sir Walter

Raleigh, also a major colonizer in the Americas, and settlers had included the militantly Protestant poet Edmund Spenser. The Catholic rebels' financial and military backing by Spain and the papacy had made the question of 'planting' one of national security in the 1588–1604 Spanish war, and this fear of foreign 'meddling' in a Catholic Ireland had continued. The issue of 'planting' was thus always implicitly linked to Anglicization and imposing an 'English "social and legal system headed by a loyal elite of 'English' (in manner or ethnicity) and Protestant gentry, though this was patchy at best in Munster where a form of compromise evolved with many local Irish small landowners surviving. Indeed, tension seems to have been low in 1630s Munster – so Charles' imposition of a centralizing governor calling land-titles into question was an avoidable disaster.

The major revolt in Ulster in the late 1590s, led by the Earl of Tyrone (head of its ancient kingly O'Neill dynasty) had duly led to a systematic policy of colonization in Ulster under James VI and I, with the City of London and other mercantile 'projectors' involved – hence turning Derry into the Anglicised 'Londonderry'. James was already bringing his Gaelic lords of the Hebrides under 'modern' law and central control, and crushing 'brigand' clans like the Macgregors. The 'threat' of sinister European Catholic plotting to inflame the remaining Irish Catholic magnates and their feudal tenants into rebellion had continued to loom over English Protestant opinion through the Thirty Years' War – coupled with ambitious would-be settlers' desire for extra Irish lands and profit. Indeed, the whole danger of an externally-imposed and culturally (and religiously) alien elite living on top of a 'powder-keg' of resentful, culturally conservative 'natives' in Ireland has a parallel to the situation in (Slav, Protestant) Bohemia, crushed and partially settled by the Germanic Habsburgs (Catholic) in and after 1620. Now the threat of the Long Parliament launching a new wave of settlers seems to have pushed a network of elite Irish Catholics (some officers who had some experience of fighting overseas in the Thirty Years' War) into pre-emptive action. Unlike in Scotland, this was not directly the result of Royal policies – apart from Wentworth threatening to confiscate 'illegally' held lands on a greater scale than his predecessors. But, crucially, the crisis came to a head at a time when Charles' attempt to impose greater centralization (and raise money) by Wentworth post-1633 had upset the normal political 'balance' in the Anglicised areas of Ireland between the Dublin government, its newer Protestant 'New English' settlers, older semi-Anglicised Catholic landowners of medieval Anglo-Norman ('Old English') origin, and 'native Irish' lords of ancient 'Celtic' dynasties. Lacking a large army or administration (or much income from a rural economy), Dublin had long relied on co-operation with the various regional landowners as its effective agents, raisers of troops (their tenants) and revenue, and 'eyes and ears'. But the remorseless and confrontational Wentworth had proceeded to undermine and challenge many legally defective titles to land-holding held by the 'New English', as much for reasons of profit by selling off those confiscated as for centralism, and to interfere in the usual localist autonomy of the Protestant Church. He particularly clashed with the greatest of the 'New English' plantation profiteers in Munster, the Earl of Cork (head of the Boyle dynasty), invaluable as a local 'strongman' in practical politics but too defiant of strict legal procedure for Wentworth's liking. Having raised fears of his partiality for the Catholics by no crackdown on recusancy fines, offended many of the Protestant landowners on whom local government relied, and come to rely on the Catholic 'Old English' for support in the Irish Parliament, he then delayed in formally putting their cherished special legal privileges (the 'Graces') into statute law and challenged their land-titles too. Did this push some into rebellion? His plans for extra plantation, now in Galway, and belated rapprochement with the Ulster planters also disillusioned Catholics about his goodwill. If time had been on his side and he had had adequate money (which he was piling up) this 'push' for a new, centralised order might have worked, but the political developments in England led to his recall in 1640 as we have seen. He was succeeded by what amounted to a rudderless 'interim' regime – and thus the absence of a demonstrably energetic and capable commander in Dublin who could crack down on rebels quickly. Would the plotters have dared to act had they faced Wentworth?

The idea of the Irish rising being by 'loyal' rebels, in Charles' name and to preserve his throne, has been assumed to be a polite fiction – covering its treasonous intent and included so as to enable 'Old English' Catholics loyal to Charles (not to his Parliamentary coercers) to join in the plot. But it may well have been genuine, at least in the minds of its proposers, and the rumour of the militant Parliamentary zealots deposing Charles is an indication that the plot was aimed at a Parliament dominated by pro-Covenanter peers and MPs, not at his government 'per se'. The heirs of the 'Puritan' City merchants who had 'planted' Ulster in the 1600s as a 'godly' work designed to evict Catholicism there – men like Pennington and Maurice Thompson – were now the allies of the Warwick group. It was assumed that a new plantation was in the offing, and the rising was designed to thwart this by restoring the evicted Catholics to their lost territories; there were arguments that the previously loyal Catholics were absolved from their support for the King as his legal government had been usurped by a hostile 'Puritan' Parliament. Alternatively, some argued that the rebels were aiding the King by taking on his usurping challengers.[40] Lord Maguire, one of the leaders, claimed that the crucial incident was Parliament's appointment in August of the new Lord Lieutenant, the Earl of Leicester, as he was reckoned to be potentially as oppressively Protestant (and fond of confiscating Catholic land) as his grandfather, Sir Henry Sidney, had been in the 1560s.[41] Two other feared figures were Essex, the new Lord General and son of the Elizabethan commander against the Ulster rebel Tyrone in 1599–1601, and the new 'Master of the Ordnance' Lord Newport, his half-brother – who would be in charge of raising any new army.

The plot centred on the O'Neill clan and their tenants, kin and hereditary dependants to the late Earl of Tyrone (leader of the last great Irish rising in the 1590s, and exiled 1607). His kinsman Sir Phelim O'Neill headed the plotters within Ulster, and was in correspondence with Tyrone's exiled son John and nephew Owen Roe O'Neill; it centred on 'planted' towns in Ulster taken from the O'Neills. It was aided at Court by the O'Neill's' relative Daniel O'Neill, an army officer serving Charles, whose plotter brother Con used him to endeavour to arrange a Royal licence for recruiting Irish soldiers (officially for Spain in the Netherlands, in fact to be armed ready to revolt in Ulster). There was in any case some degree of assistance or approval by émigré Irish Catholic officers in Spanish service who arrived in Ireland in June 1641 to recruit troops for the Spanish army through the services of Spanish ambassador Cardenas in London, though it was later claimed by Lord Maguire that only three of them were involved. Some appear to have backed out of it when they heard of the risky plan to seize Dublin. If there was any contact between the Court and the plotters, Daniel O'Neill was the obvious link.[42] Due to the Parliamentary order disbanding Strafford's 8,000-strong Irish army, there were plenty of demobilized officers drifting around ready to turn on

Parliament. In the first week of October, with unemployed officers being ordered out of London, placards appeared denouncing Parliament for betraying the King and the nobility.[43] Anti-'Junto' feeling was thus being organised. Although later Royal use of Catholic rebels against Parliament was to encourage 'back-dated' Parliamentary belief that Charles was using Catholic Irishmen to attack them in 1641 it is not impossible; as we have seen, he was already prepared to use the Scots army, so why not Irishmen too?

In a further complication, the Tyrone rebellion had been the occasion for the crowning achievement in Protestant iconography of the 'Warwick circle' member Essex's late father. The late earl had been seen off to conquer the rebels in 1599 amidst great enthusiasm in London, mentioned in the prologue to Shakespeare's 'Henry V', but had failed to defeat the Tyrone rebels, had signed a controversial truce without Royal permission after becoming bogged down by guerrilla attacks, and had returned to England to disgrace, rebellion, and execution. His son, the current Earl of Essex, was to become a much-mooted leader for the new expedition against the latest rebellion in 1641–2 – and was feared by his sovereign for his potential to stage the attempted coup or military intimidation that his father had threatened towards Elizabeth in 1599–1601. The threat posed to Irish Catholics by the Earl of Essex's militancy as an army commander as well as the general confiscatory tone taken in Parliament was probably a useful propaganda weapon to win over 'moderates' loyal to the King personally. When the rebellion occurred the rebel Lord Mayor of Limerick, Dominic Fanning, was to drink the King's health and claim his faction were loyal to him but it was the Protestant English Parliament who were the real rebels. In County Leitrim the rebels went further and alleged that the 'rebel' Puritan MPs had already deposed Charles and selected a replacement so the Irish had to rescue the proper King.

The run-up to the 'Grand Remonstrance': the effects of its timing at a point of fears for Protestantism.

The aristocratic leadership of the 'opposition' had coalesced around the Earls of Warwick, Bedford (until his death in May), and Essex, Lords Brooke and Saye and Sele, and the heir of the Earl of Manchester, Lord Mandeville. These men, with the less certain support of other peers alienated from the King and his 1630s Court favourites (e.g. Pembroke and Hertford), had organised the attack on the Royal prerogative and Royal ministers in the Lords since November 1640, and now in the autumn of 1641 had to decide their attitude to 'Root and Branch'. Their 'party' (nicknamed the 'Junto' after the Spanish term for 'council'), was now more divided; some, such as Warwick, Saye and Sele, and Mandeville, were Calvinist zealots likely to vote against the bishops. Crucially Bedford, whose interests seem to have been more constitutional than religious, was dead. Other former 'moderate' backers of the King, like Northumberland and the ambitious and wavering Hamilton, had swung to their side that summer. They were backed up regularly in the Commons by Pym, Hampden, St John, and by assorted MPs chiefly known for their zeal on religious matters, men such as Sir Arthur Haselrig (Brooke's brother-in-law) and Denzel Holles who would persevere in broadly Presbyterian sympathies right through the coming conflict until 1660-1. (Holles, less militant about waging war on the King, would be in favour of peace in 1643.) Would their unity continue or would enough votes drift back to the King to block religious reform? The main legislative measures Royal critics had demanded had been passed and the King had seemed to be co-operative. MPs like Hyde and Colepeper accepted Royal office out of fear that the radical 'extremists', led by Pym, were going too far. The Commons votes on religion since late May had been much less decisive than the earlier ones on curbing the Royal prerogative; the first reading of the bill to abolish bishops had been passed narrowly and pro-Royalist MP Edward Nicholas thought it stood no chance of becoming law.

There was a provincial pro-Anglican reaction in favour of the King, now that the main 'abuses' had been reformed and the Irish Rebellion presented a major outside threat of 'Popish' massacre. The issuing of Parliament's ordinance of 8 September for the removal of superstitious imagery from churches had led to sporadic iconoclasm, albeit only where sponsored by militant local clergy or gentry (e.g. Herefordshire MP Sir Robert Harley, later a Parliamentary commander, who smashed up the village cross at Wigmore on the 27th). The precise extent of this iconoclasm has been examined by David Cressy, but cannot be exactly reckoned;[44] the perception of Parliament-sponsored innovation and anarchy was however important (as in 1642) in rising 'Royalism'. It was especially implemented by self-appointed 'Puritan' vigilantes in London, a hive of radical congregations, and Nicholas reported hopefully to the King on 5 October that this 'insolent carriage of the schismatics' was seriously annoying many in the City.[45] Simultaneously, the usurpation of the normal 'official' appearance of formal Acts of Parliament for printed recess orders of the Commons, where their 'Recess Committee' chairman Pym was named, led to the first pointed jokes about 'King Pym'.[46] More seriously on a practical level, the Parliamentary moves to disband the Royalist army at York by laying off potentially dangerous officers backfired when it led to some of them turning up in London, searching for employment and hostile to Parliament. These 'reformadoes' first appeared in October, and some of them were to be recruited by the King and his 'hard-line' courtiers to his armed forces in the capital in the winter – giving him confidence for his 'fight-back'.

The King's reviving political fortunes at Westminster were now co-ordinated in his absence by the Clerk of the Privy Council, Nicholas. Early in October he wrote on his master's behalf to a dozen or so peers who had shown their alarm at 'Root and Branch' by their voting on 8–9 September, including the Earls of Bath, Huntingdon, Devonshire, Newcastle (removed from his guardianship of the Prince of Wales in favour of Hertford) Northumberland and sacked ex-ministers Lords Cottington and Coventry.[47] These and the bishops could be expected to form the nucleus of a Royalist 'party' in the Lords when the Houses re-convened on 20 October, and Nicholas' conduit to the bishops was ex-Treasurer Bishop Juxon of London.[48] The five vacant sees were now filled with men who Nicholas described as 'of whom there is not the least suspicion of favouring the Popish party'.[49] – Ralph Brownrigg was married to Pym's niece and John Prideaux was the Calvinist Professor of Divinity at Oxford. Nicholas clearly understood how to use the 'middle ground', and on 22 October the reassembled Commons saw the 'opposition' attempt to remove the bishops as a factor in Lords votes as Holles proposed reviving the question of impeaching those thirteen bishops who had backed Laud's notorious canons in 1640.[50] This was coupled with a bill from Sir Gilbert Gerard (St John's wife's uncle) to bar bishops from all secular offices, including the Lords.[51] The revival of the impeachment was defeated, with some of the peers 'targeted' by Nicholas leading their defence. But while a coherent Royal 'party' defended the current Church in the Lords, the 'opposition' also moved on to a bold attempt to establish a Parliamentary veto over all appointments to offices of state, a major part of emasculating Royal power and one not coincidentally won by the Scots Parliament from Charles on 16 September. On 28 October William Strode seconded the proposal, warning that without such a veto the King (or his councillors) could undo all that any Parliament achieved, and others referred to the alleged ancient precedents for such control (which Pym had been researching in the recess).[52] The precedents for such a control of the King's choice of appointments by a self-appointed clique of his detractors dated back to 1258 (Henry III) and 1310 (Edward II), even if in those times it had been solely nobility rather than MPs who ran the resultant councils. The successful opposition to this as a reform too far was led by Hyde, and all that was agreed was to send a petition to the King concerning 'evil counsellors'.[53] It seemed to both Nicholas and Hyde that the 'opposition' attempts at further secular and religious reform had been blunted and this might be permanent; could the King even think of dissolving Parliament on his return home?[54]

The third kingdom's civil war begins: and unbalances politics at Westminster?

Unfortunately the Irish revolt changed all this – for now the question arose of who was to control the army sent to suppress it. The coincidental timing of the Irish revolt, co-ordinated by Catholic conspirators in Ulster (led by Sir Phelim O'Neill) to occur on the night of 22–3 October, was also vital to the inflaming of English opinion and encouraging concerned MPs to listen to the lurid demands for further anti-'Popish' measures by their own Protestant militants. It was by chance that several different Irish plots were underfoot that autumn, and that all were able to come together (without news leaking out) and make the intended outbreak more extensive, dangerous, and – in terms of the English reaction – apocalyptic. Expropriated Ulster landowner Rory O'More's plot to seize back Catholic lands by force was co-ordinated with the plot by ruined local Catholic peer Lord Maguire to seize Dublin Castle, arrest the senior English officials, and arrange for the Irish Parliament to declare for Charles but against his confiscatory Parliament; and both were linked to the plot by the O'Neill's to bring in Irish exiles in Spanish service.[55] Ironically, the – serious, political – intention of the O'More plot in seizing Dublin was a

Catholic Irish version of the situation already achieved by their Protestant Covenanter enemies in another of Charles' kingdoms, and the ideal for which Warwick's group were striving in the third British kingdom. These diverse groups all intended to reduce the Monarchy to a figurehead which had been forced to abdicate its political and religious powers to their groupings – three different forces of 'hard-liners', representing two Protestant and one Catholic 'conspiracy' to limit monarchic power.

In a co-ordinated coup, a number of major Ulster towns were seized on the night of 22–23 October. Massacres resulted, their numbers exaggerated by lurid English propaganda in the coming months and clearly not amounting to the hundreds of thousands supposed by the victims' sympathisers. But at least a few thousand Protestant settlers were killed, in a sudden attack made more shocking by its clear pre-meditation, and aimed at 'ethnic' or 'religious cleansing' as it would be termed today. Possibly a quarter of the Protestant population was killed in County Antrim.[56] In an era used to the atrocities of the St Bartholomew's Day Massacre, the writings of John Foxe about the Marian persecutions, and lurid stories of endless Catholic plans to commit mass-murder, it confirmed Protestants' worst suspicions and led to demands for a 1599-style campaign of revenge. In fact O'Neill issued a proclamation from Dungannon on 24 October forbidding killings of Protestants but this was ignored by local enthusiasts and embittered evictees made the most of their chance to exterminate their dispossessors, as any realistic planner would have considered possible. The fact that Daniel O'Neill was serving at Court and was well-known to the Queen could be made the most of in the coming years by Parliament, although even if the Queen was aware of the intended revolt she bore no responsibility for it getting out of hand.

Armagh, Charlemont, Newry, Mountjoy and Tanagree, all important fortified positions in Ulster, fell within a few days and by 31 October Dundalk had followed; at Charlemont Sir Phelim O'Neill called on Lord Charlemont for dinner at his castle and then seized him and the fortress. Londonderry, Coleraine and Carrickfergus were not yet attacked and refugees made their way there as best they could for harassing bands of Catholics (probably as much opportunist robbers as organised rebels). On 29 November Rory O'More won the first pitched battle of the war, intercepting a government force en route to relieve Drogheda. Revolt duly spread to Leinster, which it probably would not have done but for the rebels' obvious success. All the King could do when he heard the news in Edinburgh (while on the golf-links at Leith) was to appoint the Earl of Ormonde, as his most trusted 'Old English' (Protestant) commander and a major landlord in the still-loyal south with many armed tenants at hand, as lieutenant-general in charge of a hoped-for army of 2300 infantry and 943 cavalry. But to add to the confusion the rebels were circulating a forged Royal warrant (allegedly issued in Scotland) giving them instructions to rise, which some may have believed; and rumours in England had it that the Queen was behind the revolt (possibly a garbled story about Colonel Daniel O'Neill's Court links).

The news of the mass-murders apparently reached London on Sunday 31 October, inflaming Protestant opinion against Catholics at Court as well as in Ireland. Crucially, it was brought to the Privy Council (in charge while the King was in Edinburgh) not by a Dublin governmental official but by Pym's 'planter' brother-in-law Clotworthy's 'man of business' Owen Connolly, who could be guaranteed to put the most lurid possible 'spin' on it to encourage drastic retaliation. He delivered the news to the Earl of Leicester, the Irish Lord Lieutenant, at the latter's house in what is now Leicester Square (then fields). The Council met in emergency session there, and next morning reported it in person to Parliament. The news was a godsend to the radicals, as providing an opportunity for demands for Protestant extirpation of the 'Papists' and a Parliament-controlled army to deal with the crisis – though fear and hatred of the aggressors were undoubtably genuine. The mood of horror and fear was reported by witness Bulstrode Whitelocke, and Parliament sent delegations to the City for a £50,000 loan to raise an army. But even before this date the Warwick-Pym group's offensive against the King on matters of political and religious 'reform' had resumed, as soon as Parliament returned from its recess (20 October); it did not cause but exacerbated mistrust. Now the militants' zeal was unleashed on 'Papists', as on 2 November Strode successfully proposed a bill to have recusants prosecuted at the next Assizes[57] and the Prince of Wales was removed from his Catholic mother's household at Oatlands Palace.[58] Instead his 'Governor' the Earl of Hertford (Essex's brother-in-law) took charge of him, at Richmond Palace. By association the Catholic Queen was a leading 'fifth columnist' to the radicals' minds, not unreasonably given her household's involvement in the May 1641 plots. Next day Pym recounted the details of the plot to seize Dublin Castle to the Commons – and people could be encouraged to link this sinister Popish plot with the King's machinations as this coincided with the arrival of details of the 'Incident' plot to murder Argyll and Hamilton in Edinburgh, helpfully blamed on Royal servant Will Murray.[59] The depositions against Murray were read to the Commons on 'Gunpowder Plot Day', adding to their emotive impact, after a sermon by radical preacher Jeremiah Burroughs which had compared King Charles to the ill-advised and deposed King Rehoboam of Israel.[60] Rehoboam was the son of Solomon, the name which Charles' father James I had used of himself. The hint was plain, the target was Charles I, and the perceived remedy was to control the Royal appointments to save this modern Rehoboam from his worst instincts. Burges was a friend of Pym, and presumably cleared his text and metaphors with him. Accordingly, 5 November also saw the Commons voting to empower Leicester, as the commander-in-chief in Ireland, to raise and the Ordnance commander Newport to fit out a new army to suppress the rebellion – without waiting for the King's approval.[61] Presumably it was no coincidence that the debate and vote took place within hours of the inflammatory 'Gunpowder Day' sermon, and Parliament had already set up a new sub-committee for Irish affairs to handle such matters. Next day Cromwell proposed that Essex be appointed 'Lord General' South of the Trent by ordinance, to continue in office as long as Parliament saw fit.[62] Already appointed by the King, Essex was instead to hold supreme military power in the capital and the South of England by Parliamentary authority. The challenge to Royal power was explicit if expressed in legal terms, and the choice of Cromwell to pose it (his first major action in the Parliament) was significant in retrospect. The army to be sent to Ireland was fixed on 4 November at 6,000 infantry and 2,000 cavalry. A 'watered-down' version of the proposal to make senior appointments subject to Parliamentary approval, a 'supplication' (request) not an order, was duly passed on 8 November;[63] what was not clear was what would be done if Charles ignored it. As the previous attempt to pass such a proposal had been defeated, it is clear that the 'Popish scare' was used to reintroduce it more successfully. The latter was also used to diminish the size of the King's party in the Lords by removing the Catholic peers from the latter, with the Warwick faction introducing a Lords motion to see that all statutes against recusancy were rigorously enforced so their Catholic colleagues left London. There were also threats to impeach the bishops (and thus remove their votes from the Lords) by a Commons committee, headed by St John, set up to consider this on 13 November. But the radicals were unable to secure the numbers for control of votes in the Lords as yet, as a bold plan they had formulated to send the King a 'request' to remove any Privy Councillors who the Commons vetoed or face unilateral action to do this was blocked by the King's allies in the Lords. The latter, led by Bristol, acted on instructions sent from Edinburgh by Secretary Nicholas.

Incidentally, it is notable that the aftermath of the outbreak of the Irish revolt also saw a number of 'scare stories' about similar plots in England, which presumably increased fear and thus a desire to act against all Catholic 'fellow-travellers' in Westminster. One of the most unlikely, tailor Thomas Beale's story about a group of Catholics who had arranged for each of them to kill an MP (why only one?), was supported by Pym's lieutenant John Hampden, which casts light on his anti-Catholic paranoia and so affection for 'Root and Branch' (which he had backed in May 1641).

Matters now proceeded to the submission of a long list of the King's alleged misdeeds since 1627, known (but not to contemporaries) as the 'Grand Remonstrance'. Under preparation for months, its announcement for voting now was clearly intended to back up the case for permanent control of the executive by reminding the MPs and peers (and, once it was published, the public) of Charles' incompetence and sinister fondness for 'Papist' councillors and autocratic abuse of power. Councillor and MP Edward Nicholas was duly alarmed at its implications and urged Charles to return quickly to London. The Remonstrance was seen by many MPs not in Pym's group as unnecessary – the main practical demands of the majority of MPs, the dismantlement of the apparatus of 'Personal Rule' in civil and ecclesiastical affairs, the eviction of Catholic place-holders from the administration, and the punishment of the supposed arch-villains Laud and Strafford, had been accomplished already and the King had accepted it all. The contentious matters outstanding, such as the curtailment of the bishops' powers or even their existence, were crucial to the future of the Church and nation but less urgent than dealing practically with the Irish threat – which meant agreement on funding and commanding an army.

The crucial question was whether a majority of MPs distrusted Charles enough to remove his power of senior appointments and regarded any

Church containing bishops as irredeemably corrupt. The current senior officers of State were not under suspicion for 'Popery', and Leicester, Essex, and Newport could be trusted to carry out the Irish war faithfully on behalf of Protestantism. The insistence on extra legal powers for Parliament showed a concern for the theoretical question of what would happen if Charles tried to return to his 'bad old ways' and remove the figures who Parliament had made him instal in office in 1641. Hence the careful listing of all his past 'form' since 1627 (the year of 'Forced Loans') in the 'Remonstrance'.

It is clear from the drawing up of the Remonstrance that the 'opposition' zealots believed in keeping up the pressure, not uniting with the King to organise the funding of a campaign in Ireland as a more urgent priority. Arguably their attitude to the King was inevitable given the 'Army Plot' of May and the 'Incident' in Edinburgh, as the King could not be trusted; but the deliberately aggressive tone of the 'Remonstrance', listing all Charles' past misdeeds, was clearly inflammatory. These MPs and their allied Calvinist peers were however losing votes, as the narrow passing of the Remonstrance showed. It was passed by 159 votes to 148 in the early hours of 23 November, after a fourteen-hour Commons debate;[64] its publication was banned but this did not exclude manuscript copies being passed around. It was important in rallying support for the Remonstrance that sufficient waverers still distrusted the King despite his agreement to the bills of reform and the execution of Strafford, and in that context Charles' actions in November 1641 were helpful to Pym. After returning from his late summer trip to Scotland he showed no practical sign of a conciliatory attitude – crucially in his alterations in Court appointments. Peers connected to the 'Junto' had lost not gained influence, as with the dismissal of Pembroke from his posts. The dismissal of the elder Sir Henry Vane from the Secretaryship of State in early December was a blow to hopes of 'opposition' influence in the government. Charles did publish a reply to the 'Grand Remonstrance', assuring that he was the defender of the established constitutional order against factional innovations – a 'first' for him in response to the recent rise in pro-'opposition' pamphleteering, showing his awareness of the need to seek public support and probably prompted by Hyde or Colepeper.

The Remonstrance made the restriction of the bishops' powers and abolition of Church ceremonial integral to the future, and spoke in paranoid language about a 'plot' against the fundamental laws and liberties of the kingdom throughout the current King's reign. Blame was allocated to Catholics at Court, Jesuit spies, and others in the pay of foreign powers and all the 'crimes' against the subject in 1629–40 were listed. Its 'narrative' was designed to induce a fear of the King as untrustworthy and in need of permanent coercion in its listeners, and the tone taken clearly showed that the men who had drawn it up were expert in the detail of the counter-manoevures of King and critics in Parliament in 1625–9 and hostile to episcopacy. Its mode of address thus polarised opinions, and it was only narrowly passed by eleven votes – possibly the insistence on adding the abolition of bishops to the 'essential' reforms was too contentious and ran an unnecessary risk. Even after its late-night passing there was a violent quarrel in the Commons over whether or not to publish it and thus appeal to public opinion for support. It could have been defeated by a few more defections, whether or not Hyde's account is to be taken seriously when he says that Cromwell told him that if it had been defeated he would have left the country in disgust (presumably to emigrate to Massachusetts or Rhode Island).[65] Pym's faction would not have been intimidated or disheartened into abandoning the attack on the bishops, but their defeat would have been rallying-point for MPs and peers who had been alarmed by the demonstrations and petitions in favour of radical Church reform. As it was, they dropped some of the most contentious religious clauses (e.g. an attack on the 1559 Prayer Book) from the final text in order to secure extra votes.

The King could have listened to moderates in Lords and Commons in order to reach a settlement and isolate Pym's faction further, appearing the injured party who was keen to get agreement on the command of an army to tackle the Irish rebels but held up by the malcontent minority in Westminster. He now had capable advisers able to read the mood of the Commons and know what would win over the majority, particularly men like Colepeper and Hyde – if he would listen to them rather than rash belligerents such as Goring. This strategy of using offers from Commons allies who feared anarchy or an insolent encroachment on their King's 'honour' and were more loyal to their King than obsessed with religion had been used before, with Wentworth in 1628–9. Hyde was now the King's principal Commons ally, voicing the fears of moderates that the House needed to get on with resolving its quarrels by compromise and turning to the more important Irish issue. But would the King fail to secure enough votes this time, as he had done with the Petition of Right on the previous occasion? The narrow outcome of the vote on the Remonstrance shows that the issue could have gone either way – and that any conciliatory moves on grants of office or religious promises by the King would have increased Hyde's support in the Commons. The major concession of his allowing Essex to lead the Irish campaign would have been beneficial to Charles' reputation but potentially risky for the future, given the Earl's links to the Warwick circle and the precedent of the Earl's father's disloyalty in 1599–1601.

The grants of Court posts to some disaffected nobles since May (e.g. Hertford and Essex) had shown the latter that Charles was willing to accept their rights so it would be counter-productive to carry on pressurizing him through their MP allies. But, as seen by the dismissal of Pembroke, this policy had its limits and no major ministerial posts had been made available. Moreover, did Essex regard himself as the servant of Charles or of the Houses of Parliament, and would he and the King have clashed over this at some point? For those peers backing 'Root and Branch', religious reform was essential but their accepting major office would leave them in a dilemma if Charles ignored it. Should they resign and lose influence over policy? One significant non-noble ministerial 'opposition' recruit, Vane, was now dismissed (27 November); his 'opposition' MP son (Sir Henry Vane junior) lost his post as Treasurer of the Navy, the sole Secretaryship of State was given to the loyalist Sir Edward Nicholas, Pembroke was refused the expected Lord Stewardship, and Essex's term as 'Lord General' South of the Trent was not extended in a 'raft' of measures taken as Charles returned to London.[66] But his haste to return led to him meekly accepting all the 'hard-line' Covenanter nominees to his Scots Privy Council, the Scots judiciary, and the Scots Parliament's 'standing commitees' (which governed while it was not in session) – and this surrender over appointments could encourage the 'Junto' to think he would give in to this requirement within England next.

The recent furore over the 'Grand Remonstrance' and the rise in pro-Royal voting seems to have added to Charles' confidence that support was rising and he could milk the fear of anarchy. Accordingly his re-entry to London on 25 November (which John Adamson sees as a 'stage-managed' Royalist rally)[67] saw him escorted by large numbers of armed men amidst fulsome declarations of loyalty; his troops included men from the disbanded army at York which Parliament had feared would back Strafford that spring.[68] Logically, the arrival of these men implied that Charles was in a stronger military position to coerce Parliament. In his reply to the 'loyal addresses' by the City grandees (headed by the pro-Royal new Lord Mayor elected in September, Richard Gurney) Charles assured his adherence to Protestantism as established in the reigns of his two predecessors. The 'narrative' of resistance to 'innovation' was thus firmly rewritten to imply that it was 'Root and Branch', not Charles' own Laudian reforms, that was innovatory and hence to be resisted.[69] The 'opposition' peers boycotted the parade, which was implicitly aimed at winning City support at their expense; and indeed the election of Gurney as Lord Mayor and presence of some of their own Artillery Company troops in the procession implied threats to their control of the capital. To add to the potential use of London by the King, bands of disbanded troops from the York army, the 'reformadoes', were lurking in the City despite orders to return home, and were hostile to Essex and Holland as 'traitors'; they could provide 'foot-soldiers' for a coup, though their wilder spirits were somewhat of a political liability. Hyde/Clarendon indeed traced the origin of the use of the name 'Cavalier', from the Spanish *caballero* for 'gentleman', to the time of this parade; it served to stimulate loyalist aggression by these malcontents towards the 'traitors' at Westminster and a desire for revenge on them.[70]

The reinvigorated Charles firmly declared on his return from Scotland that the issue of the bishops was non-negotiable, and even dared to raise the question of a life grant of tonnage and poundage (which would remove a major financial weapon for future Parliaments) at the Privy Council meeting on 11 December.[71] The settlement with the Scots in August had weakened Charles to the point of ineffectiveness in Edinburgh, but it had the advantage of meaning that Argyll's party had no excuse for intervening in England with their army. Providing that Charles kept to his terms with the Scots and did not go back on the spring 1641 reforms in England, they had no legal right to declare that he had breached the treaty and attack him in support of Warwick's group's religious demands. Moreover, there was now the Irish crisis to consider. In Scotland, it meant that the Covenanters' co-religionists in Ulster were under attack and their main military consideration had to be to support them, not attack

Charles – though the Scots Parliament suspiciously refused to assist the King in raising troops for Ulster before he left Edinburgh and would only send troops on their own terms. (The first Scots troops did not arrive in Ulster until March 1642 despite the urgency of defence.) In England, the outbreak added to the Scots treaty in making Leslie's army unlikely to come to Warwick's group's aid if they came to blows with the King. It was a valuable argument for the King and his MP allies in urging the assembled political 'nation' to put differences aside and reach a settlement. The triumphalist attitude of the 'opposition' in its nominee Essex's appointments to senior command in his gathering army for the Irish expedition could also stimulate anger from those excluded – the three regiments in the initial force of 3,500 men were to be commanded by him (which was not an unusual 'perk' for the commander), Clotworthy, and Richard Boyle, the son of Strafford's foe the Earl of Cork and brother of Warwick's son's fiancée.[72]

Seizing control: both sides 'up the stakes'. A hard-nosed struggle that was bound to lead to confrontation, if not to the 'Five Members' raid on the Commons?

The way of postponing the resolution of the Church crisis until after the Irish war indeed lay at hand, in the form of the assembly of Church divines which the Remonstrance called for to determine its future. This could be granted as a concession to reassure Parliament, even if the King had no intention of letting his critics dominate it or determine the agenda. His first speech to Parliament on 2 December assured that he supported and would maintain the extant reforms, but gave no promises for the future[73] – which meant principally the delayed Church settlement, finance and 'illegal' Royal courts largely having been sorted out. His official reply to the Remonstrance on 23 December was duly conciliatory,[74] but was soon nullified by the action he took against the 'Five Members'. In fact the pro-Royalist MPs had sought to stop the Remonstrance from being printed, as it could inflame opinion in favour of its 'narrative' of a long list of Royal oppression and Church 'Popery' which needed permanent curtailing; the vote to print it was carried (by 135 to 83) on the 15th by a devious manoeuvre by Clotworthy to raise the issue after many MPs had gone home.[75] The potential for aggression by the Warwick-Pym faction over the remaining matters of contention, particularly the Church, was shown on 3 December when Pym successfully carried a motion warning that if outstanding bills were not passed – which the current 'Royalist' Lords majority made difficult – then the Commons and 'such of the Lords that are more sensible of the safety of the kingdom might join together'.[76] Technically this would only be to make a dignified protest to the King, but between the lines it implied that the frustrated 'opposition' would unite the two Houses in one legislative body so that their own votes could outnumber the refractory Lords – a clear instance of legislative 'cheating'. The Commons were also asked to draw up plans for the defence of Hull and Newcastle, implicitly against the King as much as against the Scots, and on 7 December Haselrig introduced a bill to transfer the power to grant the commissions of the commander-in-chief (now held by Essex) and of the Lord Admiral (currently Northumberland) from King to Parliament.[77] This was temporarily abandoned after protests in the Lords, but another plan for Parliament to take command of the county militia (the spring 1642 plan in embryo, thus in existence before the King's attack on the 'Five Members') enraged moderates Lord Lyttleton (Lord Keeper) and the Earl of Manchester (Mandeville's father) as unprecedented and dangerous.[78] This 'Militia Bill', drawn up apparently by St John and vesting the militia's command in each county in the 'well-affected nobility' whose members no doubt Parliament would specify, received its second reading on 24 December.[79] It was carrying the 'control of the armed forces by Parliament' plan of June 1641 in the 'Ten Propositions' into effect, now that a war was immanent – but an Irish war, not a civil war as had been feared then. At the same time, the campaign to drive the bishops – and their votes – out of the Lords continued with the presentation on 12 December of a massive City petition for this action, drawn up by radical merchants led by Alderman Fowke, to Parliament.[80]

The legislative and implicitly the military offensive was thus being taken by the Warwick-Pym group well ahead of the King's 'attack' on the Five Members; the King had every excuse to retaliate to save his remaining prerogative powers. There was also the matter of the noisy 'spontaneous' demonstrations at Westminster in favour of the removal of the bishops from the Lords; Hertford's steward Edward Kirton claimed to have evidence that the ubiquitous John Venn of the Honourable Artillery Company was organising them and Lord Digby, a 'hard-line' courtier now in favour, claimed that Lord Mandeville had encouraged one demonstration to attack Whitehall Palace.[81] Lord Mayor Gurney was ordered to stop demonstrations before they reached Westminster, but does not seem to have been very effective;[82] the more drastic Royal action of appointing the well-known militant 'reformado' Sir Thomas Lunsford to command the Tower of London in place of 'opposition' supporter Sir William Balfour on 22 December implied a possible military 'strike' on the City.[83] There was now a danger of either side, fearing the other's intentions, making a rash or decisive move to save their cause which could lead to violence. Moreover, time now seemed to be on the King's side – on 12 December he issued an order for all MPs and peers not at Westminster to attend the next session on 12 January, and most of these were reckoned to be 'Royalist'.[84] Provided that many of the leading former 'opposition' peers of the 1630s could be permanently won over to the King's side by adding to their offices and influence at Court and/or moderates could be panicked by the 'Junto's plans to gain control of the army and miltia, they could swing over their supporters in the Commons to back the King. The crucial factor was the latter doing nothing to alienate them and revive their distrust; the problem lay with his personal stubbornness and openness to the 'hard-line' Court faction around the Queen. The latter always had an advantage from her personal access to her husband, as did the impatient aristocratic hot-heads who formed the nucleus of the original 'Cavalier' party that winter. (The 'reformadoes' now loafing around taverns in the City provided them with more manpower for a coup than in May.) A few conciliatory Royal gestures, such as making the staunchly Calvinist John Williams the new archbishop of York in November, could help – although Charles' current quarrel with the Earl of Pembroke was an indication of his continuing capacity to harbour grudges and alienate useful 'power-brokers'.

The break in opposition unanimity and the rising number of pro-Royalist MPs in the House that autumn presented problems to advocates of compromise – not least that it restored the King's confidence and belief that he would have majority Commons support for a show of strength. His regret at abandoning Strafford that May to Commons and rowdy popular pressure for execution, in violation of earlier assurances, was another factor in wanting to restore his position by a show of force against the men who had killed his faithful minister. He feared, with reason, that the long-alienated Warwick (and Saye and Sele, Brooke, and Essex) would be insufficiently respectful of his right to initiate policy once they had secured office. The Parliamentary plans to require him to subject appointments to Lords and Comons approval were thus a proven sign of a political threat by the 'Junto' to control of affairs.(and to his 'honour'). The 'Junto' had been prepared to plot with the rebel Scots and gather an illegal armed assembly of peers in London in 1640, and would only be content once he was a political nullity. Their aggressive Calvinism also made it inevitable that they would seek to dismantle the Church (which would have the added attractions of secularising Church lands, which they could buy up, and removing the bishops' 'bloc vote' from the Lords). Charles thus had every reason to keep the leaders of the 'opposition' peers away from Court and office in winter 1641–2, and without admission to such positions of power the 'Junto' would not rein in their militant MP allies. Indeed, they clearly did not trust the King at all and no offer of posts would allay that; the 'Incident' in Edinburgh (made the most of by Pym in the Commons on 5 November) showed them that Charles was capable of anything.

Who was most to blame? Did the 'Junto' deliberately try to panic Charles into over-reacting?

Bolstered in December by a firm move to take control of the Tower of London arsenal and the first mustering of armed troops in the capital to prepare to overawe or take on the City crowds and urged to a determined course of action by the Queen and her allies, the King now endeavoured to strike against the radical leaders. Technically, it was not an attempt to close down Parliament as in May 1641; he was staying within the constitution and not defying the Act which kept Parliament in session as long as it so desired this. The Scots precedent of the 'Incident' should be remembered; he had attempted to have Argyll, Hamilton, and Lanark arrested (if not killed) by Cochrane's men in Edinburgh in mid-October in a similarly bold 'strike' at his critics, and the plan's co-organiser Roxburgh was now at Whitehall. On 16 December, the French ambassador (the Marquis de la Ferte-Imbaud) reported that a Court decision had been taken on the 12th to prepare for impeaching and beheading 'several of the leading Parliament-men' – presumably by this means of creating a majority in Parliament for it.[85] Other spectators such as Papal agent Rosetti believed a military coup to seize the Tower was being planned; possibly both were in Charles 'mind, the military option being backed by the Goring-Jermyn Court 'hotheads'. The often-overlooked order of 12 December raises a major issue – why did Charles not wait until 12 January before acting against his enemies? Had he initiated the planned arrests for impeachment only after enough 'loyal' MPs and peers returned, he could have expected to win the votes on these matters. Was he forced into premature aggression before 12 January by the pressure being put on him by the 'Junto' – who wanted to trap him in this way? Or was it a case of Goring's group winning him over?

The return of an 'opposition' majority to the Common Council in the City despite the election of Gurney as Lord Mayor led to renewed mob intimidation of Parliament by anti-episcopal demonstrators, with a crowd led by militant Alderman Fowke delivering a huge petition against episcopacy to the Commons on 11 December.[86] On the 15th the militants in the Commons secured the vote to print the 'Grand Remonstrance' – which Charles furiously opposed – by the simple expedient of waiting until most MPs opposing them had gone home and rushing a motion into action. Denzel Holles threatened the Lords with an appeal to the people if they continued to hold up the Commons' proposals on who should control the Irish campaign, implying openly that the Pym faction would unleash a mob on them;[87] this speech (21 December) went further than any threats back in May. The 'opposition' had just triumphed at the City's Common Council elections, which would have given them confidence about assembling such a crowd; and in reply the King dismissed Deputy Lieutenant of the Tower William Balfour, still in 'place' since his involvement in the May plot to free Strafford, by the fiery officer Colonel Thomas Lunsford, a hot-headed 'ultra' among the 'Reformadoes' who had been in the Army at York until November. This threatened another Royal coup to seize the Tower and turn its guns on the City; but such a provocative security-measure was only a logical reaction to Holles' threats although the Commons' latest sermon by Stephen Marshall (22 December) portrayed them as Daniel threatened with destruction by 'Nebuchadnezzar' – meaning. the King.[88] The news that Balfour was to be sacked, delivered to the Commons by militant Dorset MP Sir Walter Earle (later a Parliamentarian commander) on 21 December, could imply that the Commons were about to be cast into the 'lions' den' like Daniel by an angry King.

A series of mutual escalations now followed, increasingly turning to the use of blatant force – in which the 'Junto' had led the way by the City demonstrations. Charles surprisingly backed down over Parliamentary anger against Lunsford and replaced him with Sir John Byron, but sacked Newport as the Governor of the Tower; he thus annoyed both sets of 'hard-liners' at once. The Christmas recess (25–6 December) saw more rioting and on the 27th bishops arriving for the sitting of the Lords were jostled by an angry mob. Surprisingly, the anti-Laudian 'hero' John Williams was booed, presumably for accepting the Archbishopric of York. This amounted to 'betraying' his cause.[89] This was a contrast to Williams' triumphant reception after his return from exile a year earlier and normally he was regarded in London as a praiseworthy victim of the 'Papist" Laud, but it may have been spontaneous by 'low-level' protesters not arranged by his ex-allies Warwick and Essex (or Pym) to show their displeasure at his political moderation in allying with 'Papist' fellow-bishops. The suspicion arises that the 'Junto' Calvinist peers and/or Pym were backing the riots to drive these staunch pro-King voters out of the Lords. Only two bishops turned up on the 28th. Most bishops now declared that they dared not come to the Lords any longer so they did not recognise any bills passed by Parliament, and after their 'Protest' (led by Archbishop Williams, who had evidently deserted the 'reformists') was presented to the Lords the 'Junto' led a furious attack on them for impugning the legality of current legislation passed by Parliament without them (30 December). They were duly arrested for an alleged insult to the latter.[90] The arrests could be couched in legalistic language as reacting to an insult to Parliament, but it was a blatant political act by the Warwick faction to remove them from their rights to vote in the Lords whatever the King wanted. Probably Digby was behind the failed attempt to block the legality of any legislation passed by a Warwick-run Lords; logically the organisers of the riots wanted to secure the 'Junto's clear control of the Upper House to rush through anti-royal and anti-episcopal legislation.

The move to impeach the bishops was a clear sign from the pro-Calvinist faction that they intended to force the issue of the episcopate on Charles, and the 'opposition' control of the City Common Council elections enabled easier mustering of a zealous City mob at a trial in

Westminster Hall to secure conviction (as with Strafford). There was a rumour, arising from MPs meeting secretly in the City, that the Catholic Queen would be impeached next – possibly played up by Pym in the hope of inflaming the King into a confrontation.[91] On the 27th a Commons attack was made on the veteran but now pro-Royal 'opposition' peer, the Earl of Bristol, and next day his alleged crimes were listed by Hotham, Haselrig, and Strode and demands made to remove him from the Privy Council;[92] a committee duly began preparing a petition for this on the 29th.[93] The threat of new prosecutions could be used as evidence that the Commons radicals were going too far in infringing the King's powers, provided that it was handled properly; the attack on Bristol went beyond removing Catholic peers and bishops from the Lords and implied that any peer who defied the 'opposition' cold be added to the list. Such radical proposals would not necessarily win enough Commons votes to succeed, unless the City apprentices besieged Parliament again to intimidate opposition. It was suspicious that Warwick now proposed that 600 of the troops being raised for the Irish war should be assembled immediately in London; they would be available until they sailed for use by the Lords-nominated Irish commanders (e.g. Essex) for use against the King.[94] In fairness to Warwick, the King was undeniably concentrating troops at Whitehall (and building a temporary barracks) around the New Year,[95] so anticipating a military confrontation was not just a 'scare tactic' by the 'junto'.

One of the main dangers to the Royal cause lay in Parliament using its legal powers to arraign people for contempt of its authority, which could frighten off Royal supporters from raising troops without Commons approval. (Pro-Royalist MP George Digby was charged with this in January and had to flee abroad.) The King needed to be able to prove that it was Parliament abusing authority rather than him – which was not helped by evidence of wild talk at Court about arresting MPs or by leaks about his attempts to hire troops from Irish Catholic peers. The dismantling of the Royal prerogative, and the flight of the sternest Royal 'prerogative' judges who had implemented Charles' will in the 1630s but now feared Parliamentary vengeance, made it difficult for Charles to be able to put out legal opinions that Parliament was abusing its powers. The Attorney-General, Sir Edward Herbert, was more loyal than his deputy Oliver St John but seems to have been intimidated into inaction until the impeachment attempt of 3 January. Herbert bears a heavy responsibility for his failure to challenge Parliament's usurpation of legal authority, but was presumably scared for his own job – and the King should have appointed some new pro-Royal judges to stiffen Herbert's resolve and isolate pro-'junto' Solicitor-General St John.

When Parliament reassembled after Christmas the 'Royalist' Digby put forward a motion on 28 December that it was not able to operate freely – due to intimidation by the crowds – and legislation was thus now invalid.[96] This was an attempt to lay the legal basis for cancelling any forthcoming Commons or Lords votes that defied the King, as on impeaching or abolishing the bishops or on 'Root and Branch', and was carried out in concert with Archbishop Williams' protest about the bishops' exclusion. Had it succeeded, the result would have been deadlock but no more embarrassing anti-Anglican votes however many MPs or peers were won over or pressurised into following Pym and Warwick. But the vote was lost by four, and the Lords voted to suspend and arrest those bishops who had voted for it – which indicates that the majority of peers still had faith in the right of this Parliament to decide on future governance, not that all who voted thus were totally won over to 'Root and Branch'. Had the vote been won, the King would have been able to produce a legal basis for the closure of Parliament or – if 'moderate' MPs objected to that and he needed it to raise money – its removal to somewhere outside London. There were plenty of precedents for that, as lately as 1625, though then owing to plague not disorder; and in 1644 Charles was to use this argument about intimidation invalidating a 'free' Parliament in summoning MPs to Oxford. Probably the hand of Hyde can be seen behind this idea. Now, ironically, the moderate new Archbishop Williams' presented the bishops' petition to the King complaining that their exclusion from the Lords, after mob violence, meant that Parliament was no longer free (and thus its votes were invalid).[97] The petition was presented to the Lords (rather feebly) by Lord Keeper Lyttleton on the 30th, but 'oppositionists' could rally votes by arguing that the bishops were insulting the House by implying that no vote was valid without their presence; as a result the Lords joined the Commons for an indignant joint session which ended with orders for the bishops' arrest for treason.[98] This further inflamed the King and Court, and retaliation followed.

Attorney-General Herbert, a man not noted for his boldness – he had never defied the radicals by ruling their moves illegal throughout 1641 – finally announced to the Lords that Charles wished to impeach the 'Five Members' on 3 January – and that disloyal peers such as Warwick, Saye and Sele, Brooke, and Holland should not be appointed to the Lords committee investigating the charges.[99] But the failure to act on this quickly lay with Lord Digby, who did not as planned call for an immediate Lords vote. The announcement of the impeachment had been sudden and pre-empted 'opposition' organisation of votes; if a vote had been taken immediately the motion could have succeeded and then the accused would be liable to immediate arrest. Possibly Digby had reckoned (accurately?) that the Lords vote would be lost, given that House's attitude to the bishops' actions on 28–30 December and the absence of the bishops' votes, and wanted more time to win peers over. The Commons rallying to the five despite a Lords vote for impeachment would have led to a useful charge of them defying the will of their fellow-House, which could be manipulated to the King's advantage. Instead, the Lords did not act and the accused could co-ordinate their reaction. The simultaneous raids by Royal officials on the accused's residences to look for written evidence was denounced in the Commons as a breach of privilege – but the actual impeachment was not yet condemned.[100] When the command for impeachment was brought to the Commons, in a non-provocative way by a respectful Sergeant-at-Arms, it was not drawn up in precise legal terms and so enabled its targets' faction to argue that it was not written in definitive enough terms for a formal reply.[101]

Royal supporters were not necessarily sure of enough votes in either House to push through an impeachment, but the delays while the attempt was debated would cause a useful halt to other contentious (religious) measures. Whatever their strategy, the initiation of proceedings enabled the legal authorities – the King's men – to impound the accused's papers, as was commenced with the raids on their lodgings on the 3rd. Hopefully, written evidence would be found of their treasonous dealings with the Scots in 1639–40, and/or enough evidence be amassed against their peer allies to arrest or blackmail the latter. Hyde apparently wanted more peers named as the accused – which would have decapitated their faction in the Lords during the investigation and been more likely to produce evidence in their homes but would have increased votes against their prosecution by adding to outrage. The Warwick group had sought to add to their voting-strength in the Lords by removing the bishops; now the King's supporters sought to reverse this by removing the leading Calvinist peers.

An attempt to seize the 'Five Members' followed, but its propaganda value for the 'junto' was added to by the King leading the armed incursion into the Commons in person. The moment when Charles decided to resort to a personal raid is unknown; possibly the Commons proposal (put by Strode, one of the 'Five Members') to remove the Queen's attendant Capuchin Friars from her London residence at Somerset House on 3 January[102] made her determined on quick action. Perhaps she feared that her attendants at Court would be next and told Charles to do something quickly. The introduction of expert cannoneers to the Tower on the evening of 3 January,[103] which caused panic in the City, implied that the King believed they could be needed to confront rioters – in reaction to his intended arrests? The accused MPs' homes had been raided by men of the King's new Guard at Whitehall, sealing up their papers ready for a search for evidence, on the 3rd, and rumours of immanent military action next morning led to the Commons sending Nathaniel Fiennes to Whitehall to investigate. The men of the new Guard who were hanging around the Guard/Great Chamber in the Palace were apparently waiting in readiness for orders, and after Fiennes' return action followed. In mid-afternoon the King emerged from his apartments and called on them to follow him, and a Royal armed descent on Parliament followed. Charles carefully avoided taking his troops into the Commons chamber, but this did not alter the dramatic nature of the 'insult' to the Commons, which his detractors could play up enthusiastically. In addition, he left himself open to looking foolish as he vainly strained his eyes to check along the Commons benches for the miscreants and observed that the 'birds had flown'. By personally resorting to open force he placed himself in the role in which Pym had been portraying him by implication, as the ally of the violent, pro-Catholic clique around the Queen associated with the 'Army Plot' in May 1641 and the instigator of the treacherous 'Incident' plot in Edinburgh in October. Having recently sought to turn the weapon of legality against the radicals – by showing that they were coercing Parliament – he now firmly placed himself as its enemy, causing anyone who clung to the supremacy of 'Parliamentary privilege' to rally to Pym. Presumably he hoped that most MPs would be relieved at a chance to be rid of the 'troublemakers' and reach a settlement, or that radical MPs' defiance of his proposed impeachment would be a useful political tool in another attempt to argue that Parliament was under constraint (and thus its measures should be invalidated). But the Commons' sense of corporate unity caused a revival in Pym's group's support when Charles arrived himself to request that those MPs accused of treason be surrendered.[104] The Commons had asserted its right to be consulted before accepting such a demand on the 3rd, though they promised to consider it if it was properly legal. Refusing to wait for five days for a reply as they requested and considering that he had failed to dispose of them constitutionally, he made the fatal error of leading his troops to arrest them in person. Traditionally he was supposed to have been goaded to it by the Queen calling him a coward.[105] His personal leadership of the expedition made it far easier for his victims to win support against him in the role of the oppressor than if a courtier had led the troops; in the 'Incident' in Edinburgh it had been Lord Roxburgh who was the 'front man' and who could thus be blamed for it all by the devious King.

It caused a massive rallying of Commons opinion to men who had been haemorrhaging support only weeks previously, along with the City sheltering them in defiance of the King.(Lord Keeper Lyttleton had refused to sign the warrants, so he must have had doubts about the move – what if he had managed to calm the King down and urge a delay?) The Royal participation and use of troops was evidently an attempt to overawe the MPs; last time the King had forced confrontation with the Commons, over its sudden dissolution in 1629, radicals had slammed the door in his messenger's face and held the Speaker prisoner to legitimise their condemnatory votes. Presumably the use of a body of soldiers was not merely to give him the necessary 'dignified' attendant escort but to deal with any lingering rioters or to prevent MPs slamming the door on his messenger again, and his presence should be guaranteed to dissuade all mannerly MPs from disorderly conduct. Arguably, sending a posse to arrest the MPs and allowing a repeat of their disorderly defiance in 1629 would have done more good to his cause in placing the 'Five Members' in the legal wrong for coercing Parliament. According to Ambassador Guistinian's despatch on 7/17 January the trigger for Charles' action was the Lords' order reversing his sealing up the papers of the 'Five Members' for investigation;[106] but this (or the insult to the Queen in expelling her friars) did not need his personal attention. Perhaps the presence at his side during the 'raid' of Lord Roxburgh is significant, given that the latter had been involved in the 'Incident' as proposed supplier of the troops to take Argyll and Hamilton into custody. The troops used were commanded by a Captain William Fleming, son of the Earl of Wigtown and a friend of Montrose. If it is more than rumour that Pym was tipped off by allies at Court, namely the arch-intriguer Lady Carlisle who was sister to the 'moderate' (and later Parliamentarian) Earl of Northumberland, it is apparent that the King did not observe enough secrecy about his plans in advance. (The source for the Lady Carlisle story is reliable though later – the 1650s diarist Thomas Burton, quoting what well-connected radical MP Haselrig told him. On the Royalist side, Sir Philip Warwick said Lady Carlisle was Pym's mistress).[107] Essex was at Whitehall but unawares of the plan. Some less naïve courtier, aware of the danger of gossip leading to a 'leak' if not that Lady Carlisle was unreliable, would have been well-advised to ask the King to place armed guards in a barge on the Thames off Whitehall Stairs to intercept any boat heading downstream from Westminster to the City. The escaping MPs would have been caught and taken into custody – and not on Parliamentary premises. But the King lacked such shrewd advisers, not having a cynical 'eminence grise' to hand as Elizabeth had had William Cecil and Walsingham or James I had had Robert Cecil.

The coup was properly organised unlike in May, with the more reliable Westminster militia being told to take over guarding the House from the pro-Pym City guards and the Inns of Court volunteers being told to stand ready. Showing more leadership than he had done in Edinburgh where he had left the proposed action to Captain Cochrane and Lord Roxburgh and remained in a position to deny involvement if it failed, Charles also cleverly made his nephew, the Elector Palatine, accompany him to the Commons and so seem to endorse his action. The ambitious young Elector Charles Louis, elder brother of Prince Rupert and son of the highly popular 'Winter Queen' Elizabeth of Bohemia, had been on friendly terms with leading 'opposition' peers like Essex since his arrival in London to seek aid in the summer, though they were of political use to him as ralliers of a Lords vote to give him aid and of military use as potential generals of an expeditionary force. Rumour had it that the Elector was less loyal to his uncle and was hoping for the chance of a crown if Parliament broke with and deposed Charles, though this was never proved.[108] But if he had had the nerve or ambition to absent himself from Whitehall during the crisis and so present himself as a potential rival to the King, the latter's flight in January could have enabled the more aggressive Calvinist peers to consider him as a possible military and political figurehead for their cause against a distrusted and treacherous King. The idea of setting up the Elector, a Stuart and a Calvinist, as the head of the 'Parliamentarian' cause in 1642 is one of the more intriguing scenarios of the crisis, but his uncle's co-option of him in January – and his acceptance of it – made him less attractive to the 'Junto'.

Pym and his colleagues fled in time due to a warning that the King was coming to arrest them, a Captain Langrish spotting the Royal entourage as it entered Old Palace Yard and informing the five's friends. They apparently slipped out by a back door to the water-gate to flee by boat; it was a sign of Royal insouciance that the King had not thought of sending a boatload of his men downriver from Whitehall Stairs to guard against this. A strategic thinker such as Strafford would not have been so lackadaisical. There may have been a 'leak' in Whitehall too, though if so with only minutes to spare. If Lady Carlisle was involved it was rather ironic; she was simultaneously an agent for Cardinal Richelieu and was supposed to be having an affair with Pym. (Was she the original behind Alexandre Dumas' 'Milady De Winter' in the *Three Musketeers* books?) The most defiant MP, William Strode the younger, had to be forcibly removed by his colleagues – and if he had stayed to face the King his arrest by the Royal guards would have been another propaganda coup for Pym who knew exactly how to exploit such evidence of the Royal threat to subjects' liberties. With the Commons forgetting its recent divisions and reunited against his violation of constitutional norms by leading troops into the House, wavering peers and MPs shown that the King could not be trusted to support the national assembly of his subjects against the influence of sinister pro-Catholic 'plotters', and the unruly City in a tumult again so Whitehall was unsafe, the King received a hostile reception as he attempted to persuade the Common Council to do its duty in a public harangue by him at the Guildhall on the 5th.[109] The implacable hostility to an untrustworthy and plotting King shown in the Remonstrance seemed justified. The King's opponents now turned to open resistance – the tactic which the Calvinist peers had planned in summer 1640 and once again physically centred on the City. Charles was able to enter the City physically, but seems to have been baffled as to what to do next when he failed to secure co-operation or submission. He had more troops at his back than he had possessed during the crisis over executing Strafford, but not enough for a prolonged search of or intimidation of London. As with the warning which the 'Five Members' had had, the Court was inferior in terms of intelligence; a bribe to some City figure to find out the location of the fugitives and a quick descent (at night?) by armed 'Cavaliers' on their hideout could still have secured their persons while leaving Warwick's peers at large to condemn it in the Lords in retrospect.

Confrontation between King and opposition. Charles' flight

Parliament's 'Committee for Privileges', in contact with the fugitives, now met in the City daily under the protection of the 'Trained Bands' while the King visited the City to make a stern address at Guildhall that failed to win over the largely sullen crowds. Nobody tipped off the King as to where the fugitives could be found. On the 7th, the command of the Bands was removed from the Lord Mayor by the Commons and given to a committee of MPs and aldermen. The combined Commons and Lords 'Committee for Irish Affairs' – run by the 'Junto' under commander-in-chief Essex – was empowered to sit during a short, self-declared Parliamentary recess to organise defence, and duly issued weapons from the Tower to two regiments en route to Ireland which were conveniently assembling in London. The regiments' commanders, Pym's brother-in-law Clotworthy (an Ulster 'planter' so a legitimate person to take control on military grounds) and Lord Conway, were loyal to the 'opposition'. On the 10th, the new City 'Common Council' met and gave command of the Trained Bands to the 'Junto' loyalist Philip Skippon – putting these 10,000 men under 'opposition' leadership. The Royalist Lord Mayor was now a cipher, and the City lost. That day, with the fugitive MPs expected to return to Westminster soon under City protection and large crowds passing through Whitehall to assist them, Charles chose to take the course of personal safety over military confrontation and fled his capital to Hampton Court.[110] The beds were not ready as he had not given the staff there any notice. On 13 January he went on to Windsor Castle, from whence he left on 7 February for Dover to escort the Queen on the first stage of her journey abroad (with the Crown Jewels to pawn) to seek funds for war. In typical fashion, his progress across Kent was not accompanied by any determined effort to station enough troops at the huge, strategically vital Dover Castle to stop Parliament seizing it in the manner that the Scots Covenanters had overrun his castles at Edinburgh and Dumbarton in 1639 – but unless he had called in local Royalist gentry to help he would have had to dangerously diminish his own escort of guardsmen to do this. A Royalist MP, Colepeper, boldly proposed a Commons motion on the 12th inviting the King to return but was told that the 'Five Members' must be freed from the treason-charge first. The King did not offer this concession until some weeks later.

The initiative passed to the radical leaders who now had physical control of London, troops to hand, and a majority in the Commons to pass further measures consolidating their position; peers and MPs who doubted the wisdom of their confrontational policy had no alternative source of power to rally to. On the 11th a large body of Buckinghamshire freeholders (around 5,000), allies of local hero Hampden and possibly organised by him, arrived in London with a petition demanding that the country be put in readiness to fight for the liberties of Parliament, probably in response to news of the attempted arrests.[111] The idea caught on or was used by Commons organisers; thirty-six of the thirty-nine counties had submitted similar 'spontaneous' petitions by May, though how representative they were is another matter. The idea of national rallying of support for the attacked Commons was clearly in the air, and it fitted in with the notion of Parliament (not the King) as representing the nation. In the Commons, Pym and his group seized the initiative; on 15 January Cromwell and others recommended the setting up of a committee to organise defence, which was passed; this committee then proceeded on the 18th to recommend calling out the militia by ordinance, without waiting for the usual Royal signature to make the 'Militia Bill' an Act. In matters of extending civil control by Parliament, on the 17th the 'Committee of the Whole House' recommended dismissing all the current Privy Councillors whether the King wished it or not and appointing reliable ones – which could hit 'moderate' men as well as the 'hard-liners'. In matters of extending control over the Lords, Pym kept up the pressure by handing in four county petitions for excluding the bishops and Catholic peers from the Upper House.

The religious issue was also played up while the chance existed to press the 'Root and Branch' line, this time with increased use of the 'democratic' argument in the form of petitions – no doubt organised by local enthusiasts claiming to speak in the name of all the community. On 25 January a petition from Colchester, in a well-known 'godly' county with Warwick as the local magnate, was handed in asking for revision of the 1559 Prayer Book, and on the 31st an unusual initiative saw a petition signed by thousands of women in and around London asking to have the kingdom put in a state of readiness for war due to the current threat. This first involvement of women may have reflected their prominence in radical City congregations, 'ahead' of the current trend among the anti-Laudian local activists; there were assorted vocal female agitators emerging there such as Anna Trapnel. The existence of militancy in Essex is clear, and was also stoked by fears of 'Popish massacre' plots after the Irish rising; that spring and summer were to see a wave of assaults on local Catholics. A popular demonstration against rumours that local Royalist Sir Charles Lucas intended to seize Colchester led to the participants occupying the streets (an imitation of the 'defensive' actions of the protesters at Westminster in May and late December 1641?) and sacking his house; his staff were beaten-up by riotous radicals. Fear of the Catholics attacking English Protestants as they had done in Ireland led to a series of anti-'Popish' scares and lurid rumours across the country, and as a pre-emptive measure what amounted to 'lynch law' was enforced by local pro-Parliamentary magistrates against convicted priests with public executions. Technically priests were required to keep out of England on pain of execution so this was legal, but the King usually suspended sentences; this time the local authorities acted on their own initiative.

There were other county petitions in favour of keeping the existing Church hierarchy, with thirteen counties handing in such requests between November 1641 and May 1642; their Cheshire organiser was MP Sir Thomas Aston, who published a 'Remonstrance Against Presbytery' in May 1641 and insisted that the county's petition for Church reform was unrepresentative and had been put together by a radical clique. Needless to say all such unwanted evidence of pro-episcopal feeling was ignored by the Commons, and a Kent petition in defence of the bishops

Missed Chances or Inevitable Showdown? 257

and opposition to the illegality of the Militia Bill in March 1642 was sentenced to be burnt by the public hangman.[112] There was a good deal of intimidation by the victorious radicals, using the constitutional 'dignity' of Parliament as the embodiment of the realm to punish what in the Royal case would have been *'lese majeste'*; even MPs such as Kentish moderate Sir Edward Dering were arrested for injudicious comments about their actions. Thrown out of the Commons on dubious grounds by the radicals, Dering (who had been backing 'Root and Branch' in May 1641) returned home to take his revenge by assuming control as chairman of the county 'Grand Jury' (23 March) to draw up a petition in favour of the existing Church government and liturgy. This time the local pro-Parliamentarian gentry who turned up at the meeting, led by Sir Anthony Weldon and Sir Michael Livesey, were outnumbered and had to withdraw;[113] in other counties they prevailed. It seems that putting on a show of numbers and force was essential to securing leadership of many counties' official reaction to events in and orders from Westminster. It is possible that the amount of anti-Catholic propaganda printed at this time, which had the excuse of reports of atrocities from Ireland, was deliberately increased by the Pym-Warwick group to encourage 'hard-line' attitudes on the Church. The number of pamphlets on this issue collected by the bookseller Thomas Thomason in London rose from 15 per cent of his purchases in October 1641 to 28 per cent in December and over 30 per cent by the spring. The existence of genuine panic and religious zeal to purge 'Popery' cannot be denied, but encouraging this atmosphere of panic enabled the Parliamentarian 'hard-liners' to intimidate opposition by implying that anyone who did not support them might be a Catholic sympathiser.

The King remained within reach of London for a few weeks, thus encouraging negotiation, and had too few troops to take the initiative though Sir Thomas Lunsford and George Goring managed to seize the arsenal at Kingston-upon-Thames while he was in Middlesex (12 January). On the 20th he asked Parliament by letter to state their terms; there was no immediate reply. The King showed some goodwill by accepting the bills to remove the bishops from the Lords and to raise an army for Ireland when the Lords sent them to him on 13 February, but refused to touch the Militia Bill as too great a surrender of his powers; Parliament passed it anyway as an ordinance (i.e. temporary law without Royal assent) on 3 March. This gave them the power to direct the county

Lords Lieutenant to raise troops and put them and the Trained Bands under Parliament's authority – if these men obeyed their orders. The King, however, refused to sign an order to allow his arsenal at Hull to be sent to London, allegedly for the Irish war but no doubt for Parliamentary use if it came to war in England. A battle for 'hearts and minds' now began, and the official Parliamentary printed explanation of events duly played up the King's evil intentions (supported by his 'Papist' allies) to execute the entire Parliamentary leadership after a wave of arrests[114] – based on what evidence was unclear. The public execution of two priests at Tyburn in late January 1642, followed by more in March, was a clear indication that the authorities – unlike the King – knew their 'duty' in enforcing the penal laws and played up their credentials to the populace.

The removal of Charles from London saw a return to the situation that Warwick's group had been planning in summer 1640, with the 'opposition' in control of the capital with its militia and the King in retreat without an army to call on immediately. This time, however, the King's critics had no need to seek the calling of a Parliament to back them legally; one was already in being. The King had also breached 'privilege' in entering the Commons with armed men, albeit technically only to enforce arrests for a legal charge of impeachment, and the defiant faction in control of London could claim to be defending the constitution as they would not have been able to do in an armed 'stand-off' in 1640. Their propaganda notably continued to present their cause as being 'for King and Parliament', open rebellion being likely to detract from their support; the fiction was maintained that Charles was a puppet of 'evil councillors' in need of rescue. But as the King had signed up to peace with the Scots in August 1641 Parliament did not have a Scots Covenanter army to hand in Northumberland and Durham to call upon, and could if necessary order his army in York south.

With the two 'camps' physically separated the chances of moderates on either side negotiating a settlement were drastically reduced though Charles showed no sign of haste in heading north for York. Luckily for the King, his peace-treaty with the Scots of August 1641 was holding as long as he did not meddle with Argyll's ascendancy and the Covenanters were preoccupied raising troops to save their co-religionists in Ulster. (The first detachments of Leslie's army sailed there in April.) The English 'opposition' could not expect the Covenanters to come to their rescue as in summer-autumn 1640, giving Charles time to add to his own forces in the North of England. Had the Irish crisis not been a distraction, Argyll and his allies would have been more of a threat to the King and more useful to the latter's enemies in London. But even without the existence of two opposing armies as yet, only a Royal surrender to the radicals' terms – a temporary handover of political control of the administration and army to them and abolition of the episcopal Church, as seen in the 'Nineteen Propositions' – could have avoided ultimate war. The King was now seen as provenly treacherous, and the 'Parliamentary' leadership would only accept his complete political and military neutralisation – the terms forced on him in Scotland in August 1641. John Adamson sees this as a coherent and long-term political objective of the 'Warwick group' from 1640, with the untrustworthy and 'pro-Catholic' King made a powerless 'Doge' subject to his counsellors as in Venice. The Venetian parallel may have been played up in 'opposition' figures' talks with that state's ambassador to flatter him; classically-educated nobles and gentry had other, Greek parallels for a limited monarchy to use as precedents.

Religion had been the main issue for a breach, but was not the only one – Parliament asserting control of appointments showed that the 'Junto' would not trust Charles to keep to any terms, and the armed descent on the Commons seemed to prove their point. Possibly Warwick, Essex, Brooke, and other Calvinist enthusiasts, regarding religious reform as paramount and the King unwilling to deliver this, had never expected Charles to do their bidding without coercion and the events of January 1642 just enabled them to carry their point with less convinced MPs and peers. In that case, the attempted 'coup' in arresting the 'Five Members' gave the more radical 'opposition' leaders the physical backing and the legal excuse to rally support for a programme of legislative long-term coercion of the King. What is unclear is whether the crucial 'opposition' moves of mid-late December 1641 to control all senior administrative and military appointments and drive their enemies out of the Lords had always been intended; the 'Venetian' hypothesis for their ideal constitution would suggest that something like this was a goal for Warwick and Essex (even for Bedford?). Would they have chanced their arm on these proposals had they not had rising fear of a Royal backlash available to boost their voting-strength? Or was confrontation on these matters inevitable? Crucially, what would have been the effect if large numbers of peers and

MPs who were absent from the Houses had obeyed the King's summons to turn up on 12 January? They could also have been intimidated by the City crowds, as those present in Westminster had been in May and late December 1641; but if Charles had had their support someone such as Digby might well have won a vote alleging that Parliament could not now meet safely. The 'constitutional' path to withdrawal of the Royalist party from Westminster in January 1642 would have been a wiser one than the real-life withdrawal after a botched armed raid on the Commons.

On 20 January Hampden introduced a Bill to secure the forts and ports in the hands of people that Parliament could trust, a direct challenge to the King's rights as commander-in-chief albeit based on the earlier 'Ten Propositions' plans which had been a 'fall-back' position for the radicals since May 1641. On the 31st Sir John Hotham carried out the first act of pro-Parliamentary military defiance in securing Hull without waiting for the Bill to pass. (His similarly-named father was to be Governor but as MP for Beverley, Yorks was still in London; it was reckoned later that Hotham junior was told to keep an eye on his lukewarm father for possible disloyalty.) Parliament introduced a Bill to take over control of the militia from Royally-appointed Lords Lieutenant, which was sent to the King for signing on 5 February, and as he delayed doing so sent a threatening Declaration to him proposing to take such measures by their own authority. By now their relations with the King had degenerated into mutual mistrust and insults, although he sent a conciliatory letter from Canterbury on his way back from Dover saying that he would rule according to law – which did not include the illegal Militia Bill – and would not use force against Parliament. By the time he reached Theobalds House, the Cecil estate in Hertfordshire handed over to James I in exchange for Hatfield House in 1607, he was still refusing to sign the Bill; but he was prepared to drop the treason-charges against the 'Five Members'. (Possibly this was a manoeuvre to make it seem more unlawful if Parliament then moved against Lord Keeper Lyttleton, still in London.) On his northwards journey (at Newmarket) another Parliamentary delegation accused him of complicity with wicked courtiers in planning a foreign invasion,[115] presumably a reference to the Queen's plans to hire troops in Holland. He was officially requested to return to London, but this was clearly an empty gesture and he carried on with his journey North via Cambridge. His reception at the latter was poor, with bystanders calling on him to return to London; there seems to have been unease at his abandoning his capital as the visible sign of a slide into war.

In a letter of reply to Parliament from Hinchingbrooke House Charles alleged that he was only heading for York in order to establish a more convenient base for the reconquest of Ireland, and repeated his unanswered request of 20 January for a statement of their terms (the general tenor of which, i.e. surrender of the civil and military offices and abolition of the bishops, was already obvious). On 19 March he arrived in York, where he was funded by the principal Catholic magnate of South Wales, Lord Glamorgan, as he set up his Court there; loyal MPs and peers arrived from London, among them Hyde, Colepeper, and Viscount Falkland, thus increasing the physical separation into two camps. An army was now to be raised, with appeals for men (by the traditional medieval means of letters of summons in 'Letters of Array' as Charles did not have Parliament or the judges 'lined up' for a more 'modern' summons) and money. The Earl of Lindsey (Robert Bertie), former titular commander of the fleet, was appointed commander-in-chief – a dubious choice given his lack of experience or flexibility as a battlefield commander, and more reflective of his social eminence and Charles' personal confidence. Charles also talked unrealistically of going to Ireland to fight the Catholic rebels there with Ormonde, no doubt intending to use the troops in the latter's army in England afterwards; Ormonde wrote back to persuade him not to do so.

This was to be the start of many such royal efforts to bring into play the forces of his 'outer' kingdoms to change the balance of power in England in the next six years – an imaginative and flexible strategy but one which would lead the increasingly desperate King into all sorts of impractical schemes. Worse, it would add to Charles' ingrained habit of promising something to one of his potential allies – or in later years an opponent who he was seeking to win over – and simultaneously or a little later offering something entirely different to their rivals. Nor was there any sign of embarrassment by Charles at the apparent deception – he was the King and he was answerable only to God. The mixture of muddle, improvisation, a lack of experienced men on hand (or called in) to advise the King who could match a general like the Scots' Alexander Leslie, and inadequate planning for a potentially long war were ominous signs of what was to come in the 1642 campaign and indeed during the first couple of years of war. The latter was, however, a new and unwelcome experience for England in 1642, there having been no major well-matched domestic military clash there since the 1487 battle of Stoke between the Tudors and the Yorkists. The 'Great Rebellion', as Clarendon was to call it, was seen by many observers (including him) as a storm that had come from a clear sky – but as the preceding narrative has shown, this was not strictly true and problems had been building up for decades. The complexities and inadequacy of Early Stuart government plus bad luck in timing for Royal appointments and initiatives were largely to blame – but the King had made more blunders than his father or Elizabeth had done and this was to persist until he was throwing away the chances of a settlement with his foes (or escaping abroad) weeks before his execution.

Notes

Chapter One
1. On Charles and Buckingham persuading James to let them go to Madrid in 1623 and Cottington's opposition: Clarendon, History (1888 edition) vol 2 p. 20–32; on Charles' leading role in the idea, see Earl of Kellie to Earl of Mar, 25 February 1623, in HMC Mar and Kellie Papers p. 153, and Venetian ambassador's comments in Calendar of State Papers Venetian 1621–3 p. 804; on the farcical 'disguised' journey through Kent and arrests, see Mainwaring to Zouch, 22 February 1623 in NA: SP 14/138/58 and Lord Conway to Brooke, 3 March 1623, NA: SP 14/139/26. On the celebrations in London after the mission's failure, see Clarendon, *History*, vol I p. 22: *The Letters of John Chamberlain*, ed. N. McClure (2 vols, Philadelphia 1939), vol 2 pp. 55–7.

    On James' alleged warning to Charles in 1624 about him giving Parliament encouragement to impeach ministers that would later be used against him, see Clarendon vol 1 p. 44.

    On the questions of a rising 'arc' of confrontation between Charles and sections of the politcal elite (or not) in 1625–9 and on the rival interpretations and evidence of 'Whig Historians' vs the 'Revisionists': see Kevin Sharpe, *Faction and Parliament: Essays in Early Stuart History* (New York, Methuen 1985) and L. J. Reeve, *Charles I and the Road to Personal Rule* (Cambridge University Press 1989).

    On Charles and Parliament in 1625–6: S. R. Gardiner, *Debates in the House of Commons* 1625, Camden Society 1877, pp. 67, 81–2, 106–7. CSPVenetian 1625–6, pp. 128, 217; J. Hacket, *Scrinia Reserata: -A Memorial offered to the great deservings* of John Williams, DD, 1693, vol 2, p. 16, 27. and Sir John Eliot, *Negotium Posterorum*, ed. A B Grosart (1881) on rival views of the dissolution of the 1626 Parliament. Commons Journal vol I, p. 814 (on Wentworth vs Buckingham in 1625). HMC Supplement, p. 295. Clarendon, *History of the Great Rebellion*, ed. W. D. Macray (Oxford 1888), vol I pp. 13–14. S.R. Gardiner, ed, *Debates in the House of Commons in 1625* (Camden Society, 1873) pp. 55, 110, 115, 117. National Archives: S.P. 15, Addenda, no. 521 f. 83; F. C. Dietz, *English Public Finance 1558–1641* (1964 reprint) p. 227. Robert Ruigh, *The Parliament of 1624* (Cambridge, Mass. 1971) p. 215; Harvard University, Houghton Library: Spring Mss. (English Mss. 980), 19 March 1624. Thomas Fuller, *The Church History of Britain*, ed J Nicholls vol iii (London 1868) p. 365 and HMC Supplementa: Mar and Kellie Mss. Report (1930) p. 226 on Buckingham being accused of poisoning James I. Conrad Russell, 'Parliamentary History in Perspective 1604–29', in *History*, 61 (Feb 1976), pp. 1–29.

2. Lords Journal, vol 3, pp. 435–6; Hacket, *Scrinia*, vol ii pp. 13–14; Laud, *Works*, vol iii, p. 14; CSPV 1623–5, p. 160.

3. On Anglo-French terms in 1624–5: *Memoires Inedites du Comte Leveneur de Tillieres*, ed M. C. Hippens (Paris 1863) pp. 83–4; *Memoires du Cardinal de Richelieu* (Paris

1912–27), vol v, pp. 18, 38–9, 85–9. On Charles vs Eliot: W. Notestein and F. Relf, *The Commons Debates* for 1629, Minneapolis, 1921, pp. 252–7.
4. R.R. Heele, *A Bibliography of Royal Proclamations*, Oxford 1910, p. 1566.
5. Rushworth, *Collections* vol I, pp. 651–4.
6. Ibid p. 664; Notestein and Relf, p. 11.
7. SP 16/14/41-52; Rushworth, *Collections* vol I, p.662.
8. CSPV 1628–9, pp. 579–81; Acts of the Privy Council 1628–9.
9. *The Letters of John Chamberlain*, ed. Neil McClure, Philadelphia 1929, p. 629.
10. On Charles' determination to secure payment and belief in his acting in the national interest over the forced loan, see NA: SP 16/3/116 and SP 78/79/13–14 (Charles' letter on the loan to Louis XIII).

    On the constitutional issues surrounding the 'Forced Loan', see R. Cust, 'Charles I, the Privy Council and the Forced Loan' in *Journral of British Studies*, vol 24, no 2 (April 1985) and Mark Kishlansky, 'Tyranny Denied: Charles I, Attorney-General Heath and the Five Knights' Case 'in *Historical Journal*, vol 42, no 1 (May 1999) especially p. 61.

    For Eliot, see J. Forster, *The Life of Sir John Eliot, 1590 to 1632*, 2 vols, Longmans 1864; especially vol 2, p. 227 on Eliot's death and burial. Also: D. Hulme, *The Life of Sir John Eliot*, 1590 to 1632, London 1957.
11. William Camden, *Annals of Queen Elizabeth*, 1675, p. 270.
12. S.P. Dom. iii 28.
13. *Proceedings in the Parliaments of Queen Elizabeth I*, ed. T.E. Hartley, Leics. UP 1981, 2 vols, vol I pp. 145–9.
14. SP 14/24/183.
15. See Poison at Court: the Overbury Murder.
16. Clarendon, *History of the Rebellion*, vol I, p. 44; and Conrad Russell, *Parliament and English Politics 1621–9*, pp. 190–5.
17. S.R. Gardiner, *History of England 1603–42*, vol vi, p. 83.
18. 'A Declaration of the True Causes which moved His Majesty to assemble and dissolve the last two meetings of Parliament', London 1626.
19. Gardiner, vol vi p. 83.
20. Ibid p. 110.
21. See Roger Lockyer, *George Villiers, Duke of Buckingham 1592–1628*, Longman 1981.
22. HMC Lonsdale Mss. 'Notes on Parliament' pp. 4–6, 8–9, 13, 18–28; and David Harley, 'Political Post-Mortems and Morbid Anatomy in seventeenth century England', *Social History of Medicine* 4 (1994), pp. 1–28. The episode was brought up in Parliament in 1626.
23. Rushworth, *Collections*, vol I, p. 357.
24. Lords Journals pp. 576–7.
25. Lockyer, *Buckingham*, pp. 306–8.
26. British Library : Additional Mss. 6703, ff. 45–8; Harleian Mss. 1583, f. 37. Calendar of State Domestic Mss. vol xvi, ff. 11, 32; Sir John Glanvil, *The Voyage to Cadiz in 1625* (Camden Society, London, 1883) pp. 33–42.
27. S.R. Gardiner, ed, *Debates in the House of Commons* in 1625, pp. 98–9; Lockyer, pp. 380–5 and 396–401.
28. J. Foxe, *Book of Acts and Monuments*.
29. CSPV 1625–6 p. 604; Clarendon History vol I, p. 69.

30. JS McCauley, 'Richard Montagu: Caroline Bishop 1557–1641', Cambridge Ph. D. 1961.
31. 1625 *Parliamentary Debates*, ed. W. Notestein, pp. 49 and 62; *The Life of the Renowned Dr. Preston...*, ed. EW Harcourt, 1885, pp.92–5 and 117. The most often quoted example of this promotion of order and harmony is the Court masque 'Coelum Brittannicum' by Thomas Carew, staged in February 1634.
32. See Kevin Sharpe, 'Criticism and Compliment' pp. 232–43.
33. As n. 32.
34. Sharpe, pp. 179–82 and R.M. Smuts, 'The culture of absolutism at the court of Charles I', Ph D, Princeton 1976.
35. Sir W. Davenant, *Dramatic Works*, ed. J. Maidmont and W.H. Logan, 1872–4, vol 2, pp. 312–25, and Roy Strong, *The Illusions of Power*, p. 79. Sir J Harington, *Letters and Epigrams*, ed. N McClure, Philadelphia 1930, pp. 119–21.
36. Peter Heylyn, *A Short View of the Life and reign of Charles I*, 1658, pp. 6–7; William Lyly, *Life and Death of Charles I*, 1651, repr. 1774, pp. 177–8. BL Rawlinson Mss. D 392, pp. 356 ff.
37. Sir J Harington, *Letters and Epigrams*, ed N McClure, Philadelphia, 1930, pp. 119–21.
38. B.L. Rawlsinson Mss. D392, pp. 356 ff.
39. Oxford: Bodleian Library Mss: English History, c. 28, ff. 549–67.
40. J. Berington (ed), *The Memoirs of Gregorio Panzani*, Birmingham 1793, pp. 137, 198, 246; Kevin Sharpe, The Personal rule of Charles I, pp. 306–8.
41. K.L. Lindley, 'Lay Catholics in the Reign of Charles I', in *Journal of Ecclesiastical History* 22 (1971), pp. 119–22; Panzani Memoirs, p. 206.
42. K. Sharpe, 'Archbishop Laud', in *History Today* 33 (1983), pp. 26–30; W. Lamont, Godly Rule, p. 65.
43. F. Boss (ed), *The Diary of Thomas Crosfield*, 1955, p, 63.
44. Works of Laud, vol. ii; Sharpe, Personal Rule, pp. 285–6.
45. W.H. Hutton, *Archbishop William Laud*, 1895, p. 132.
46. Laud, *Works*, vol ii, pp. 259–60.
47. Laud's 'Conference with Fisher', in *Works*, vol ii, p. 218.
48. *Works*, vol vi, pt I, p. 259.
49. The term was coined by Nicholas Tyacke and is the central thesis of his book *Anti-Calvinists*.
50. Lancelot Andrewes' non-promotion is probably the main example of James' caution. See H. Trevor-Roper, *Catholics Anglicans and Puritans*, Fontana 1997, pp. 40–120 for discussion on 'Laudianism and Political Power'.
51. Cited by Trevor-Roper, as n. 50.
52. See discussion in Antonia Fraser, *The Gunpowder Plot: Terror and Faith* in 1605.
53. See H.C. Porter, Reformation and Reaction in Cambridge, Cambridge 1958, p. 576 ff; K. Sharpe, 'Archbsihop Laud and the University of Oxford' in H. Lloyd James, V. Fezell and B. Worden (eds), *History and the Imagination*, 1961, pp. 146–64.
54. See *NDNB* article on George Abbot.
55. Rushworth, *Historical Collections*, vol ii, p.7.
56. Clarendon vol I, p. 115.
57. Sharpe, *Personal Rule*, pp. 351–63.
58. Gardiner, *History of England 1603–42*, vol vii, pp. 319–20.
59. 'A Divine Tragedy lately Acted', quoted in Sharpe *Personal Rule* p. 355.
60. B. Whitelocke, *Memorials of English Affairs*, pp. 17–18.

61. Sharpe, pp. 116–19, 242–5; National Archives: C. 115? M 36?8434; Bodleian Library: Bankes Mss. 16/7; Gardiner, vol vi, pp. 86, 282; Pettit, Royal Forests, pp. 46, 52, 66–7, 88, 282.
62. Conrad Russell, ibid. Berkshire Record Office, Trumbull Mss. xviii, f. 104; xix, f. 36.
63. See P.Olander, 'Changes in the mechanism and procedures for control of the London press, 1625–37', Oxford Universty B. Litt. Thesis, 1976, chs. 1 and 2.
64. Bodleian Library Tanner Mss. 299, ff. 156–156 v.
65. Tanner Mss. 67, f. 39.
66. Sharpe, pp. 648–51; S. Lambert, 'The printers and the government, 1604–37' in R. Myers and M. Harris (eds), *Aspects of Printing from 1600*, Oxford 1987, pp. 1–5.
67. See *NDNB* article on Sir Edward Coke.
68. K. Sharpe, Sir Robert Cotton 1586–1631: *History and Politics in Early Modern England*, Oxford 1979.
69. CSPD 1629–31, p. 305; PRO Privy Council Papers 2/41/99; Sharpe, Sir Robert Cotton pp. 80–2.
70. A. Searle, Barrington Family Letters 1628–32 (Camden Society 4th series, 1983 p. 257; PRO C. 115/M36/8431.
71. HMC Cowper, vol ii, p. 268
72. PRO SP 16/103/5; *Commons Debates 1628*, ed. R.C. Johnson et al, New Haven Conn. 1977, 5 vols, vol 2 p. 213.
73. HMC Mar and Kellie Papers, p. 227.
74. Gervase Holles, in his *Memorials of the Holles Family*, p.94; HMC Portland Mss. 9, p. 113.
75. *NDNB* article on the earl of Pembroke.
76. See also Neil Cuddy, 'The Revival of the Entoruage: *the Bedchamber of James I, 1603–25*' in D. Starkey et al, *The English Court from the Wars of the Roses to the Civil War*, Longmans 1987, pp. 173–225.
77. Sharpe, *Personal Rule*, pp. 105–24 and 443–62.
78. Ibid, pp. 120–2.
79. Rushworth, *Collections*, vol ii, p. 277.
80. CSPV 1632–6, p. 195: CSPD 1628–9, p. 435. On the 'projectors': CSPD 1635–6, p. 297; CSPD 1636–7, pp. 12–13, CSPD 1637–8, p. 12; H.C. Darby, *The Draining of the Fens* (Cambridge 1940) pp. 38–48; K. Lindley, *Fenland Riots and the English Revlution* (1981); Ellesmere Mss. 6748/43, 18 March 1637; John Thirsk, *Economic Policy and* Projects (Oxford 1978). For the cancellation of patents in 1639, Coke Mss. 60: 5 April 1639, National Archives: PC 2/50, f. 209.
81. CSP Venetian 1632–6, pp. 436, 466; National Archives C. 115/N8/8759; Bodleian Library: Bankes Mss. 37/18; Clarendon, *History of the Rebellion*, ed W. Macray, vol 1 pp. 132–6.
82. Bodleian Library: Rawlinson Mss. C 431, ff. 32, 34, 38, 48.
83. Sir John Coke Mss. 54: 3 August 1636. CSPV 1638–9, pp. 523, 543.
84. CSP 1638–9, pp. 523, 543.
85. D. M. Smuts, *Court Culture and the Origins of a Royalist Tradition in Early Stuart England* (Philadelphia 1987) pp. 228–9.
86. See discussion in Albion, *Charles I and the Court of Rome*.
87. Robin Clifton, 'The Fear of Catholics in England', Oxford D. Phil. thesis 1967, p. 93.
88. PRO C 115/N8/8822.

89. CSPV 1636–9, p. 69.
90. Sharpe, *Personal Rule*, pp. 158–9.
91. Clarendon, vol i, p. 164.
92. PRO C 115/M 35/8386; PRO 31/3/68, ff. 114–18; CSPDom. 1628–9, pp. 292–3; Sir John Coke Mss. 36: 10 January 1629; Thomas Birch, *The Court and Times of Charles I*, vol I p. 419; National Archives: 31/3/68, ff. 114–115v.
93. Bodleian Tanner Mss. 299, f. 84.
94. Clarendon, *History of the Rebellion*, vol i, p. 62
95. Ibid, vol v, p. 155.
96. BL Egerton Mss. 1820, ff. 114 and 164.
97. PRO SP 31/3/68, ff. 216–18; Gardiner, *History of England* 1603–42, vol viii, p. 85.
98. PRO SP 31/3/68, f. 176.
99. PRO SP 16/218/29.
100. Sharpe, p. 174.
101. See SP Salt, 'Sir Thomas Wentworth and the parliamentary representation of Yorkshire, 1614–28', in *Northern History*, 16 (1980), pp. 130–68.
102. Sharpe, *Faction and Parliament*, pp. 7–8.
103. Sharpe, *Personal Rule*, pp. 135–6.
104. Gardiner, vol vii, p. 233; Barnes, 'Star Chamber Litigants', pp. 9–13, 15; Barnes, 'Star Chamber Mythology', passim; Barnes, 'Due process and slow process', pp. 330–2.
105. British Library: Ellesmere Mss. ff. 778–9; Bodleian Library: Tanner Mss. 299, ff. 127–30, 148–60; Sharpe, *Personal Rule*, pp. 671–6.
106. PRO C 115/M36/8427.

Chapter Two
1. CSPD 1634–5, p.100; Sharpe, *Personal Rule*, pp. 548–52.
2. Lambeth Palace Mss. 943, ff. 187–8; Coke Ms. 148.
3. Clarendon vol I, p. 92.
4. BL Egerton Mss. 1820, ff. 334–334 v.
5. CSPD 1634–5, p. 162.
6. Rushworth, *Historical Collections* vol ii, p. 294.
7. Knowles, *Strafford Letters*, vol I, p. 438.
8. Sharpe, pp, 558–67.
9. CSPD 1636–7, pp. 119, 375.
10. BL Lansdowne Mss. 232, p. 34; Rushworth vol ii, p. 344.
11. CSPD 1637 p. 455; CSPD 1639–40, p. 551.
12. CSPD 1637, p. 169.
13. BL Rawlinson Mss. C 169, ff. 340 ff; CSPD 1637–8, pp. 387, 432, 488, 595.
14. CSPD 1637–8, pp. 387, 488; CSPD 1638–9, p. 295. See also Conrad Russell, 'The Ship Money Judgementss of Brampston and Davenport' in ibid, *Unrevolutionary England*, 1603–42, Hambledon Press 1990.
15. PRO SP 16/218/29.
16. BL Egerton Mss. 1820, f. 257; Clarendon Mss. no. 333.
17. Ibid, f. 139 v.
18. Egerton Mss 1820, ff. 313–15.
19. L.J. Reeve, *Charles I and the road to personal rule*, Cambridge 1989, pp. 263 and 278–9.

20. e.g. STC 23522, *The Swedish Intelligencer*, 1632; STC 2520 I r, The Reasons for which Gustavus Adolphus was at length forced to march. into Germany.
21. Firth Mss. C4, p. 518; PRO Scottish Office 1/2/54.
22. G. Burnet, *Memoirs of the Lives and Actions of James and William, Dukes of Hamilton, 1677, p.21.*
23. CSPD 1633–4, pp. 394, 398.
24. Gardiner, *History of England* 1603–42, vol vii, p. 179.
25. CSPV 1636–9, p. 307.
26. Egerton Mss. 1820, f. 267 v.
27. PRO SP 31/3/68, f. 166.
28. CSPD 1635, p. 41.
29. Egerton Mss. 1820, f. 481; Gardiner vol vii, pp. 380, 382.
30. Egerton Mss. 1820, f. 581 v.
31. PRO SP 31/3/68, ff. 243–246 v.
32. Gardiner, vol viii, p. 83.
33. PRO Sp 31/3/68, ff. 219, 243–246 v
34. Gardiner, ibid p. 102.
35. Clarendon SP i, p. 447; CSPD 1635–6, p. 314.
36. Knowles, vol I p. 417.
37. Clarendon Mss. ix, no. 740.
38. A. Colllins, *Letters and Memorials of State collected by Sir H Sidney*, 2 vols. 1746 vol ii p.435.
39. Ibid, pp. 447, 450; CSPV 1636–9, p. 96.
40. HMC Denbigh, vol v, pp. 45–7.
41. HMC De l'Isle and Dudley, vol vi, p. 81; Knowles, vol ii, pp. 48–9; Nottingham University Library: Clifton Mss. C1/C 227.
42. Gardiner, vol viii p. 205.
43. Clarendon Mss. 12, no. 952.
44. Collins, *Letters and Memorials*, vol ii, pp. 473, 474; Gardiner vol viii, p. 518.
45. PRO SP 31/3/71, f. 85; Hamilton Mss. 327, date 30 June 1638.
46. CSPV 1636–9, p. 374.
47. Clarendon Mss. 14, nos. 1084 and 1098.
48. Clarendon Mss. 15, no. 1199.
49. Clarendon Mss. 17, no. 1296; Clarendon State Papers vol ii, pp. 71–6.
50. Calendar of State Papers Domestic 1640, p. 248.
51. Clarendon Mss. 17, nos. 1314 and 1318.
52. See G. Donaldson, *Scotland: James V to James VII*, Mercat Press Edinburgh, 1998, chapter 6.
53. Donaldson, pp. 209–10.
54. David Calderwood, *Church History (Woodrow Society, 8 vols), vol vii, pp. 622–3.*
55. Donaldson, pp. 296–7; M. Lee, *The Road to Revolution: Scotland under Charles I, 1625–37*, Urbana 1981, pp. 119–37.
56. Donaldson, p. 213.
57. Donaldson, pp. 296–300, 305.
58. As n. 55.
59. Donaldson, p. 303.
60. J. Spalding, *Memorials of the Troubles in Scotland and England 1625–45*, (Spalding Club Aberdeen, 1850) pp. 35–6; BL Rawlisnon Mss. D 49.

61. Spalding, p. 36.
62. Donaldson, pp. 306–7.
63. *The Historical Works of Sir James Balfour*, 4 vols, 1825, vol ii, pp. 119–200.
64. Nat Library of Scotland: Woodrow Mss. lxxvi, f. 19.
65. Gardiner, vol viii, p. 307.
66. Woodrow Mss. lxxvi, f. 19.
67. Ibid, f. 36; Clarendon vol I, p. 138; Heylyn, *Cyprianus Anglicus*, vol ii, p. 283.
68. Donaldson, pp. 309–10.
69. Laud, Works, vol iii, pp. 428–9; Huntingdon Library Mss. HA 15172.
70. G. Donaldson, *The Making of the Scottish Prayer Book* of 1637, Edinburgh 1954, pp. 52–9.
71. Donaldson, *Scotland: James V to James VII*, p. 310.
72. D. Stevenson, *The Scottish Revolution*, Newton Abbot 1975, pp. 59–60.
73. Heylyn, *Cyprianus Anglicus*, vol ii, p. 307.
74. 'A Brief and True Relation of the Broil which fell out on... the 23rd of July 1637' in J. Leslie, Earl of Rothes, *Relation of Proceedngs* (ed J. Laing and D. Nairne), Ballantyne Club Edinburgh 1830, pp. 198 ff.
75. Hamilton Mss. 382.
76. Register of the Privy Council of Scotland, vol vi, 1635–7, pp. 483–4.
77. Coke Mss, 59; Denmilne Mss. xii, f. 31.
78. Hill Burton, *History of Scotland*, vol vi, pp. 150–2.
79. J.D. Ogilvie, 'The National Petition, October 18 1637', in *Edinburgh Bibliographical Society Publications*, vol xii, pp. 105–31.
80. Hamilton Mss. 385, date 25 Aug 1637.
81. Gardiner, vol viii, pp. 326–8.
82. Denmilne Mss. xii, f. 19; Hamilton Mss. 382.
83. Hamilton Ms. 10492: Charles to Hamilton, 25 June 1638.
84. Hamilton Mss. 10492.
85. Stevenson, *Scottish Revolution*, p. 125.
86. Denmilne Mss. xii, f. 65.
87. Hamilton Mss. 10484.
88. Hamilton Mss. 10490.
89. Coke Ms. 59; National Archives, P.C. 2/50 /233.
90. Coke Mss. 59.
91. CSPD 1638, pp. 584, 590.
92. CSPD 1638–9, pp. 351–6; Gardiner vol ix, p.1.
93. Donaldson, pp. 313–16; S.A. Burrell, 'The Covenant Idea as a revolutionary symbol in Scotland', *Church History* 38, pp. 338–50; G.A. Henderson, 'The Idea of the Covenant in Scotland', in *The Burning Bush*, pp. 61–74.
94. Hamilton Mss. 10485 and 10486.
95. Donaldson, p. 319; Burnet, *Memoirs of the Dukes of Hamilton* pp. 71–2.
96. Gardiner, vol viii, pp. 363–4.
97. Donaldson, pp. 320–1.
98. Gardiner, *Hamilton Papers*, pp. 59–60.
99. Donaldson, pp. 321–2; *Archibald Johnson of Warriston, Diary*, pp. 391–3.
100. Hamilton Mss. 10490.
101. Hardwicke SP, London 1778, vol ii p. 113.
102. Knowles, vol ii, p. 561.

103. Sir Thomas Hope, *Diary*, p. 83.
104. CSPD 1638–9, p. 327.
105. C.V. Wedgwood, *The King's Peace*, p. 250.
106. Ibid.
107. CSPD 1639, p. 3.
108. Stuart Royal proclamations, vol ii, pp. 662–7.
109. STC 21906: A Large Declaration Concerning the Late Tumults in Scotland, 1639; Rushworth vol iii, pp. 1018–39.
110. BL Add Mss. 11045, f. 1.
111. Hamilton Mss. 10520.
112. Sharpe, *Personal Rule*, p. 815.
113. Wodrow Mss. xxiv ff. 36–64; Denmilne Mss. xii, f. 32; STC 22206 ('Confession…') and 22039 ('A Short Relation…')
114. CSPD 1638–9, pp. 473, 551.
115. Ibid, p. 385.
116. Cited in Tyacke, *Anti-Calviinsts*, p. 238.
117. CSPD 1637–8, p. 27; CSPD 1639, p. 525.
118. PRO SP 31/3/71, f. 23.
119. Temple of Stowe Mss. 11, ST 1893; Hamilton Mss. 11144; Gardiner, Hamilton Papers, pp. 73–5; BL Ellesmere Mss. 6602; Knowles, vol ii, p. 351.
120. Hamilton Papers, pp. 73–5.
121. Heylyn, *Cyprianus Anglicus*, p. 260; Clarendon, vol i, p. 151.
122. Strafford Mss. vol x.
123. Balfour, vol ii, p. 323; Robert Baillie, vol i, pp. 195–6.
124. Strafford Mss. vol x: date 19 Apr 1639.
125. Baillie vol i, p. 195.
126. Wedgwood, *The King's Peace*, p. 277.
127. Knowles, vol ii, pp. 313, 318.
128. Burnet, *Lives of the Dukes of Hamilton*, pp. 121–2, 124, 137–9.
129. CSPD 1639, pp. 269, 272, 281–3.
130. Hamilton Mss. 1/90.
131. Parsons, *Diary of Sir Henry Slingsby*, p. 35.
132. BL: Rawlinson Mss. B10, ff. 36 ff.
133. BL Additional Mss. 11045, f. 45.
134. CSPD 1639, pp. 367–70.
135. Scotland Archives: Advocates' Mss. 19, part 1, f. 17; Burnet, *Memoirs of the Dukes of Hamilton*, p. 140.
136. C.S. Terry, *The Life and Campaigns of Alexander Leslie, Earl of Leven*, 1899, pp. 76, 78–9; CSPD 1639, pp. 299–301, 307, 319.
137. Advocates Mss. 19/1/17, ff. 4–5, 11.
138. Johnston of Warriston *Diary*, p. 8.
139. Hardwicke State Papers vol ii, pp. 141–2.
140. CSPD 1639, pp. 355, 370.
141. As n. 133.
142. Rushworth, Collections, vol ii, p. 957.
143. Breadabane Mss. Letters 1636–9, letter 786.; Acts of Parliament, Scotland, vol v, pp. 252–5.
144. Register of Privy Council Scotland, 1639, p.142; Burnet, p. 160.

145. Bodleian ibrary: Tanner Mss. 67, f. 126; CSPVenetian 1636–9, p. 577.
146. W. Scott and J. Bliss, eds, *The Works of Wiliam Laud*, 7 vols, Oxford 1847–60, vol. iii p. 230.
147. Huntingdon Library: Hastings Mss. 5558, 3 February 1640; CSPD 1638–9, p. 361.
148. CSPD 1639–40, pp. 109–11, 368, 420, 434; HMC x, vol I, p. 48
149. C.V. Wedgwood, The King's Peace (Collins, 1978 edition), pp. 311–12.

Chapter Three
 1. Wodrow Quarto Ms. XXIV, ff. 36–64; STC 22037 (Edinburgh 1638); Denmilne Mss. XII, f. 32; A Short Relation of the Kirk of Scotland, Edinburgh 1638 (STC 22039).
 2. Laing, ed, *Letters and Journals of Robert Baillie*, vol I, pp. 188, 199, 219, 226; Peacham, *The Duty of All True Subjects to their King*, London 1639 (STC 19505); Tyacke, Anti-Calvinists, p. 238; B. Whitelocke, *Memorials*, p. 28.
 3. CSPD 1637–8, p. 27; CSPD 1639, p. 525; Dalrymple, *Memorials and Letters*, p. 41.
 4. CSPD 1638–9, p. 337
 5. Valerie Pearl, *London and the Outbreak of the Puritan Revolution*, Oxford 1961, p. 98.
 6. Edinburgh: Advocates' Mss. 32/4, f. 8.
 7. Twysden Mss. U 47/47, Z 1, f. 142.
 8. CSPD 1639, pp. 67–8.
 9. E.g. Letters of the Lady Brilliana Harley (Camden Society, old series, 58, 1854) p.41; CSPD 1638–9 p. 361; Dorset Record Office, Bond Papers, D 413, box 22, p. 52. Stuart Royal Proclamations, vol ii, p. 297; Spalding, *Memorials*, p. 257.
10. Wodrow Ms. xxvii, f. 106; Denmilne Mss. xii, f. 36.
11. HMC Cowper, vol ii, p. 215; CSPD 1638–9, p. 563.
12. Clarendon Mss. 14, nos. 1098, 1105, 1113.
13. CSPV 1636–9, pp. 553, 555.
14. Clarendon Mss. 15, no. 1199.
15. NA: S.P. 31/3/68, f. 235.
16. Yale University: Beinicke Library, Osborn Shelves, f. 111.
17. CSPD 1640, p. 278.
18. Rushworth, vol ii, p. 894.
19. Commons Journal vol ii p. 25; Notestein, ed, *D'Ewes Diary*, p. 23; HMC De l'Isle Mss. vol vi, pp. 260–1.
20. BL Add Mss. 11045, f. 81.
21. Knowles vol ii, pp. 394–403.
22. CSPD 1639–40, pp. 446–7, 472.
23. J.H. Elliott, 'The Year of the Three Ambassadors', in H Lloyd Jones, V. Pearl and B. Worden (eds) *History and Imagination*, 1981, pp. 165–81.
24. CSPV 1640–2, p. 31.
25. BL Ellesmere Mss. 7830; PRO SP 31/3/72, ff. 141–141 v.
26. Clarendon Mss. 18, no. 1383; Clarendon SP vol ii pp. 84–5.
27. Quoted in A. Loomie 'Alonso de Cardenas and the Long Parliament 1640–9' in *EHR* 97 (1982) p. 292.
28. Clarendon Mss. 18, no. 1383.
29. Elliott, p. 175.
30. Ellesmere Mss. 78314; CSPD 1639–40, p. 158.
31. CSPVenetian 1636–9, p. 563.

32. M. Kishlansky, *Parliamentary Selection: Social and Political Choice in Early Modern England*, Cambridge 1986; and see Sharpe, *Personal Rule*, pp. 854–6.
33. Clive Holmes, *The Eastern Association in the English Civil War*, Cambridge 1975, pp. 21–5.
34. CSPV 1640–2, p. 27.
35. CSPD 1639–40 pp. 580–1
36. Huntingdon Library: Hastings Mss. 5557: 13 January 1640.
37. Clarendon vol I, p. 171.
38. Sharpe, pp. 858–9.
39. Hamilton Ms. 803, date 24Mmarch 1640.
40. CSPD 1639–40, p. 329.
41. B. Cope, *Proceedings of the Short Parliament*, pp. 115–25.
42. Ibid, p. 134.
43. E Cope, *Proceedings of the Short Parliament*, Camden Society, 4th series, vol 19, 1977, pp. 158–62.
44. Ibid, pp. 135–7.
45. Ibid, pp. 138–42; J. Maltby, *The Short Parliament Diary of Sir Thomas Aston 1640* (Camden Society, 4th series, no. 35, 1988) pp 4–5.
46. Cope, pp. 145–57; Maltby pp. 8–11.
47. Cope, pp. 164–7.
48. Cope, pp. 169–73.
49. Cope, pp. 69–70.
50. Lords Journal, vol iv, pp. 65–7.
51. Cope, pp. 175–7; Maltby, pp. 63–5.
52. Cope, pp, 177–80.
53. Maltby, pp. 85–109.
54. Cope, pp. 187–91.
55. Cope, p. 193.
56. Maltby, p. 144; Cope, p. 243; Clarendon vol i, p. 180.
57. Cope, pp. 197–8.
58. National Archives: SP 16/452, f. 131.
59. Ibid, f. 280.
60. J. Nalson, *An Impartiall Collection of the Great Affairs of State from the Beginning of the Scotch Rebellion in 1637 to the Murder of King Charles I*, 2 vols, 1682–3, vol i, p. 243; CSPD 1640, p. 119, 140–1, 144.
61. HMC De l'Isle and Dudley, vol vi, p. 219.
62. CSPD 1640, pp. 112–13, 98, 219, 500.
63. National Archives: SP 16/453, f. 36.
64. Ibid.
65. J. Denniston, ed, *Coltness Collections, Maitland Club, Edinburgh, 1842*, pp. 20–1; Burnet, *History of My Own Times*, ed Osmund Airy, 2 vols, Oxford 1897, vol I, p. 42. T. Thomson, ed, *A Diary of the Public Correspondence of Sir Thomas Hope of Craighall, Bt, 1633–45*, Edinburgh 1843, pp. 93–4.
66. Commons Journal vol ii, p. 25; PRO SP 16/453 f. 36 v.
67. CSPD 1640, pp. 154–6.
68. Lambeth Palace Mss. 943, ff. 695–6; CSPD 1640, p. 352.
69. Ellesmere Mss. 7837, 9 June 1640, and 7843, 1 July 1640.
70. STC 21919.

71. Sharpe, pp. 878–84.
72. HMC Portland Mss. vol iii, p. 63
73. Wedgwood, *The King's Peace*, p. 334.
74. CSPV 1640–2, pp. 50. 53.
75. Oldmixon, *History of England* pp. 141–3; Gardiner, *History of England 1603–42*, vol ix p. 179; Adamson, *The Noble Revolt*, pp 46–7.
76. Oldmixon, p. 144.
77. Edinburgh: New College Library Mss. X 15b 3/1, vol I f. 362.
78. Gardiner vol ix, p. 179; New College Mss. Edinburgh x, 15 b 3/1, f. 363.
79. CSPD 1640 pp. 230–1.
80. Ibid, pp. 617, 619.
81. BL Ellesmere Mss. 7847, date 8 Aug 1640.
82. CSPD 1640, pp. 297–8.
83. Ibid, p. 230.
84. Ibid, p. 617.
85. Ellesmere Mss. 7851, date 18 Aug 1640.
86. Bodleian Library Tanner Mss 65, ff. 100–100v.
87. Hamilton Mss. 1231, date 24 Aug 1640.
88. CSPD 1640, p. 603; Stuart Royal Proclamations vol ii, no. 312, pp. 731–2.
89. CSPD 1640, p. 630; Ellesmere Mss. 7856, date 29 Aug 1640.
90. Clarendon Papers ii, p. 107.
91. Breadalbane Mss: Letters 1640–9, p. 813; Gumble, *The Life of General Monck*, 1671, p. 10; Burnet, *Memoirs of Dukes of Hamilton* vol I, p. 173.
92. Clarendon Papers, vol ii, p. 210.
93. Quoted in Sharpe, p. 894.
94. Spalding, *Memorials of the Troubles*, p. 337.
95. Laing (ed), *Letters and Journals of Robert Baillie*, vol I, p. 259; CSPD 1640, p. 193.
96. CSPD 1640–1, p. 8.
97. Hardwicke State Papers, vol ii, p. 169.
98. CSPD 1640, pp. 624–5.
99. Clarendon State Papers vol ii, p. 94
100. Denmilne Mss. 1328.
101. Hardwicke State Papers vol ii, p. 170; Arundel Castle Letters no. 380.
102. Clarendon State Papers vol ii, pp. 97–8.
103. Clarendon Mss. 19, no. 1418.
104. New College Library Edinburgh Ms. xi, 15 b 3/1, vol I, f.262.
105. National Archives: SP 16/465, f. 111v.
106. Reproduced in J. Oldmixon, *History of England during the Reigns of the Royal House of Stuart* (1730) p. 144.
107. Ibid.
108. Burnet, *History of My Own Times*, ed. Osmund Airy, Oxford 1897, Vol I, pp. 45–6.
109. Clarendon Mss. 19, ff, 24–5; Clarendon State Papers vol ii, pp. 110–12.
110. BL Add. Mss. 44848, ff. 283–4 and appendix.
111. Adamson, *The Noble Revolt*, p. 79.
112. David Scott, 'Hannibal at our gate: loyalists and fifth-columnists during the Bishops' Wars – the case of Yorkshire', *Historical Research* 70 (1997), pp.269–93.
113. National Archives: SP 16/467, f. 157.
114. Ibid.

115. Sir John Birkenhead, *A Letter from Mercurius Civicus to Mercurius Rusticus, or London's Confession*, B.L. Thomason *Tracts* E 65/32.
116. Calibut Downing, A Sermon Preached to the Honourable Artillery Company, 1 Sep 1640, Thomason Tracts E 157/4; Birkenhead p. 8.
117. PRO Sp 16/467, f. 225; and see New College Library Edinburgh, Mss. X15 b 3/1, vol 1, f. 262 on threat of mutiny.
118. Clarendon Mss. 24–5.
119. Clarendon State Papers ii, p.98.
120. BL Additional Mss. 44848, app, ff. 520–1.
121. BL Additional Mss. 11045; Edinburgh: New College Library Mss. X15b, 3/1, f. 263.
122. Ibid, p. 120.
123. BL Add Mss. 23146; Nottingham University Library, Clifton Papers C 615.
124. Staffordshire RO: Dyot Mss. D 661/11/15.
125. Hardwicke State Papers iii, p. 180.
126. BL Add Mss. 11045, f. 144 v.

Chapter Four
1. See Adamson, *Noble Revolt*, passim.
2. R. Zaller, *The Parliament of 1621*, 1971, pp. 121–2.
3. Clarendon State Papers ii, p. 23
4. Notestein, *D'Ewes Diary*, p. 24; BL Additional Mss. 15567, f. 31 v.
5. PRO SP 16/476, f. 47.
6. Cambridge University Library Ms. Mm. 1/45, f. 112.
7. Kevin Sharpe, *Personal Rule*, pp. 590–3.
8. See Sharpe, *Personal Rule*, pp. 914–16.1 Bodleian Library, Tanner Mss. 306 f.292 and 495 f.92.
9. CSPV 1640–2, p. 93.
10. Byrne, *A New History of the Prelates' Tyranny*, pp. 114–15.
11. Sir Ralph Verney, The Verney Papers: Notes on the Proceedings of the Long Parliament, ed. John Bruce (Camden Society, London 1845), pp. 2–3.
12. BL Additional Mss. 15567, f. 32.
13. Prynne, *A New Discovery of the Prelates' Tyranny*, pp. 114–15; *D'Ewes Diary*, ed Notestein, p. 4; Oxford : New College Mss. 9502, 28–9 November 1640.
14. Rushworth iii, pp. 101–4.
15. Wing Mss. B 5668: Another sermon... preached before the honourable House of Commons now assembled in Parliament on 5 November 1641 .
16. *D'Ewes Diary*, ed. Notestein, pp. 313–14; E. Calmay, *A Just and Necessary Apology*, 1646 (BL Ms. E 319/25), p. 9.
17. W. Notestein (ed), *Diary of Sir Simonds D'Ewes*, p. 5.
18. BL Ms. E 463/18; Commons Journal vol ii p. 24; BL Thomason Tracts E 463/18, 'A Letter from an Ejected Member of the House of Commons to Sir John Evelyn'.
19. See CJ ii 35, and Adamson, pp. 117–19.
20. Sheila Lambert, 'The Opening of the Long Parliament', in *Historical Journal* 27 (1984), pp. 265–87.
21. Clarendon, *History of the Rebellion*, vol iii, p. 3.
22. Rushworth iii, p. 12.
23. Ibid, pp. 12–16; and BL Add. Mss. 15567, ff. 17–21 v.

24. Whitaker, *Life of Radcliffe*, p. 222.
25. BL Hart Mss. 1601, f. 5 v.
26. CJ ii, p. 21.
27. *D'Ewes Diary*, ed. Notestein, p. 6.
28. Ibid p. 5 and CJ vol ii p. 22 (Herts petition); Cambridge University Library Mss. kk VI, f. 38 (Palmer diary).
29. Whitaker, p. 292, 318; D'Ewes Diary, pp. 24–5.
30. HMC 4th report, p. 30; LJ iv p. 102; D'Ewes Diary, pp. 24–5.
31. LJ iv, p. 84; Hart, Justice Upon Petition, p. 2; Hart, 'The House of Lords and the Appellate Jurisdiction in Equity, 1640–3', in *Parliamentary History* 2 (1983) pp. 49–60.
32. BL Add. Mss. 15567, f. 31 v.
33. *D'Ewes Diary*, p. 24; Cambridge University Library Mss. Kk 38, p.34; BL Additional Mss. 15567 on Strafford's intentions.
34. Whitaker, p. 218.
35. Adamson, pp. 103–4.
36. *D'Ewes Diary*, pp. 25 and 25 n; Minnesota University Library, Mss. 137 (Peyton Diary), p.10; J. Nalson, An Impartiall Collection. vol I, p. 523.
37. Gardiner, *History of England* 1603–42, vol ix, pp. 233–4 and notes.
38. As n. 35.
39. CJ ii, p. 26; Whitelocke, *Memorials* vol I, pp. 113–14.
40. Clarendon vol I, pp. 225–6.
41. CJ ii p. 26.
42. Ibid; Lords Journal iv, pp. 88–9.
43. CSPV 1640–2, p.96; NDNB article on Windebank.
44. *D'Ewes Diary*, p. 6.
45. Adamson, chapter 5 'Bedford's Commnwealth'; *NDNB* article on Bedford.
46. *D'Ewes Diary*, p. 7.
47. Ibid, p. 146.
48. Ibid, pp. 74–5.
49. Adamson, p. 590 and n. 91.
50. Centre for Kentish Studies: De L'Isle Mss. U 1475/C 129/12.
51. Rushworth iii, p. 119.
52. HMC De L'Isle and Dudley Mss. vol vi, p. 346.
53. CJ ii p. 70; *D'Ewes Diary*, ed. Notestein, p. 265.
54. The Speech or Declaration of Mr. St. John, pp. 1–38.
55. CJ ii, p. 60; D'Ewes Diary p. 196; CSPV 1640–2, p. 27; Pauline Crofts, 'Annual Parliaments and the Long Parliament' in *Bulletin of the IHR*, 59 (1986), pp, 155–71
56. Sheila Lambert, 'The Opening of the Long Parliament' in *Historical Journal*, vol 27 (1984) p. 176–9.
57. *D'Ewes Diary*, pp. 184, 188.
58. Rushworth, pp. 167–8 (but wrong date given).
59. Sheila Lambert, 'The Opening of the Long Parliament', as n. 56, pp. 265–87; and Lambert, 'Procedure in the House of Commons in the Early Stuart Period', in *E H R* 95 (1980) pp. 776–9; Rushworth, Historical Collections, vol iii part 1, p. 155.
60. *D'Ewes Diary*, p. 280.
61. *D'Ewes Diary*, p. 109.
62. De *L'Isle* Mss. U 1475/C 114/7.

63. Nalson, vol I, pp. 735–6; LJ iv, p. 142; *D'Ewes Diary* p. 128.
64. *D'Ewes Diary*, pp. 335–6; BL Harliean Mss. 164, f. 113.; Rushworth, vol iii p. 184.
65. Gardiner, vol ix p. 281.
66. BL Harleian Mss. 6424.
67. D'Ewes Diary pp. 277–9; Westminster Cathedral Archives, A xxx, p. 1.
68. BL Harleian Mss. 6424, f. 13; Rushworth iii, pt 1, pp. 165–6; AO Meyer 'Charles I and Rome' in *American History Review* 19 (1914), pp. 13–26.
69. HMC De L'Isle and Dudley, vi, p. 385.
70. CJ vi, p. 87.
71. BL Harleian Mss. 6424, ff. 16 v – 17; Add Mss. 72433, f. 83 v.
72. PRO SP 16/473, f. 154.
73. Clarendon i, p. 247.
74. Rushworth iii, pt 1, p. 155
75. Gardiner, vol ix p. 281.
76. *D'Ewes Diary*, p. 335; BL Harleian Mss. 164, f. 113.
77. Rushworth, *Historical Collections* vol iii, part I pp. 183–4.
78. Adamson, *The Noble Revolt*, pp. 182–3.
79. Clarendon ii, p. 211.
80. Common Plea Remembrance Rolls: CP 45/314, mem. 3..
81. Staffordshire Record Office: Davenant Mss. D (W) 1778/I /1/12.
82. *D'Ewes Diary*, pp. 364–5; CJ ii, p. 87.
83. BL Harleian Mss. 6424, ff. 16v -1 7.
84. HMC De L'Isle and Dudley Mss. vi, p. 383; Centre for Kentish Studies: De L'Isle Mss. U 1475? C 114/12
85. *D'Ewes Diary* p. 501.
86. Staffordshire RO: Dartmouth Mss. D(W) 1778/1/i/14 (23 February 1641).
87. BL Add. Mss. 669, f. ¾.
88. De L'Isle Mss. U 1475/C 114/10
89. CJ ii, p. 90; D'Ewes Diary pp. 388, 394–5.
90. BL Harleian Mss. 6424,: HMC De L'Isle and Dudley Mss. vi, pp. 376, 387.
91. CJ ii, p. 97.
92. Parliamentary Archives: 20 March 1641, ff. 78–82; Gardiner ix, p. 309.
93. BL Harleian Mss. 163, ff. 163, 315 v; Centre for Kentish Studies: De L'Isle and Dudley Ms. U 1475/C 114/12.
94. Whitelocke I, p. 120; BL Harleian Mss. 6424, f. 21 v.
95. Clarendon I, pp. 320–1.
96. Adamson, pp. 230–2; BL Sloane Mss. 1467, ff. 27v – 28; BL Harleian Mss. 164 (D'Ewes), ff. 152–155v, 160; ibid 476 (Moore diary), ff. 160–169 v; BL Additional Mss. 14828, f. 131 v.; John Timmis, 'The Basis of the Lords' Decision in the Trial of Strafford: Contravention of the Two-Witness Rule', in *Albion* 8 (`975) pp. 311–19.
97. CJ ii, p. 118; BL Harleian Mss. 26, ff. 26–7; 1601, f. 55; ibid 6424, ff. 54r-v; Add Mss. 19398, f. 72; Gwydir Papers (National Library of Wales), 1683; PRO SP 16/479, ff. 55v-56.
98. CJ ii, p. 118; BL Harleian Mss. 1601, f. 56; PRO SP 16/479, f. 56.
99. Adamson, p. 242, and n. 30.
100. BL Harleian Mss. 163; J, Rushworth, *The Tryal of the Earl of Strafford... upon an Impeachment of High Treason*, 1680, pp. 552 and 638.
101. BL Harleian Mss. 164, f. 170.

102. Ibid, ff. 52 and 53.
103. CJ ii, p. 122.
104. BL Harleian Mss. 164, f. 178; CJ ii, p. 133.
105. BL Add. Mss. 11045, f. 139 v.
106. CSPV 1640–2, p. 145.
107. Napier, *Montrose and the Covananters*, vol I, pp. 365–8.
108. BL Harleian Mss. 164, ff. 183 and 186v; CJ ii p. 125; CSPD 1641, p. 555.
109. BL Harleian Mss. 164, ff. 183 v and 186 v.
110. CJ ii, p. 125; BL Harleian Mss. 164, f. 183 and 165, f. 85.; Add Mss. 31954 f. 181.
111. PRO SP 31/9/2- ff. 115, 136; BL. Harleian Mss. 6424, f. 56; Add mss. 64922, f. 24v.; Adamson p, 266.
112. CJ ii, p. 126.
113. Clarendon I, pp. 318–19.
114. CJ ii, pp. 281–2, 285.
115. Trinity College Dublin Mss. 809, ff. 5–12.
116. Clarendon, *History of the Great Rebellion* vol I pp. 320–1.
117. BL Sloane Mss. 1467, f. 39v; Add. Mss. 6424, f. 58; Harleian Mss. 163, ff. 290, 294.
118. Bray, *Evelyn Diary and Correspondence*, vol iv, p. 79; CJ ii, p. 287; BL Sloane Mss. 1467, f. 39v; BL Harleian Mss. 6424, f. 58, 290, 294 .
119. BL Harleian Mss. 477, f. 27 and 132.
120. Rushworth ii, pt 1, p. 253.
121. LJ entry for 3 May 1641.
122. BL Add. Mss. 19398, f. 72.
123. BL Add Mss. 19398, f. 72; Bodleian Library Tanner Mss. 66, ff. 83v-84.
124. BL Harleian Mss. 477, ff. 27v- 28.
125. Ibid 6424, f. 58 v.
126. LJ iv, pp. 136, 139; BL Harleian Mss. 477, ff. 43v, 45v, 47v.
127. LJ iv, p. 241.
128. National Archives: SP 16/480, f. 33v.
129. PRO SP 16/480, f. 33v; CJ ii, pp. 139–40.
130. LJ iv, p. 238.
131. BL Harleian Mss. 477, f.f. 28, 226, 242, 246, 248, 254–5, 259; CJ ii p. 132.
132. PRO SP 31/9/20,; Gardiner ix, pp. 363–5.
133. Sir W. Sanderson, *A Compleat History of the Life and Reign of King Charles from his Cradle to his Grave*, 1658, pp. 414–15.
134. CSPV 1640–2, pp. 150–7.
135. CJ ii, p. 127; Wing Mss. B 47771 A.
136. Adamson, p. 291 note 3.
137. CJ ii, p. 130.
138. LJ iv, p. 245.
139. Sir Edward Dering, *Collection of Speeches*, p. 62.
140. Adamson, *The Noble Revolt*, p. 329.
141. CJ ii, p. 178.
142. Ibid, pp. 179–80.
143. Ibid p. 159.
144. Stevenson, *Scottish Revolution*, pp. 224–5.
145. Buckminster Park, Lincs: Tollemache Mss. 37484.

146. Ibid; BL Mss. E 160/26, '"Certain Instructions Given by the Lord Montrose, Lord Napier, Lord Kerr of Blackhall'.
147. BL Mss. E 160/25.
148. HMC 9th report, appendix ii, p. 255.
149. National Archives: SP 17, case F, no. 2.
150. Adamson p, 143.
151. See Adamson, chapter 8.
152. BL Harleian Mss. 163, f. 200 v.

Chapter Five
1. CJ ii, p. 159.
2. NA: SP 16/481/21.
3. Adamson, pp, 323 ff.
4. CJ ii p. 185; CSPV 1640–2, p. 174.
5. See Judith Maltby, *Prayer Book and People in Elizabethan and Early Stuart England* (Cambridge UP 1998) pp. 238–47. For evidence that pro-Anglican petiitons could be more uncertain on keeping bishops, see Peter Lake article on the 1641 Cheshire petition in T. Cogswell, R. Cust and P. Lake, eds, *Politics, Religion and Popularity: Early Stuart essays in honour of Conrad Russell* (Cambridge UP 2003) pp. 259–89.
6. LJ iv, p. 395; CJ ii, p. 286.
7. LJ iv, p. 392.
8. BL Harleian Mss. 164, ff. 109–109v; CJ ii, pp., 283 and 287.
9. BL Add. Mss. 669, f. 3/18.
10. BL E 197/1 : 'A Collection of Speeches Made by Sir Edward Dering, Knight and Baronet, in Maters of Religion', 1642.
11. BL Add Mss. 19398, f. 72: PRO SP 16/482, f. 178.
12. James Gordon, *History of the Scots Affairs* (ed. J. Robertson and G., Grub, 4 vols, Edinburgh 1841), vol iii, p. 547.
13. Tollemache Mss. (Buckminster Park, Lincs) 3748.
14. CSPV 1640–2, p. 177.
15. Adamson, p. 350.
16. Stevenson, *Scottish Revolution*, p. 228.
17. Certain Instructions, pp.4–5; Yale University, Beinicke Library, Osborn Shelves, f b 158 f.78; and Wodrow Mss. (Nat Library Scotland) 65, f. 41.
18. Stevenson, p. 225.
19. Adamson, p. 445; CJ ii, pp. 135, 138, 180–1.
20. Stevenson, p.231; Beinicke Library, Yake University, Howard of Escrick Papers.
21. Sir James Balfour, *Historical Works, Edinburgh 1824–5*, 4 vols, vol iii, p. 45. NA SP 16/483/104; CSPV 1640–2, pp. 270–1.
22. Stevenson, pp. 234–5; Acts of the Parliament of Scotland vol v, pp 534–45.
23. BL E 173/31: S. Marshall 'A Peace-Offering to God: A Sermon Preached to the Honourable House of Commons assembled in Parliament at their Public Thanksgiving, 7 September 1641'.
24. CJ ii, p. 278; BL Harleian Mss. 164/82.
25. Thompson, *'The Origins of the Parliamentary Middle Group'*, pp. 80–1.
26. CJ ii, p. 280.
27. BL Add. Mss. 171/17, f. 4.

28. Allan Macines, *Charles I and the Covenanting Movement 1625*–41, Edinburgh 1991, pp. 202–3; Nicholas Papers vol I, p. 49; Hamilton Mss. GD 406/1/1434.
29. Adamson pp. 371 and note.
30. NA: SP 16/481, f. 483.
31. Hamilton Mss. G D 406/1/1412.
32. Stevenson, *The Scottish Revolution*, pp. 236–7.
33. HMC 4th Report, vol 1, pp. 163, 164.
34. BL Thomason Tracts E 173/13: Nathaniel Fiennes et al, 'The Discovery of a Late and Bloody Conspiracy at Edinburgh, in Scotland', 1641; Hamilton Mss. GD 406/1/1544. Coates, *D'Ewes Diary*, p. 9.
35. Balfour iii, pp. 94–7.
36. HMC 4th Report, pp. 163–9.
37. J. Hart, *Justice upon Petition: the House of Lords and the Reformation of Justice*, 1621–75, 1991, p. 65.
38. Minnesota University Library Mss. 137, f. 133.
39. Trinity College Dublin Mss. 816, f. 90; and N. Canny, 'What Really Happened In Ireland in 1641?' in J. Ohlmayer (ed), *Ireland From Independence to Occupation*, 1641–60, Cambridge 1995, p. 29.
40. Brian Mac Cuarta (ed) *Ulster 1641:Aspects of the Rising*, Belfast 1997, p. 114. Trinity College Dublin Mss. 809, ff. 5–12.
41. 'Relation of Lord Maguire', in Mary Hickson, *Ireland in the Seventeenth Century or the Massacres of 1641*, 2 vols, 1882, vol ii, pp, 341–54.
42. Adamson, pp. 378–9.
43. CSPV 1640–2, p. 225.
44. Jacqueline Eales, *Puritans and Roundheads: the Harleys of Brampton Bryan and the Outbreak of the English Civil War*, Cambridge 990, p. 115; David Cressy, England on Edge: Crisis and Resolution, 1640–2, Oxford 2006, p. 205. For the 'loyalism' of the Irish rebels, see Trinity College Ms. 829, ff. 302–5, and Canny, *Making Ireland British*, pp. 490–2.
45. Bray, *Evelyn Diary and Correspondence*, vol iv, p. 92.
46. Surrey History Centre: Bray Mss. 85/5/2/9.
47. Ibid, 85/5/2/11.
48. Ibid; and *Evelyn Diary and Correspondence* vol iv p. 94.
49. Ibid p. 92.
50. CJ ii, p. 292; BL Harleian Mss. 6424 f. 97.
51. Coates, *D'Ewes Diary*, p. 21; Harleian Mss ibid.
52. Coates p. 44–5.
53. Ibid p. 45; CJ ii, p. 97.
54. *Evelyn Diary and Correspondence*, vol iv p. 107; Coates p. 45.
55. Adamson, pp. 375–82.
56. See further, Roy Foster, *A History of Modern Ireland* 1603–1972 (Penguin 1989) pp. 86–9.
57. CJ ii, pp. 300, 302, 303.
58. Coates, p. 74.
59. Ibid, pp.74, 87; CJ ii, p. 306.
60. C. Burgess, *Another Sermon*.
61. CJ ii, pp. 304, 306.
62. Ibid. p. 306

63. Bodleian Library, Rawlinson Mss. d. 932, ff. 12v – 13 v; Coates, *D'Ewes Diary* pp. 68, 72.
64. *Evelyn Diary and Correspondence* p. 117; Rawlinson Mss. 1099 f. 19b; LJ iv p. 438; CJ ii, pp. 307, 322. Coates p. 105.
65. CJ ii p. 325.
66. Cromwell's aside to Falkland, quoted in Clarendon i, p. 420.
67. CJ ii p. 325.
68. Adamson pp. 441–3.
69. BL E 238/4: 'Ovatio Carolina' pp. 14–16; Adamson pp. 441–5.
70. BL Ms. E 238/4: Ovatio Carolina, pp. 11–12.
71. Clarendon i, p. 456.
72. Privy Council Registers xii, pp. 200–01.
73. Coates p. 127.
74. BL E 199/30.
75. Coates pp. 294–5.
76. CJ ii, p. 344.
77. CJ ii p. 330; Coates p. 228.
78. Coates p. 244.
79. Gardiner ix, p. 95.
80. CJ ii, p. 357.
81. Ibid, p. 339.
82. Coates p. 216 note; Clarendon I, p. 84.
83. BL Mss. 179/19, A 2.
84. Clarendon I, p.448; *DNB* articles on Balfour and Lunsford.
85. Wing Mss. C 2600.
86. Archives du Ministere des Affaires Etrangeres, Paris: Correspondence Politique, Angleterre, no. 46., date 16/26 Dec 1641.
87. Gardiner, 'Plan for the deliverance of Strafford', in *EHR* 12 (1897) pp., 114–16.
88. CJ ii p. 339.
89. Coates p. 330.
90. BL Ms. E 131/30.
91. Clarendon, *Great Rebellion*, vol I p. 456. See Richard Cust, *Charles I: A Political Life* (Longmans 2005) p. 301 for the manoevures of these crucial days .
92. Clarendon I, pp. 454, 471; PRO SP 16/486/110; LJ iv p. 493.
93. Coates pp. 352–3, 357.
94. CJ ii, p. 361.
95. LJ iv, p. 494.
96. NA: LC 5/135, entry for 28 Dec 1641; Signet Office Docket Book f. 181v.
97. LJ iv, p. 495.
98. LJ iv, pp. 496–7: BL Mss. 669, f.3/27.
99. MISSING
100. BL Mss. 669, f. 3/27; CJ ii, pp. 367, 368; LJ iv, pp. 496–7.
101. CJ ii p. 366; LJ iv p. 501.
102. Gardiner vol x p.238; NA: 31/3/73, ff. 10r-v; CJ ii pp. 368, 369.
103. Gardiner x p. 136. Clarendon I, pp. 471–2; CJ ii, p. 63; LJ iv, pp. 497–8.
104. LJ iv, pp. 501–2; CJ ii, pp. 366–7.
105. *Private Journal of the Long Parliament*, ed. W. Coates, A Steele Young, V Snow (New Haven and London 1982) p. 8. *Parliamentary Journal*, Jan-Mar 1642, pp. 11, 2, 25; Gardiner x, p, 138; CJ ii, pp. 368–9.

106. CSPV 1640–2, p. 276.
107. Gardiner x, p. 136.
106. CSPV 1640–2, p. 276.
107. Sir P. Warwick, *Memoirs of Charles I*, 1702, reprinted 1813, p. 225; .Russell, *Fall of the British Monarchies*, p. 449.
108. C. V. Wedgwood, 'Charles I's nephew and the English throne: the Elector Palatine and the Civil War' in *History Today*, vol 4 no. 1 (January 1954).
109. W. Lyly, *Life and Death of Charles I*, pp. 232–4; CSPD 1641–3, pp, 238, 242, 249.
110. Coates, p. 393; CJ ii, pp. 368–9; Lord Mayor's Archives: *Common Council Journal* vol 40, f. 15.
111. J. Adair, *A Life of John Hampden, the Patriot* (Thorogood 2003) p. 267.
112. Alan Everitt, *The Community of Kent and the Great Rebellion*, 1640–60, Leicester 1966, pp. 97 and 100; John Walter, *Understanding Popular Violence in the English Revolution*, Cambridge 1999, p. 322.
113. See Derek Hirst, 'The Defection of Sir Edward Dering, 1640–' in Peter Gaunt (ed), *The English Civil War*, Oxford 2000, pp. 207–25.
114. BL E 131/14: 'A Great conspiracy of the Papists against Worthy Members of Both Houses of Parliament'; Robin Clifton, 'Fear of Popery' in C. Russell (ed), *The Origins of the English Civil War*, London 1973, pp. 144–63; Clifton, 'Fear of Catholics' in *Past and Present* 52 (1971).
115. Clarendon I, p. 589; CJ ii, pp. 406, 552.

Bibliography

Primary Sources
Aubrey's Brief Lives, ed Oliver Dick (Penguin 1962).
Bodleian Library Oxford: Bankes Mss.
   Carte Mss.
   Clarendon Mss. no. 24.
   Rawlinson Mss. c956 (Holland Diary).
   Tanner Mss. no 60.
British Library: Additional Mss. 6703, 15567 (Anon, memoir of Long Parliament),18981,
   18982, 19398 (Correspondence), 23146 (Dugard diary),24465, 25465, 31116.
   Egerton Mss. 1820.
   Harleian Mss 163–4 (*D'Ewes Diary*), 457 (Minutes of the 1640–1
   Anglo-Scottish Treaty),478 (Moore Diary), 1583, 1601
   (Anonymous Diary), 6424 (House of Lords Diary of Bishop Warner), 6865 (Holles
      Diary).
   Rawlinson Mss. D392.
   Sloane Mss.
   Stowe Mss. 326.
   Thomason Tracts.
   E 94/10: Autobiography of Henry Burton, 1643.
   E 162/1-2: William Prynne, 'A New Discovery of the Prelates
   Tyranny in their Late Prosecution of Mr William Pryn, 1641.
   E 199/30: The Kings Majesties Speech the 2 day of December 1641:
   To the Honourable House of Parliament.
   E 203/1: His Majesties Declaration: to all his Loving Subjects, of the Causes which
      moved Him to dissolve the last Parliament, 1640.
Historical Manuscripts Commission: Portland Mss.
House of Commons: Commons Journals, vols 2–5.
House of Lords: Lords Journal, vols 4–6.
Paris: Archives du Ministere des Affaires Etrangeres: Correspondence Politique: Angleterre.
Calendar of State Papers Colonial: 1574–1660.
Calendar of State Papers Domestic: 1628–9, ed J Bruce (HMSO, 1859).
   1629–31, ed ibid (HMSO 1860).
   1636–7, ed ibid (1867)
   1637–8, ed ibid (1869)
   1639, ed W Douglas Hamilton (1873).
   1639–40, ed ibid (1877)
   1640, ed ibid (1880).
   1641-3, ed ibid (1887).
   CSPV 1625-6, ed Allen Hindes (HMSO 1913).

1628-9, ed ibid (1916).
1632-6, ed ibid (1921).
1636-9, ed ibid (1923).
The English Revolution, vol I : *Fast Sermons to Parliament* (Cornmarket Press, Oxford 1970).
The English Revolution: *Newsbooks*, ed. Robin Jeffs (Cornmarket Press Oxford):
  Vol 1: Oxford Royalist vol 1: Mercurius Aulicus, January–August 1643, (1971).
  Vol 2: Oxford Royalist vol 2: Mercurius Aulicus, September 1643–March 1644 (1971).
  Vol 3: Oxford Royalist vol 3: Mercurius Aulicus, April 1644–March 1645 (1971).
  Vol 4: Oxford Royalist vol 4: Mercurius Aulicus, April–September 1645 (1971); Mercurius Rusticus, May 1643–March 1644; Mercurius Anti-Britannicus, August 1645; Mercurius Academicus, December 1645 – March 1646.
Letters and Papers of Robert Baillie, ed. D. Laing, 3 vols (Edinburgh 1841–2).
Richard Baxter, *Reliquiae Baxterianae*.
J. Bruce, ed, *The Verney Papers*: Notes of Proceedings in the Long Parliament, temp Charles I, from memoranda by Sir Ralph Verney (Camden Society 1845).
Thomas Carte, ed, *Collection of Original Papers* (London 1839).
The Letters of John Chamberlain, ed. N. McClure (Phildelphia 1929).
Earl of Clarendon (Edward Hyde), *History of the Great Rebellion*, ed. W. D. Macray (Oxford 1888).
State Papers Collected by the Earl of Clarendon, ed. R. Scope and T. Monkhouse, 3 vols (Oxford 1767–86).
Commons Debates 1621, ed. Wallace Notestein, F. Relf and H. Simpson, 7 vols (New Haven 1935).
Commons Debates in 1625, ed. S. R. Gardiner (Camden Society 1873).
Commons Debates in 1628, ed. R. C. Johnston et al (New Haven 1977).
The Commons Debates for 1629, ed. Wallace Notestein and F. Relf (Minneapolis, 1929).
Ester Cope and Wilson Coates, eds. *Proceedings of the Short Parliament* of 1640 (Camden Society, 4th series, vol 19, 1977).
The Correspondence of John Cosin, 2 vols (Surtees Society 1888).
The Writings and Speeches of Oliver Cromwell, ed W CABbott, vol 1 (Cambridge Massachusetts 1937).
David Dalrymple, Lord Hailes, ed, *Memorials and Letters Relating to the History of Britain in the Reign of Charles the First* (Glasgow 1766).
Sir John Eliot, *Negotium Posterorum*, ed. A. B. Grossart (1881).
The Diary of Sir Simonds D'Ewes, ed. Willson Coates (1942),ed. Wallace Notestein (New Haven, US, 1925).
Memorials of the English Civil War: Correspondence of the Fairfax Family, ed. R. Bell, 2 vols (1849).
Thomas Fuller, *The Church History of Britain*, ed. J Nicholls (London 1868).
S. G. Gardiner, ed, *Parliamentary Debates in 1610* (Camden Society, London, vol 18, 1862).
—— ed. *Debates in the House of Commons in 1625* (Camden Society, London 1873).
—— ed, *Constitutional Documents of the Puritan Revolution 1625–60* (1889).
——, 'Plan of Charles I for the deliverance of Strafford' in *English Historical Review*, vol 12 (1897) pp. 114–16 .
J. N. Gilbert, ed., *History of the Confederate War in Ireland by Richard Bellings*, 7 vols (Paris 1882–91).

P. Gordon of Ruthven, *Short Abridgement of England's Distemper* (Spalding Club, Aberdeen 1842).
J. Hacket, *Scrinia Reserarta: A Memorial* Offered *to the Great Deservings* of John Williams DD (1693).
W. Haller, ed, *Tracts on Liberty in the Puritan Revolution, 1638–47*, 3 vols (New York 1934).
The Hamilton Papers, ed. S. R. Gardiner (Camden Society 1880).
Sir John Harington, *Letters and Epigrams*, ed. N McClure (Phildelphia 1930).
T. E. Hartley, ed, *Proceedings* in *the Parliaments of Queen* Elizabeth *I* (Leicester UP 1981).
R. R. Heele, *A Bibliography of Royal Proclamations* (Oxford 1910).
The Autobiography of Lord Herbert of Cherbury, ed. S. Lee (London 1886).
Peter Heylyn, *A Short View of the Life and Raigne of* Charles *I* (1658).
Cyprianus Anglicus, or *the Life and Death of... William Laud* (London 1668).
Historical Manuscripts Commission: Bath Mss: Harley Papers vol 2 (1907)
  De l'Isle Mss, vol 5: Sidney Papers (1962)
  Egmont Mss. part 1 (1905)
  Fourth Report, part 1 (1874)
  Fifth Report, part 1 (1876)
  Eighth Report, part 1: Digby Mss (1881)
  Lonsdale Mss: 'Notes on Parliament'.
  Ormonde Mss.
  Portland Mss.
  Supplement: Mar and Kellie Mss. Report (1930).
Sir Ralph Hopton, *Bellum Civile* (1902 edition).
Memoirs of the Life of Colonel Hutchinson (London 1806).
M. Keeler, *The Long Parliament 1640–I* (1954).
William Laud, *Works* (Oxford 1847).
Hamon Lestrange, *The Reign of King Charles* (1655).
The English Levellers, ed. Andrew Sharp (Cambridge Texts in the History of Political Thought: Cambridge UP, 1998).
The Memoirs of Major-General Ludlow 1625–1672, ed. C. Firth (Clarendon Press 1894).
The Journal of Sir Samuel Luke, ed I G Philip, 3 vols (Oxfordshire Record Society, 1950–3).
Margaret Cavendish, Duchess of Newcastle, *Memoirs of William, Duke of Newcastle and his Wife Margaret*, ed. Sir C. Firth (London 1907; also the 1913 edition pub. by J. M. Dent).
Memoires du Cardinal Richelieu (Paris 1912–22)
National Archives: Privy Council Papers, vol 2.
  State Papers vols 14 (James I), 16, 31 (Charles I), 78 (France), 84 (Holland), 99 (Venice).
  E 158/2: The Declaration Showing the Necessity of the Earl of Strafford's Suffering.
  /17: The Earle of Bedfords Passage to the Long Parliament, May? 1641.
  E 417/19: A Brief and Perfect Relation of the Answers and Replies of Thomas, Earl of Strfford.
The Oglander Memoirs: Extracts from *the Manuscripts* of *Sir John Oglander, Knight*, ed. W Long (1888).
The Memoirs of Gregory Panzani, ed. J. Berington (Birmingham 1793).
Sir Charles Petrie, ed, *The Letters, Speeches and Proclamations of Charles I* (Cassell 1935).
Memoirs of Prince Rupert and the Cavaliers, ed. Eliot Warburton, 3 vols (London 1849).

J. Rushworth, *Historical Collections*, 8 vols (London 1659–1700).
——, *The Tryall of Thomas, Earl of Strafford, Lord Lieutenant of Ireland* (London 1680).
Sir Walter Scott, ed, *Secret History of the Court of James I*, 2 vols (1811).
Scottish Record Office: STC 19505, 22037, 22039
Spalding Memorialls of the Troubles in Scotland, ed. J Stuart, 2 vols (Spalding Club Aberdeen 1831–2).
Joshua Sprigge, *Anglia rediviva... being the history of the ... army under Sir Thomas Fairfax*, 1647 (reprint Oxford 1849).
The Earl of Strafford's Letters and Despatches, ed. W. Knowles, 2 vols (1739).
Stuart Royal Proclamations, vol 2: 1625–46, ed. J. Larkin (Oxford 1983).
Verney Papers: Notes of Proceedings in the Long Parliament *tempore Charles I* (Camden Society, 1845).
J. Vicars, *England's Parliamentary Chronicle*, 3 vols (1643–6): vol 1, Jehovah-Jireh. God in the *Mount*; vol 2, God's Ark overtopping the World's Waves; vol 3, The Burning Bush not consum'd.
Sir Edward Walker, *Historical Discourses upon several occasions*, ed. H Clopton (1705).
Sir Philip Warwick, *Memoirs of the Reign of Charles I* (1702, reprint Edinburgh 1813).
Webb, J, *Memorials of the civil war... as it affected Herefordshire and* the *adjacent counties*, ed. T.N. Webb, 2 vols (1879).
Bulstrode Whitelocke, *Memorials* (Oxford 1853).
George Wishart, *Memoirs of Montrose* (London 1893).

Secondary Sources
H. Abell, *Kent and the Great Civil War* (Ashford 1901).
John Adair, *Cheriton 1644: The Campaign* and *the Battle* (Kineton 1973).
—— *Roundhead General*: the Campaigns *of Sir William Waller* (Sutton 1997).
John Adamson, 'The "Vindiciae Veritatis" and the Political Creed of Viscount Saye and Sele' in *Historical Research* vol. 60 (1987).
—— *The Noble Revolt: the Overthrow of Charles I* (Phoenix 2007).
H. Atkin and W. Loughlin, *Gloucester in the Civil War* (Tempus 1992).
Gordon Albion, *Charles I and the Court of Rome* (1935).
G. E. Aylmer, 'Attempts at administrative reform, 1625–40' in *English Historical Review* vol 72 (1957), pp. 229–58.
—— *The King's Servants: the Civil Service of Charles I* (1961).
A. R. Bayley, *The Great Civil War in Dorset 1642–1660* (Taunton 1910).
Thomas Birch, *The Court and Times* of James *I* (1849).
M. Braddick, *God's Fury, England's Fire: A New History of the English Civil Wars* (Allen Lane 2008).
H. N. Brailsford and C. Hill, *The Levellers and the English Revolution* (Cresset 1961).
D. Brunton and H, Pennington, *Members of the Long Parliament* (1954).
J. Bruce and D. Masson, eds, *The Quarrel between the Earl of* Manchester *and Oliver Cromwell; An Episode of the English Civil War* (Camden Society, new series, vol 12, 1875).
E. Broxap, *The Great Civil War in Lancashire* (Manchester 1910).
Nicholas Canny, *Making Ireland British* 1580–1650 (Oxford 2001).
S. D. Carpenter, *Military Leadership in the English Civil War 1642–51* (London 2005).
Thomas Carte, The *Life of James, Duke of Ormonde*.
Charles Carlton, *Charles I: The Personal Monarch* (Routledge 1983).

Peter Clark, A. G..R Smith and Nicholas Tyacke, eds, *The English Commonwealth: Essays in Politics and Society Presented to Joel Hurstfield* (London 1979).
M. Coate, *Cornwall in the Great Civil War and Interregnum 1642–1660* (Truro 1963 edition).
T. Cogswell, *The Blessed Revolution: English Politics and the Coming of War 1603*–1624 (Cambridge UP 1989).
W. Craven, 'The Earl of Warwick: a speculator in piracy' in *Hispano-American Historical Review*, vol 1) (1930) pp. 457–79.
Patricia Crawford, *Denzel Holles, 1598–1680: A Study of his Political Career* (London 1979).
David Cressy, *England On Edge: Crisis and Revolution, 1640–2* (Oxford 2006).
Richard Cust, 'Charles I, the Privy Council and the Forced Loan' in *Journal of British Studies*, vol 24, no 2 (April 1985).
—— Charles I: A Political Life (Longmans 2005).
Richard Cust and Ann Hughes, *Conflict in Early Stuart England: Studies in Religion and Politics 1603–42* (1989).
——, *The English Civil War* (London 1997).
F. C. Dietz, *English Public Finance 1558–1641* (1964 edition).
Barbara Donagan, 'The clerical patronage of Robert Rich, Earl of Warwick, 1619–42' in *Proceedings of the American Philosophical Society*, vol 120 (1976, pp. 388–419.
Peter Donald, 'New Light on the Anglo-Scottish Contacts of 1640' in *Historical Research*, vol 62 (1989).
——, *An Uncounselled King: Charles I and the Scottish Troubles*, 1637–41 (Cambridge UP 1990).
——, *The Bishops' Wars: Charles I's campaigns against Scotland 1638–40* (Cambridge UP 1994).
Graham Donaldson, *Scotland: James V to James VII* (1965).
F. T. R. Edgar, *Sir Ralph Hopton: The King's Man in the West 1642–53* (Oxford UP 1968).
Timothy Eustace, ed, *Statesmen and Politicians of the Stuart* Age (Macmillan 1985).
Mark Fissel, *The Bishops' Wars: Charles I's Campaigns Against Scotland 1638–40* (Cambridge UP 1994).
Kenneth Fincham, *Prelate as Pastor: The Episcopate of James I* (Oxford UP 1990).
J. Forster, *The Life of Sir John Eliot 1590 to 1632*, 2 vols (Longman 1867).
Roy Foster, *A History of Modern Ireland 1603–1972* (Penguin 1989).
Anthony Fletcher, *The Outbreak of the English Civil War* (Edward Arnold 1981).
S. R. Gardiner, *History of England 1603–42*, 10 vols (1883–4).
——, *History of the The Great Civil War* (Windrush Press, 1988 reprint).
Peter Gaunt, ed, *The English Civil* War (Oxford 2000).
Geraint Jenkins, The *Foundations of Modern Wales 1642–1780 (Oxford UP 1993).*
M.A, Gibb, *The Lord General: A Life of Sir Thomas Fairfax* (1938).
G. N. Godwin, *The Civil War in Hampshire* (1882).
J. Hexter, *The Reign of King Pym* (Cambridge, Massachsuetts 1941).
Caroline Hibbard, *Charles I and the Popish Plot* (Chapel Hill, North Carolina 1983).
Christopher Hill, *Puritanism and Revoluton* (Penguin 1968).
—— *The World Turned Upside Down: Radical Ideas During the English Revolution* (Penguin 1975).
—— *The English Bible and the Seventeenth Century Revolution* (Penguin 1993).

Derek Hirst and Richard Strier, eds, *Writing and Political Engagement in Seventeenth Century England* (Cambridge UP 2000).
Clive Holmes, *The Eastern Association in the English Civil War* (1974).
D. Hulme, *The Life of Sir John Eliot* (London 1957).
H. F. Kearney, *Strafford and Ireland 1633–1640* (London 1958).
Mark Kishlansky, 'Tyranny Denied: Charles I, Attorney-General Heath and the Five Knights' Case' in *Historical Journal*, vol 42, no 1 (March 1999).
William Lilly, *Life of Charles I* (1772).
Keith Lindley, 'Lay Catholics in the Reign of Charles I' in *Journal of Ecclesiastical History* vol 22 (1971) pp. 119–22.
—— *Fenland Riots and the English Civil War* (London 1982).
—— *Popular Politics and Religion in Civil War London* (Aldershot 1997).
Patrick Little, 'The Earl of Cork and the Fall of Strafford 1638–41, *Historical Journal*, vol 39 (1996), pp. 619–35.
Roger Lockyer, *Buckingham: the Life and Political Career of George Villiers, Duke of Buckingham 1592–1628* (1981).
A. J. Loomie, 'Alonso de Cardenas and the Long Parliament 1640–8' in *English Historical Review*, vol 97 (1982).
Alan Macinnes, *Charles I and the Making of the Covenanting Movement, 1625–41* (Edinburgh 1991).
Brian Manning, ed, *Politics and the English Civil War* (1973).
Florence Memegalo, George Goring (1608–57): *Caroline Courtier and Royalsit General* (Ashgate 2003).
T. L. Moody, F. X. Martin and F. J. Byrne, eds, *A New History of Ireland*: Volume III, 1534–1691 (Clarendon Press, 1991 edition).
John Morrill, Blair Worden, and Ian Gentles (eds), *Soldiers, Writers and Statesmen of the English Civil War* (Cambridge UP, 1998).
The New Dictionary of National Biography, ed. C. Mathew (Oxford UP 2001).
Valerie Pearl, *London and the Outbreak of the Puritan Revolution: City Government and National Politics 1625–43* (Oxford 1961).
Michael Perceval-Maxwell, 'Protestant faction, the Impeachment of Strafford and the Origins of the Irish Civil War' in *Canadian Journal of History*, vol 17 (1981) pp. 135–53.
T. O. Ranger, 'Strafford in Ireland: a Revaluation' in Trevor Aston, ed, *Crisis in Europe, 1560–1660* (London, 1965).
L. J. Reeve, *Charles I and the Road to Personal Rule* (Cambridge UP 1989).
F. Relf, *The Petition of Right* (Minneapolis 1917).
Stuart Reid, *Crown, Covenant and Cromwell: The Civil Wars in Scotland, 1639–51* (Pen and Sword 2012).
Richard Richardson, *The English Civil War: Local Aspects* (Sutton, 1997).
Conrad Russell, 'The Theory of Treason in the Trial of Strafford', *English Historical Review* vol 80 (1965).
—— *Parliaments and English politics 1621–9* (Oxford UP 1979).
Clayton Roberts, 'The Earl of Bedford and the Coming of the English Revolution', in *Journal of Modern History*, vol 77 (1949).
Trevor Royle, *Civil War; The Wars of Three Kingdoms 1638–60* (2005).
Robert Ruigh, *The Parliament of 1624* (Cambridge, Mass. 1971).
Conrad Russell, 'Parliamentary History in Perspective 1604–29' in *History*, vol 61 (1976) pp. 1–19.

—— *Unrevolutionary England, 1603–42* (Hambledon Press 1990).
—— *The Fall of the British Monarchies, 1637–42* (Clarendon Press 1991).
C. Thomas-Sandford, *Sussex in the Great Civil War and the Interregnum 1642–1660* (1910).
David Scott, '"Hannibal at our gates": Loyalists and Fifth-Columnists during the Bishops' Wars: The Case of Yorkshire' in *Historical Research*, vol 70 (1997) pp. 268–93.
——, *Politics and War in the Three Stuart Kingdoms* 1637–49 (2003).
Kevin Sharpe, ed, *Faction and Parliament: Essays in Early Stuart History* (Oxford UP 1978).
—— 'Archbishop Laud' in *History Today* 33 (1983) pp. 26–30.
—— *The Personal Rule of Charles I* (Yale UP 1992).
—— and Peter Lake, *Culture and Politics in Early Stuart England* (*Problems in Focus*, Macmillan 1994).
Alan Smith, ed, *The Reign of James VI and I* (*Problems in Focus*, Macmillan 1973).
W. F. Snow, *Essex the Rebel* (Lincoln, Nebraska 1970).
David Starkey et al, *The English Court from the Wars of the Roses to the English Civil War* (Longmans 1987).
David Stevenson, *The Scottish Revolution 1637–44* (Newton Abbot 1973).
Lawrence Stone, *The Crisis of the Aristocracy 1558–1641* (Oxford 1965)
—— *The Causes of the* English *Revolution* (1972).
C. S. Terry, *The Life and Campaigns of Alexander Leslie, Earl of Leven* (London 1899).
Colin Tite, *Impeachment and Parliamentary Procedure in Early Stuart England (*1974).
Margot Todd, ed, *Reformation to Revolutioin: Politics* and *Religion in Early Modern England* (New York, 1995).
Howard Tomlinson, ed, *Before the English Civil War: Essays on Early Stuart Politics and Government* (1983).
Geoffrey Trease, *Portrait of a Cavalier: William Cavendish, First Duke of Newcastle* (Macmillan 1979).
Hugh Trevor-Roper, *Archbishop Laud* 1573–1645 (1962 edition).
—— *Catholics, Anglicans and Puritans* (Fontana 1989).
Nicholas Tyacke, *Anti-Calvinists: The Rise of English Arminianism c. 1590–1640* (Oxford UP 1987).
David Underdown, *Somerset in the Civil War and Interregnum* (1973).
Malcolm Wanklyn and Frank Jones, *A Military History of the English Civil War, 1642–6: Strategy and Tactics* (Longmans, Harlow 2005).
C. V. Wedgwood, *The King's Peace, 1637–41* (Collins 1955).
Penry Williams, *The Tudor Regime* (Oxford 1979).
J. N. Willis-Bund, *The Civil in Worcestershire (1642–6) and the Scottish Invasion of 1651* (Birmingham 1905).
D H Wilson, King James VI and I (1956).
A C Wood, Nottinghamshire in the Civil War (Oxford 1937).
Peter Zagorin, The Court and the Country: The Beginning of the English Revolution (Oxford 1969).
R. Zaller, The Parliament of 1621 (Berkeley and London 1971).

Index

Abbot, George, archbishop of Canterbury 34, 40, 42, 48, 52, 55
Abbot, Robert, brother of above 40
Adamson, John, historian 30, 33, 134, 150, 166–8, 170–1, 176, 188, 190–1, 199, 206, 212, 259
Alexandra Feodorovna (Alix of Hesse), empress of Russia 65
Andrewes, Lancelot, bishop of Winchester 46–8
Anne of Austria (Spain), queen of France 16, 65–6
Anne of Denmark, queen of Scots/England 7, 28, 39
'Arminius' aka van Arnim, Cornelius, Dutch theologian 34, 39, 42–6, 48–9, 51
Ashburnham, John, Royal aide 184
Astley, Sir Jacob, Royalist officer 99
Aston, Sir Thomas 128, 256
Aston, Sir Walter, ambassador 81

Bacon, Sir Francis, philosopher/Lord Chancellor 31, 33, 56, 186
Balfour, William, Royal official 194–5, 201, 243–5
Balmerino, lord 94, 220
Balthazar Carlos, prince of Spain 122
Bancroft, Richard, archbishop 43, 46, 48–9
Bani Sadr, Abolhassan, revolutionary President of Iran 191, 203
Bankes, Sir John, lord chief justice 179
Baro, Peter, theologian 51
Barrington, Sir Thomas 197, 199, 214
Bastwick, John, Calvinist cleric viii, 24–5, 58, 65, 154
Beaton, Cardinal David, Scots chief minister 86
Beecher, Sir William 36
Bellievre, French ambassador 83, 133
Bernhard of Saxe Weimar, German prince/general 120
Bernini, Giovanni, sculptor 66
Bertie, Robert, earl of Lindsey 261
Billingsley, Captian William, Royalist officer 194
Birkenhead, Sir John, Royalist journalist 141
Blount, Mountjoy, earl of Newport, Royal official/Parliamentary ally 185, 195, 199–200, 204, 206–7, 230, 244, 249, 259
Burton, Henry, Calvinist cleric viii, 20, 24–5, 53, 58, 65, 73, 77, 154, 160, 162, 171

Boleyn, Anne, queen of England 30
'Bond of Association', the (1584) 196, 209
'Book of Sports', the 52–3
Bor(r)oughs, Sir John 158
Bourke, Ulick, marquis of Clanricarde 72
Boyle, Richard, earl of Cork 72–3, 227, 241
Boyle, Richard, relative of above 241
Bridgeman, John, bishop of Chester 52
'Brig O'Dee', battle of (1639) 110–11
Brooke, Robert, lord, Parliamentary leader 109, 119, 131, 134, 144, 162, 185–8, 195, 199–200, 204, 206–7, 230, 244, 249, 259
Brownrigg, Ralph, preacher 52, 231
Buchan, John, writer 217
Burlamachi, Philip 64
Burnet, Gilbert, cleric/historian 139
Burroughs, Jeremiah, preacher 206, 231, 235
Burton, Thomas, diarist/MP 252
Byron, Sir John, Royalist general 138, 246

Caesar, Sir Julius, Italo-English financier 54
Campbell, Archibald, seventh earl of Argyll 98, 104
Campbell, Archibald, eighth earl and marquis of Argyll, Covenanter leader 93, 98, 100–01, 103–6, 111, 114–16, 195, 202–3, 217–23, 235, 240, 244, 252, 258–9
Campbell, John, lord Loudoun, cousin and ally of above 126, 134, 198, 202, 222–3
Capel, Sir Arthur, Royalist officer 164
Cardenas, Alonso de, Spanish ambassador 122
Carew, Thomas, poet 40
Carey, Lucius, viscount Falkland, courtier and Royalist 174, 177, 192, 200, 261
Carey, Sir Robert 41
Carleton, Sir Dudley, secretary of state 32
Carr (Kerr), Robert, earl of Somerset/favourite of James VI and I 11, 26–7, 60, 176
Catherine de Medicis, queen of France 24
Cave, Sir Richard 221
Cavendish, William, earl and marquis of Newcastle, courtier and Royalist general 113–14, 185, 205, 231
Cecil, Sir Robert, earl of Salisbury/secretary of state/lord treasurer 11, 28–9, 49, 61, 252
Cecil, William, lord Burghley, father of above/secretary of state/lord treasurer 33, 62, 252
Cecil, William, second earl of Salisbury, son of Sir Robert C 122
Charles I, king of England/Scots vi-ix, 3 – 146, 149 – 262.

Charles II, prince of Wales and king of England/Scots vi, 124, 161, 198, 205, 231, 234
Charles IX, king of France 24
Charles Louis, nephew of Charles I, Elector Palatine 80–1, 84, 120, 175, 182, 221–5, 252–3
Chevreuse, Marie, duchesse de, lady in waiting to queen Anne of France 65–6
Christian IV, king of Denmark 59
Clotworthy, Sir John, Ulster 'planter'/MP 121, 154, 157, 165, 167, 183, 196–7, 208, 234, 241
Cochrane, Colonel, ally of Montrose 223, 244, 252
Coke, Sir Edward, attorney-general/judge/legal writer 13, 27, 53, 55–8, 129, 181
Coke, Sir John, secretary of state 19, 82, 84, 97, 117
'Commonwealthsmen', the 62
Connolly, Owen 234
Conway, Sir Edward, later Lord C, Royal official 31, 84, 97, 121, 132, 135–8, 254
Conyers, Sir John 176
Colepeper/Culpeper, Sir John, Royalist 164, 214, 230, 237, 255, 261
Corbet, bishop of Norwich 52
Cottington, Sir Francis, chancellor of exchequer /treasurer/courtier 64–8, 78, 122, 138, 166, 231
Covenant, the, Scots National (1638) 97–101, 116, 118, 131
Cotton, Sir Robert, antiquarian and collector 55–7
Coventry, Thomas, lord keeper 20–1, 76, 117
Craddock, Matthew 166
Cranfield, Lionel, earl of Middlesex/lord treasurer 11, 13, 15, 21, 27, 31, 33, 55, 59, 170, 179, 186
Cressy, David, historian 230
Cromwell, Oliver, Parliamentarian leader and general 141, 151, 163, 183, 192, 197–8, 211, 214, 221, 235, 238, 255
Cromwell, Thomas, earl of Essex, minister of Henry VIII 181

Danton, Georges Jacques, French revolutionary leader 191
Darley, Henry, officer 140, 151
Davenant, John, bishop 53
Davenant, William, playwright 40, 179
De La Pole, Michael, earl of Suffolk/minister to Richard II 185
De La Pole, William, minister to Henry VI 149, 181, 185, 193
De Montfort, Simon, earl of Leicester/reformist baron and coup leader 135, 156
Dering, Sir Edward, MP 215, 257
Devereux, Robert, earl of Essex, Elizabethan courtier and general (ex. 1601) 47, 60, 83, 152–3, 228–9

Devereux, Robert, earl of Essex, son of above/'opposition' peer and Parliamentary general viii, 27, 47, 60–1, 109, 113, 141, 143, 152–3, 155–6, 175–6, 184, 191, 193, 195, 197, 201, 204, 208, 216, 221, 228–9, 234–5, 237, 239, 244, 247, 259
D'Ewes, Sir Simonds, MP/diarist 169, 172m, 191, 215
Digby, George, courtier/Royalist organiser and officer 170, 174, 177, 191, 200, 242, 246, 248
Digby, John, earl of Bristol, ambassador/courtier, father of above 6–7, 9, 21, 34, 41, 144, 152, 156, 191, 205, 236, 247
Digges, Sir Dudley 20, 34
Donaldson, Gordon, historian 91
Do(o)rt, Synod of (1619) 34, 39, 43, 50–1
Downing, Calibut, preacher 140–1, 151
Downs, battle of the (1639) 84
Dudley, Robert, earl of Leicester/favourite of Elizabeth I 18, 34, 47
Duns Law, battle of (1639) 112–14, 132, 137
'Dupes, Day of' (1630) 66
Durie, John, theologian/traveller 52
Dyott, Sir Richard 144

Earle, Sir Walter, MP/Parliamentarian leader 23, 131 171, 186, 245–6
Edward I, king of England 22, 133
Edward II, ditto 206, 232
Edward III, ditto 22
Edward VI, ditto 62
Egerton, John, earl of Bridgewater 58
Eliot, Sir John, MP and critic of Charles I 14, 17–23, 25–6, 29, 32, 35, 41, 58, 75, 77, 150, 156
Elizabeth I, queen of England vii-ix, 4, 10, 16, 18–26, 28, 30, 32–8, 41, 43, 46–7, 50–2, 55–6, 61–2, 149–53, 173, 196, 214, 221, 225, 252, 262
Elizabeth, 'Winter Queen' of Bohemia/Electress Palatine 6, 9, 16, 27, 50, 78, 80, 252

Fairfax, Sir Thomas, Parliamentarian general 90
'Falstaff, Sir John' 109
Fanning, Dominick, lord mayor of Limerick 229
Fawkes, Guy, plotter 61, 195
Felton, John, assassin of duke of Buckingham 25
Ferdinand II, Holy Roman Emperor/king of Bohemia and Hungary 6, 9, 79, 81–2
Ferte-Imbauld, marquis de, French ambassador 244
Fiennes, Nathaniel, MP/Parliamentarian organiser 129, 139, 176, 178, 222, 250
Fiennes, William, lord Saye and Sele, father of above/'opposition' peer 23, 35, 62, 75, 109, 119, 127, 129, 131, 134, 139, 144, 149–52, 171, 175–6, 178, 204–8, 221, 229–30, 244, 249

Index 291

Finch, Sir John, Speaker of Parliament/Lord Keeper 17, 19, 21, 77, 117, 125–8, 174, 204
Fitzalan-Howard, (St.) Philip, earl of Arundel 23
Fitzalan-Howard, Thomas, earl of Arundel/earl marshal 20–1, 23, 33–4, 66, 81–2, 96, 98–9, 109, 111, 117, 130, 138–9, 151, 216
'Five Knights', the 23
'Five Members', attempted arrest of (1642) 250–3, 255, 259
Fleming, Captain William 252
Fowke, Abraham, alderman of London 242, 245
Foxe, John, Protestant author and polemicist 38, 47, 233
Francois Hercule, duke of Anjou/Alencon 24
Frederick, Elector Palatine 6, 9, 16, 27, 50, 78
Frederick Henry, Dutch stadtholder 175, 182, 190, 202
Frost, Gualter, later Parliamentarian secretary of state 131

Gardiner, Samuel Rawson, historian 4, 166–7, 177
Gardiner, Stephen, bishop of Winchester/lord chancellor 64
Garraway, Sir Thomas, lord mayor of London 131
Geddes, Jenny, Edinburgh protester 93
Gerard, Sir Gilbert 231
Giustinian, Venetian ambassador 123–5, 212, 251
'Glorious Revolution', the 29
Glynne, John, lawyer and later lord chief justice 175, 187, 189
Gondomar, count, Spanish ambassador 6–7, 9, 26, 152
Goodman, Godfrey, bishop of Gloucester 133
Goodman, Father, Catholic priest 175
Gordon, George, marquis of Huntly, Royalist commander 96, 101–2, 106, 110–1, 115
Gordon, Lewis, lord Aboyne, son of above 110–13
Goring, George, hard-line Royalist leader 109, 185, 216, 238, 245, 257
Graham, James, earl/marquis of Montrose, Covenanter/Royalist commander 90, 98, 100, 102, 106, 110–11, 115, 118, 202–3, 207, 217–20, 222–4
Graham, William, earl of Menteith 89
'Grand Remonstrance', the (1641) 236–9, 241, 253
Grey, lady Katherine, presumed heiress to Elizabeth I 21
Grey, lady Mary, sister of above 21
Grimston, Sir Harbottle, Parliamentarian 125–6, 165, 168, 174, 178
Grindal, Edmund, archbishop 43
Grotius, Hugo, Dutch jurist and philosopher 48
Gunpowder Plot, the 8, 49, 152, 162, 195, 235

Gurney, Sir Richard, lord mayor of London 240, 243, 254
Gustavus Adolphus, king of Sweden 78–80

Hamilton, James, marquis/duke of H, Royalist courtier and general 79, 81–2, 88, 93, 95–8, 101–5, 109–11, 114, 116, 176, 179, 190, 203, 223–4, 230, 235, 244, 252
Hamilton, Sir James 223–4
Hamilton, Sir Thomas, earl of Haddington 85, 89
Hamilton, William, earl of Lanark/second duke of H 244
Haselrig, Sir Arthur, Parliamentarian leader 125, 187, 189, 200, 212, 219, 230, 241
Hastings, Henry, earl of Huntingdon 47
Hatton, Sir Christopher, Elizabethan favourite and lord chancellor 31
Hawkins, Sir John, Elizabethan naval officer and organiser 32
Hay of Kinfauns, Sir George, later earl of Kinnoul 85
Heath, Sir Robert, attorney-general 17, 23, 173
Henderson, Alexander, Covenanter leader 94, 97, 99, 105, 114, 116
Henri III, king of France/Poland 24
Henri IV, king of France/Navarre 9, 65
Henrietta Maria, daughter of above, queen of England/Scots 15, 22, 24, 31, 39–40, 44–5, 59, 64–8, 81, 83, 107–8, 112, 117, 119, 122–3, 131, 155, 184, 194, 196–7, 207–8, 212, 216, 234, 243–4, 250–1, 254–5, 260
Henry III, king of England viii, 134, 140, 156, 180, 206, 232
Henry VI, ditto viii, 169, 185, 206
Henry, prince of Wales (d 1612) 5–8, 20, 30–1, 41, 59, 85, 176
Herbert, Sir Edward, attorney-general 247–51
Herbert Philip, earl of Montgomery/Pembroke 61, 121–2, 151–2, 174–5, 207–8, 216, 230, 237, 239, 243
Herbert, William, earl of Pembroke, brother of above 10, 13, 33, 42, 61, 151
Heylyn, Peter, biographer of Laud 44, 49, 9102, 109
High Commission, court of 54, 160, 204
Hill Christopher, historian vii
Holborne, Robert, lawyer 776
Holles, Denzel, parliamentarian leader 17, 23, 167, 176, 192, 199, 207, 212, 230, 245, 250–2
Hooker, Richard, bishop and theologian 41, 44, 54, 214
Hopton, Sir Ralph, ambassador/Royalist general 75, 79–81, 83, 120, 126, 174, 177, 200
Hotham, Sir John, later governor of Hull 199, 260
Howard, Charles, lord H of Effingham and earl of Nottingham, lord admiral 14, 32

Howard, Frances, countess of Essex/Rochester, courtier 11, 26–7, 60, 176
Howard, Henry, earl of Northampton/lord privy seal 26
Howard, Thomas, fourth duke of Norfolk (ex. 1572) 18, 34
Howard, Thomas, earl of Suffolk/lord treasurer 26, 29, 33, 59
Howard, William, lord H of Effingham, lord admiral 32
Howard of Escrick, William, lord 139, 144, 222
Hyde, Sir Edward, earl of Clarendon, secretary of state/lord chancellor 7, 27, 52, 67, 74–5, 109, 125, 161, 164, 167, 176, 192, 200, 232, 237–40, 249, 261–2

'Incident', the (Edinburgh plot 1641) 223–4, 235, 237, 244, 250–1

James III, king of Scots 96
James V, king of Scots 86
James VI (Scotland) and I (England), king vii–ix, 4–15, 17, 20, 22–3, 26–34, 37–50, 52, 54–6, 59–60, 71, 85–91, 94, 100, 152–3, 162, 164, 176, 179, 181
James VII (Scots) and II (England), king 134, 145
Jefferies, George, repressive lord chief justice 58
Jermyn, Sir Henry, courtier and Royalist hard-liner 184, 194, 208, 216, 245
Jervoise, Sir Thomas 107
Jessop, William, secretary to Providence Island Company 151
John, king of England viii
Johnson, Lyndon Baines, US President 32
Johnston of Warriston, Archibald, Covenanter leader 100, 102, 104, 114, 190–1
Joshua, Israelite leader 100
Juxon, William, bishop of London/lord treasurer 64, 91, 98, 105, 154, 231

Kerr, Robert, earl of Roxburgh 223, 251–2
Kerr, Walter, Royalist officer 223–4
Kishlansky, Mark, historian 4, 124
Knox, John 39, 45, 48, 86, 97, 105

La Rochelle, siege of (1627–8) 35–7, 99
Laud, William, bishop of London/archbishop of Canterbury viii, 15, 20, 38, 41–6, 49, 51–6, 64, 67, 76, 82, 88, 91—2, 109, 114, 117, 119, 121–5, 131, 133, 138, 149, 151, 154, 156, 158–63, 166, 170–3, 177, 183, 210, 214, 246
Leighton, Alexander, cleric 58, 163
Leslie, Alexander, general 79, 98, 110–11, 114–16, 121, 124, 197, 220, 222, 258, 261
Leslie, Walter, earl of Rothes, Covenanter leader 93–4, 98, 100, 103, 106, 110–11, 114–16, 121, 131, 136, 198, 241
Lilburne, John, democratic agitator 163

Littleton/Lyttleton, Sir Edward, lord keeper 178, 248, 260
Livesey, Sir Michael 257
Louis XIII, king of France 9, 14, 16, 36, 65–6, 79–80, 106, 122–3
Louis XIV, king of France 66
Louis XVI, king of France vii, 50–1, 191, 203
Lucas, Sir Charles, Royalist officer 256
Lunsford, Sir Thomas, Royalist officer 143, 245–6, 257

Macdonnell, Randall, earl of Antrim/Ulster settler leader 104–5
Magna Carta 5, 23, 57
Malvezzi, Virgilio, Spanish ambassador 122
Manners/Villiers, Katherine, duchess of Buckingham 11
Manning, Brian, historian 169
Mansell, Sir Robert, admiral 14, 35
Mansfeld, count, mercenary commander 13–14, 28
Marie Antoinette, queen of France 65
Marie de Medicis, queen of France 65, 117, 167
Marshall, Stephen, preacher 221, 245
Marten, Henry, MP and republican 197
Mary I, queen of England 25, 38, 47, 55, 64, 225
Mary, queen of Scots 5, 30, 39, 45, 47, 86, 99, 217, 224
Mary of Guise, mother of above, queen and regent of Scots 86, 93, 95, 107
Mary, princess of England/Scots and wife of Dutch stadtholder 65, 122, 175, 182, 190, 194
Masham, Sir William 214
Maximilian, Elector of Bavaria 81
Maynard, Sir John, lawyer 118
Mazarin, Cardinal Giulio/Jules, French chief minister vii
Maurice of Nassau, prince, Dutch stadtholder 50
Melville, Andrew, Scots Calvinist cleric 37, 45, 86
Mildmay, Sir Henry, MP/official 165, 199, 214, 221
Monck, George, Royalist and later Parliamentarian officer 137
Montague, Edward, lord Mandeville/earl of Manchester, Parliamentarian leader 134, 144, 152, 176, 196, 205–6, 223, 229–30, 242–3
Montague, Henry, earl of Manchester 20, 134, 138, 152, 223, 242
Montague, Richard, Anglican cleric and controversialist 39, 42
Montague, Walter/'Wat', Catholic convert 68
More, Sir/St., Tudor lord chancellor 19, 181
Moses, Israelite leader and lawgiver 97, 100
Murray, Will(iam), Royal aide 223

Napier, lord, ally of Montrose 202, 219
Neile, Richard, archbishop 41, 46, 49
Nero, Roman emperor 45
Newburn, battle of (1640) 136–7, 143, 194, 220
Newbury, first battle of (1643) 200
Nicholas II, emperor of Russia vii, 12, 50–1
Nicholas, Sir Edward, secretary of state 117, 161, 211, 223, 230–1, 236, 239
Noy, William, attorney-general 62, 75–6

Olivares, count-duke de, Spanish chief minister 9, 12, 79, 83, 120
O' More, Rory, 1641 Ulster rebel leader 232–3
O'Neill, Daniel, Royal officer 183, 228, 234
O'Neill, Hugh, earl of Tyrone/Irish rebel leader 70, 226–9
O'Neill, Owen Roe, 1640s Catholic rebel general 228
O'Neill, Sir Phelim, leader of 1641 Ulster rebellion 228, 232–3
Osborne, Sir Thomas 99
Osborne, Sir Thomas, earl of Danby and duke of Leeds/lord treasurer 161
Overbury, Sir Thomas, Jacobean courtier and murder-victim 26, 60
Overton, Henry 171

Panzani, Gregory, papal envoy 44
Paulet, John, marquis of Winchester, Catholic grandee 108
Peacham, Henry, writer 118
Pen(n)ington, Isaac, City of London merchant 162, 194, 199, 228
Percy, Algernon, ninth earl of Northumberland, moderate Parliamentarian/courtier 117, 122, 124, 127, 130, 132, 136, 138, 164, 169, 176, 179, 183, 187, 189, 197, 205–6, 221, 242
Percy, Sir Henry, son of above, Royalist activist 145, 184, 206, 208
Percy/Hay, Lucy, countess of Carlisle, court figure and reputed intriguer 164, 169, 252–3
Percy, Thomas, seventh earl of Northumberland 34
'Petition of Right', the (1628) 23
Phelips, Sir Robert 13–15
Philip II, king of Spain 24, 195, 224
Philip IV, ditto 6, 12, 67, 122–3
Pindar, Sir Paul 108
Porter, Endymion, Catholic courtier and art-collector 68
Poynings' Act (1494 Ireland) 224
Preston, John, 'Puritan' cleric 34, 40–2, 66, 178
Prideaux, John, university theologian/preacher 40, 51, 231
Providence Island Company, Caribbean colonial/privateering venture 75, 77, 83–4, 151, 221
Prynne, William, Calvinist controversialist viii, 20, 24–5, 44–5, 55, 58–9, 65, 118, 154, 160, 162, 171
Pym, John, Parliamentrian leader 19, 29, 121, 125–9, 131, 139, 149, 152, 154, 157, 159, 162, 164–7, 169, 171, 174, 176, 179–80, 183, 187, 189, 191, 195, 200–04, 207, 211–12, 221, 230–1, 234–8, 241–4, 247–50, 252–3, 255

Radcot Bridge, battle of (1387) 141
Raleigh, Sir Walter, adventurer and courtier 7, 20–3, 225–6
Reve, LJ, historian 79
Rich, Henry, earl of Holland, courtier/moderate Royalist 81, 84, 111–14, 121, 124, 127, 138, 144, 150, 152, 183, 189, 205, 216, 240, 249
Rich, Sir Nathaniel 16, 221
Rich, Robert, earl of Warwick, brother of Henry R, Parliamentary and pro-Covenanter leader viii, 16, 25, 35, 37, 68, 75, 77, 79, 83–4, 108, 118–21, 124, 126, 128–31, 134, 138–44, 149, 151, 155–6, 162, 166–8, 170–1, 173, 176, 180, 182–5, 187, 189–90, 193–7, 200–09, 212—17, 219, 221, 223–4, 228–30, 234, 240–1, 244, 246–7, 249–50, 258–9
Richard II, king of England viii, 141, 165, 168–9, 178, 206
Richelieu, Armand-Jean, cardinal de, French chief minister vii, 14, 16, 36, 65, 78–82
Robert II, king of Scots 89
'Rod, Black', Parliamentary official 17, 19
Roe, Sir Thomas, ambassador to Mughal empire 68, 78, 80, 222
Rolle, John, MP 18, 20
'Root and Branch', scheme to reform Anglican Church 37–8, 173, 175, 177, 180, 191, 200–01, 205, 211–12, 215, 221, 236, 239–40, 248, 256
Rous, Francis, theologian/MP/half-brother of Pym 19, 152
Rudyerd, Sir Banjamin, MP 126–7, 174, 178, 221
Rupert of the Rhine, prince/Royalist general 120, 252
Russell, Conrad, historian 4, 30, 54, 169, 206
Russell, Francis, earl of Bedford, Parliamentarian leader 47, 62, 77, 84, 119, 125–6, 129, 134, 139, 144, 149–50, 152, 164, 167, 169–70, 174–80, 182, 187–93, 198, 201, 204–6, 208–11, 216, 229, 259

Saul, king of Israel 183
Sejanus, minister of emperor Tiberius 25
Selden, John, MP and author/legal expert 56–7, 63, 73
Seymour, Edward, earl of Hertford/duke of Somerset/regent for Edward VI 38, 123, 153
Seymour, Edward, earl of Hertford, son of above 21
Seymour, Thomas, lord Sudeley/lord admiral 30
Seymour, William, earl of Hertford, moderate Parliamentarian 1119, 139, 144, 152–3, 175, 205, 230–1, 234, 239

Sharpe, Kevin, historian 4, 51, 57
Shakespeare, William 109, 229
Ship-Money/SM fleet 63, 69, 73–8, 80–1, 109, 118, 121, 125, 127–8, 149, 151, 156–7, 159, 164, 168–71, 178–9, 182, 192, 199–200
Sidney, Robert, earl of Leicester/lord lieutenant of Ireland 82, 169, 171
Skippon, (General) Philip, Parliamentarian officer 141, 254
Slingsby, Sir Henry 107, 112
Soloman, king of Israel 162, 235
Somerset, Henry, marquis of Worcester, South Wales Catholic magnate 108, 183
Spenser, Edmund, poet and colonist in Ireland 226
Spottiswoode, John, archbishop 89–91, 94–5, 100
St. Bartholomew's Day Massacre (1572) 24, 167, 233
St. John, Oliver, Parliamentarian legal expert/solicitor-general 27, 73, 134, 140, 151, 163, 167, 169, 171, 173, 176–9, 186, 192–3, 200–01, 205, 216, 230–1, 236
Stapleton, Sir Philip, Parliamentarian leader 187, 197, 223
'Star Chamber', the, Privy Council judicial committee 54–5, 57–9, 62, 154, 204
Stewart, John, lord Traquair, adviser to Charles I 81, 94–5, 97, 101–2, 111, 115–16, 122, 126, 137, 202–3, 217
Stewart, John 219–20
Stewart, Colonel Walter 202–3, 207, 218
Stoke, battle of (1487) 262
Stuart, Arbella, cousin and possible heir to Elizabeth and James VI and I 153
Stuart, Esme, duke of Lennox, minister of James VI and I 31, 88
Stuart, Esme , junior, son of above 88
Stuart, Henry, lord Darnley, murdered father of James VI and I 224
Stuart, James, duke of Lennox/son of Ludovick S 88, 101, 203, 208, 218–19
Stuart, Ludovick, duke of Lennox, brother of above, adviser to James VI and I 88
Stubbes, John, Elizabethan controversialist viii, 24–5
Stubbs, William, bishop/historian 4
Suckling, Sir John, poet and Royalist activist 193–4

Taylor, John, ambassador 81–3
Temple, Sir John 171
Thomason, George, collector of political pamphlets 213, 257
Thompson, Maurice, City of London merchant and Parliamentarian ally 140, 142, 228
'Three Musketeers', the, novel 16, 253
Throckmorton, Elizabeth, lady-in-waiting/wife to Raleigh 21
Tiberius, Roman emperor 25

Toiras, marshal de, French general 36
Tresilian, Sir Robert, lord chief justice to Richard II 27, 165, 168–9
Twysden, Sir Roger 119
Tyacke, Nicholas, historian 46

Urban VIII, Pope 66
Ussher, James, archbishop of Armagh 173

Vane, Sir Henry, senior, secretary of state 79, 117, 122, 126–9, 131, 138, 144, 169, 184, 187, 199, 207, 237, 239
Vane, Sir Henry, junior, Parliamentary leader 176, 178, 184, 186–7, 207, 211, 239
Venn, John, Hon. Artillery Company official 140, 191, 242
Villiers, George, first duke of Buckingham, minister to James VI and I and to Charles I 6–16, 19–23, 25–7, 31–7, 39–40, 42, 45, 50, 56, 59, 66–7, 69, 88, 104, 120, 156, 170, 179, 186, 216
Villiers, Susan, sister of above, countess of Denbigh 42

Waller, (General) Sir William, Parliamentarian officer 204
Warwick, Sir Philip 252
Wedderburn, James, Scots bishop 91–2
Weldon, Sir Anthony 257
Wentworth, Peter, Elizabethan MP 20
Wentworth, Sir Thomas, earl of Strafford, minister of Charles I 13–15, 58, 62, 64, 68–75, 96, 98, 104–5, 110–11, 114–17, 121, 123–8, 131, 133, 135, 137, 140, 143, 154, 157–8, 161, 165–71, 174–6, 179–205, 207–12, 218, 226–8, 237, 243, 247, 253
Weston, Richard, earl of Portland/lord treasurer 15, 17, 19–20, 64, 67–8, 80, 154
Wharton, Philip, lord, Parliamentarian 176
Whitelocke, Bulstrode, Parliamentarian lawyer 118, 185–6, 234
Whitgift, John, archbishop of Canterbury 37–8, 43, 46, 52
Widdrington, Sir Thomas 192
William II, Dutch stadtholder 175, 182, 190, 194
William III, king of England and Scots/Dutch stadtholder 134
Williams, John, archbishop/lord keeper 13, 15, 37, 42, 154, 156, 162, 173–4, 183, 197, 199, 205, 209, 243, 246, 248
Wilmot, Henry, lord 136–7
Windebank, Sir Francis, secretary of state 57, 66–8, 80, 8, 107, 122, 126, 138–42, 145, 157, 161, 166–7, 174, 204
Woodhouse, Sir Thomas 185
Wotton, Sir Henry 67
Wren, Matthew, bishop 41, 53, 133, 158, 177, 213
Wyatt, Sir Thomas, Tudor rebel 30